David's Song

David's Song

Betty Bunsell Franklin

authorHOUSE®

AuthorHouse™
1663 Liberty Drive
Bloomington, IN 47403
www.authorhouse.com
Phone: 1-800-839-8640

Published by AuthorHouse   10/16/2012

ISBN: 978-1-4772-3780-9 (sc)
ISBN: 978-1-4772-3781-6 (hc)
ISBN: 978-1-4772-3782-3 (e)

In memory of

RMR
Tidworth, 1944

My thanks to

Gill and Mike

Without whom this book would never have been written, and to the rest of my family for their encouragement and support.

Chapter 1

February 1944

It had rained during the night, washing away most of the snow that had lain since the beginning of February. What remained now hugged the kerbstones where it had been swept from the pavement, the dirty slushy lumps slowly melting in a weak sun. It was still bitterly cold as Mr Phillips, the manager of Burton and May of Northampton, walked down Milford Hill into Milford Street, wondering how many more mornings he would be taking this journey, treading the same pavement, passing the same houses and shops, turning the same corners. He should have retired two years ago, but the head office had asked him to stay on until the war was over. Young men to train as managers were hard to find, most of them being called up when they were eighteen for the services or war work in the factories or down the mines.

He turned into Market Street at eight thirty as most of the shopkeepers were getting ready for the day's trade. He said, "Good morning," to those who were in sight as he passed the hardware store, the teashop, and the optician's and then arrived at his own shop. He walked into the small arcade formed by the display windows fronting the pavement. From a bunch of keys, he picked the one that opened the lock on the shop door, thinking as he often did, that anyone wishing to break in could simply ignore the lock and kick in the glass panel, which comprised most of the door. He picked up the pint of milk from the doorstep, noticing as he did so that the cream had frozen, pushing up the cardboard disc so that it sat on top like a flat cap.

Inside, the air was chilled. He switched on the lighting, walked over to his desk, and put the milk and his attaché case down. Taking a box of matches from his pocket, he walked over and lit one of the two gas convector stoves that were placed each end of the shop. In the corner, by the door, stood a long wooden pole with a hook on the end. It was used to pull the awning over the windows to keep the sun off the display but served also to open and close the blackout curtains. Having done this, he went to the back of the shop, lit the other heater, and pulled back the curtain from the window overlooking the backyard. Going back to the desk, he opened the case took out a small canvas bag, unlocked a drawer, and tipped in the float money. He picked up the milk and walked through to the staffroom, slipped the galoshes from his shoes, took off his outdoor clothes, and hung them on the peg behind the door. Before he did anything else, he was going to make a cup of tea and have his first cigarette of the day from his ration of five.

It was warmer in the shop when he returned. He looked at his watch—nearly nine o'clock. The letter box rattled, and a sheaf of mail dropped onto the doormat. He walked over, picked it up, took it back to the desk, and shuffled through it. It was mostly bills, but one that caught his eye was in a buff envelope—obviously from head office—with "Open Immediately" stamped in red. He opened it and read:

> Arrangements have been made between the War Office, Board of Trade Department, and the US Army representatives to supply US Army officer personnel with regulation US government shoes. Consignments are being sent to all Burton and May retail outlets. You are required to display these shoes in a prominent position both in the shop interior and display window. We must emphasize that these goods must be *sold only* to US Army officers, who must produce a valid chit of permission to purchase. This covers the coupon value. *Cash only* will be acceptable on transaction. Display cards will be sent to you with your consignment.

Mr Phillips sighed and laid the letter down on the desk. So, American army officers were going to be able to buy shoes for no coupons. Americans! They were gradually taking over the place. At the bus station, cinema queues, restaurants. More money than our boys had and a better uniform. And the girls they attracted, he gasped at the thought—common little tarts, walking along the streets with painted faces, smoking and chewing gum, hanging around the American Red Cross on the High Street. He was glad in a way that he and Dora had never had children. It was not that they had not wanted them; it just hadn't happen. He supposed that he would have had grandchildren by now, growing up, perhaps in the forces or a granddaughter open to the temptation of the flashy uniforms and the free spending of money. He hoped so much that the two younger members of his staff would not have their heads turned by these soldiers from overseas. But what could he do? Only warn them that any misbehaviour that reflected on the shop would mean instant dismissal. He hoped it would never come to that.

Now. What about these shoes? He looked around the shop, wondering where would be the best place to show them. A long, narrow showcase extended the length of the floor space, dividing the gents' department from the ladies', and this end would do—right inside in front of the door where they could be seen at once. At the moment, the showcase displayed a variety of slippers, little felt booties in red or blue for tiny tots, plaid slippers with ankle straps for small girls, tab fronts for boys and men, fur trimmed for ladies or turned back collars. Underneath the showcase were the cupboards containing boxes of slippers now depleted after the Christmas rush. Some of the ones on show could now go underneath. The front of the showcase held the "luxury" slippers, leather fur lined velveteen with leather soles and a small heel for the ladies. So few luxury items were available in this time of trade restrictions, the slippers had sold like hotcakes. The few that remained could now go on top with the others, leaving space for the American officers' shoes. He went over to the door and unlocked it. The staff would be arriving soon and another trading day would begin.

***

Ina Welland studied herself in the long mirror on her wardrobe door. She turned to make sure her stocking seams were straight and then turned back to glance at her reflection once more. She was not completely satisfied with what she saw. She wished she was prettier and had the slim petite figure and naturally blonde hair that her friend Stella had and that boys were as quickly attracted to her as they were to Stella. She was told that she had nice hair. She put her hand to her head and ran it down each side. Her hair

3

was dark brown and fell in loose waves to her shoulders where it ended in curls. And it was all natural, she consoled herself. She did not go in for the fashions of the day of wearing her hair in "rolls" at the side of her face and a bunch of curls on top. She had tried a style once, with her hair swept back and a roll on her forehead. It had met with her father's disapproval so she had not tried it again. She picked up a large hair-slide from her dressing table, caught the hair at the nape of her neck, and fastened it with the slide. She brushed her hands down her wash-weary jumper and skirt, telling herself that no one was going to notice them under the overall she wore at work and that everyone else was in the same boat anyway.

Downstairs in the warm living room, she took her place at the breakfast table. Her twelve-year-old brother, Clive, was already seated with his nose in a comic. Hilda Welland came in with two plates of reconstituted dried egg, pan-scrambled, on toast.

"Put that comic away, Clive, and eat your breakfast."

Clive did as he was told. Picking up his knife and fork, he surveyed the table. "No brown sauce?"

"No," his mother replied, "not until I go to the shop. You'll have to make do with tomato."

"Not keen on tomato."

"Then you'll have to go without. Now get on and eat it, or you're going to miss your bus."

Hilda turned to her daughter. "Are you riding your bike to work?" she asked.

"I thought I would; the roads are pretty clear," Ina said.

"Well, be careful. They may still be a little icy, and don't forget, it will be dark when you come home tonight."

***

The air was cold when Ina set off from home. A slight, easterly wind had gotten up, with the promise of a freeze if it continued. Stella's bus had not come in when she'd arrived at the bus station. She leant her bicycle against the wall and knotted her head square more securely under her chin and waited. She had a self-confident personality that sometimes overshadowed Ina. Even at her youthful age, she had an effect on the male sex, which was not lost upon her and which she used to her advantage. She was not promiscuous in the sexual sense, but she liked the admiration she received.

Ina was not jealous of her friend but sometimes envied the ease with which she gained attention from any group of boys they occasionally met. Stella usually had first choice of an admirer, and Ina did sometimes wish that her own figure was not quite so generous and her hair so dark.

Nevertheless, in spite of the war going on around them, the girls had a fairly pleasurable life. These small encounters with local boys who were not old enough for the services were usually casual and short-lived. The bus came in, and Stella jumped onto the pavement. Her long blonde hair was rolled round a wadding band, which went most of the way around her head. She caught up with Ina, and together they walked along Endless Street towards Market Street. When they reached the shop, Stella opened the door wide to let Ina and her bicycle through. There was no other entrance to the shop, and the only access to the back was through the shop itself. They went through the door at the other end of the shop and into a small back room. Here was an enclosed toilet and a sink with a cold tap. A wide bench stood against one wall with shelves above, where Mr Phillips did the small repairs—putting rubber stick on soles, stapling buttons onto children's shoes, or hammering steel tips into boys' shoes, toe, and heel; punching new eyelet holes in straps, inserting heel grips, and putting the shoes of the bunion-footed matrons on the stretcher. Overhead were two shelves that held an assortment of newly labelled shoeboxes ready for a new consignment of shoes, which came in paper bags.

The boxes were used over and over again, having blank labels put on them as soon as they were empty. Shoeboxes were seldom given away with the shoes. Beyond this small room was the staffroom and, beyond that, a second, large enough for a sitting room, with a small kitchen adjoined. Upstairs were three bedrooms. Mr Phillips and his wife had lived on the premises when he had taken over the shop as manager, but there being no back way and having to go through the shop each time Dora Phillips had to go out proved inconvenient, and they had rented a house in Shady Bower. The rooms were left empty in spite of the scarcity of living accommodation. The difficulty of access made them exempt from enforced occupation. The girls hung their outdoor clothes up on the coat stand. Vera Jenner, the third salesgirl, entered the room.

"Hello," said Ina. "Have a good weekend?"

"Yes," Vera replied. "George and I went to my auntie's in Bristol. She hadn't met him before. She's my mum's aunt really. She's quite old, nearly eighty."

"Will she be going to the wedding?" asked Stella.

"No; that's why we went to see her yesterday afternoon."

Vera's wedding to her fiancé had been arranged for the coming August. She was a quiet girl, rather shy to the point of timidity. Ina wondered at times how she had managed to attract her George, having herself met him and having considered him quite nice-looking and much more outgoing than Vera. She had felt a stab of envy.

The morning passed fairly uneventfully, and there were few customers. When a Southern Railway delivery horse and cart drew up outside, Ina and Stella could safely leave to Vera whatever serving was necessary and concentrate on the two sacks of returned shoe repairs the carrier brought in. Shoe repairs, except for the minor ones done by Mr Phillips in the back room, were sent to the factory at Northampton. Customers leaving their shoes for repair were given the perforated section of a numbered ticket; the other section was then tied to one of the shoes. When they were returned from the factory, they were taken to the back room beyond the staff room and placed on the floor in numerical order. It was a rule that, if they were not collected within six months, they could be sold for the price of the repair. There was a pair of shoes in Ina's size, tan and white brogue court shoes with a Cuban heel. She had tried them on and asked if she could have them. She had two months to go and was keeping her fingers crossed. That morning, the carrier brought two canvas sacks of repaired shoes. Ina and Stella dragged the sacks into the back room, opened them, and tipped the contents onto the floor.

"It's your turn today," Stella said with a grin. She picked up the empty sacks and took them back through the shop to the waiting carrier.

Ina crossed though the names in the second book; that way, a glance would tell if a customer's shoes were indeed back. Losses of shoes were a most rare occurrence, usually through some slip up with the cards. Ina looked at the brogue court shoes, stepped out of her own, and put the brogues on. She walked up and down. They were real leather, not utility, might even be pre-war. They hadn't been made by Burton's, and she couldn't make out the name of the maker, as the print on the insole had been worn away. She took them off and put her own shoes back on. Going through the staff room on her way back to the shop, she saw that Mr Phillips was at the table doing his paperwork. He had a cup of tea by his elbow and was smoking another of his ration of five Player's through a cigarette holder.

"Your shoes are still there then, Miss?" He called them all Miss, except for Mrs Gray, who was always called Mrs Gray.

"Yes," Ina replied.

"You'll have a good pair of shoes there and all for 1s.6d." He smiled.

"And no coupons." She smiled back.

***

Two stools stood in front of the row of chairs where a woman was sat. The woman stood up and viewed her feet in the small standing mirror, speaking to Vera about the shoe she was trying on. Vera answered "yes" or "no" without much attempt to help the woman choose from the pile of shoes that were gathered around her. At the back of the shop on the left-hand side was a window overlooking a small backyard that let light into the shop. Underneath was another showcase, on top of which were three chromium-plated stands; these were to display ladies' stockings; men's and children's hosiery was carefully placed on the base, while drawers underneath were filled with backup stock. From this, Ina and Stella were filling in empty spaces left by Saturday's trade. Stella looked in Vera's direction.

"She's so slow," she remarked. "I wonder she ever manages to make a sale! Talk about being the first sales."

"She did get two tags last week," Ina told her.

"Tags" were fixed to shoes priced over £2.0s.0d and worth 1s.0d in commission to whoever sold them. Vera, being the eldest and having been at the shop longer than Ina or Stella, was granted the privilege of being the first to serve.

"Goodness knows what George sees in her. He must do all the talking," Stella went on.

"She may be different with him. She's not bad looking," Ina told her.

"I know. I'll give her that, but a good-looking bloke like George! I'd have thought he'd have gone for someone with more 'go' in her."

Ina didn't answer. Without confiding in Stella, Ina had thought much the same. On the first occasion that she had met Vera's George, she had regarded him as having a very likeable personality; he wasn't a bit shy like Vera, and yes, he was nice-looking.

***

At ten o'clock, Mrs Gray breezed into the shop. Mrs Gray was always breezing, her stoutness belying her mobility. She was an active little body but nevertheless never seemed to get much done.

"Did you come down Castle Street this morning?" she asked Ina.

"Yes. Why?"

"Did you see anything?"

"Like what?" asked Ina, puzzled.

"Tell you when I come back into the shop." And she was gone to hang her coat up.

"What's she on about?" asked Stella.

"Beats me," Ina replied.

Mrs Gray spared no time hanging up her coat and getting back into the shop.

"You didn't see anything at all?" she asked Ina.

"No. What was I suppose to see?"

"Well, you know Ern's on nights at Sarum Engineering. Last night, there was a fight outside the Castle Arms between American soldiers and our boys. Ern and some more of them went outside, and the place was full of military police, theirs and ours, and civvy police. Ern said there was broken glass all over the street. It was a right riot."

"It must have been cleaned up when I came along Castle Street. I didn't notice anything, though if I had heard of it, I might have looked for something."

"Nothing but trouble, these Yanks. If they're not taking English girls, they're causing fights."

"How do you know our boys didn't start it?" asked Stella. "There's good and bad in all of them."

"Well," went on Mrs Gray, "I don't remember anything like the streets of Salisbury are now. It's no pleasure to go anywhere these days. My neighbour was walking his dog over the fields the other night and nearly fell over a couple."

"Couple of what?" asked Stella.

"You know. A Yank and a girl. It's disgusting!" snapped Mrs Gray

"He got a good look at them then." Stella smiled.

"It's not funny, Miss Auden," said Mrs Gray huffily.

"I know," Stella replied. "But I dare say it was going on long before the Yanks came."

"Oh. So you're on their side!"

Stella could see that Mrs Gray was getting out of her depth so decided to change the subject. She turned to Mr Phillips. "Mr Phillips, can we put out the spring stuff?"

"It's a bit early, isn't it?" he answered.

"I just thought it would cheer people up to let them see spring's on the way."

"Very well, do so if you want to."

Stella went through the shop and came back after a while dragging a large cardboard box. This held the seasonal decorations. The spring ones consisted of sprays of waxed cherry and apple blossom, daffodils in small pots, and cardboard cut-outs of lambs standing in daisy filled grass.

"Shall we dress the windows?" asked Vera, suddenly coming to life.

"Yes if you like. I'll put a couple of things in my window," Mr Phillips said.

Between the few customers coming in, the women managed to spread the spring symbols around the shop, placing a lamb by the hosiery with sprays of apple and cherry blossom and two pots of daffodils. Next was the centre display. Up went two more lambs, sprays, and daffodils.

"Doesn't that look a bit odd?" asked Vera.

"Why?" asked Ina.

"Well, among the slippers. Ought to be sandals," Vera said.

"We'll have sandals in soon, and people still wear slippers indoors all year round."

Vera just shrugged.

"What do you want in your window, Mr Phillips?" asked Ina.

"Oh. Just a few of the sprays and a couple of the daffodils," he answered. "I don't think the lambs would go down very well in the gent's window."

The shop door opened, and in came Dora Phillips. She was a thin birdie woman who wore a long brown corded coat with an Astrakhan collar. On her head she wore a velveteen beret-like hat after the style of an ice bag. She usually came to see her husband sometime during the day, morning or afternoon, and he took advantage of her appearance to have another cup of tea and a cigarette.

"I'll do my window later," he said and gave the till keys to Vera.

"Are you going to do your window now?" Stella asked Vera.

"Yes, I'll have a lamb and some sprays and daffs."

The windows were accessed by narrow doors either side of the main door. Vera took what she wanted and stepped into her window. A customer came into the shop, and Mrs Gray stepped forward. Ina and Stella finished their decorating, putting the box aside for Mr Phillips to take his share. Vera didn't really like being in the window. She was always afraid of knocking over the display, although it was kept to a minimum of shoes, mostly size 3. She placed the lamb in the corner and put the sprays gently on the glass stands. She heard tapping on the window and looked round. Two American soldiers stood looking through, smiling at her and beckoning for her to come out. Flushing to the roots of her hair, she escaped from the window, flew across the shop floor, and disappeared out the back. Startled, the others looked after her.

"What's got into her?" said Stella, and suddenly she knew.

The two GIs came into the shop. One of them asked, "Hey there, where's the pretty girl who was in the window?"

Mrs Gray, whose customer had gone, went up to them. "She's not here; she's gone. Go away, or you will get her into trouble."

"Hell, ma'am, we had no such intentions. We only wanted to have a little word with her."

"Go away," hissed Mrs Gray. "If our boss comes in, he will not be very happy."

"What's the matter with you British? Don't you want to be friendly? We only wanted a little word." He turned to Stella and Ina who were looking on. "What about you two? You ain't gonna turn your backs on a couple of GIs who have come over to help you win the war" he declared with a challenging grin.

Stella came up to them. She could smell drink on them and knew she'd have to tread carefully in case they turned nasty.

"Look, guys," she said, "we've got nothing against you, but our boss doesn't like us having men in the shop. He's very old-fashioned, you know? We'll all get the sack. You wouldn't want that, would you? The girl's getting married soon to a soldier in the airborne anyway, and both of us have boyfriends." She hesitated and then said, "They're marine commandos; otherwise"—she smiled at them—"you might have been in with a chance."

"Okay, little lady. Get the picture. Hope to see you around sometime, eh?"

"Yes of course."

"You sure are missing out on a treat."

"I'm sure I am."

They were walking towards the door, and she opened it for them.

"Cheerio," said the one who had been doing the talking. "That's what you Brits say, isn't it?"

"Cheerio," Stella replied, adding under her breath, "and a soldier's farewell to you."

He looked at her a little uncertainly and then, turning to his companion, said, "Aw, come on; let's go get some chow."

They went through the door and walked unsteadily into the street.

"I'll go and tell Vera the coast is clear," Ina said and went through to the small back room just as Vera came out of the toilet.

"Have you been in there all the time?"

"They really embarrassed me," said Vera. "I couldn't go into the staffroom because of Mr and Mrs Phillips being in there. They'd have asked what was wrong."

"Well it's all clear now," Ina told her.

"Will you finish off my window, just in case they come back?"

"All right," replied Ina. "I'll tell Mr Phillips you felt a little dizzy."

"Won't he suspect something?"

"I shouldn't think so."

"What if they're outside when I go home dinner time?"

"They'll be long gone by one o'clock. They were off to get something to eat."

***

The rest of the morning passed uneventfully, and at twelve o'clock, Ina and Stella had their lunch in the staffroom, usually sandwiches—tomato with paste or cheese toasted by the gas fire. After, they would have a stroll around town, getting back at one o'clock, in time for Vera to go home and Mrs Gray, who didn't take a full hour, to have her sandwiches. Mr Phillips usually went to a nearby restaurant. In the staffroom, the gas fire was already lit on a low flame. Stella bent down to raise it, and they both opened their sandwiches.

"What have you got in yours?" asked Ina.

"Cheese. You?"

"Cheese." Ina took the toasting fork off the hook by the fireplace, while Stella plugged in the electric kettle to make tea.

"Are you doing anything tonight?" Stella asked.

"No, not particularly, probably write to Teddy."

"Do you think he gets all your letters—yours, your gran's and his mum's?"

Ina sighed. "I don't know. They go somewhere I suppose. I'd like to think he gets some of them, even if he can't reply."

"It's wicked isn't it? Your aunty must be desperate for news. She often has such a sad look on her face," Stella said. "It makes me feel sad too. I hope the war's over by the time Terry's old enough to go. How old is he?"

"He will be nineteen in May," Ina said. "He's never been called up because he's on the railway."

There was silence for a while and then, Ina said, reflectively, "I wonder how long it will be before we go into France?"

"My dad reckons it will be about May some when."

Their lunch finished, they strolled along Queen Street and crossed the marketplace towards Style & Gerrish. Once there, they paused in front of a window display of dresses, skirts, and blouses.

"I could do with a new dress," said Stella, "but even if I had the money, I wouldn't have the coupons. You're lucky in a way with your aunty Nell being a dressmaker."

"I still can't afford to buy the material," replied Ina, "and my coat took the rest of my coupons, even though it was a Christmas present from my mum and dad."

"It's a nice coat, though," Stella told her. "Brown suits you."

"I can only wear it Sundays," said Ina, "and I had this old navy thing when I left school."

"I've had mine that long," replied Stella, "and it's the only one I have."

Ina suddenly started. She had seen reflections in the window.

"What's up?"

"It's those two Yanks who came into the shop," said Ina, "and they're coming this way."

"They wouldn't recognise us now would they?" Stella asked. "They weren't that sober."

"We'll have to give them the slip. I don't like the look of either of them, especially that one with a face like a pudding."

"Where are we going to slip to?" asked Stella.

"One place they can't follow us—down the ladies' toilets!"

They turned with their backs against the direction the American soldiers were walking, and crossing over the road, they reached the public toilets in the marketplace and ran down the steps. When they reached the bottom, Ina said. "I haven't got any pennies. Have you?"

Stella took her purse from her handbag and took out two pennies. She gave one to Ina. They selected two toilets next to one another, put their money into the slots, went into the toilets, and closed the doors.

"How long do you think we're going to be in here?" Ina called.

"Not too long I hope. We'll give them a few minutes and then go up. They'll have probably cleared off by then."

"I've just thought of something funny," said Ina.

"What?"

"They've got us hiding in the lavs, just like they had Vera."

They both laughed.

***

After a while they came out. They stopped halfway up the steps as two women came down.

"Excuse me," Stella said to them, "have you noticed any American soldiers waiting about up there?"

One of the women turned and went back up the steps. "Can't see any," she said.

"Good. Thanks very much." Then to Ina, she said, "Come on; with a bit of luck we've outwitted them."

"Funny that," the woman said to her companion. "Thought girls were falling over themselves for the Yanks, instead of getting rid of them."

"Probably got two more waiting around another corner," her companion replied.

The girls hurried back to work and reached the shop with five minutes to spare. They did not tell Vera they had seen the two Americans, just that the way was clear for her to go home.

"Let's hope Pudding Face and his pal really have gone," said Ina.

Chapter 2

It was quite dark by five thirty. Mr Phillips had pulled the blackout curtains across the door and the fanlights over the window doors and the window at the rear of the shop. There was no fear of a sudden rush of customers, so he and Vera did the cashing up. At six o'clock, he put his hand under the door curtain and turned the "open" sign to "closed". Ina went through to the staffroom and pulled the curtains across the window before turning the light on. Stella and Vera followed her and changed into their outdoor clothes. Just enough natural light remained for Ina to fetch her bicycle and test the shaded front and rear lights. They said goodnight to Mr Phillips and went off in different directions.

Although Ina usually met Stella in the mornings, she went straight home after work, going along Fisherton Street and turning right at the Wessex garage to take the Devizes Road. She went round the back way of her house, pushing her bicycle before her and leaning it against the shed while she opened the door to wheel it inside, to make sure her father would be able to take his cycle out when he went to work that night.

"Hello, Ina." The voice came as she was walking up the path to the back door, and it startled her. She turned and saw Harold Daley, the son of her next-door neighbour.

"Oh. It's you," she said.

"Fancy coming to the pictures one night this week?" he asked.

"Not after last time!" she replied emphatically. "I don't like being pawed about, and you won't get a second chance."

"Go on. You know you enjoyed it."

"That's what you think!"

"I suppose it would be better if I wore my army cadet uniform. You girls go for uniforms now. Anyway I shall be called up soon, and I'll have a proper uniform. Perhaps you'll feel differently then."

"I don't think so." Ina had reached the back door.

"Stuck up cow!" Harold called as she went inside and shut the door.

"What's the matter with you?" asked Hilda Welland as Ina came into the room. "You've a face enough to turn the milk sour."

"Oh," replied Ina. "It's that Harold pestering me to go out with him again. I had enough the first time."

"Didn't he behave himself then?" asked Hilda.

"No, Mum, he didn't; hands all over the place. It was revolting and made me feel sick. I don't like him anyway."

"According to Mrs Daley, he gave you the push." Hilda smiled.

"Then he is a liar. Anyway, Mrs Daley would say that, wouldn't she? Always on about how well he has done in the cadets and how he'll get quick promotion in the army. She is always going on about her kids. You'd think Maureen was the only one to be a civil servant at Southern Command or have an RAF sergeant for a boyfriend."

"Well," said Hilda, "that's Cissie. She was always the same, even at school, but I wished I'd known before what Harold did. I'd have had a word with her."

"Don't go saying anything now," Ina told her. "It'll only spoil your friendship with her."

"Friendship! She just hangs on to me because we were at school together, but we weren't really friends. I think she just wants someone to go to whist drive with. She bores so many people."

"Well, you stuck it for five years," laughed Ina.

"I thought I had seen the last of her when we had left school. I never dreamed she'd live next door to us. There, I suppose she's not so bad really. Lay the table will you?"

"What have we got for tea?"

"Spam fritters with mashed potatoes and peas. There wasn't enough left of yesterday's joint to do anything with."

"What time's Dad getting up?" asked Ina.

"He should be getting up now. Give Clive a call. He's in the front room doing his homework."

Ina went into the front room to see the twelve-year-old at the small side table with his schoolbooks.

"Dinner's nearly ready," she said.

"I've just finished. It's really cold in here. My fingers are like ice," replied Clive.

"Can't spare the coal for two rooms, Clive," called Hilda, who'd overheard. "I told you to start directly when you came in from school. You could have had the dining table all to yourself."

Jim Welland came into the room and sat down at the dining table.

"Cold up in that bedroom," he said giving a shiver.

"Another one complaining of a cold room," said Hilda. "I've just told your son, not enough coal to heat all the rooms. Anyway, it's nearly spring; the warmer days will be coming."

She went into the kitchen and came back with the last plate and set it before her husband.

Jim turned to Clive, who sat nearest the radio. "Switch the wireless on, son."

Clive leaned over and turned the knob. An American voice came over the airwaves announcing a singer and the song she was going to sing.

"Ina!" Jim turned to his daughter. "Have you had that AFN programme on again? Why don't you turn it back to the Home Service when you've finished?"

"It wasn't Ina, Dad. I turned it on when I came home from school," Clive said.

"What on earth do you want to listen to a Yankee programme for?" asked his father.

"I just put it on for the music," Clive replied.

"Flaming Yanks!" Jim cried. "They're taking over this country."

Clive tuned the radio to the Home Service, and they finished their meal in silence except for the radio giving out the last of the news. When they had all finished, Hilda began clearing the table. Ina got up from her chair to help her mother, Jim sat in his chair by the fire reading his paper, and Clive spread comics over the table and became absorbed. Ina helped her mother wash up and put the crockery away. They had just come out of the kitchen into the living room when the back door opened and a voice called out

"Coo-e-e-e. Can I come in?"

"Oh, no," groaned Hilda quietly.

"What does that blooming woman want now?" said Jim.

"Have you finished eating?" the voice came again.

"Yes," replied Hilda resignedly. "Come in."

The woman who came in was tall and thin, with hennaed hair and carmine lips.

"Did you want something, Cissie?" asked Hilda.

"No, but I must tell you, I've got some exciting news."

"Oh! What's happened then?"

"It's Maureen and Keith," replied Cissie. "They're getting engaged at Easter. Isn't it smashing?"

"Very nice," said Hilda. "Give them my congratulations."

"We're having a bit of a party, and we're hoping his aunty can get down."

"His aunty?"

"Yes. She brought him up. His parents both died when he was young."

"Oh, that's a shame." Hilda tried to put a little sympathy into her voice.

"I think she's pretty well off," Cissie went on. "Got a big house. She'll leave it all to Keith."

"Maureen's a lucky girl," said Hilda.

"Yes. He's such a nice boy. One more promotion, and he'll be a warrant officer. Of course, Harold should get quick promotion when he joins the army you know."

"Yes, so you've said."

"I do wish he could get a nice girl." Cissie gave Ina a sideways glance, which wasn't lost on Hilda.

"A really nice girl who'll appreciate him," Cissie went on.

"Girls like that are hard to find," interposed Jim from the depths of his armchair. "He'll have to snap one up before a Yank gets to her."

Cissie gave a forced laugh. "Well, I must go; had to give you the good news."

She went out of the living room into the kitchen. "See you Wednesday night then, Hilda. Will your mum-in-law be going to the whist drive?"

"Yes. As far as I know."

"Very good for her age, isn't she?"

"She's seventy-two," replied Hilda. "She's got a few more miles to go yet."

"Yes, well, see you Wednesday then."

"Goodbye, Cissie."

Hilda saw her out and came back into the living room.

"For heaven's sake, bolt the back door," said Jim, "in case she has anymore 'good news' to tell us. She really gets on my box."

"She's not bad really," said Hilda, "but I must admit, Nell and I get fed up with her at the whist drive sometimes. She'll be telling everyone about Maureen and Keith on Wednesday."

Jim was rolling a cigarette. "He's a lot older than she is, isn't he?"

"I don't know that I've ever noticed," Hilda replied. "I haven't seen much of him."

"I only noticed him when Alb brought him down the legion."

"Are you going down there tonight, Jim?" Hilda asked.

"No. Not now. Not with having to leave here at 9.30."

"Can I have AFN on again?" asked Ina.

"I suppose so. Don't know why you want that rubbish on. What's the matter with Vera Lynn or Ann Shelton?"

"I won't have it on too loud."

"You'd better not. And don't forget," Jim said, waving a finger at her, "I shall want to hear the nine o'clock news."

Six o'clock . . . seven o'clock . . . eight o'clock . . . nine o'clock, thought Ina. *Come ten o'clock, he'll be word perfect . . .*

***

When Ina fetched her cycle from the shed the next morning, she discovered that the front tyre was very flat. "Damn," she swore. Knowing she would have no time to mend the puncture, she rushed back into the house. Clive had already left for school, and her mother was bustling about tidying up before it was time for her to go to the milk factory, where she worked five days a week, 10.00 a.m. to 4.00 p.m.

"I've got a puncture. I'll have to get the bus."

"You'll have to get a move on, then."

Ina went out of the living room into the hall.

"If you're going out the front way," Hilda called, "don't slam the door. Your father's in bed."

Ina closed the front door as quietly as she could and ran down the path, through the gate, and down the road towards the bus stop. Ina saw a few people waiting for the bus, which cheered her up, as she knew it would give her more time. She looked behind her and saw the bus coming towards her. She reached the bus stop just as the bus pulled up. She followed the other passengers and sat on one of the left-hand side seats. The bus moved off, and the conductress came along the aisle for the fares. She was a peroxide blonde, her hair piled upon her head, her cap flattened on top like a pancake. She was chewing gum with her mouth open; when she took Ina's fare and gave her the ticket, Ina noticed her fingers were dirty and the bright red varnish on her nails was chipped and peeling. *Must be handling all those coppers*, thought Ina.

***

Ina got off the bus outside Style & Gerrish and crossed the Blue Boar Row. The smell of animals wafted from the market. Hurdles enclosed cattle, sheep, and pigs. Lorries, with their backs open, fringed the square, and auctioneers were walking around with their sticks, poking and prodding the animals. Down one side were rows of cages stacked one on top of another, holding chickens, cockerels, pigeons, rabbits, and kittens. Ina skirted the market square and saw Stella walking opposite her along Queen Street. She hailed her, and Stella crossed the road to join her.

"Where's the trusty steed this morning?" Stella asked.

"Puncture. I had to catch the bus."

"I waited for you a little while and then I came on—thought you might be ill or something."

"No." Ina fell into step with Stella as they crossed the canal into Market Street. "I didn't notice it until I got the bike out this morning. I should have asked my mum to leave a note for my dad to see if he could fix it for me. It'll be dark when I get home tonight, and I shall get moaned at if I bring it in the kitchen."

"Nothing exciting happened last night then."

"Like what?"

"Oh, I don't know." Stella sighed and then went on: "I babysat for Jean last night. Eric's on leave, and they went for a drink. He has to go back Friday, and I don't suppose she'll see much of him again before he goes to France."

"He's no idea when it will be, then?" Ina asked.

"He said everything's geared up for it. They're probably waiting for the right conditions."

"What would they be?"

"Beats me."

***

They reached the shop, and a new day began. Tuesday could be quite busy, being a market day, when the farmers from the outlying farms and country people would come into town for various purchases. By the time the girls were ready, the shop was beginning to fill up.

Later in the morning, an American soldier came in accompanied by a woman.

"You have some navy suede court shoes in the window, 22/11d. Have you got them in a size 6?" asked the woman.

Mr Phillips called Vera. "Miss. Young lady would like the navy suede court shoes in a size 6 please. Will you serve?"

Vera indicated a seat for them both and fetched the shoes. The woman tried them on, walking up and down.

"How do they look, Bob?"

"Okay, honey, okay. Do you want those?"

"Yes, please."

The woman gave the shoes to Vera, who put them into a paper bag

"We don't get the box, then?" the American asked.

Vera hesitated, and Mr Phillips said, "If you would like the box, then we shall give it to you. We really do like to keep them and relabel them for the next consignment."

"No, no," said the American holding up his hand. "We don't mind at all, do we, honey? Guess it's because there's a war on. The bag will do nicely. How much for the shoes?"

"It'll £1.2s.11d please, and seven coupons," Vera told him.

He gave Vera the one pound and searched in his pocket for the loose change.

"I have three shillings. I hope that's enough."

"Yes, thank you," said Vera. "You have some change."

"And seven coupons," he said with a smile. "We must not forget the coupons."

He turned to the woman. She handed her coupon book to Mr Phillips, who cut out the required amount and then handed it back to her with the penny change. They thanked him and went out of the shop.

"She's onto a good thing," Mrs Gray remarked. "Wonder what else he's going to buy her? That's all those girls want Yanks for—to spend money on them."

"Oh, for a Yank with dough," whispered Stella to Ina.

The woman who was being served by Ina grinned and said, "And so say all of us!"

***

When Ina got home from work that night, her father was already up and sitting in his chair.

"Your puncture's mended," he said.

"Oh, thanks, Dad. I didn't think you'd know about it."

"I didn't," replied her father. "Clive did it."

"Oh, thanks, Clive." She turned to where he was sat reading a comic. "I owe you one".

"I shan't forget," he said with a grin.

Hilda came in from the kitchen. "Get the table laid, Ina, and for goodness sake, Clive, get your head out of that comic and help your sister."

Clive got up reluctantly to get the cutlery from the sideboard drawer.

Jim said, "I don't know about you, I'm sure, Clive. Here you are, a grammar school boy, and you've always got your nose in a comic."

***

Wednesday was early closing day and also ordering day; that is, no shoes were actually ordered, but on special sheets they did a sort of stocktaking. On the sheets, they wrote the job number of the shoe, the colour, if it was suede or leather, heel size, and shoe size, and it was left to the warehouse in Northampton to decide what shoes to send to restock or whether to send a new line that may have come in. Mr Phillips usually filled in the gents' sheets, and Vera, the ladies'. Ina did the children's and Stella the sundries—shoelaces, polish, suede cleaner, inner soles, heel grips, and shoe dyes. Stella also did the hosiery.

Vera did not know all the ladies' shoe numbers off by heart so went inside the window to get them from the shoes. This she hated, now especially, since the incident with the American soldiers. Ina had filled the ladies' sheets in, in Vera's absences and had kept the numbers in her head. She offered to go outside and write down the numbers on a piece of paper for Vera to transfer to her sheet. Mr Phillips made no comment. As long as the job was done, he did not interfere.

At one o'clock, the shop was shut and the girls left. On this occasion, Ina accompanied Stella to the bus station, pushing her bicycle along the road. When they arrived, Stella's bus had not come in, so they stood there for a while talking. Ina was in no hurry to get home. Her mother would be at work, Clive in school, and her father in bed. As she stood with Stella, she noticed an American soldier standing alone nearby. People were passing by in front of and behind him, but he did not seem to notice their existence. Ina felt a surge of something akin to pity for him. He was here, miles away from his home and family. Soon he would be going to war, and there was no one to wish him luck or kiss him goodbye.

As if he felt Ina's eyes on him, he turned suddenly and took a couple of steps towards the girls. "Pardon me," he said, "but am I in the right place for the Tidworth bus?"

"Yes," said Stella. "It should be in soon. I'm waiting for it myself."

"Do you live in Tidworth?" he asked.

"No," Stella replied. "I get off the bus just after Amesbury."

"I've been through Amesbury when I've come in by truck," he said. "Some of our guys get off there."

"Well, here's the bus," said Stella, pointing.

Ina stayed until Stella and the American were on the bus and noticed, with a smile, that they sat together. She turned with a wave of her hand, mounted her bicycle, and cycled along Endless Street, along the Blue Boar Row and into Fisherton Street.

***

Ina found a note on the kitchen table in her mother's hand when she got in:

I've put a vegetable casserole in the oven. I'll make dumplings when I get in. Light the oven at four o'clock on a low gas. Please do some potatoes. There's a letter from Avril on the mantelshelf. I'll be home about four thirty.

Mum

Ina took the letter down from the mantelshelf. Avril wrote regular but not very long letters.

Dear Mum, Dad, and all.

Good News. Brian and I have Easter off, and we can both get home. Will let you know when we shall be coming. I haven't much to report, except, guess what? I've got a stripe so I'm a LACW. Shall soon catch up with Brian, who's just got his second stripe.

She went on to say what she had been doing and how she was looking forward to being home. She had been in the WAAF just over two years, volunteering to be with Brian, who had gone into the RAF in 1940 at eighteen years of age.

Ina put the letter down and automatically turned on the radio, tuning into the AFN programme and making sure it was playing quietly, as her father would still be in bed. It was good that Avril and Brian were getting a bit of leave together. All the time Avril had been in the WAAF, she had never managed to be stationed anywhere near Brian, and weekends together had been few and far between. Only once had they had seven days leave together to spend at home.

Ina peeled some potatoes and put them in a saucepan of water. She decided she would have a bath and wash her hair. She went upstairs into the bathroom and turned on the Ascot over the bath, filled up an enamel jug with hot water from it, and washed her hair while the bath was filling up. She heard her father getting up and called out to him.

"I'm in the bath, Dad. Did I wake you up?"

"No," he called back. "I didn't sleep very well."

***

Jim went downstairs into the living room. He had emptied the ashes from last night's fire and had relaid it when he had gotten home that morning. If he lit it now, the room would be warm when Hilda and Clive came in. He put a match to the paper and soon the dry sticks were crackling. By the time Ina came downstairs, the fire was well alight with a little coal and a couple of logs.

"Want a cup of tea?" she asked.

"Yes, please, duck," her father said. "I want to get down to the allotment and call into your gran's on the way home."

Ina sat by the fire, towelling her hair and listening to the radio. Her father made no comment about the programme. He finished his cup of tea and then went up to the bathroom to wash. When he came down again, he got into his overcoat, fetched a large canvas bag from the kitchen, and went out of the back door.

"Give my love to Gran and Aunty Nell," called Ina.

He waved and said, "I'll be back before five o'clock" and opened the shed door to get his bicycle.

***

Clive came in from school at four-thirty. His cap was on the back of his head and his socks were gradually working their way down to his ankles. He threw his satchel into the corner. "No Mum yet?"

"No. She should be in soon. You'd better get upstairs and change out of your school clothes."

"I shall be glad when I get out of these trousers," Clive grumbled. "Short trousers at my age he complained. I'm nearly thirteen and still in short trousers! My knees are sore with cold."

"Well, that's your school uniform," said Ina, smiling. "If you had to be clever clogs and get yourself into Bishop's School, you must put up with it."

"No sympathy." Clive went upstairs, and Ina laid the table.

They had tea a little earlier on Wednesday nights, as Hilda went to the whist drive at the Legion Hall with her mother-in-law and sister-in-law and, of course, Cissie Daley. By the time Hilda arrived home, the fire was blazing in the grate. Ina had put another log on and the living room was cosy and warm. Hilda made the dumplings, took the casserole out of the oven, popped the dumplings in, and put the casserole back. She put a match to the burner under the potatoes.

"Did you salt the spuds?" she called to Ina.

"Yes," Ina called back.

"You'd better give Dad a call."

"He's already up. He's gone down to the allotment and was going to call in to see Gran."

"I hope he won't be late," Hilda said. "I shouldn't think he could see much down there. It's getting dark now." She was just serving up when Jim came in. "Oh, good," she said, "you're just in time. How's Mum?"

"She's fine," replied Jim, "all raring to go gambling tonight."

"It isn't gambling."

"Well, you hope to win a prize don't you?" He laughed and took his place at the table.

***

The Legion Hall was at the bottom of the road; Nell and her mother usually met Hilda there. Hilda was partnering Cissie, and they took their places at one of the tables. After a little while, the MC blew his whistle, and play began. Every so often, they would move tables, taking their scorecards with them. Silence prevailed until the whistle blew for break time, when they had tea or coffee and a biscuit.

Now was the chance Cissie had been waiting for. She regaled the others at length with the details of Maureen's impending engagement to her airman, and the three sat with polite attention, even Hilda, who had heard it all before. At last, the woman responsible for the catering and her assistant came to collect the cups and saucers, and then the whistle blew, and play once more commenced.

At the end of the game, they gave in their scorecards. Hilda and Cissie had both won prizes. Hilda's was a compendium set, which would look very nice in the fire grate in the front room, and Cissie's, a table lamp.

"Look!" she cried. "Just the thing for Maureen's bottom drawer."

***

After Hilda had gone out, Clive got his satchel onto the table and removed the books.

"Got much homework tonight, son?" asked his father.

"Too much!" replied Clive.

Jim sat in his chair by the fire reading the *Railway Magazine*. Ina got her mother's workbox out and proceeded to put new elastic in a pair of knickers, sew some more ribbon straps onto a petticoat, and darn a pair of stockings. There was no sound, apart from the ticking of the clock and the fire crackling in the grate. She suddenly thought of the lonely

American soldier and wondered if Stella had made a date with him. She was just a little envious of the way Stella just smiled at a chap to have him falling at her feet. She wished she had Stella's unselfconsciousness and easy repartee.

***

When she met Stella off the bus the next morning, she asked "How did you get on with the Yank?"

"What do you mean," Stella asked, "get on with him?"

"Well. Did he date you?"

"No!"

"Well" exclaimed Ina. "What a surprise"

"He was very nice," said Stella, "offered to pay my fare. But I told him I had a season ticket. Anyway, he was married; talked to me of his home in Kansas and showed me photos of his wife and kids"

"Were you disappointed?"

"No! Of course not. He was too old for me anyway. He was in his late twenties at least."

***

It was the next Monday morning that the consignment of shoes came. Four large cardboard boxes were dumped by the railway carter on the floor in the ladies' department. Eager hands ripped open the packaging. There might be a chance of a new line and not just replacements for the stock sold. One packing case was comprised entirely of men's shoe boxes. The American officers' shoes had arrived complete with place cards and price tickets.

Chapter 3

March 1944

Ina and Stella had not gone dancing on Saturday night. It had been very busy at work, and both had declared a preference for going to the pictures. Stella stayed over at the Wellands, and in the morning, after breakfast, went with Ina to get the Sunday papers. They walked to the paper shop and got a copy each of *The Pictorial* and *News of the World*. Stella bought some chocolates with the last of her sweet coupons and two bunches of daffodils, still in bud, for Mrs Welland from the bucket outside the shop doorway. The sun was bright, and as yet, the sky cloudless. The easterly wind had dropped, and it was quite pleasant, providing one was warmly wrapped up. The girls decided to go for a walk after lunch and set off at about two twenty with no real aim in mind except to be back by five o'clock when it would be teatime. They decided to go and call in to Ina's grandmother and her aunt Nell.

"Hello," called Ina, opening the back door.

"Is that you, Ina?" called her grandmother. "Come on in."

"Stella's with me," Ina added.

Her grandmother and aunt were sitting by the fire listening to the radio. Mrs Welland moved to turn it off.

"No, don't do that", said Ina. "We're not stopping long."

"Hello, Mrs Welland," Stella said.

"It's nice to see you again, Stella. Are all your family well?"

"Yes, they're fine at the moment, thanks." Stella replied.

"Your mum and Mrs Daley were lucky Wednesday night," put in Nell to Ina.

"I don't reckon I will be able to go to whist drives much longer,'" said old Mrs Welland. "My legs just won't get me up that hill." She was referring to Ashley Road.

"That's a shame" said Ina. "You like your whist drives, Gran."

"Well, we shall have to see," replied the old lady

"Where's Uncle Sid and Terry?" asked Ina.

"Terry has gone to the TA, and Uncle Sid's at work. We might get used to our husbands being on the railway, me and your mum," replied Nell.

"It's something you never really get used to," said Mrs Welland. Her husband had been an engine driver like Ina's father and Uncle Sid. "I know, I had a few years of it."

Stella and Ina joined in some more small talk then left and went on their way.

***

"Do you want to go anywhere in particular?" said Stella.

"I would like to have a good look at that blouse in Bloom's window," Ina answered.

They made their way into town and walked along the New Canal towards Bloom's.

"That's the one," said Ina pointing to a cream silky blouse with embroidery on the turned back collar and the breast pocket.

"Crumbs, Ina" cried Stella. "It's 9/11d!"

"I know, but I have got nearly seven shillings in national savings, and I might be able to borrow a few bob off of my dad, and I am hoping I can scrounge some coupons off of Mum."

Stella walked slowly back along the canal, looking in the shop windows.

Suddenly she stopped and then hurried back to Ina. "Don't look now," she said, "but there're two Yanks over there, and they are coming towards us."

"Not Pudding Face and his mate."

"No. They look all right."

Ina turned round and allowed herself to look. The Americans were definitely coming towards them, and they were both smiling. Ina was suddenly struck by the appearance of the taller of the two. *He must,* she thought, *be nearly six feet tall.* He was slender with light brown hair showing under his forage cap and a slightly tanned face. They moved closer, and soon she was looking into a pair of amber-coloured eyes. A slight smile was raising the corners of a generous mouth.

Oh, crummy, she thought. *He's beautiful.*

The shorter of the two had dark tight curly hair and the bluest eyes Ina had ever seen set in a face of ruddy complexion.

"Pardon me, ladies, but are we going in the right direction for the cathedral?" said the dark one.

Ina felt a stab of disappointment. So, that was all they wanted—directions.

"Yes," said Stella, "you go straight along this road, turn left, and you will see an archway. You go through there and you are in the cathedral grounds."

"We'd take it as a great favour if you would accompany us," the American went on. "Or are you doing something else?"

"No," replied Stella. "We won't mind showing you around."

Ina knew that she herself would have shown the tall young man around anywhere he wanted—Stonehenge, Old Sarum, the infirmary, the swimming baths.

Please, she pleaded in her mind, *don't let Stella choose this one!*

"Guess we'd better introduce ourselves," the shorter American continued. "I'm Joe, and this is my buddy, David."

So that was his name, David.

"I'm Stella," Stella told him, "and this is my friend, Ina."

"Ina?" said the one named David. "I never heard that name before. Is it English?"

"I don't know," replied Ina. "I've never thought about it. I don't know why my mum called me Ina. Perhaps she read the name in a book. I expect there're other Inas about."

"Well, then, Ina, can I walk with you?"

"Yes of course." He wanted to walk with her! Not Stella—her!

She looked at her friend. The look on Stella's face made Ina think that David would have been her first choice. However, they started along the canal, Joe and Stella in front and Ina and David behind. David made no move to hold her hand or offer her his arm, although she noticed Stella already had her arm through Joe's and they were chatting away together like old friends.

"Do you live in Salisbury?" asked David.

"Yes, not far from here. Stella comes from Amesbury or just outside Amesbury. She works in Salisbury though, with me—in a shoe shop. Is this the first time you have been here, in Salisbury?"

"No. I've been here a couple of times. Mostly we settle in Tidworth."

"That's where you're stationed?"

"That's right" he exclaimed "We haven't been in England long. We've come from Italy."

"Italy?"

"Yes, that's where we finished up when we left North Africa."

"Where do you come from in America?"

"Alabama."

"Where the stars fell."

"You know that song." It was a statement more than a question.

"My auntie Nell has a record of it. She used to play her records a lot before the war."

"Not now?"

"No. Not much. Some of Vera Lynn's. Everyone plays Vera Lynn."

"Popular lady."

"I listen into the AFN programme as well."

"So you know all the latest songs then?"

"Yes, my dad goes potty because I don't change the programmes and he misses a bit of the news."

***

They had reached the end of the Canal and turned the corner.

"Hey," said David, "there's the Red Cross Club. I know where I am now. That's the top of the spire above the archway."

"That's right. You've seen it before, then?"

"It was pointed out to us, but it was dark, and we couldn't see it properly. We came by truck before. We caught the bus today and got off at the bus depot. We didn't really know where we were. Then we saw you girls and reckoned you would tell us."

"Did you think we might go with you?" Ina asked.

He smiled down at her. "We hoped you would."

They went through the High Street gate and walked towards the cathedral.

"It's mighty impressive," said David, "all that green around and those houses; it's all so quiet and sort of . . . old-fashioned, I guess."

"You must have cathedrals in America," said Ina.

"Yes, I guess so, but not where I live. I saw a cathedral in Italy, but it was in the middle of town."

"Most people settle," explained Ina, "and then build their cathedral. Salisbury did it the other way around—cathedral first and the town after."

Joe and Stella stopped and waited for them to catch up.

"Are we going in?" asked Joe.

"Sure, why not," replied David.

***

They entered the cathedral, and both men bought a guidebook. Ina and Stella pointed out the things of interest. It was quiet in the lofty interior, and they found themselves whispering.

"So," said David. "This building's seven hundred years old. We wouldn't have anything that old in the States. I can't imagine what America looked like then."

"Full of buffalo and wigwams, boy," said Joe.

"Are people really buried in those tombs?" David asked.

"Yes," said Stella, "but I don't expect there's much left of them now."

"And all those battle flags. You British sure have fought some battles in your time." said David.

"And we've lived to fight another day," Ina put in.

"I guess you have at that," he smiled.

They walked the length and breadth of the cathedral and then outside and through the cloisters.

"Do you come here much?" David asked Ina.

"Not often," she said. "I can't remember when I last came. I think I was still at school. I remember one time coming here to sing carols. All the schools came and the school choirs sang with the choristers."

"Were you in the school choir?"

"I was, as a matter of fact. I gave up when I left school. I just sing to the wireless now."

"The wireless?"

"Well, radio, then."

They came out the cloisters and walked through the top gate into the grounds and along by the houses that flanked the road.

"Who lives in these houses?" asked David.

"Clergy, mostly, or anyone connected to the cathedral, or anyone rich enough to buy."

***

They walked back through the High Street gate. It was there that David offered her his arm. She noticed, then, the triangular flash on his sleeve.

"Are you in a tank regiment?" she asked.

"No, I'm a dog-face—foot soldier. We're an infantry division attached to the 2nd Armoured Division. We go with the tanks."

Ina wasn't quite sure what he meant. "Oh," she said uncertainly.

"We walk single file either side of the tank, unless we're on patrol."

This time she understood.

"Have you been with a GI before?" he asked.

"No—not with a British soldier either," she replied.

They passed the Red Cross Building.

"I don't suppose you've been in there?"

"No. I haven't."

Ina noticed a few Americans with girls going in and coming out.

"Maybe we could go in."

Ina hesitated. "I don't know if we have time," she said.

"Why? Do you have to be somewhere?"

"We have to go home for tea," she explained. "My mum will be waiting."

"Home for tea?" he repeated. "And what are you having for your tea?"

"Betox sandwiches and a sponge cake made with dried egg powder."

"Betox! What's Betox?"

"It's like a beef paste that you spread on bread."

"Sounds delicious."

"You're poking fun at me," she said.

"No, honey, I wouldn't do that."

Stella and Joe stood on the corner of High Street, waiting for Ina and David to catch up.

"They have to go home for tea," said David.

"Hey! That's a shame" Joe exclaimed. "Any chance we can see you after?"

"Don't see why not," replied Stella.

"How about we meet the girls somewhere later and take in a movie?" asked David.

"Fine by me," answered Joe.

"Is that okay with you two?"

"Yes," said Stella answering for both of them.

"Where will it be then?" asked David.

"The Gaumont's easiest. You can meet us outside," said Stella. "Anywhere else and you might get lost."

"So, where's this Gaumont?"

"It's in the canal where you first met us."

"Yeah! I'm with you," said Joe. "We'll be waiting for you there. What time?"

Stella paused and looked at Ina.

"Six thirty?" suggested Joe.

"Yes we can make it by then," said Ina.

"Okay, then," said Joe. "Six-thirty it is. How are you getting home?"

"By bus," said Ina. "It goes from the marketplace."

"Okay," said David. "We'll see you to your bus."

They walked across the market. A Devizes Road bus was in. The girls clambered on board and had hardly sat down when the conductress rang the bell and the bus pulled away. They waved to the boys as they passed by.

They waved back, and Joe blew a kiss.

"Well, what do you think of them?" asked Stella as they journeyed along.

"I like David," said Ina. "I think I could go steady with him."

"Joe's a lot of fun," said Stella. "Are you going to say anything about them being Yanks when you get home?"

"No fear" exclaimed Ina. "I can just imagine my dad's reaction. I should be locked up for a week!"

"I shan't say anything to my dad and mum either," said Stella. "They've never actually said they didn't want me to go out with Yanks, but I don't think they'd be too happy."

"I don't like deceiving my mum and dad, but I do like David, and I want to see him again," said Ina.

"Fair enough then. Mum's the word."

***

There was a sponge cake for tea but no Betox sandwiches. Hilda had spent points on a large tin of pilchards, which they had with tomatoes and a lettuce from the allotment greenhouse.

"What are you doing after tea?" Hilda asked the girls.

"We thought we'd go to the pictures," said Ina.

"Perhaps Clive can go with you," suggested Hilda.

"Oh! Well . . . ," started Ina, feeling colour rise to her cheeks.

"Oh, I see! Got a couple of boys. Who are they this time?"

As sharp as a knife, Ina answered, "They don't live in Salisbury; they come in from Stella's way."

"So you know them, Stella?"

"Yes, Mrs Welland."

"Well, be careful what you're doing. Dad and I are going down Gran's for a game of cards. I thought Clive would get bored."

"I don't want to go to the flicks with those two," stated Clive. "I'd rather go along to Roger's."

"Well, all right, then, but come on home at nine. You have to be up for school in the morning."

***

It seemed to Ina that the time to leave for the bus back into town would never come. Up in her bedroom, she and Stella renewed their makeup, and Ina took a brown paisley scarf out of her drawer. Out of a little box, she selected a brooch made with fuse wire, worked round with wool and then shaped to look like a small bunch of flowers. On impulse, she took her bottle of Devon violets scent and tipped a little onto the brooch.

"What are you doing?" asked Stella.

"Making sure I smell nice," Ina replied.

"I thought scent was supposed to be worn on you not on your brooch."

"Smell," said Ina, pushing the brooch towards her.

Stella bent her head and sniffed the brooch. "Doesn't smell too bad at all," she said "You'll knock him out."

Downstairs, they put on their coats. The paisley scarf went nicely with Ina's brown coat. She folded it into a triangle and placed it round her neck with the point hanging down the back and the two ends tied loosely under her chin.

"Right," she said, "I'm ready."

***

They got off the bus in the market and crossed over Queen Street.

Please, please, let them be there, Ina prayed inwardly. David had an effect on her that she would not have thought possible. Getting to the corner, she wanted to close her eyes but felt them drawn towards the Gaumont. They were there, standing outside the door.

"Glad you came," said Joe.

"Didn't you think we would?" asked Stella.

"We hoped so," was his reply. "And here you are."

Ina felt David take hold of her hand. "It's a wonder there isn't a queue," she said.

They went through the doors.

"Where to now?" asked Joe. "Wanna go upstairs?"

"If you like," said Stella.

"Okay. Upstairs it is."

"Can we not go to the back?" asked Ina. "I hate going down those steep steps in the dark. I'm frightened I'll fall."

They went upstairs and David asked her if she wanted chocolate or candy.

"No, thanks," Ina answered. "We have no sweet coupons."

"Oh, I forgot!" said David. "They're on ration too. Next time I'll bring you some from the PX." Then looking down at her said, "There is going to be a next time, isn't there?"

"Hope so," She murmured.

***

They gave their tickets to the usherette, who guided them to their seats at the back of the cinema, and settled down to watch the film. David took her hand again and drew it through his arm. Joe's arm was around Stella's shoulders, but Ina preferred David to hold hands. When the show was over, they came out to the street.

"Anywhere we can go for something to eat?" asked Joe.

"Not much choice of places," replied Ina. "There's the Bib and Tucker by the bus station, or there's the restaurant in the Gaumont."

"I guess we'll go to one of those then," said Joe. "Which is the best place?"

"It depends on whether you want red-and-white-check tablecloths and steel cutlery or white tablecloths and silver-plated cutlery."

"Well," said Joe, "I guess we could go back inside and give it a try"

They turned and went back inside and found their way to the restaurant. They were shown to a table by the waitress and given a menu.

"The meal of the day is roast beef," remarked Joe. "Roast beef, roast potatoes, and Yorkshire pudding. What's Yorkshire pudding?"

"Flour, eggs, and milk mixed to a batter," explained Ina.

"Like pancakes?" asked David.

"Yes, but it's not fried. It's poured into very hot fat and placed in a hot oven. Then it rises up."

"I guess anyone would 'rise' up if they were poured into hot fat and put in an oven," remarked Joe.

"Roast beef is the traditional Sunday dinner," said Ina. "Nearly all our meat ration goes on that."

"We have roast beef at home," said David, "not every Sunday, but we do have it."

"Sure," said Joe. "We have it at home sometimes, but not with the roast potatoes. I guess they're put in hot fat and cooked in the oven too."

It did not seem odd to the girls that they had already had one Sunday dinner. The prospect of another was too good to miss.

During the meal, Stella turned to Joe. "I don't know your second name," she said.

"It's Smith," said Joe.

"Really?" said Stella. "I didn't think it would be something like Smith. I thought you would be a Joseph Finkleheimer III or something."

"No, ma'am," replied Joe. "Just plain old Joe Smith. I wouldn't have it any other way. The way I see it is there must be a hundred other guys in this man's army named Joe Smith, and if there's a bullet with my name on it, I have a 99 per cent chance of it finding one of those other guys and not me. What's your name, anyhow, Stella what?"

"Auden," Stella replied.

"Ain't never heard of that," said Joe.

David turned to Ina. "I'm David Easton," he said, "E.A.S.T.O.N."

"My name's Welland. Ina Welland," Ina told him.

He put out his hand. "I'm pleased to meet you, Ina Welland."

She took his hand and shook it. "Likewise," she said.

***

There was a fine drizzle falling when they came out of the Gaumont into the canal.

"How are you getting home?" asked David.

"I can catch a bus from the market. Are you going back to Tidworth by bus?"

"Yes, we got return tickets."

"You'll go back on the same bus as Stella, then."

"Yeah, sure, she goes to Amesbury, doesn't she?"

"She gets off a couple or two stops after."

When they reached the market, Ina called out, "Goodnight," to Stella and Joe as they crossed over to the bus station.

"I'll catch you up," David called after them. Turning to Ina he said, "How long before you bus comes?"

"Fifteen minutes."

"You'll get soaked. You'll spoil your nice coat. I'll get you a cab."

"No, it's okay, really."

"No, there's a cab rank over there; c'mon." He caught hold of her arm and propelled her towards the rank. He saw her into a taxi, and she told the driver where she wanted to go.

"How much?" asked David, putting his hand into his pocket.

"No, it's okay. Honest," protested Ina.

"No. Come on. Settle yourself down. I'm paying."

"It's three shillings on a Sunday night, mate," said the driver.

David gave him the money, said, "Goodnight," to Ina and made his way towards the bus station. The taxi moved away from the kerb, and it wasn't until Ina was halfway home that she realised they'd made no arrangements to meet again.

***

The next morning, Ina met Stella off the bus as usual.

"Did you make any arrangements to meet the boys again?" she asked.

"Yes, of course I did," said Stella, "Wednesday evening. They can't get into town before 7.00. They're coming by transport, so I said we'd meet them at the bottom of the road to the baths, about seven o'clock."

"That's all right, then. I was a bit worried. I thought they didn't want to see us again."

"I think you're really 'gone' on David, aren't you?"

"I suppose I am."

"Don't get too fond of him, Ina. Don't forget; they'll be going to fight in France soon, and that's the last we'll see of them"

"I suppose so," Ina answered despondently.

"Cheer up, gal. There's plenty more fish in the sea."

"I don't want anyone else," said Ina in a small voice.

"Come on, Ina! You've only known him for a day."

"I know how I feel."

"Well, watch you don't get hurt. Blokes like them usually get loads of girls."

***

They had reached the shop and were surprised to see Mrs Phillips there, putting the float into the till. "Mr Phillips has a very heavy cold," she explained. "I don't want it to turn to flu, so I persuaded him to stay in bed. I've seen to the blackout and lit the heaters. If you can manage until lunchtime, I'll come down then."

"I'm sorry he's not well," said Stella. "I expect we shall be all right. It's fairly quiet on Mondays."

Vera came into the shop.

"Mr Phillips is unwell," Mrs Phillips told her. "Miss Auden thinks you'll be able to manage, and I'll be in lunchtime."

"Yes, that's all right. Sorry to hear about Mr Phillips."

"Well, if I make him stay in bed today, he may be well enough to come in tomorrow. I must go on. I want to go to the chemist's on my way home."

***

The morning passed without incident. The girls weren't terribly busy, but about eleven o'clock, the Southern Railway carrier called with another consignment of goods from the warehouse. The shop staff helped him bring the large boxes in, and then set to unpacking. One by one, the boxes were emptied and checked off against the invoice.

"Oh no" exclaimed Vera, diving down into a box. "Not those wooden soled sandals again!"

Last year, they'd had several pairs as a "try out". They looked very good at first and came in red, tan, navy, and white, but the wooden soles did not stand up to the English climate and, after being worn in the rain a few times, had cracked. Nearly all of the sandals had been brought back and refunds had been given.

"I suppose I'll have to put them out," grumbled Vera.

"We'll have to alter the displays," said Mrs Gray.

"I've got some children's' sandals here," said Ina.

"I hope I've got some sandals different from the wooden ones," put in Vera.

Further boxes revealed ordinary sandals and a new line in ladies shoes, a brown court with a Cuban heel at 22/11d.

"They're nice," said Ina, "I could do with a pair like that to go with my brown coat. I'm fed up with lace-ups."

Her own consignment of children's shoes were stacked away on the shelves, ranging from babies' soft soled ones to black patent ankle straps and brown bar shoes for girls and brown and black lace-ups for boys. She saw Vera put a pair of the brown court shoes on the display stand and wondered if there was any possibility of her having a pair to try on.

"Vera," said Ina, "could you let me have a size 5? I want to try a pair on lunchtime."

Vera found a pair of size 5 shoes and gave them to her.

"They're 22s.11d, Ina," Stella told her. "Reckon you're going to afford them?"

"I'll talk nicely to my dad," said Ina, but without much conviction.

***

Mrs Phillips came at twelve o'clock, and Ina and Stella went to the staffroom, Ina taking the shoes. She tried them on and walked up and down. "I'm going to reserve them," she said.

39

They often did this with shoes they liked so that they could get the money together with no fear of the shoes being sold, providing they were not reserved for too long. After they had eaten, they left the shop and wandered along Market Street and down the canal. Here, they paused before Bloom's window and gazed at Ina's blouse.

"How much money do you have in National Savings stamps?" asked Stella.

"Just 15s.6d and it's taken me ages to save that. What with the savings woman coming around Friday nights and my Christmas club down the Legion, it doesn't leave me much out of 7s.6d."

"Haven't had many tickets lately, have we? You'd think we'd get staff discount, wouldn't you?"

"Well one thing is for sure, I'm not going to afford the shoes and the blouse."

Chapter 4

Ina finished her tea and helped her mother wash up and put away the china and cutlery.

"Mum?" she said.

"Yes?"

"There were some brown court shoes come in today. I tried a size 5 on, and they fitted me a treat. They'd go ever so well with my brown coat!"

"Are you going to buy them?"

"I've got them on reserve. I've got 15/6d saved up."

"How much are they?"

"They're 22/11d."

"Oh! Ina!"

"I know it's a lot, but I'm fed up wearing my brown lace-ups all week and Sundays."

Hilda sighed, "I don't know," she said. "It's a lot to fork out."

"It's only 7/11d extra," Ina said.

"Only 7/11d!" cried Hilda.

"Would Dad lend it if you asked him?"

"I don't know. There's Clive's uniform to get before Easter. I have to do that bit by bit. He grows out of everything so quickly." She looked at Ina. "Do you really want them that much?"

"Yes I do."

"Oh, all right, then. They want us to go into work Saturday morning so you will have to wait till I get paid."

"Thanks, Mum!" said Ina.

"Good job the new coupons are out, or you wouldn't have had them anyway."

Lunchtime the next day she went to the post office and cashed in her stamps.

"All of it?" asked the man behind the counter.

"Yes, please."

The man grunted, and Ina suddenly felt guilty. The savings were supposed to be helping the war effort. When she and Stella got back to the shop, Mr Phillips had returned and was in his workshop, putting on some stick-on soles and heels.

"Do you feel better now?" Ina asked.

"Yes, thank you, Miss. Everything all right while I was off?"

"Yes," replied Ina. "Has Mrs Phillips gone?"

"She had some shopping to do, and then she was going on home. I gather the consignment was satisfactory."

"Yes."

"Miss Jenner wasn't very pleased about having more wooden-soled sandals, I take it."

"No."

"Well, I did mention it to the area manager, and I know for a fact that other shops have had the same trouble. But there's probably some left in the warehouse and they're trying to get rid of them."

"We shall just have to see if we can sell them, then," Ina replied. Then she added, "Mr Phillips, I have a pair of brown court shoes on reserve. Could I take them on a deposit?"

"When can you pay for them?"

"I can give you fifteen shillings now and pay the rest next Monday."

"It isn't strictly business, Miss. If I do it for you, I must do it for the others, and goodness knows where we shall end up."

"Yes. I see," said Ina, disappointed.

"Well" considered Mr Phillips "just this once, but don't make a habit of it."

"Oh, thanks, Mr Phillips."

Ina went straight to the staffroom and hung up her coat. She told Stella her news.

"Why do you want them so badly?" Stella asked.

"I want them for tomorrow," explained Ina.

"Oh, I see!"

***

When Stella went back into the shop, Vera left for lunch, unaware of the arrangement for the shoes, and Ina thought it best not to say anything to her or Mrs Gray. She showed the shoes to her mother when she got in from work that night.

"Where did you get the money from?" asked Hilda.

"Mr Phillips let me bring them home. I paid him the 15/—I had in savings and I said I'd give him the rest on Monday."

"Ina!" said Hilda crossly. "I wish you hadn't! I don't like you owing money like that; it's not right. Why the hurry? Couldn't you have waited?"

"I suppose so," mumbled Ina. What could she tell her mother? That tomorrow she was on a special date with a GI?

"I've got a few bob towards Clive's clothes. You can have 5/—of that, and you will have to find the rest yourself and pay it off tomorrow morning."

"Thanks, Mum."

"And you can do a bit of ironing for me."

Ina paid for the shoes the next morning and handed her book of coupons to Mr Phillips.

"That's all settled then," remarked Stella, when Mr Phillips went out to the workroom.

"I wish I could still have the blouse."

"If wishes were horses, beggars would ride," said Stella. "Don't be greedy. Anyway, if you had the blouse you'd want a new skirt, and you could go on forever."

"Oh, to have the war over so that we could have what we like when we like."

"That will be the day."

"Anyway, I've still got two bob to last me till Friday," said Ina.

"I expect I could lend you a penny or two," said Stella.

"I shall be okay," Ina replied.

***

It seemed as though that Wednesday morning would never end. At last, they shut up shop. Ina arranged to meet Stella off the bus, which should get into town at about six thirty. It would enable them to go to the ladies' in the market for Stella to repair her make-up and comb her hair after her journey.

At five minutes to seven, they walked along Castle Street. Ina felt her heart beating, and she was sure her face was pink. They saw David and Joe standing there before they reached the meeting place. Ina went up to David, and he took hold of her hand.

"You look very nice," he said.

"Thanks." Ina smiled.

"Well, what are we doing then?" asked Joe. "Want to go to a movie or something?"

"We could walk back into town and see what is on at the Regal?" offered Stella.

This they did, crossing the road and going into Chipper Lane. The queue was quite long outside the Regal.

"It's hardly worth waiting," Stella said. "By the time we get in, it'll nearly be over."

"Okay," said David. "Where then?"

"I'd like to go to the Red Cross if that's okay with everyone," Joe put in.

"Sure, if the girls agree," said David.

"I want to see Sharkey if he's there."

"Sharkey?" asked David. "What do you have to see him for?"

"He owes me."

"Why do you have anything to do with that guy? He's bad news."

"I want to get what I'm owed before he blows his pay."

***

They made their way towards the Red Cross Club. Inside, it was pretty crowded. As they headed for the bar, they passed the dance floor. There was a speciality dance in progress, a young GI and a girl were jitterbugging to the band, and people had edged away from the centre of the ballroom to give them plenty of room. They were the only dancers on the floor. The audience watched until it was over and everyone clapped. The band then played again, and several couples took the floor.

"Want a dance?" Joe asked Stella.

"Why not!" answered Stella.

Ina could feel her feet tapping. She looked at David, and he understood her look.

"Gee, Ina, I'm sorry, honey; I don't dance!"

"Never mind," she said.

"Are you sure? You can dance with someone else if you want to."

"No. It's all right. To tell you the truth, I have new shoes on, and they pinch a little bit."

"Let's sit down somewhere. I'll go get some drinks. What will you have?"

"Lemonade, please."

"Lemonade! Nothing stronger?"

"No—I'm not really old enough to drink alcohol."

"How old are you, then?"

"Seventeen."

"Sweet seventeen," he smiled. "Stella too?"

"Yes. I was seventeen at the end of last month and Stella the beginning. There's not much between us."

"Well, since we are getting on familiar terms, I'm twenty, twenty-one in November."

He went to get the drinks and, when he came back, said, "They didn't have any lemonade; I've got you a Coke. Is that okay?"

"I've never tasted it," Ina said.

"Take a sip. If you don't like it, you can leave it. I won't mind."

She took a sip. "It's all right," she said. "Not bad at all."

"That's fine!" He sat down.

"What did you do in your spare time at home?" she asked.

"Oh, went to the 'shack'. That's where most of us hung out. Played pool, mostly."

"No dancing?"

"Well, maybe a hop at the diner."

"I've seen that at the pictures." Ina stood up. "I must take my coat off. It's getting warm in here."

She draped the coat round the chair and then looked down at him. "They're playing a slow foxtrot," she said.

"A slow what?"

"Foxtrot." She put her hands towards him. "Come on," she said, "have a slow dance with me."

"Honey, I told you, I can't dance."

"You'll be able to dance this. Let me show you. Come on, David."

He stood up. "Okay, okay," he said. "But don't blame me if your toes get trodden on!"

"Put one hand on my waist and I'll put my hand on your shoulder. Then hold my hand up like this." She held his hand up. "Now move from side to side, like this—just follow my movements."

They gyrated for a while. A female vocalist had joined the band and her voice came through from the ballroom to where they were in the bar.

Long ago and far away, I dreamed a dream one day . . .
And now, that dream is here beside me . . .
Once the sky was overcast, but now the clouds have passed . . .

They were swaying in harmony now. David looked down at her. "This really is dancing, is it?"

"Yes, it's a 'smoochie' dance." Ina looked up into his face.

"A smoochie dance! In that case, oughtn't I to be kissing you?"

"In front of all these people?"

"Who cares about people!" He bent his head and kissed her lips gently.

The vocalist sang:

You're here at last . . .

They seemed lost to the world, slowly gyrating in the small space between the table and the wall.

Chills run up and down my spine. Aladdin's lamp is mine . . .
The dream I dreamed did not forsake me . . .
Just one look, and then I knew . . .
That all I longed for long ago . . . was you . . .

"Hey, boy" Joe called boisterously, cutting through the atmosphere "I thought you couldn't dance!"

"If this is dancing," replied David, "I might get to like it."

Stella sat down.

"More drinks?" asked Joe.

"Beer for me, Coke for Ina,"

"Coke for you?" Joe asked Stella.

"Don't know; what's it like?"

"Have a sip of mine," said Ina.

The dance came to an end. She and David took their places at the table.

"Did Joe find Sharkey?" David asked Stella.

"No, I don't think so," Stella answered. "I didn't see him talk to anyone."

Joe came back with their drinks on a tray and set them down on the table. Some more people came up to the bar.

"There's Sharkey," said Joe. "Pardon me while I go and see him."

"Don't get into any bother, Joe," said David, concerned.

"No bother," answered Joe and went back to the bar to talk to a short, squat American, who turned to greet him.

"Pudding face!" exclaimed Stella. "That Sharkey is pudding face!"

"So it is," said Ina.

David turned to her. "You know that guy?"

"Yes—no—yes—well, Vera, the girl who works with us, was dressing her window. Sharkey and his pal started to knock on it. They put the wind up her, and she flew through the shop and shut herself in the toilet."

"Sharkey's enough to scare anyone," said David.

"Well," Ina went on, "he and his friend came into the shop. They were both the worse for drink, and we had a job to get rid of them. Stella managed to persuade them to go in the end. We were frightened the manager would come back into the shop and think we'd encouraged them."

"He's one mean man," said David. "I don't know why Joe has anything to do with him."

"What does Pudding Face owe him money for? Or shouldn't I ask?" said Stella.

"Joe beat him in a poker hand."

"Does Joe gamble?" asked Stella.

"No, not real heavy, or at least, not that I've noticed. Guess it was a lucky streak he was on. Sharkey turned mean and refused to pay up, so Joe said he would catch up with him some other time. Looks like now is the time."

"I hope there isn't going to be trouble," said Stella.

Ina had a sudden vision of them all being carted off to the police station. But Joe came back and took his seat at the table.

"Did you get the money?" David asked.

"Yes, sure did!" replied Joe, patting his hip pocket. "Twenty-five bucks. It was like taking candy from a baby."

"What did you say to him?"

"I just told him to watch his butt when we were on manoeuvres with live ammo."

"You wouldn't do anything like that?" said a horrified Stella.

"Don't you ever worry about your Uncle Joe, honey," he said patting her hand, "Guys like Sharkey don't like being backed into a hole in front of other guys!" Then he changed the subject. "Do you like your Coke?"

"Yes," she replied, "it's not bad. How are your shoes?" she asked Ina.

"I took them off to dance," said Ina.

"You'll be sorry you did that," Stella told her.

***

Jim Welland was on two till ten. He said he would get something to eat at the canteen, so Hilda went to the whist drive knowing she had no need to worry about a meal for him. Clive had gone to his friend's house. She told him she'd call in for him on her way home. It meant a late night for him, but she didn't want to leave him by himself. Ina obviously was on a date; otherwise she didn't usually go out Wednesday nights. Hilda said as much to the others when they were having their half-time break from playing and immediately wished she hadn't.

"You don't think it's someone you wouldn't approve of?" Cissie asked.

"I shouldn't think so," answered Hilda, a trifle tartly. "I trust Ina."

"Well, you never know these days. That's why I'm glad Maureen has a nice steady chap that she can bring home."

"I'm sure it's not serious," replied Nell.

"She's only seventeen," said old Mrs Welland. "Hardly the age to start courting."

"Anyway," said Hilda, "I trust her with young Stella. I think they both have their heads screwed on the right way; it isn't as though she's out every night, only tonight and weekends. She works hard all week. I don't want to be the heavy-handed parent and have her resenting me."

"Oh no!" agreed Cissie. "Of course, Maureen's twenty-one. You'd expect a girl to be ready to settle down at that age—which reminds me"—she leaned forward conspiratorially—"I've been looking at that youngest Purdy girl, and if she's not expecting, I'll eat my hat. She's going to be just like the other one—pile of trouble with another on the way by the end of the year. I blame her and him. They shouldn't have allowed their girls to go about with the Yanks; asking for trouble that is, just asking for it. They have those Yanks in the house and all. What do they think the girls get up to?"

The whistle blew for the restarting of the game.

"Saved by the whistle," muttered Nell as Cissie walked back to the card table.

"If she does have to eat her hat," said old Mrs Welland, "I hope it chokes her."

She knew that Nell, even after all these years, still felt Teddy's illegitimacy keenly, although he was a good boy, always had been, and Sid did not favour him less than his own son. If only they could hear one way or another if Teddy was dead or alive. The strain was unbearable. There were probably hundreds of mothers in the same boat. She had liked Eddy, Teddy's father, both she and her husband. It was just a shame he had been killed. And now—all these young Americans far from home—she wondered if there would be many girls who would suffer the same as Nell had done.

Chapter 5

On Saturday, the shop was busy. Quite a few mothers were bringing their children in for new shoes. Ina liked serving the children. She always used the special rule to measure their feet. It annoyed her greatly when some mothers with boys tried to fit their feet into a size 5 shoe because 6 came into the men's sizes and were, therefore, more coupons. It didn't happen very often, but when it did, it saddened her.

She was always aware of the toddlers since, once, whilst fitting shoes for one tot it had started to wee, and it had gone all over the chair and stool.

The girls' black patent ankle strap shoes brought back memories of before the war when she and Avril had worn them at Easter time. Easter then had been a special occasion when her mother had bought material for summer dresses, and Aunty Nell would make them up on her Singer sewing machine—gingham check for school and flower patterned for Sundays. With their straw hats trimmed with small artificial flowers, the Welland girls were always smartly turned out.

However, after several sales had been made and just before lunchtime, Ina served a woman accompanied by a badly behaved child. There wasn't much choice in children's shoes—black or brown, lace-ups for boys, bar shoes for girls. Here was a spoilt girl who insisted on having red shoes.

"The lady doesn't sell red shoes," explained the mother.

The child kicked off the bar shoe that Ina had placed on her foot.

"Yes she does!" the child cried. "There are red ones in the window."

"Those are ladies' shoes," explained Ina.

"I want a pair," said the child.

"They wouldn't be in your size."

For a while, quite a battle raged between mother and daughter.

"They won't fit you. They're ladies' shoes, and they're not suitable."

"I want them," insisted the child. "I want to try them on."

Ina said, "They start at a size 3, and you take a size 1."

"I don't believe you," said the child.

By now, Ina was starting to feel cross, but she knew she must keep her temper. Other people were waiting to be served, and they were muttering between themselves.

Mr Phillips, having just finished serving, came over. "Anything wrong, Miss?" he asked Ina.

"The little girl wants to try on the red shoes that are in the window. The smallest size we have in those is size 3," she replied.

Mr Phillips turned to the mother. "They're ladies' shoes, Madam," he said. "Size 3 is the smallest; they will be much too big for her."

"I want to try them on," the girl said, her voice just short of a scream.

"Very well," said Mr Phillips, nonplussed. "I'll fetch them for you myself."

He fetched them from the window and gave them to Ina to put on the girl's feet. Besides being too large, they were most unsuitable shoes for a child of her age. They had a Cuban heel and a bow on the instep. The shoes fell off.

"Get the smaller ones!" demanded the child.

"I've already told you," said Mr Phillips, "these are the smallest size we have."

The girl burst into a rage of tears. This time, the mother had had enough. She put the girl's own shoes back onto her feet, pulled her out of the chair, apologised to Ina and Mr Phillips, and then dragged her daughter out of the shop.

"Hope you don't get too many of those," remarked the woman who took her place.

"No, thank goodness," said Mr Phillips. "But we daren't loose patience with them. Today's children are tomorrow's customers."

"My daughter," said the woman to Ina, "will have a pair of brown bar shoes, size 1, and she won't be getting anything else."

***

Although each girl was responsible for keeping stocked her own department, they would serve any customer who was waiting, man or woman. So when Ina went up to an elderly, military looking gentleman and asked if she could help him and he told her he wanted a pair of brown brogues in a size 9, Ina felt elated. If she sold them, she would get a shilling ticket, as they cost nearly £3 a pair. She fetched the shoes for him, helped him out of his old shoes, and fitted him with the brogues. He walked up and down, looking at his feet in the small freestanding mirror by the counter.

"Yes, they're fine," he said. He sat down and took off the shoes; Ina helped him put his own shoes on again.

"Have you another pair size 9?" he asked.

"Yes, there is another pair," said Ina.

"Good. I'll have the two pairs."

Ina took the shoes to the counter, removed the tickets, and put the shoes into bags.

Two shilling tickets! she thought. She gave him the shoes. "That's £5.5s.0d please."

He gave her a large white five pound note and a ten shilling note. "You can keep the change," he said.

"Oh, no, really!" she protested.

"I insist," he said.

"I don't think we're allowed tips," Ina replied.

"Well, I will come over to the cash desk with you and see if we can persuade your manager to let you accept it."

Ina wrote out his receipt in her paragon cashbook and took the receipt and carbon copy with the money over to the cash desk. Mr Phillips looked mildly surprised; £5 notes were very rare.

"I did tell the young lady she could keep the change. She was so helpful."

"Thank you," said Mr Phillips. "It's very kind of you to say so. We don't usually encourage our assistants to accept money, but you're obviously pleased with Miss Welland's service, and I would not like you to be offended."

"That's all right then," the man said.

Ina flushed red and said, "Thank you very much, but I really didn't do anything."

"You gave very good service," said the man. "I appreciate it. One doesn't often come across it these days." He moved towards the door. "Goodbye to you."

"Goodbye, sir," they both replied.

When he was gone, Ina still stood there with the money in her hands.

"Go on then," said Mr Phillips. "Go and put the money in your purse."

"I ought to share it with the others really," said Ina.

"You were the one he gave it to," Mr Phillips told her.

"I'll have to tell them."

"That's up to you."

"I've got two 2s.0d tickets; I'll give them 1s.0d each," she decided.

Mr Phillips said, "I'm sure they'll be very pleased," noticing that her act of generosity obviously did not include Mrs Gray.

Ina went into the staff room and put the money into her purse. She told Stella about the money when they went to lunch.

"No!" said Stella emphatically, "I don't want you to give me 1s.0d. That was your commission. Anyway, it will go towards your blouse, won't it?"

Later that lunchtime, they went round to Bloom's, the idea being that Ina could put a deposit on the blouse, but it had gone.

"Bother," said Ina.

"Save it until you see something else," said Stella.

"No, I'll give it to my mum. It will help me to pay back the money she gave me towards the shoes."

"How are the shoes now?"

"Now that I have worn them to work since Wednesday, they're all right."

"Well, that's something then."

***

On Saturday night, they met the boys as usual. This time, they had to wait for them; Joe and David had come straight from work, and the trucks weren't due in till seven o'clock.

"I feel conspicuous standing here," said Ina.

53

"Me, too," replied Stella. "I think we will have to try and arrange somewhere else to meet."

They saw the trucks coming along Castle Street.

"Oh Lord," said Ina. "Let's walk down the street a bit."

They walked towards town looking back every so often until the last truck had turned right into the road leading to the car park. Soon the boys came into sight, and the girls turned to meet them. Stella had arranged to go dancing at the Assembly Rooms with Joe. Ina and David were going to a film. They had all arranged to meet up at the Bib and Tucker at ten o'clock. David took Ina's hand in the Regal Cinema and drew it through the crook of his arm. He put his other hand in his pocket and fetched out two candy bars.

"What's that?" she asked quietly.

"Hershey Bars," he whispered. "Candy and chocolate—we don't need coupons."

***

They came out of the Regal just as Joe and Stella came along Endless Street. David and Ina crossed the road, and all four went into the Bib and Tucker.

"So this is the red check café," said Joe as they took their seats.

Stella picked up the menu. "The steak and kidney pie looks all right." She gave a sigh. "We don't have that at home anymore."

"I wonder they have it here," put in Ina.

"Steak and kidney pie sounds okay to me," said Joe. "I'm hungry."

Ina turned to David. "All right with you?" she asked.

"Sure thing," he replied. "If you girls don't get to have it at home anymore, now's your chance to make up for it—though I can't say I rightly knows just what it is."

"Don't expect too much," Ina went on. "Cafes and restaurants are rationed the same as we are."

"I guess that makes them pretty restricted in what they can serve up," Joe said.

"Yes," Ina agreed.

Stella asked, "What time does your transport go back to Tidworth tonight?"

"Eleven thirty," Joe replied.

"We shan't have to linger on," Ina said.

"No," replied Joe, "or my fairy godfather will be bust me down to private."

"What are those stripes for under the other ones?" asked Stella.

"I'm a staff sergeant," explained Joe.

Ina looked at David and touched the one stripe on his arm. "You're a lance corporal," she said.

"A lance corporal? Is that what you call a soldier with one stripe?"

"What do you call yourself?" she asked.

"PFC," David replied. "Private First Class. I'm newer at the game than Joe."

"How long have you been in the army, Joe?" Ina asked him.

"I joined in '38," said Joe, "when I was nineteen. I couldn't get a job, and I was a growing boy who needed three square meals a day and someone to buy my clothes for me."

"And you?" she turned to David.

"I got drafted just after Pearl, a few months into '42. They dragged me in kicking and screaming."

"I don't believe that" she exclaimed.

"Well" he paused "maybe not as bad as that."

"He's a good shot," said Joe. "Took to a rifle as if he was born with one in his hand."

David laughed. "I shot before the army claimed me," he said.

"What did you shoot?"

"Anything that got in my way—rats, skunks, snakes."

"Snakes!"

"Yes a few."

Ina looked at him. "I don't know whether to believe you or not," she said.

"Get on and eat your pie and fries before they get cold." He grinned.

***

When they finally left the Bib and Tucker, the boys walked the girls to the bus stop.

"You'd better be going on. We'll be all right," said Stella.

"Are you sure?"

"Yes, of course."

"Don't get off with any GIs," said Joe. "They can't be trusted." He kissed Stella good night.

David bent down and kissed Ina on her lips. "Looking forward to spending most of the day with you tomorrow," he said. He kissed her again.

The boys crossed the road and walked along the Blue Boar Row. When they reached the corner, they turned and waved before they were out of sight. Ina almost felt a sense of emptiness. Roll on tomorrow! She found herself wishing the invasion of Europe wouldn't happen, at least not yet.

***

Hilda had taken her shopping bag to work. When she left at four o'clock, she made her way to the co-op grocery shop where the family was registered. The hardest thing she found about rationing was what to put in Jim's sandwiches. Sometimes he would go to the canteen, depending upon which shift he was on, and then she didn't have to bother.

Cissie was in the shop when she entered. Sighing inaudibly, she returned her neighbour's greeting.

"You must be excited about your Avril coming home for Easter. Jim told Albert all about it. Nice for her and her boyfriend to get some time together. That's the trouble nowadays; young people have to do their courting from a distance. What is her boy?"

"A corporal," answered Hilda.

"Really? He's getting on then."

"Avril has her first stripe as well, now," said Hilda and then wondered why she had bothered to mention it.

"Jolly good!" said Cissie. "Did I tell you Maureen got promotion?"

"No, I don't think so," Hilda answered, adding under her breath, "but you are going to tell me."

"She is a section leader," said Cissie. "She has several people working under her."

"She has done very well," Hilda replied. She liked Maureen. Maureen, fortunately in Hilda's estimation, took after her father.

"Well, I suppose a lot of it is down to her going to South Wilts," said Cissie. "Neither of your girls passed for the grammar school, did they?"

"No. Only Clive," replied Hilda. "Pity Harold didn't get through."

"It doesn't really matter," Cissie said. "Once he is in the army, he will get on well enough. They think a lot of him in the cadets."

***

The door opened, and in came Mrs Purdy. She was a short stout woman in her late forties, who always wore a crossover pinafore and a man's flat cap on her head. Hilda said hello to Mrs Purdy; Cissie ignored her. Cissie had been served and had packed her shopping away.

"I'll wait for you," she told Hilda and then added, "You must be proud of Avril. I know I am of Maureen, and Ina's a nice girl. It's so good to know your daughters have grown up into decent young women."

She spoke quite loudly, and Hilda, slightly embarrassed, paid for her purchases. Mrs Purdy went up to the counter and put her ration books down.

"There you are," said Cissie once they were out of the shop. "She had a green ration book. That's for an expectant mother. It's either that youngest one or the other one's having another."

Outside the shop, a baby lay in its pram. Cissie bent over it. "You poor little soul," she said.

***

Ina and Stella had arranged to meet the boys at two thirty at the usual place, although they had mentioned finding a more suitable rendezvous. During that Sunday morning, Ina looked in her wardrobe.

"There's not much choice in here," she said to Stella.

Stella was wearing a dress and coat that she had borrowed from one of her older sisters. She wore her hair with a deep wave on top, the sides rolled up kept in place with hairgrips. The long blonde locks at the back of her head were caught up in a large hair-slide. Ina toyed with the idea of putting her own hair up at the sides but thought better of it. Stella's dress showed off her slim figure and, just for a while, Ina felt inferior. She took a brown tweed dress from the wardrobe and put it back again.

"What about the pink dress?" asked Stella. "I haven't seen you wearing that one at all."

"It's a second-hand one," explained Ina. "Mum bought it from someone at work for me, but I don't know if I like it or not. I've only worn it once."

"Try it on," Stella urged.

Ina slipped out of the skirt and jumper she had on and pulled the pink dress over her head and hips.

"It looks nice, Ina," said Stella. "I don't know why you don't like it."

The dress was fine wool with gentle pleats falling from the waist; it had a self-covered belt, a V-neck, and elbow-length sleeves. Ina looked at herself in the long mirror on the wardrobe door. "No, it doesn't look too bad, does it?"

She turned this way and that; it somehow made her look slimmer. Why hadn't she noticed it before? "I ought to have something around my neck," she said.

"Haven't you got a necklace?" asked Stella. "I'm sure I've seen you wearing one."

"I had some beads, but I've broken them."

Neither girl had much in the way of jewellery. Costume jewellery was a thing of the past, unless you paid the earth for it.

"Mum might have something," said Ina.

They went downstairs. Hilda was in the kitchen making a cup of tea, and she turned as the girls walked in.

"Oh, so you're going to wear that at last," she said. "I didn't think you liked it."

"I want some beads, Mum. Can I borrow some of yours?"

"There're those coloured glass ones that look like crystal."

"Can I borrow those, then?"

"I suppose so."

She picked up the tray full of cups and saucers and took them into the living room. "Would it be rude to ask who you are going to meet today? Seeing as you won't be home for tea."

"Those two boys who live Stella's way," replied Ina. It was sort of true; Tidworth was Stella's "way".

"What do they do for a living then?"

"Work on a farm," put in Stella without batting an eyelid.

***

Ina went back upstairs to take off the pink dress, feeling a bit happier.

After lunch, when the crockery was washed up and put away, Ina and Stella went back upstairs to the bathroom to wash and change. Ina put on clean underclothes and slipped into the dress again. She liked it even better now and wondered what she had disliked about it in the first place. The necklace went well with the dress. She had put on some Pond's vanishing cream under her face powder, and she used a pink lipstick. She had brushed her hair until it shone. The boys were waiting for them when they reached the meeting place.

"Anything special you girls want to do?" asked Joe.

"Well, as it's a nice day, I thought we go for a walk by the river," said Ina. "You don't mind walking, do you?"

"Lady," said Joe, "you're talking to two dog faces who go on a twenty-mile hike in full kit, so what's a little stroll."

They walked along Castle Street under the bridge and made their way to the meadows. The river ran quietly between the banks, and they followed its course easily, taking their time. The days were getting a little warmer now; the trees were in green bud, and in the hedgerows, the blackberry bushes were in flower. Wild violets hid among the grass by the bank. Now and then, the water rippled with the feeding fish. Two swans and their cygnets swam down the river, and a brood of mallard chicks were trying to climb up the bank, their little bodies scrambling to find a foothold.

"Hey," said David, "look at those little fellas. They're quite cute, aren't they?" He looked around. "It is sure a beautiful day," he remarked.

"Still gets chilly in the evenings," said Ina.

"Yes, I guess."

***

They walked in silence for a little while, and then Ina asked: "What's Alabama like?"

"Oh, I don't know, big, bigger than England. I live right down the south, a place that is hardly on the map, but I was mostly in Florida."

"Florida?"

"Yes, it's the next state."

"What did you do there?"

"Worked in the orange groves, picking and packing and loading the crates onto trucks."

"Did you like it?"

"It wasn't too bad. Money was good. I was with my brother."

"You worked together?"

"Yes, me and Todd."

"That's an unusual name."

"It was my mother's maiden name. That's why she called him Todd. He's older than me."

"Where is he now?"

"He's in the navy, in the Pacific on a carrier. He joined in 1940."

"Not because of the war then?"

"No, we weren't in the war then. But the orange picking days were coming to an end."

"Was he at Pearl Harbour?"

"No. He escaped that, but it was pretty bad. His ship put in there a while after."

"We know what its like. We have had our harbours and dockyards bombed."

"Yes, I guess you have all been through a pretty bad time. Have you had any bombs dropped on Salisbury?"

"Some in 1942 but not much damage fortunately."

"London had it bad."

"Yes, and lots of other places—Liverpool, Manchester, Hull; all the way down to Southampton, Portsmouth, and Plymouth."

"I guess we are lucky at home to not have had all of that."

"Let's hope it stays that way." She looked at him. "Have you got any more family?"

"Yes, my mom; a younger sister, Thelma; two younger brothers, Mike and Johnny, and my stepdad."

"You're father died then?"

"Yes, when I was twelve. It was during the Depression. Have you heard of it?"

"Yes. I don't think things were all that good here."

"Well, times were hard for my mom; she got a job waiting on tables in a diner. That's why Todd went to Florida. There wasn't any work going around us, and the place in Florida wasn't too far away. I left school when I was fifteen and joined him. Shouldn't have left really, but I think the authorities turned a blind eye. They knew how things were and how poor people were. My mom got married again just before Todd left for the navy."

"And you get on all right with him?"

"Yes sure. He's a regular guy. Good to my mom and the kids. If it weren't for him, Thelma wouldn't be at college. She's nearly eighteen, and with a bit of luck, the two boys will follow her. I only wish I had had a bit more education. I can read and write and add up, but I'm not much good at geography and history and that kind of thing."

"I left school at fourteen. So did Avril, my sister. She's in the WAAF now; that's the Women's Auxiliary Air Force. Her fiancé is in the RAF, but they have never managed to be at the same station."

"That's tough."

"They see a bit of each other when they have the same weekend free, and they are both home for Easter. Brian's home is in Harnham, just outside of Salisbury. I have a brother called Clive. He's twelve and goes to grammar school. He's the brainy one."

"We have grammar school."

"I think ours are more like your high school."

"Were you allowed to leave at fourteen?"

"It's the official school leaving age. They were going to put it up to fifteen before the war started, and then they changed their minds. What do you want to do after the war?"

"Probably go back to Florida."

"To the orange groves?"

"Not especially. I would like to go in for something where I could be my own boss. I wouldn't mind breeding turkeys."

"Turkeys?"

"Yes. There's a call for turkeys back home. Thanksgiving, July Fourth, Christmas. Don't you have turkeys at Christmas?"

"We are lucky to have chicken," laughed Ina.

"Yes, I guess you are at that."

"Did you have good times in Florida, you and Todd? Is that why you would like to go back?"

"Yes, we had good times. Todd came by an old Pontiac pickup, and we drove down to the beach sometimes or we'd just drive around."

"Is it hot in Florida?"

"Yes, pretty hot. It rains sometimes. But it can be dusty; depends where you are."

They had walked across fields and climbed over styles, and Ina said, "I'm getting warm."

"There is an old tree trunk over there," said David. "May be we can sit there for a while?"

"Yes, all right," agreed Ina. "I'm going to take my coat off."

They sat on the trunk, and Joe and Stella caught up with them.

"Chickening out then?" said Joe. "Is there room for anymore?"

"Find your own tree trunk," said David, grinning.

"I will do that, then," said Joe.

***

Ina took off her coat, laid it carefully on the ground by the tree trunk, and sat down.

"Do you mind if I unbutton my jacket?" asked David.

"No, of course I don't. Why don't you take it off?"

"I would be improperly dressed," he answered with a smile and sat down on the tree trunk beside her. "That's a nice dress you have on," he said. "And those beads are real pretty."

"They are my mum's; she let me borrow them."

"You look real good, Ina; you're a real pretty girl."

"Me? Pretty? Stella's the good-looking one."

"Stella? I guess Stella is pretty too, but you mustn't sell yourself short. You are very attractive."

"But Stella is blonde and blue-eyed and has a good figure."

"You've got a good figure."

"I'm a bit plump."

"I don't like skinny girls, and I like the way you do your hair. It's nice like that, loose. I'm not keen on those rolls girls have all over their heads; it doesn't look natural."

"You're old-fashioned." She smiled.

"Guess I am," he said, "but I prefer your hair like that. You remind me of Rita Hayworth."

"Rita Hayworth has red hair."

"Not in the black and white movies."

They sat in silence for a while, until David said, "I've known you a whole week."

"Our first anniversary," she answered.

"I feel like I've known you a long time." He paused for a while and then said, "I like you a lot, sweet pea."

"I like you a lot too, David. What was that you called me?"

"Sweet pea."

"Wasn't that the baby in the Popeye cartoons?"

"It's also the name for a pretty girl, especially if she is wearing a pink dress and pretty beads."

He put his hand under her chin and lifted it upwards. He leant forward, and he kissed her. "Is there anyone else, Ina?"

"No," she answered.

"Then you are my girl?"

"If you like."

"I like."

A gentle breeze blew up, and Ina shivered.

"Getting cold?" David asked.

"No, not really. I just had that sensation, like someone walking over my grave. Have you heard of that expression?"

"I sure have. I get it myself sometimes."

Joe and Stella were walking back towards them.

"Didn't you find a tree trunk?" asked David.

"Yes," said Joe, "a beauty, only it was hanging way over the water."

"I guess we can make room for you," David said.

"I reckon we will be heading back," said Joe. "This here Limey girl says she's dying for a cup of tea."

"Okay," said David. "Ready when you are." He stood up.

"You are improperly dressed, soldier," said Joe with mock severity. "Do up your jacket, or I'll put you on KP."

"Yes, Sarge," said David, saluting.

"What's KP?" asked Stella.

"Kitchen patrol," David told her. "It's a punishment—peeling potatoes, peeling onions, cleaning pans."

"How awful," said Stella in mock horror.

***

63

Ina and David walked in front of Stella and Joe.

Along the way Joe suddenly burst into song.

I'm gonna buy a paper doll
That I can call my own.
A doll that other fellows cannot steal . . .

"Does he often start singing like that?" asked Ina.

"Yeah, now and again," David told her.

"Do you sing?"

"Sometimes. We all sing when we are walking alongside the tanks or going on a route march, but they're not the kind of songs you can sing to a young lady." He grinned.

"Don't you know any songs you can sing to a young lady?"

"One or two, maybe. I could sing you one I learnt. Don't know where I heard it. Someone else was singing it, and I picked up the words I guess. Don't know if I got the words right or maybe the tune even . . ."

"Sing it anyway."

"Okay, if you say so. It's sad. Might make you cry."

"Now you're teasing me."

"Try me."

He looked at her, still smiling at her, and began to sing:

"Goodbye, Mary, I must go."
Said the lad, "Now don't grieve so,
"For 'tis duty calls for me far across the sea."
"Take these autumn leaves of gold,"
Said the maid. "We'll never grow old.
"Always wear them next to your heart
"And think of me."

The next verse told how the lad arranged to come back another autumn and meet her down the lane under the old oak tree. David's voice was pleasant, with his deep southern accent lending it warmth. There was then the chorus:

"I'll be there, Mary, dear, I'll be there
"When the perfume of the rose fills the air.

"By that old tree grand and tall
"When the leaves begin to fall.
"I'll be there, Mary, dear, I'll be there."

He sang two more verses and then the chorus again.

"I think they were lovely words," Ina said, "even though they are sad. What's the name of it?"

"Darned if I know; or if I did, I've forgotten."

David suddenly stopped. "Are we going back a different way?"

"Yes, it's a shortcut. There's a little bridge that goes over the stream. We'll wait there for the others to catch us up, and we'll decide what we are going to do next."

"I think Stella wanted a cup of tea," said David.

"Well, we shall find one somewhere."

"The Bib and Tucker?"

"Probably." She laughed.

***

They had reached the small bridge and stopped. David leaned over the handrail. Ina stood beside him looking into the stream.

"Did you know," said David, "that if you look at the flowing water long enough, it seems like you are moving forward?"

"So it does," answered Ina. "You learn something different every day."

The others came up and stood beside them.

"We came back a different way," said Joe. "How far away from town are we?"

"Not far," said Ina. "Castle Street Bridge is just over there." She turned to Stella. "Stella, I was just thinking, wouldn't this be a good place to meet rather than Castle Street?"

"Yes I suppose so," replied Stella. "Would that be all right with you two?"

"Yeah, if we can find it," said David.

"Well, as we go back, you will see Castle Street is only the other side of those trees," Ina told him.

"You don't like waiting in the street?" remarked Joe.

"No, we feel—well, you know, as if we are waiting to be picked up," explained Ina.

"That's understandable," said Joe. "This little bridge suits me."

"Let's go get this cup of tea," said David.

They started walking.

"I don't know if the Bib and Tucker will do just drinks," Ina said. "They might expect us to have a meal."

"Well, we can handle a meal if you like," said Joe. "But we were saving our appetites for this evening—to take you girls for dinner at that restaurant in the Gaumont."

"There's a little teashop behind the bus station," said Stella. "They may be open."

They were. It was just a small place. In the window was a card with "Teas" written on it, and on the glass panel of the door, a sign said "Open" and underneath "Please mind the step".

Ina pushed the door open, and a bell rang. They went inside. There was no one else in the tea shop, so they were able to sit at a table for four.

A woman came in. "Yes?" she enquired.

"Do you and David prefer coffee?" asked Ina.

"No, tea will do for me," replied Joe.

"And for me," said David.

"We'll make Englishmen of you yet." Stella laughed.

"Four teas then, please," Ina said to the woman.

"Anything to eat?" asked the woman.

"What do you have?" asked Joe.

"Toasted teacake; bread, butter, and homemade jam; chocolate Swiss roll; and packets of four biscuits."

"The biscuits are what you call cookies," Stella explained.

"Guess cookies will do for me," replied Joe.

They all settled for "cookies". The woman took a tray of biscuits from the counter and put it on the table for them to choose. She then went out of the room and, in a few moments, came back with a tray of steaming tea in thick china cups with teaspoons in the saucers.

"Sugar on the table," she said.

"So you think you will be able to find the bridge?" asked Stella of Joe.

"Yeah, I don't see why not," Joe replied, grinning at her.

"We'll find it okay," put in David.

"I know a riddle about a man on a bridge," Joe remarked.

"What is it?" replied Stella.

"Well," Joe went on, "there was this man standing on a bridge, and he jumped into the river. What I want to know is, where was he when he jumped?"

"On the bridge," said Stella.

"No," Joe said. "That was before he jumped."

"In the river," put in Ina.

"No, that was after he jumped."

"In the air, then," said Stella.

"No; that was after he jumped."

"All right, clever clogs," said Stella. "What's the answer then?"

"I'm darned if I know," said Joe. "It's been bugging me for years."

They finished their Sunday by going once more to a film at the Gaumont and then for a meal in the restaurant. Afterwards, Joe saw Stella to the bus station and waited with her until her bus came in, and David walked Ina to her bus stop. The boys joined up again when the girls' buses had gone, and walked along Castle Street to catch their transport.

"Where was he when he jumped!" said David. "The times I've heard that old chestnut!"

***

The foursome fell into a routine. Wednesday nights they went into the American Red Cross on High Street. Sometimes Joe and Stella danced, and sometimes Ina managed to persuade David to slow foxtrot with her. He seemed to know now how to follow her steps, although he would not try anything else, and he persuaded her to dance a few times when she was asked by someone else.

They formed a group with some more Americans and their girls, just for the time they were in the Red Cross Club. The two soldiers who seemed the friendlier with David and Joe were named Virgil and Bob. Of the two, Virgil was the more outgoing. He was not very tall and quite slender but darkly handsome. Ina never questioned his ancestry but presumed he was of Italian descent or somewhere in that region. When Virgil and Bob came into the Red Cross, they were, mostly accompanied by two different girls. They heard that Sharkey had been banned for head butting one of the barmen, and the girls felt something akin to relief. Stella was still sure that he would recognise them from the shop.

Saturdays, they usually went to the cinema. Sometimes, Stella and Joe went dancing, but mostly it was a film. When they did go dancing, David asked Ina if she wanted to go with them, as he didn't mind if she did, but she convinced him that it was himself she wanted to be with and she would rather go to the cinema. Sundays were the days Ina looked forward to most of all. They spent all afternoon together, just walking. Sometimes they went over the meads and along the river, where they had gone that second Sunday. Then they either had a meal or went to the cinema again. Wednesdays and Saturdays proved awkward initially. When they had decided to meet at the bridge, they had reckoned without the fact that the evenings would be fairly dark and, in the blackout, it would be difficult for the boys to find their way. They had managed it however and, as Joe said, without a compass.

***

One Sunday, they caught a bus to Harnham; Ina said she wanted to show them Salisbury from Harnham Hill. They walked along the brow taking in the view.

"It's great," said David. "I wish I had some binoculars."

"See over there," said Ina, pointing, "that tall chimney stack? It belongs to the milk factory, where my mum and auntie Nell work."

"A milk factory?" said David.

"Don't say that in America you get your milk from cows."

"Oh. So it's a comeback you have heard before!"

"There's the infirmary, and of course you have a good view of the cathedral."

"I don't think we have got any views like this where I live. Most of the scenery is rugged. We have small towns, a church maybe, and a general store and a livery stable, a small hotel and clothes shop; most of the houses are isolated. Our neighbours are about half a mile away."

"How do you get about?" Ina asked.

"Drive. Most people have a car of some sort."

"And horses? Does anyone ride them?"

"Sure, those who keep them for pleasure riding. Not so many as used to. My old grandma had a pony and trap she used to go round in."

"Did you ride on a horse?"

"No. Not me. I prefer four wheels."

"So you drive then?"

"Sure, I drive. Been driving since I was ten—practised in the family car, but I couldn't go on the main road. I drove licensed first when I was seventeen."

"What happened to the car you and your brother had?"

"I had it when Todd joined up, and then I let my other brothers have it."

Stella and Joe were nearly out of sight.

"Do you want to catch them up?" asked Ina

"No. They may want to be on their own." He turned to her: "Shall we set here for a while?"

"Yes, if you like."

They sat on the slope that formed the hill, and Ina said, "How old is Joe?"

"Joe? He's twenty-four."

"He's young to be a staff sergeant, isn't he?"

"One of the youngest in the army I should think. But he is seasoned—saw action in Mexico and the desert. He is an old hand."

"Where does he come from?"

"Georgia. It's where the 2nd Armoured is based."

"I learnt a song about Georgia, when I was at school."

"Did you?"

"Yes. It was called 'Marching through Georgia'." Directly she said it, she felt that she shouldn't have.

"Well, don't sing it in front of Joe; it's a Civil War song."

"I didn't realise it," she mumbled.

"'Sherman's dashing Yankee boys will never reach the coast. So the saucy rebels said but 'twas an idle boast.' That's it, isn't it?"

"Yes."

"Well, we were the rebels who got licked by the Yankees. We still get referred to as 'Johnny Rebs'. It's meant as an insult, but I pay it no heed now."

"Do you get called that in the army?"

"Now and then, but nearly all the guys in our outfit come from the Deep South. When the Stars and Stripes go up, we might get asked if we have bought our confederate flag with us."

"The war was over the slaves, wasn't it?"

"So they say. But I guess there was something else behind it. It was all political—the North and South divide, the Mason-Dixon Line. We were in Dixie. The Yankees freed the Blacks okay; lots of them went up north and found there were places where they still couldn't use the same lodging houses or bars as the whites or shop in the same stores. They ended up with jobs no one else wanted. They were no better off than they were in the South, except maybe they got paid for what they did—hardly enough to keep themselves, though."

"But they weren't slaves anymore, were they?" Ina replied.

"Listen, sweet pea, forget a lot you've heard. Yeah, some of the slaves were treated really rough, but mostly they had a roof over their heads in the old days and were fed and clothed." A hard note had crept into his voice.

"I'm sorry," she said. "I shouldn't have said anything, should I?"

"It's just that you don't understand, Ina. You haven't had the same problem in your country. It's what I've been brung up with. I don't know anything else. It's my background. It's in the way I lived, and I can't help it if it makes you feel bad."

She felt tears pricking her eyes. She stood up, and he stood up with her.

Stella and Joe were coming back, walking towards them. Before they reached them, David caught hold of Ina's hand.

"Sweet pea," he said, "I'm sorry. I had no right to get sore with you. I know you didn't mean anything by it; you just got me in a raw place. I feel bad now to think I might have hurt you."

"It's all right, David," she told him. "I was a bit tactless. I just didn't think."

"I don't want to be bad friends with you, honey. I like you too much. Forgive me?"

"You must forgive me too."

"Let's forget it ever happened."

"Where to now?" asked Joe, as he and Stella reached them.

"Back to town I guess," said David.

"Okay. Let's go, then," said Joe.

They reached the road and started to walk along. Ina saw a bus approaching.

"Quick!" she cried. "We might get to that bus stop before the bus."

They sped along the road, reaching the bus stop just as the bus pulled up to let a passenger off. Laughing breathlessly, they boarded the bus. Ina got her purse out of her handbag.

"You don't have to do that," protested David. "How much to town?" he asked the conductress. She told him. He reached into his pocket and bought out some coins. "Four, please."

Once they had reached the city centre, Ina asked what they were going to do next.

"We could go to a movie or go for a meal. I don't think you girls will have time for both," said David.

"Meal, then," said Joe. "Roast beef of old England with potatoes roasted in hot fat. That's it, isn't it?"

"Might have changed the menu," Stella told him.

"In that case," said Joe, "we'll take pot luck"

***

When Ina met Stella off the bus the next morning, she told her about her near quarrel with David.

"I don't know much about their Civil War," said Stella, "but you seem to have touched a nerve. If David's lot lost the war they may still feel bad about it."

"It was when I mentioned the slaves he changed. I wish I had never said anything. I shall know better in future, but it shows I still have things to learn about him."

Halfway through the morning, a well-dressed woman came into the shop waving the stub of a repair ticket. "I'm so sorry," she said. "I forgot all about these. I hope you haven't sold them!"

She gave the stub to Vera, who took it out to where the repaired shoes were kept and came back with the brown and white brogue court shoes.

"Sorry, Ina," Vera said, when the woman had gone. "Looks like you have lost your shoes."

***

The evenings were drawing out, and when Ina and Stella met the boys, it was light enough for them to be clearly visible instead of shadowy figures. Ina usually went down Ashley Road, the end of which brought her near to the bridge. She didn't feel keen on going to the American Red Cross that Wednesday night. She wasn't comfortable with some of the girls who went there; also, she knew she was walking a fine line. At any time, she might bump into someone who knew her, and if her father found out about David, there would be fireworks. Nevertheless, there was nothing she could say without upsetting the plans of the others.

As she reached the bridge, she saw Stella, but only one other figure—Joe. She felt her heart quickening, and a fear clutched her. He hadn't come! He had taken what she had said to heart. He must have thought about it and decided not to see her again.

When she reached them, Joe said, "Dave can't make it tonight, honey. He's been confined to camp."

"What's he done?" she asked

"Nothing. He's in quarantine. He gave me this letter for you."

He handed her an envelope. She opened the letter with hands that trembled a little. The light was still not all that good, but she managed to make out his words. She read.

My dear Ina

I am sorry I can't see you tonight, but I am in quarantine, and I'm not allowed off camp. We have had an outbreak of measles, and I didn't know if I have had them or not, so I had to send my mom a cablegram yesterday and ask her to cable me back. I don't expect I shall hear until tomorrow or the next day. If all goes well, I shall be okay for Saturday. But if I don't turn up at the bridge, you will know I'm not clear. Will miss you, sweet pea.

Love,
David

Ina breathed a sigh of relief.

"You two go on," she said. "I'll go back home."

"There is no reason to do that," Stella told her.

"No. You go on. I don't want to spoil your evening," protested Ina.

"You won't spoil anything," said Joe. "I've always wanted to spend time with two pretty girls on my arm. What say we give the club a miss tonight and go to a movie?"

"All right by me," said Stella.

"Yes, all right. I'll come," Ina added.

That night, before she went to bed, she read David's letter again. In spite of him saying that he had not had much schooling, his writing was distinctive and his spelling good. She kissed his signature and then placed the letter back into the envelope and put it in the drawer of her night table.

Chapter 6

April 1944

Hilda had managed to save enough points and coupons to make sure she could put on a reasonably good spread for Easter. She had ordered a leg of lamb, though it probably wouldn't last through to Easter Monday. Bacon had been forgone so that she could get a small bacon joint for the Monday. The allowance of corned beef could be mixed with fried onion and cooked chopped vegetables to make a pie. Points had been spent on two large tins of fruit salad and a large tin of evaporated milk.

When she arrived at the milk factory Wednesday morning, Gladys Parker, a workmate, came up to her. "I was wondering, Hilda, would your Ina be interested in buying a costume? It belonged to my sister, but she can't get into it anymore. She wants ten bob for it."

Hilda looked at the costume and said, "I'll take it home. She can try it on."

***

Ina had peeled potatoes, and there was a cabbage from the allotment, cut up and soaking in another saucepan.

"Thanks, Ina," Hilda said. She put the package on the table.

"What's that?" Ina asked.

"It's for you, if you want it." Hilda handed her the parcel. "Open it and see."

Ina put her hand inside the bag and pulled out the costume. "Where did you get it from?"

"Off of Glad Parker, who works at the factory. Her sister wants to sell it; she can't get into it anymore."

Ina shook the suit out. It was a dark blue bird's-eye tweed. The skirt was gored, and the jacket had blue self-covered buttons down the front.

"How much does she want for it?"

"Ten bob." said Hilda.

"I don't know if I can afford it." Ina sighed. "I drew out my money for the shoes."

Hilda sighed. "You can have that five bob back that you gave me, and perhaps your dad will give you the rest."

Ina stood up and slipped out of her working skirt. She pulled the costume skirt over her head and down over her hips.

"It fits a treat," said Hilda. "Try the jacket on."

Ina slipped her arms through the sleeves and buttoned up the jacket. "I'll go upstairs and look at it in the mirror."

She dashed upstairs to her room and stood in front of the long mirror on her wardrobe door. She turned sideways, first one way and then the other. She got her hand mirror off the dressing table and, turning with her back to the long mirror, tried to gauge what it looked like from the back. Then she went downstairs.

"What do you think, Mum?"

"It looks very nice. You look a treat in it, and that white blouse that Avril gave you should go well under the jacket."

Ina took the costume off and put her old skirt back on.

"Are you satisfied with it?" asked Hilda.

"Yes, I like it. I can have it then?"

"Yes. I expect Dad will go halves with the rest; it'll only be half a crown."

Ina took the costume back upstairs, found a hanger in the wardrobe, and hung it up.

When she came downstairs again, Hilda said, "You haven't got anything planned for Easter holiday, have you?"

"Not so far, why?"

"It'll be nice to have you here. As Avril is going over to Brian's for Easter Sunday, I thought we could have a small party Easter Monday. I've asked Gran and them to come to dinner and tea."

"I'll be there," replied Ina.

She had made no definite plans to meet David as yet, and it would hardly be fair to let her mother down after she had been so generous about the costume. She was, however, left with one problem. What was she to do about shoes? Would brown shoes go with the dark blue? They would have to do; another pair was out of the question.

***

Avril and Brian arrived together on Thursday evening. They had arranged to meet at Waterloo Station and catch the Exeter train to Salisbury; from there, they caught a taxi to the house on Devizes Road. Avril's suitcase was not large. She, like Brian, was obliged to wear uniform, especially travelling to and from their bases. But she brought a couple of dresses with her and a pair of light shoes. It did not take her long to put her things away.

Her sister and Brian were there when Ina came home from work. Brian stayed for tea, and then went home to his parents in Harnham. Avril and her family spent the evening catching up on each other's news. Ina told Avril about the Purdy girls and Cissie Daily's comments about them.

Later that night, when they were both in bed, Avril asked how Stella was, how work was going, and if she, Ina, had a boyfriend.

"Yes," said Ina, "his name is David. He comes from out Stella's way. She goes with his friend."

"Have you brought him home yet to see Mum?"

"No, it's not that serious."

"It's just as well. You should be having lots of boyfriends at your age. I like your costume. Where did you get it from?"

"It's not a new one. Glad Parker at the milk factory had it for sale. It was her sister's, and she couldn't get into it anymore."

"She's putting on weight! What, with all this rationing!"

"She's expecting," replied Ina. She didn't tell Avril that it was an American soldier's baby.

"Did you manage to pay for it all right?" Avril asked.

"It was 10s.0d. Mum gave me five, and Dad gave me 2/6d."

"Have you got something to wear under it?"

"That white blouse you gave me with the turned-out collar."

"Do you manage all right for money? I know you don't earn a lot."

"It's a bit of a struggle sometimes. I try to put 1s.0d in National Savings and 1s.0d in the Legion Christmas Club, but it only leaves me 5s.0d, unless I sell a pair of shoes over 30s.0d. I get 6d commission or 1s.0d if I sell a pair over £2.0s.0d."

"Do you sell many of them?"

"Not really."

"Would you like my navy shoulder bag?" asked Avril.

"Don't you want it anymore?"

"No. Brian bought me one for my birthday—a black one. The blue one used to clash with my uniform. It should go nicely with your costume."

"Did you bring it home?"

"Yes, but wait until morning. We had better settle down; otherwise, Dad will be knocking on the wall."

***

The navy blue bag was round in shape with a zip fastener going halfway round. It was quite roomy inside and comfortably held Ina's make-up bag, her hand cream, comb, purse, and notebook and pencil. There was a little pocket inside, which would hold her latchkey and her identity card. Her old handbag was a two-strap black patent leather affair that she had had when she first left school and was now showing signs of wear. The shoulder bag would not go very well with her brown coat, but beggars could not be choosers.

"Here is a little Easter present for you," said Avril later the next morning and gave Ina half a crown.

"I can't take all that!" Ina protested.

"Yes you can. Don't be daft."

"I haven't got you anything."

"That's okay. I don't want anything. Just to be home and be with Brian is enough for me."

Good Friday was a quiet day. They had hot cross buns at breakfast and a precious boiled egg, cod with white sauce for lunch, and for tea, finished off the hot cross buns.

***

Ina took her "new" handbag to work on Saturday.

Stella admired it.

"It should go nice with my new blue costume, I want to go into Woolworth's dinner time," Ina said, "to see if I can get a blue hair band."

"I want to go to the market to get a new lipstick refill," said Stella.

The market had fewer stalls now than there had been before the war, but some enterprising vendors still rented a stall and carried on trading. The cosmetic stall sold a good range of make-up, though not the real quality brands. There was rouge, face powder, eye make-up, lipstick refills and nail varnish, vanishing cream, and cold cream. There were powder compacts and lipsticks in cases; but these were expensive. Most girls bought the loose powder and lipstick refills and used their existing compacts and lipstick cases. There were also powder puffs on small coloured georgette squares the size of a handkerchief. They were 1s.0d each. Ina bought one with a blue floral pattern. Stella chose and paid for her refill. As they moved from the stall, Ina caught sight of a pair of shoes on a second-hand stall. This stall usually did a brisk trade on a Saturday. The skirts, dresses, and blouses were not suitable for Ina or Stella, but this time they approached the stall and Ina looked over the shoes. She found a pair of blue suede shoes with a Cuban heel.

"Look," she said to Stella, "those would go with my costume. I wonder if they're my size."

"Size 5 they are," said the lady stallholder, "and two bob to you."

"That's my size!" Ina said. She slipped off her own shoes and tried them on.

"They are fine," she said. "I'll have them."

The woman took them and wrapped them in a sheet of newspaper. Ina stepped back into her own shoes and handed over the 2s.0d.

"They're a bit scuffed on the toes," Stella said as they walked away.

"Never mind," Ina replied. "Perhaps Mr Phillips will have some idea on how I can clean them up."

"Bit of a cheek," said Stella with a grin, "taking a pair of second-hand shoes that you bought in the market into a shoe shop."

"I'll just say I want some advice for Avril," said Ina.

"Ina Welland! You're getting to be a right little storyteller. What if he sees the parcel?"

"I'll just say its fish and chips!"

***

They went into Woolworth's, and Ina got her hairband. Back at work, Ina asked Mr Phillips what he recommended for scuffmarks on suede shoes.

Mr Phillips said, "Give them a gentle rub with emery paper, and then hold them over the spout of a steaming kettle. When they are dry, clean them in the normal way with suede cleaner."

Ina managed to fork out for a small bottle of blue suede cleaner with a foam-topped brush.

"When are you going to wear those shoes with the outfit?" asked Stella.

"I'm saving all of it till tomorrow," said Ina.

Chapter 7

That Saturday night, David was at the meeting place.

"Mom's cable came this morning," David said, "and I'm all clear. I had measles when I was two years old, so how was I supposed to remember?"

They walked arm in arm along Castle Street. Girls were still hanging around at the entrance leading to the car park where the trucks came in, waiting for GIs.

"I see what you meant when you said you didn't want to hang around here," remarked David. "It looks a bit—" He paused and then said, "well, you know what I'm getting at."

"Yes, I do," said Ina.

"You wouldn't do it, would you—stand there, I mean. You're a nice girl. I'm glad you're my girl."

"I thought you would choose Stella when we first met."

"Stella? Why should I have chosen Stella?"

"Because she is prettier than me, and the boys seem to go for her."

"I chose to walk with you. I told you before; don't sell yourself short."

"All right." She smiled. "I'll remember."

"You're different from the girls back home."

"In what way?" she asked.

"Well . . . mostly, they are brash and forward. They have a lot to say, and they always want to be the boss."

"Did you have a lot of girlfriends back home?"

"Not really; one or two, maybe. Nothing I couldn't forget if I wanted to. I guess that makes you my first regular girlfriend."

"I'm glad to hear it," said Ina.

Joe and Stella had stopped. Ina and David caught up with them.

"Is there any other place to go apart from the movies or the dance hall?" asked Joe.

"I'm afraid there isn't a lot going on here. There's a theatre on Fisherton Street, but you have to book in advance for a seat," Ina told him.

"Well I guess we might as well go to the Red Cross, and you girls can watch us play pool," said Joe.

"They'd get bored, wouldn't they?" asked David.

Oh hell, I didn't want to go to the Red Cross thought Ina.

***

Ina and Stella followed the boys into the Red Cross, and Ina just hoped there wouldn't be anyone in there she knew. The poolroom held two tables, neither of which was vacant. There were chairs placed around the room, so they settled down to wait. There seemed to be quite a few would-be players already waiting for a table. At last, Joe got up.

"I've had enough," he said. "We might as well go to the bar."

The bar was packed. There was no getting near it.

"What did you do in the evenings before you met us?" asked Stella.

"Went into Tidworth and took in a movie or went into a pub. We didn't come into Salisbury much. In fact, we haven't been in England that long," answered Joe.

"Why don't we find a quiet little pub out of town?" suggested David.

"We aren't really allowed in pubs until we are eighteen," said Ina.

"You look eighteen to me," Joe told her,

"Do you think we'll both pass for eighteen then?" asked Stella.

"Anywhere," replied Joe.

"What if anyone asks to see our identity cards?" Ina put in.

"Identity cards? Do you civilians have to carry identity cards?" David looked horrified.

"Yes," Ina told him, "and they have our date of birth on them."

"It might make a difference if we stuck to soft drinks," suggested Stella.

"That's better," said Joe. "Where to now?"

"If we went into one of the little side street pubs, it would probably be okay," Ina offered and then added, "just this once."

***

They walked along Milford Street and turned from there down a side street. There was a small pub tucked away in the middle of a brewery. They pushed the door open and entered. Once inside, they saw that it was obviously patronised by just the local community. There was not a uniform in sight. At first they were greeted with silence, but as they walked towards the bar, the talking began again. Underneath the two patterned windows on the front outside wall ran a long cushioned bench, fronted by a trestle table. The girls sat down there while David and Joe waited for the landlord to serve them. When he was free, he came over to the boys.

"Yes, gents, what can I get you?"

"Two small glasses of beer, please, and two glasses of lemonade."

The landlord pulled the pumps, and the beer flowed into the glasses. He then filled the two smaller glasses with lemonade and placed all four glasses on a tray.

"Right," he said. "That will be 1s.4d."

David paid the landlord, while Joe took the tray and put it on the table in front of the girls. When they were all seated, the boys began to take an interest in their surroundings. There was a darts match in progress at the other end of the bar, and at a table nearby, two elderly men were playing dominoes. Under a sign saying "Gambling Strictly Prohibited", four men were playing cribbage.

The landlord, with no customers to serve at that moment in time, leaned across the bar. "Where are you stationed then?" he asked.

"Tidworth," Joe told him.

"Been in the country long?"

"Since February. We came from Italy."

"Italy, eh! They soon capitulated when the Allies got there, didn't they?"

"I don't think they are a warring nation," said Joe. "They seemed pretty glad to see us."

"When do you think the balloon is going up then?"

"Can't really tell," said David.

"I was in the last lot," said the landlord. "I was in Belgium; fought in most of the battles—Passchendaele and the Somme."

"I never understood how we managed to keep out of it for so long," said Joe. "My dad went in 1917. He got wounded, but not seriously."

Two men came up to the bar, and the landlord turned round to serve them. As he drew their beer, one of the men turned to Joe and David.

"You blokes fancy a game of arrows?" he asked.

"Arrows?" queried Joe.

"Darts; you and your mate against me and mine."

"Why not," answered Joe. "Our game might be a bit different from yours, but we will give it a try." He turned to David. "Okay by you?"

"Sure," replied David, "but the girls will be left here on their own."

"They can come over," said the man, "there's plenty of room."

The girls picked up their drinks, bags, and coats and followed the boys to the other end of the bar where the dartboard was. They sat on two seats close to two middle-aged women. The darts game started, and everyone looked on.

"Your boyfriends seem like a couple of nice blokes," said one of the women.

"They are," said Ina. "We are very lucky."

"Do you want any crisps?" Stella asked.

"Yes, if they have any."

Stella went up to the bar, where a woman, probably the landlord's wife, stood.

"Have you any crisps?" she asked the woman.

"Yes. How many packets would you like?"

Stella looked over to where David and Joe stood waiting their next turn at darts.

"Do you two want any crisps?"

"Crisp what?" asked Joe.

"Potato crisps."

"Oh you mean potato chips."

"No, chips are what you have with fish."

"Now you have confused me."

"Oh," said Stella, "potato chips then. I shall never get you to speak English."

The woman laughed. "Four packets of crisps, then."

"Yes, please."

David and Joe lost the first leg, which wasn't surprising, as the game did vary from the one they knew. The second leg they won, but the third leg they lost again.

"Hard luck boys," said one of the women. "Played well though, didn't they."

"Yes," said Ina, "they didn't play too badly."

"You haven't been in here before, have you?" the woman went on.

"No," answered Ina, "my friend and I don't go into pubs, but this seemed a nice quiet place, and there is not much to do in Salisbury, is there? We usually go to the pictures or go and have a meal. We wouldn't go into the pubs in town, anyway. There always seems to be trouble there, so we are better off somewhere else."

"Do you go to that place on High Street?" asked the other woman. "The American Red Cross?"

"We sometimes go in there on Wednesday nights," answered Stella. "It's quieter then. Saturday night isn't very good. All the rough girls seem to get in there; they hang around the door waiting for GIs to take them in."

"Sensible girls; best to keep away from there on Saturday nights."

The boys bought another round of drinks, including their darts partners and the two women. They sat chatting for a while, and then Stella exclaimed suddenly, "It's a quarter to ten. I'll miss my bus."

"Aren't you staying with Ina tonight?" asked Joe.

"No," Ina replied for her. "My sister is home on leave, so Stella has lost her bed."

"Come on, then," said David. "We'll be on our way."

They drank up, the girls got into their coats, and with a goodnight to the others, the four of them left the pub.

"That was a real good night," said Joe. "They were real nice people."

"Yes, I enjoyed my game of darts," said David, "even if we did lose."

***

When they reached the bus station, Stella's bus was in. She climbed aboard and sat down by the window; she turned to wave at them. The conductress rang the bell, and the bus moved off. David and Joe walked Ina over to the market.

Ina said to David. "Are you coming in tomorrow, Easter Sunday?"

"Sure," said David.

"How about Easter Monday?"

"Monday?"

"It's a holiday," said Ina

"No," said David, "I shall be working as usual. We don't usually get holidays in the army. Why did you ask anyway?"

"Mum's having a bit of a party. There will be my sister and her boyfriend and my granny and my dad's sister and her son. So I said I would stay home."

"That's okay then," he said. "I'll see you tomorrow, anyway."

When they got to the bus stop, Ina's bus was not in. David put his hand into his pocket and pulled out two half crowns and held them out to her. "Get a cab home," he said.

"No. You can't keep paying out for taxis for me," protested Ina.

"Do as you are told," he replied.

Once more she was propelled towards the taxi rank.

"I shall not want all of that," she said. "The taxi fare is only 2s.0d."

David went up to a taxi. "Can you take this young lady home?" he asked.

"Where to?" asked the taxi driver.

"Devizes Road," said Ina.

"Right, hop in," he said.

David made her take one of the half crowns.

"There you are," he said. "Off you go. I will see you tomorrow."

He and Joe waited until the taxi pulled away and then crossed the road into Castle Street.

"What do we do now?" asked Joe. "The transport doesn't go until eleven o'clock."

David stopped. "Might as well go back to the Red Cross," he said. "At least we can sit down in comfort until it's time to get the transport."

***

Sunday morning Ina asked her father if he had any emery paper she could use.

"What do you want emery paper for?"

"It's to rub the scuff marks off of some suede shoes."

"You'll find some in my toolbox in the shed. Watch what you are doing in there. Don't knock into the bikes and don't make a mess."

She went up the back garden to the shed, found the toolbox, and took out a sheet of emery paper. She shut the toolbox carefully and put it back in the right place. She avoided the bikes, shut the shed door, and as she came out, heard Harold's voice over the fence.

"I have got my call-up papers," he said.

"Oh have you?" Ina replied.

"Got to report for my medical next Monday."

"I hope you get on okay." Ina tried to sound interested. "What are you going into?"

"Army," he said, "seeing as I've been in the cadets all this time. I would like to go in the commandos, but I might get put in the Royal Artillery when I've done my basic training. Lots of Salisbury blokes do." He grinned at her. "Any chance of a date on my first leave?"

Ina began to walk away.

"Better than smelly old farm yokels," he called after her.

She smiled to herself. If only he knew.

Once back indoors, she took her suede shoes into the kitchen and put them onto the draining board. She picked up one and gently rubbed it with the emery paper, surprised to find that it really did make a difference. She did the same to the other shoe and then filled the kettle up and put it on the gas stove to boil. When steam came from the spout, she held first one shoe and then the other into it, turning them around so each was covered with steam. Hilda came into the kitchen.

"What on earth are you doing?" Hilda exclaimed.

"I'm trying to get the scuff marks off these shoes."

"Whose are they—Avril's?"

"No. Mine," replied Ina.

"Where did you get them from?"

"I bought them in the market yesterday."

"Off the second-hand stall?"

"Yes. They were only 2s.0d."

"Ina!"

"Well. I thought they would go better with my costume than my brown ones."

"I don't like the idea of you having shoes that someone else has worn. You may have had some of Avril's clothes handed down to you, but you never had her cast-off shoes."

"Well I couldn't afford another new pair, could I?"

"I don't know!" said Hilda. "Goodness knows what you will be up to before this war is over. You ought to know better working in a shoe shop. Hurry up and turn that kettle off. We can't afford to waste gas."

***

Ina waited for her shoes to dry. Just before lunch, she had a wash and changed her underclothes but put her everyday skirt and blouse back on. After lunch, she helped Hilda wash up and put the dishes away.

"I'm going to meet Stella later," she informed her mother.

Upstairs in her bedroom, she put on the bird's-eye skirt and the white blouse. She had a pair of artificial silk stockings and very carefully pulled them up her legs. She wished she had some nylons but didn't like to ask David to get her some. She pushed her feet into the now dry and quite presentable suede shoes; slipped on the jacket, putting the collar of the blouse outside; and did the buttons up. She looked into the long mirror and was quite pleased with what she saw. She ran downstairs and into the living room.

"Well?" she asked her mother. "Do I look all right?"

Hilda looked critically at her daughter. Ina had swept her hair back off of her face, and her wavy locks were kept in place by her new hairband. "You look very nice," she said. She suddenly realised that Ina was really quite grown up, and she sighed a little under her breath.

***

When Ina reached the bridge, the others were there.

"I'm not late, am I?" she asked.

"No, you're okay. We met Stella in Castle Street," David told her.

"What are we going to do today then?" asked Stella.

"I thought we could go up to the old castle and walk around the rings," replied Ina. "It's only up Castle Road."

"Where's Castle Road?" asked Joe.

"It runs on from Castle Street under the railway bridge."

"Is there really a castle up there?" asked David.

"No," replied Ina, "there was, but it's just ruins now."

They started to walk along the road and had nearly reached the gates of Victoria Park, when Ina said, "We can go through here and come out the other end."

They went through the gates and started to walk along the gravel path between the lawns with the sign saying, "Keep off the Grass" and the shrubberies and flower gardens.

As they walked along the path, David said, "You look very nice, Ina. I haven't seen that outfit before. Is it new?"

"Oh. No," she said. "It's just that I haven't worn it before." She felt herself growing a little pink, although it was not untrue. "Now that it's spring," she said, "I want to wear something different from my brown coat."

"It can't be very easy for you to have many clothes—not with having to pay coupons for them," David said.

"No," replied Ina. "To tell you the truth, David, I bought the costume from a woman my mum works with."

"Well, there's no shame in that. I nearly always had to wear something that belonged to someone else when I was a kid, and you do have a good excuse. We were pretty poor in those days. I told you, didn't I?"

"Yes you did," replied Ina, "and these shoes I bought for 2s.0d off a market stall." She explained how she had smartened the shoes up.

"You're a clever girl, sweet pea. I'm proud of you," said David, looking down and smiling at her.

"My sister, Avril, gave me the blouse and the handbag."

"You're a lucky girl to have a nice big sister."

"Money can be a problem," Ina went on. "I give my mum most of my wage, not that it is very much. I keep 7s.0d for myself. Mum misses Avril's money now she is in the WAAF. Clive is her biggest expense; he grows out of his clothes so quickly. He has to wear a school uniform and have sports equipment."

"Just seven shillings!" David mused. "That's about a dollar. That's not much" he exclaimed.

"I manage. Dad helps me with big things like coats, not that I have a coat very often. He gives me money sometimes when he works overtime, but he has to be careful because they are still paying off the house."

"You know, if you want any money, you only have to ask me. I wish I could buy you things, nice clothes and shoes, but I don't have the coupons!"

Ina flushed. "I don't want you to give me money, David. I would only feel embarrassed, and I would feel cheap as well. I wouldn't be any better than those girls who just go with American soldiers for their money."

He looked down at her with a wry smile on his face. "I think maybe there's a bit of difference there! I wouldn't think badly of you. Guys like to buy pretty things for their girls."

"It's all right," said Ina. "I get by. Avril gave me some summer dresses before she went into the WAAF, and I have had a couple of new dresses. We wear overalls at work, so it doesn't matter if I am a bit shabby underneath it. At least I know what I wear is clean."

***

A band was playing at the bandstand. It was a silver band from one of the outlying villages, the players being either too old or too young or otherwise exempt from military service. The four of them joined other people who were stood there listening. The gardens around them were now in their early bloom; daffodils and narcissi, grape hyacinths, and wallflowers and winter pansies filled the borders. In the small garden plots dug into the grass were more daffodils, growing alongside tulips, anemones, and primroses. They stayed for a while listening to the music and then walked through the grounds, making their way through the playing fields, past the sports pavilion, and then out of the top gates back into Castle Road and towards the old castle. They walked up the sloping grassy field and onto the rings. Ina pointed out the lay of the castle and parts of the ruined walls. They looked down from the top of the rings into the deep ravine below.

"That was the moat," she said.

"It's quite a view from up here," said David, "something like the other hill we climbed—Harnham? That was it wasn't it? And there really was a castle here? How long ago?"

"About seven or eight hundred years; I'm not quite sure."

"What happened to it?"

"I don't really know. We were taught all about it in school, but I don't think I could have been paying much attention at the time. I know they didn't use it for anything in the end because of the difficulty of getting water up from the river to the inhabitants of Old Sarum. It just fell into ruins. Then about the twelfth century, somebody reckoned we needed a new cathedral. I forget who it was. They said they would shoot an arrow into the air, and wherever it fell, they would build the new cathedral there."

Joe pointed. "And that's the cathedral way over there," he said. "Must have been some shot. It wasn't Robin Hood was it?"

"No." Ina laughed. "Robin Hood was from the north."

A stiff breeze had blown up.

"Guess we had better start making our way down," said David. "It's getting a might windy, and I don't want to be blown off into the moat."

As they turned to go, Ina pointed across the Stratford valley. "See those houses going along that hill," she said.

"All those little houses," said David.

"Yes. That's the road I live in."

"You're not so far away from home, then," said David.

Joe caught sight of the Old Castle Inn. "Would that be a pub?" he asked.

"Yes," said Ina, "but it won't be open now. It's only open from twelve to two on a Sunday. It won't be open again until this evening."

"That's a pity," said David. "It looks a nice place."

"Some bars are open all day back home," said Joe.

"They couldn't do that here," Ina said with a laugh. "They'd use up their whole ration in two days."

"So, beer is rationed, too!"

"Well . . . not exactly," Ina said. "But beer, spirits, and cigarettes are in short supply and have to be eked out."

"How do you know all this?" asked Joe. "Are you a seasoned drinker?"

"No, I get my information from my dad. He goes to the British Legion Club, and they serve drinks there."

"Is it like the Red Cross?" asked David.

"Something," Ina told him. "It was originally for ex-service men from the 1914-18 war, but today's troops use it as well now. The legion people make poppies to sell for people to wear on Armistice Day, marking the end of the First World War—11 November 1918 to be exact."

"Was your father in the first war?" asked Joe.

"Yes," Ina answered. "He was called up in 1915, when he was eighteen. He came home in 1919. He made friends with another soldier and brought him home because he had nowhere else to go. My gran took him in to live with her. He and my dad joined the railway. They're both engine drivers now, like my granddad was."

"What we call engineers," David put in.

"Do you? Well, I suppose it's the same thing."

"Did he stay with your grandma?"

"Yes, my granddad died in the flu epidemic. After a few years, Uncle Sid and my auntie Nell, dad's sister, got married, so they still live with

Gran." She thought it best not to go into any more detail, not to mention Teddy.

They walked on until they came to the meadows and then to the bridge.

"Back where we started," remarked Joe. "Why don't we take a stroll by the river again?"

The mallard chicks were now almost fully grown. The cygnets were now nearly as big as their parents; they had shed most of their down and were now sporting new white feathers. It was pleasantly warm. The two men had taken off their overcoats and draped them across their arms.

David suddenly stopped. "I almost forgot," he said.

He put his hand into his overcoat pocket and drew out some Hershey bars. He handed one each to Ina and Stella.

"Happy Easter," he said. And then he asked Joe, "Want one?"

"Sure," Joe said, "if there's one to spare."

Their footsteps led them away from the bridge until they were walking along the towpath. They had not gone far when Joe, once more, burst into song:

I'll be down to fetch you a taxi, honey,
Better be ready by half past eight

"There he goes again!" laughed Stella,

"Honey," Joe told her, "if I didn't sing sometimes, well . . . I reckon I'd just sit down and cry."

Although he smiled as he spoke, Ina felt a slight chill creep over her. She had seen the newsreels of wounded soldiers being brought back from Dunkirk. Although she wasn't very old at the time, she was still aware, even at thirteen years of age, that they must have suffered somewhat. Joe and David had already seen action—seen their buddies hurt, killed even. She pushed her arm through David's and caught hold of his hand in both of hers. He looked at her quizzically.

"You okay?"

"Yes." Then she whispered, "Sing me that song."

"Song?"

"About Jack and Mary."

"You sure?"

"Yes."

91

"You won't cry all over me?"

"Promise."

He sang, and it was when he came to the last two verses that she thought she might break her promise, but she listened quietly and intently to the words.

See the lad with an empty sleeve
Of his comrades taken leave.
He was home once more the transport had come back
If she loved you long ago,
She'll not love you less I know.
And one arm will do to hold her to you, Jack.

It was autumn time again as he wandered down the lane.
And under that old tree, he found a grave
Then he knelt in silent prayer, for the one he loved slept there.
And the tears fell on the golden leaves she gave.

This time, Ina joined in the chorus with him.

"I'll be there, Mary, dear. I'll be there . . ."

They walked in silence for a while; she thought about the words of the song. If Jack had come home and Mary was still alive, what would she have done? Would she have loved him still as much?

Impulsively, she said, "She would have loved him the same, wouldn't she? If I loved someone that much, it wouldn't make any difference to me if he lost an arm or a leg—"

"You reckon?"

"No. Honestly. If—" She had been about to say that, if he was wounded, it would make no difference to her. But that was presuming, and she did not know the extent of his feelings for her. Instead, she finished, somewhat lamely, by saying, "There's a lot of men who have already come back from the war. Some may have lost both limbs or been burnt when their planes crash-landed. I expect their wives have gone on loving and caring for them—"

"Yeah, wives, maybe. Not so sure about girlfriends, though. They can easily opt out. Anyhow, I wouldn't want to be that badly wounded.

I'd rather get it outright—blown sky high or a bullet through my head, something quick and easy that I knew nothing about. I couldn't stand to go through my life as a cripple."

She had not withdrawn her arm from his, and now she laid her head against his shoulder.

"Hey, C'mon" he exclaimed. "We shouldn't be having talk like this! Here I am, on a nice day walking along with my girl. I can't think about what might happen, Ina. I gotta do what I was trained to do. I had my scraps on the way here. I'm not especially brave, but if somebody sticks a gun in my hand and says, 'Go shoot a German,' then I guess I have to do that thing. Bad things happen in war, but good things happen too, like meeting you."

"I shall miss you when you go, David."

"I shall miss you too, sweet pea. Will you write to me?"

"Yes, of course, if you want me to."

"We all like to get letters from our girls. You're not writing to any other boys, are you?"

"No, only to my cousin, Teddy. We all write to him. We don't know if he gets our letters. He's in a Japanese POW camp, and my auntie hasn't heard from him for two years."

"That's tough, Ina. Guess there's a lot of our guys who are in those camps. I think Mom gets worried about Todd, you know, in case his ship gets sunk by a torpedo or hit with one of those kamikaze pilots and he ends up in one."

"You'll write back, won't you?"

"Sure. You'll have to be patient with me though. I'm not one of the world's greatest letter writers. Mom's always going on that she doesn't hear from me regular. A lot depends on where I am and how tied up I am. I'm not much good at putting things into words, but I'll do my best."

Chapter 8

"It's no good," said old Mrs Welland. "I just can't get up that hill. You'll have to go without me."

"But, Mum," protested Nell, "they're expecting us, and knowing Hilda, she's probably gone to a lot of trouble."

"One less won't make any difference."

"I'm not leaving you here on your own."

"I shall be perfectly all right!"

"We'll help you, Mum," Sid told her. "I'll take one arm, and Terry can take the other."

"That won't make any difference, Sid. I just haven't got the energy to climb all up Ashley Road."

"Gran," suggested Terry, "why don't we go down the road and along Meadow Road? We could go up Gas Lane. That's not such a steep hill, and perhaps we can get a bus to Uncle Jim's."

"Right," said Sid. "I'll get the timetable."

He opened a drawer, took out the timetable, and began to leaf through it. "Here we are. Devizes Road . . . leaves market . . . gets railway station . . . gets to Wessex . . ." He folded the book up.

"They run quarter to and quarter past the hour—Sunday service. If we leave now and take it steady, we should get the quarter past eleven."

"Come on, Gran. Don't forget, it will be downhill all the way coming home," encouraged Terry.

"Oh, all right. Get my coat. I'll take my stick. Me," she muttered, "having to walk with a stick!"

***

The old lady was greeted warmly by her daughter-in-law.

"Come on in to the front room, Mum. We've got a bit of a fire going. Ina's got the kettle on for a cup of tea."

Avril and Brian were all ready in the front room on the sofa. They got up and ushered her to a fireside chair.

"Well!" she enquired. "How are you both then?"

"We're fine. Thank you, Gran," Avril told her.

"Your dad tells me you've got a stripe then, Avril."

"Yes, Gran. And Brian's got a second one, so now he outranks me again."

"You'll have to mind your Ps and Qs then, won't you!" Her grandmother smiled.

Hilda had gone through into the kitchen. Nell followed her.

"Anything I can do, Hilda?" she asked.

"No, I don't think so," Hilda replied.

"I'm just making a cup of tea, Auntie," Ina said, putting a tray of cups and saucers on the small kitchen table.

"You'd better find out if the men are going down the legion before you pour any for them," warned Hilda, and, as if he had heard, Jim came into the kitchen.

"We're going down the legion," he said.

"Now, how did I guess that?" Hilda asked.

"Can I come, Dad?" called Clive.

"Yes, hurry up!" said Jim. "Just don't make a nuisance of yourself down there." Turning to Hilda, he said, "I'm going to pop into Alb's on the way to let him know we're going down."

"I think they've got Maureen's Keith home this weekend," Hilda told him. "It'll be interesting to know if they do get engaged."

"Well I'm not going to stick my neck out and ask him," Jim replied, "just in case."

"Don't forget, Jim," Hilda told him, "dinner is at two. Don't be late!"

Ina poured out the tea, put three cups on the tray, and took them into the front room for her sister, grandmother, and herself.

When she had gone out of earshot, Hilda said, "I think she's got a boyfriend—someone special this time."

"Not brought him home yet then?"

"She told Avril it wasn't serious."

"She hasn't asked to bring him home yet then?"

"No . . . It would be nice to know what he's like. He comes from Stella's way as far as I can make out. Stella goes out with his friend, so the chances are, her family know them. They're obviously not old enough for the forces yet. I'm not really worried about her, Nell. She's seventeen, and I can't rule her life now. She's sensible. God knows Jim's lectured her enough."

Nell gave a wry smile. "Warned her to behave herself or she'd end up like her auntie Nell?"

Hilda flushed slightly. "Well . . . I suppose he might have mentioned what might happen to her if . . . well . . . you know. Nell, I'm sorry. I didn't mean to drag all that up."

"I know, Hilda. I'd feel the same if I had a daughter Ina's age. But Jim's never really forgotten or forgiven, has he? I sometimes think it was hard on Teddy, trying to understand why his uncle Jim made more fuss of Terry than he did of him."

"Do you think he did, then, Nell?"

"That's how it used to look to me! Perhaps it was a shock to come home from the war and find his sister holding an Australian soldier's baby. No. I wouldn't like Ina to go through what I went through, not when there are the likes of Cissie Dalcy about. When she goes on about Mrs Purdy's girls, I can't help feeling she's taking a swipe at me. There were plenty of Cissie Daley's about in my time! But you stuck by me, Hilda, and Mum and Dad and most of the girls at the milk factory."

"I think Jim is as concerned about Teddy as the rest of us. He says sometimes that he wishes they'd get a move on and get rid of the Japs."

"Does he?"

"Yes, honest." Hilda touched Nell's arm and said, "Come on. Let's go into the front room with the others. There's nothing in here that can't wait a while."

***

Old Mrs Welland greeted their arrival with, "I was just asking Avril when she and Brian were getting married."

"Not until after the war, I hope," Hilda replied, "or she won't have a reception with a two-tier cake and all the trimmings!"

"No. Brian says we wait until the war's over."

"There won't be any utility wedding for Avril!" put in Ina. "When we go over to France and capture Hitler and have got him locked up in the tower of London, then we can go to town, can't we, Avril?"

The old lady turned to Ina. "How are things in the shoe shop then Ina?"

"Oh, all right, Gran."

"Do you get any nylons in?" Avril asked.

"What, nylon stockings? No never see those. We get pure silk sometimes. But they go like hotcakes, and they're too expensive for me."

"What do you wear, then?" Avril went on, "The ones you've got on now look nice."

"They're only lisle," Ina told her.

"Lisle? They look fully fashioned."

"Well," Ina grinned, "that's a trick of the trade. We turn them inside out, cut the fringes around the back of the heels off; the seams are now on the outside, so they look like fully fashioned."

"That's crafty!" Avril said.

"I thought young gals painted your legs to look like stockings," said the old lady.

"Stella did once, Gran," Ina replied. "She got some special stuff; it was quite dear. She put it on, and her sister drew a line up the back of her legs with an eyebrow pencil. It rained that day when we went out, and all the colour ran. Her legs were all streaky, and we had to go down to the ladies' lavs so she could go into the wash and brush up. The attendant down there charged her four pence instead of tuppence because she took a long time getting it all off."

***

At a quarter to two, the men came back, bringing with them a few bottles of pale ale and, by the courtesy of Brian, a bottle of sherry for the ladies and the obligatory bottle of Tizer for Clive.

Hilda called from the kitchen, "Jim! Will you and Clive bring down a couple of chairs from upstairs?" And to Avril and Ina, she added, "You two girls can lay the table. You'll have to pull the leaves out and use the big tablecloth. Don't forget the felt. It's in the cupboard. I don't want the table marked."

Jim and Clive came in with the chairs.

97

"We going to have enough chairs?" asked Jim.

Hilda had come into inspect the table. "We can have the two out of the front room."

She studied the table. "Do you think nine of us will get around that, Jim?"

"It's going to be a tight squeeze" Jim said.

"We could get the small table from the other room," Hilda went on.

"I can sit at that, Mum," chipped in Clive.

"All right, then. It'll be a bit of a squash."

But it was settled. And while Avril and Ina placed the cutlery and cruets on the tables, Hilda and Nell dished up the meal. Hilda's fears that the joint would not go round were unfounded.

"This is so nice," commented old Mrs Welland, "the family altogether for once." Then her face clouded, and she said, quietly, "except for Teddy not being here."

"Let's hope this is the last wartime Easter we shall have, Ma," Sid said, "and by next Easter we shall have our boy back home."

"I expect once we get going in France, it won't be long before the Japs cave in," Jim said comfortingly.

It was not a profound statement, but Nell was grateful.

Sid turned to Brian. "You got any idea when the balloon's likely to go up, Brian?"

"Me? No. They don't tell us anything. I don't suppose they know themselves. It's going to take some time in doing—getting everyone across the channel."

"I should say so," agreed Jim, "a darn sight more than going over in '14 or the BEF in '39."

"Wonder where they'll land?" Sid said. "France? Belgium?"

"Might be Holland," Jim offered.

"Shouldn't think so," answered Brian. "Not enough ground cover for troops.

"You could be right, there," the other two agreed.

Avril looked up at Brian. "I'm glad you're not air crew," she said. "At least you won't be going over there."

"I shouldn't be too sure about that," he told her. "Maybe not with the first wave, but once they've established a foothold, they'll be building runways. I could be sent over then."

"But you've already been abroad once!" she protested.

"That makes no difference. If I get drafted, then I have no choice but to go"

Ina looked down at her hands, clasped tightly in her lap. *If they stick a gun in my hand and tell me to go shoot a German, then I have to do that thing*, David had said.

Hilda rose up from the table. "If everyone's finished," she said, "I'll get the afters."

"What have we got, Mum?" Clive asked.

"Apple pie and custard, all right?"

Ina and Avril got up to give her a hand. Once the afters had been dished up and served, Jim refilled the men's glasses. "You ladies want anymore sherry?" he asked.

Ina and Hilda declined; Avril, Nell, and old Mrs Welland pushed their glasses forward to be recharged.

"By the way, Jim, did Maureen's Keith go down the legion with Alb?" Hilda asked.

"Yes. He was there."

"Did he say anything about getting engaged?"

"You women!" said Jim. "Don't you ever think of anything except getting some poor blighter hitched for life?"

"Well did he?"

"No. Not to us he didn't."

"I should think if they had, Cissie would have dragged Maureen round here to show off the ring," Nell told her.

Hilda shrugged. "Perhaps he hasn't given it to her yet."

Brian asked, "Has she known him long?"

All eyes turned to him. Hilda was the only one to speak. "Don't really know. About six months I would say. Why?"

Brian hesitated for a moment and then said, "I don't know if I ought to say anything, but I've seen him before."

"Have you, Brian?" asked Hilda.

"It was at my first station when I first joined."

"He didn't seem to recognise you," Sid told him.

"No. Well, I was part of a new intake, and he was an LAC. I'm sure it's him." Brian looked slightly uncomfortable but continued, "I think he's a married man."

"Strewth!" Jim gasped. "There's a turn-up for the book!"

"What makes you think that?" asked Avril.

"There was some sort of trouble at the camp. You know how word gets around. You can't help overhearing these things. It involved a girl in the village, and then his wife came down, and there was a bit of a ding-dong. A lot of blokes knew he was carrying on with this girl and that he was married. I think he had kiddies, but I'm not sure how many."

"Do you think Maureen knows?" asked Avril.

"If she does, then she hasn't told her mother," Nell replied.

"I can't see Maureen having anything to do with a married man," Hilda put in. "She's such a quiet little thing."

"You know what they say," her mother-in-law said. "Still waters run deep."

"No. I can't see it," Hilda told her. "She'd be too frightened her mother would find out to keep a secret like that."

Ina felt herself flushing and hoped no one noticed. Wasn't that what she was doing? Keeping David secret?

"Do you think we ought to say something?" Hilda asked Jim.

"No, I don't" he said, emphatically. "We keep out of it"

"I could be wrong," Brian said. "I wouldn't like to put a spanner in the works."

"No," Jim went on. "Best to say nothing, though, mind you, I did think he was a lot older than the girl."

A silence fell upon the group, which the old lady broke by saying, "That apple pie was a treat, Hilda. You make a lovely bit of pastry."

Everyone murmured their assent.

"I wish my pastry turned out this well," Nell said. "You have a real knack, Hilda."

Hilda grinned at her sister-in-law. "I'm glad everyone liked it. I really didn't know how it would turn out. I was running short of margarine, so I used dripping!"

***

When the table was cleared and the washing up done, Avril suggested they go for a walk. Hilda declined, saying she would keep her mother-in-law company and have tea for them when they returned. Jim and Sid declined on the grounds that walking wasn't good for them at their age. Brian said he'd go to keep Avril company.

"Got you under her thumb already then, son!" commented Jim, wryly.

Terry was going so that Clive wouldn't feel left out, and Ina and Nell decided that the fresh air would do them good and help their lunch go down.

"Where did you think of going?" Ina asked Avril, thinking in her heart, *Please don't say the meads.*

"How about a walk up the road and then down the avenue into Wilton?" suggested Avril.

They all agreed and set off.

The day was warm, with very little breeze. They walked by gardens filled with flowers of spring and trees in early bud. Terry and Clive walked in front, Avril and Brian behind them, Ina and Nell at the rear.

"Do you remember before the war when you were small and we used to go for walks on a Sunday?" Nell asked.

"Yes. I do," Ina replied.

"Gran would come with us then," Nell went on, "and your dad and Uncle Sid, if they weren't working. Terry would toddle along beside Teddy, and Clive would be in his pushchair. You and Avril used to look very smart. Your mum bought the material, and I made you both your Sunday dresses. You wore straw hats with daisies round the brim."

"And white socks and black patent leather ankle strap shoes."

"Your mum and dad didn't have much money in those days, but you always looked nice. I know your gran was worried when Jim qualified as a driver and he bought the house."

"He still moans about paying the mortgage!"

They both laughed. Then Nell said, "You look nice in that costume. Is it the one you bought from Glad Parker's sister?"

"Yes. But I wish I had another blouse to go with it besides this one."

"I'll tell you what. Do you remember that dark blue dress I had—the one with the turned-back collar?"

Ina said she did.

"Well, I spilled some fat down the skirt. My own fault, but I couldn't get it out. If I cut the top off to just under the waist, I reckon it would go nicely under your costume. Would you like me to do that for you, then?"

"Yes, please!"

"Right, directly I get a few minutes I'll get the machine going. It won't take long."

***

At the bottom of the avenue, they crossed the road. Avril stopped and called back, "Do you want to go right into Wilton or go back?"

The others elected to go into the town. They went through the park, passing through the flowering shrubs and the spring flowers, along by the river, and back onto the road. They strolled through the town.

"I wonder if we can get a cup of tea?" Avril said.

"It doesn't look as though there's anywhere open," Brian told her.

"I think we ought to be heading back," said Nell. "Your mum will have the tea ready, and we don't want to be late."

They walked back the way they had come. Ina looked at Avril and Brian walking along hand in hand. A feeling of envy crept over her, and for a moment, she felt near to tears. Why couldn't David be walking with her? Did Avril know how lucky she was to be with her boyfriend? No one had ever discouraged their courting. She remembered the first time Avril had brought him home. She had been fifteen years old and Brian seventeen. They had both been working in Lipton's then. Brian was in the Air Training Corps. He had looked very smart in his uniform and was already talking about going into the RAF. The family had readily accepted him, her mother and Gran and Auntie Nell. Nice boy. Well mannered. So was David. Polite, considerate, kind, smart, nice-looking, and . . . a Yank.

"I really enjoyed that walk," remarked Nell as they reached the house.

Inside, the table was laid for tea. Nell had bought some fancy cakes and brought them up to her sister-in-law. Hilda had managed a chocolate sponge cake and had cut cold bacon sandwiches and cheese and tomato rolls. In a glass dish were the contents of a tin of fruit salad, in another, a jelly, at which Nell cried, "Jelly, Hilda!"

"I made it with some gelatine I found and some orange squash," Hilda explained.

"You've done us proud, Mum," said Avril.

***

"What do you think about us going over to Tidworth on Sunday?"

Ina and Stella were sat opposite each other in the staffroom.

Ina looked up at Stella, a slight frown on her face. "Do you think they'd want us to?" she asked.

"I don't see why they shouldn't'," Stella answered.

"They might think they've seen enough of Tidworth," Ina said.

"I get a bit fed up prowling around Salisbury."

"What makes you think that Tidworth will be any better?"

"Well, if it's no better, at least it will be different."

Ina considered further. "I don't know how much the bus fare is," she said.

"Can't be much more than about 3/6d return," Stella told her.

"Not much more than 3/6d!" cried Ina.

"You'll get your pay Friday night. We'll just keep away from Woolworth's and the market."

"Oh. All right," Ina conceded. "We'll ask them Wednesday night and see what they say."

***

On Wednesday night, they went to the American Red Cross. Ina wasn't keen but voiced no objection. She was wearing her suit and the blouse that Nell had made from the dress. It looked quite presentable. David told her he liked the blouse, and this time, she did not tell him its origin.

They sat at a table where Virgil and Bob were sitting. David and Joe each had a glass of beer, and the girls had cola.

The band struck up, and Joe turned to Stella. "Wanna dance?"

They both stood up, and Joe whisked Stella off to the dance floor.

"Don't you dance then, David?" asked Virgil.

"Me? No. I'm no hoofer."

Ina felt a stab of disappointment. She was on the brink of telling Virgil that David had made the effort before, but she held her tongue, lest she should embarrass him in front of his friends.

Virgil turned to Ina, but said to David, "Do you mind if I dance with Ina?"

"No, if she wants to dance."

103

To Ina, Virgil said, "Would you like to dance?"

Ina glanced at David. His face was impassive. She thought, *He doesn't seem to care one way or another.* She stood up and followed Virgil to the dance floor.

Then she heard David call out, "Don't forget to bring her back—soon!"

Virgil grinned at Ina. "Who is it he doesn't trust? You or me?"

The band was playing a quickstep, and although the American way of dancing was slightly different, Ina found she could follow Virgil's steps quite easily.

"You dance very well," he told her. "Do you go dancing a lot?"

"No. Not a lot lately."

"Pity Dave doesn't dance. He doesn't know what he's missing."

She didn't answer, and the subject seemed closed.

"You know," he said, "Ina's a pretty name. Don't think I've heard that before; Ida, maybe, like Ida Lupino. Are you Dave's regular girl?"

She hesitated a moment. Was she? He hadn't mentioned anyone else.

"Yes, well . . . we've been going out together a few weeks."

They danced on in silence until the music stopped, and Virgil took her back to David. Stella and Joe followed them.

Back at their table, Joe asked Virgil and his friend if they wanted a drink.

"No. We're off," Virgil said. "Got a couple of girls to meet at seven thirty."

"You won't be coming back then?"

"Shouldn't think so," Virgil said. "It's heavy."

"Okay then. See you around."

When Virgil and his friend had gone, Stella said, "We've something to ask you two."

"You have?" said Joe.

"What do you think about us coming over to you next Sunday?"

Joe furrowed his brow. "To us? At Tidworth do you mean?"

"Yes."

"What do you want to come to Tidworth for? Ain't nothing there that you haven't got here."

"We thought it would make a change—somewhere different for us instead of Salisbury."

"Well. Okay then, sure, if that's what you want. Have you been to Tidworth before?"

"No," said Stella. "We can come over in the afternoon. We'll find out the bus times and let you know Saturday night."

"Okay, we'll meet you off the bus."

***

As David waited with Ina at her bus stop later that night, she said. "What did Virgil mean by 'heavy'?"

David looked at her with raised eyebrows. "You don't know?" he asked.

She shook her head.

"It means they have some place to go . . . like . . . maybe one of them has a house . . . Jeeze! Ina. Why did you have to ask me a question like that?"

For Ina, the penny suddenly dropped. She clamped her hand over her mouth and felt the colour rush to her face. "Sorry," she said through her fingers. "I suppose . . . I . . . think perhaps I know."

David laughed and said, "What do you know. I got me a girl who can blush!"

***

On Saturday morning, the regional inspector came.

"I haven't come on spec to make an inspection," he said to Mr Phillips. "I had to pass through Salisbury today. My wife asked me to get her some coffee from Stoke's, so I thought I'd pay you a visit and cadge a cup of tea."

"I'll make it for you," said Mrs Gray condescendingly and followed the two men through the shop.

"She wants to earwig on their conversation," sniffed Stella.

"Probably going to tell Mr Phillips we're in for a raise."

"You wish!" said Stella.

***

Mrs Gray bustled about boiling water, fetching cups and saucers and pouring milk into the little used milk jug.

"Sugar?" she asked the inspector.

"No thank you, not for me," said the inspector. "I gave it up when rationing started."

Mr Phillips put his hand in his pocket and took out a small packet of saccharin tablets. "I'm afraid I still give in to my sweet tooth," he said sheepishly.

"How are things going anyway?" asked the inspector. "Are the American officers' shoes selling?"

"Well . . . a little slowly," Mr Phillips answered reluctantly. "But there, it's still early days."

A small frown creased the inspector's forehead. "Hmm," he said. "They had plenty of publicity in the officers' messes. Anyway, your display is very satisfactory. I noticed it as I came through."

Mrs Gray was making a show of pouring out the tea through a tea strainer. When she had finished, Mr Phillips said, "Thank you, Mrs Gray," and she knew she had been dismissed. As she went out of the room, Mr Phillips would have taken a wager on her creeping into the workroom and listening to their conversation through the door.

The inspector was continuing. "There is another matter I may as well bring up while I'm here, and that is about the wooden-soled sandals. I'm afraid we've had one or two complaints from various branches. Apparently, in some circumstances, the soles show signs of cracking—probably due to wearing them in the rain. Northampton suggests that the wooden soles be removed in these cases and a leather sole fitted, making like an ordinary sandal. They can do that at the factory."

"Won't that make them rather expensive?" asked Mr Phillips.

"Well, it will still mean a good sandal for less coupons. But," the inspector went on, "they'd soon know if the wood had been cracked deliberately, so anyone trying to fox them would just get their sandal back unaltered."

"Is there plenty of leather about, then?"

"I wouldn't say plenty exactly, but Northampton doesn't seem to have any problems so far."

"Perhaps they're slaughtering more cattle to sell to the American cook houses for beef."

If the inspector noticed the slightly sardonic note in Mr Phillip's voice, he showed no sign. Instead he declared he must get on.

They both rose, just as the door opened and Mrs Phillips came in.

"Ah! Your good lady wife! It's very nice to see you again, Mrs Phillips."

He stretched out his hand and shook hers, enquired after her health, and expressed regret at having to leave so soon.

"I'll see you out," said Mr Phillips. Both men went out of the staffroom.

***

Mrs Phillips felt the teapot. She decided that the tea was still warm enough. She fetched another cup from the kitchen, poured herself tea, and sat down, resting her elbows on the table, with the cup nestled between her hands. She sipped the tea slowly and contemplated the two things that were puzzling her. Why had the regional inspector paid an impromptu visit to the shop, and why, as she had come into the workroom from the shop, had Mrs Gray, who had been standing by the sink, turned suddenly, gone beetroot red, and scuttled back into the shop.

***

The three girls were serving when Mrs Gray returned to the shop, so she had to wait before she could regale them with what she had overheard. At least it gave her face time to resume its normal colour. She was expecting them to gather around her with baited breath, hanging onto her every word. But, the time had passed. When the shop had finally cleared of customers, they showed no interest whatsoever in what she had to say.

She made a valiant stab at the subject. "The inspector went on about your wooden-soled shoes, Miss Jenner."

Vera looked at her but said nothing.

"He said," Mrs Gray went on, "up in Northampton, they were considering taking off the broken wood and replacing it with leather."

"Why didn't they put leather soles on in the first place and have a decent sandal?" asked Stella.

"I don't know," Mrs Gray said irritably. "I suppose it's one way of getting them for less coupons."

"Make them expensive," Ina put in.

"I wouldn't be able to afford them," Stella said.

"Me neither," said Vera.

Mrs Gray was losing ground. At that moment, the shop door opened, and in came a short, tubby, middle-aged man with a balding head and a fleshy nose. It was Mr Gray. Mrs Gray motioned him to follow her to the rear of the shop, where they then stood by the hosiery display talking 'sotto voce'.

"Suit each other, don't they?" remarked Ina.

"Like two fat peas in a pod," agreed Stella.

***

Later that morning came a busy period. Ina was the only one who had finished serving when two American officers came through the shop door. Ina gave a quick glance in the direction of Mr Phillips. He was just on his way to the workroom to put rubber soles on the pair of gent's shoes that he had just sold. Ina went forward to the Americans and asked if she could help.

"Yes. Surely," one replied. "Those officers' shoes you have for the US Army—I'd like to try a pair on, please. My English size is 8. Do you have them in that size?"

"Yes," Ina replied. "If you care to take a seat, I'll get you a pair to try on."

The officer took a seat, saying to the other American, "What about you, Bill? You got your permit for a pair?"

The other officer took a seat beside him. "Yes. I might as well get a pair, as we're here." He took a small notebook out of his pocket, opened it, and glancing up to Ina, said, "It says here that my size is 9."

Ina took down the shoeboxes, opened them, and gave each officer his relevant size. She also handed each of them a shoehorn. Bill put his notebook back into his pocket and took a shoehorn from her.

"These little books help us with our conversions," he explained. "I haven't got the hang of your currency yet."

"Don't worry," Ina told him. "I'll help you with it."

The shoes fitted. Both men said they were comfortable. They put their own shoes back on, Ina wrapped each pair. Mr Phillips had finished putting on the rubber soles, and his customer had paid and left the shop.

He was now standing by the cash desk. The two officers followed Ina across the shop floor to the desk; the permits and money were handed over, and change and receipts were given.

"Thank you very much, gentleman," Mr Phillips said. "I hope you find them satisfactory."

"Thank you," said the first American. "Your young clerk has been very helpful."

After they'd gone, Mr Phillips put the permits in the desk drawer. Ina went to her receipt book, pinned her two tickets to the carbon copies, and then passed them to Mr Phillips, who put them on the bill hook.

"That was a good sale, Miss—2s.0d!"

"Yes," she answered, her cheeks a little pink. Two shillings! It was almost her fare to Tidworth.

***

The day had turned chilly, and grey skies were in evidence. Ina had put on her one good skirt, a jumper her mother had knitted (when she had managed to get hold of some wool), and her brown coat. By the time she and Stella reached the bridge, it had started to rain. She put her scarf over her head. She wished she had brought her umbrella; it was old and shabby, but it would have kept the rain off her coat. The boys were wearing their raincoats.

David offered to put his around her shoulders. "I don't want you to get your nice coat wet," he said.

"No. It's all right. It's not raining that hard," she told him.

"You sure?"

"Yes. Really."

"I guess it's a movie and then supper," said Joe. "And we have to tell you, we shan't be able to see you tomorrow, so you're trip to Tidworth will have to wait a while."

"Why? What's happening?" asked Stella.

"We gotta go some place tomorrow on exercises," replied Joe. "Don't know where, but it will take all week. We gotta get wherever, make camp, and start Monday."

Ina turned an anxious face to David. "Will you be back by next Sunday?"

"I hope so, sweet pea."

"How shall we know if you're back? We don't want to go all the way to Tidworth next Sunday and you're not there." Stella was as anxious as Ina.

"We'll find some way of letting you know," Joe replied.

They walked along Castle Street, turned into Chipper Lane, and ended up going to the Regal.

Chapter 9

May 1944

Monday morning—the week seemed to stretch endlessly in front of Ina and Stella.

"What are we going to do all week?" Stella moaned.

"I don't know, but it will give me a chance to catch up on some sewing," replied Ina.

She had spent Sunday going through her summer clothes. There was nothing she could reject. All she had in her wardrobe was still serviceable, at least for wartime conditions. She sighed. The same old stuff, year in year out—well, perhaps not so bad. But nothing she hadn't worn many times before. At lunchtime, her mother had asked her if she was going to meet Stella. She had replied that Stella was going to see someone. Hilda had not questioned her further but instead said, "You'd better bring those clothes downstairs. I'll put them through the wash tomorrow—get rid of the smell of mothballs."

***

The day had been reasonably bright when Ina set off from home that morning. The early May sun sent a light mist rising from the pavement. In the afternoon, it suddenly grew dark.

"I don't think there's any fear of an air raid," Mr Phillips remarked. "But I think I'll draw the blackout curtains just in case there's an eager warden about."

There was not enough natural light coming into the shop, and the light at each end was usually sufficient for them to see by. Now, he turned all the lights on, and the shop took on the aspect of a winter's day. A loud clap of thunder made them all jump.

"Good Lord!" cried one of the customers. "That was just like a bomb! I thought for a moment, I was back in Southampton during the blitz."

They did not see any lightning but the sound of a downpour of rain reached them.

"It's chucking it down!" Stella commented.

"I hope it eases up before home time," Ina said anxiously. "I didn't bring an umbrella."

"I shouldn't have thought you could manage to hold an umbrella and ride your bike," Mrs Gray chipped in.

"I should have left my bike and caught the bus home," explained Ina and then added, thoughtfully, "I've still got to get to the market though, to get the bus."

"Look's like we're all going to get wet, then, doesn't it?" sighed Vera.

***

At five o'clock, when Mrs Gray went home, the rain had eased off. It held off long enough for Stella to reach the bus station and Ina, the infirmary, before the heavens opened once more. By the time Ina arrived home, her coat was damp and her headscarf wet through.

"Get on upstairs and take your wet things off," Hilda told her, "and dry your hair. I'll have to put your coat around the fire tonight and hope it dries by morning."

"I hope it does. I don't want to wear my best brown coat tomorrow in case it rains again and ruins it. I wish I had a mac, Mum," Ina wailed.

"You can always wear one of Dad's old railway macs," Clive told her.

"I can do without your clever clog comments," Ina retorted.

"All right, you two, that's enough," Hilda said.

Ina shrugged out of her coat and hung it up on a hook on the back door instead of taking it into the hall. As she made her way upstairs, Hilda called after her: "Don't be too long; tea's ready."

"What have we got?" asked Clive.

"Mutton stew and dumplings. And I made the dumplings with suet!"

"Not dripping then?" Clive asked.

"Stop being cheeky and lay the table."

***

Ina went to bed that night before her father came home. Bearing in mind the old adage that you never ask a man for anything on an empty stomach, Hilda put his supper in front of him. She waited until he had finished and was sat, in his chair, rolling a cigarette. Only then did she say, bluntly, "Ina needs a raincoat."

"That girl thinks money grows on trees," he grumbled.

"Be fair, Jim. She does very well with her money, and she does pay her way."

"What. When she wants clothes every five minutes!"

"She's not that bad! She doesn't earn all that much at the shop."

"A darn sight more than I had at her age."

"Times have changed, Jim. You know things are dearer now."

"She'd be better off working in a factory. Why don't you get her into the milk factory?"

"She's happy at the shop. Besides, what happens when the war is over and the factories aren't needed for war work anymore? A lot of workers will be thrown out onto the street like they were in 1919. You and Sid were lucky to get on the railway; some poor devils were on the dole for years."

"If the war goes on until she's eighteen, she may not have a choice, and it's just cost a small fortune to kit Clive out with a new school uniform, let alone having to fork out for a gabardine for him in September." Jim threw the remains of his cigarette into the fire.

"How much is a new mac likely to cost?" he asked, tetchily.

Hilda shrugged. "Don't know," she said vaguely. "Two or three pounds."

"Gawd almighty!"

"I could always get one from your mum's club man."

"I don't know if I like that idea. I don't approve of tallymen."

"You wouldn't have had what you had years ago if your mum hadn't had him."

113

Jim sighed. "Have it your own way," he said, "but, just remember, I don't want a lot of debts hanging over our heads. And don't make a habit of it."

"I can help her pay towards it," Hilda told him.

"Right! You do that, and make sure she pays her share."

***

The next day, the rain held off. Ina's coat was dry enough for her to wear, although it smelt a little musty. She thought it might be the smoke from the fire. Hilda had stoked up the fire before she went to bed and had put the fireguard in front and Ina's coat on the back of a chair as near to the fire as was reasonably safe.

"I'll get it cleaned when the weather gets better," she had said.

At work, Hilda saw Nell and asked her if her mother would get the tallyman to call on her.

"Mr Johnson? Yes, I'll ask Mum."

Hilda told Nell of Jim's reservations.

"He always was a stick in the mud, and you do go to work. I was always glad of Mr Johnson when the boys were little. Quite a few people round our way deal with him. He usually calls round about six. He doesn't bring anything with him now, not with petrol being rationed. He rides his bike to collect his money, but you have to go to his house to choose want you want. I'm not quite sure where he lives now, as he moved. He will put you straight when he calls." Nell responded.

***

Wednesday evening around half past six, a knock came at the door. Hilda opened it to a small, rather thin little man with a droopy moustache. He introduced himself. "I'm Mr Johnson. You are Mrs Welland's daughter-in-law."

"Yes."

"You wanted me to call. I believe your daughter wishes to see some of my stock."

"She needs a raincoat," Hilda told him.

"Well. I don't carry any stock with me—"

"So I understand."

"If you could come with her to my house, she might find something suitable."

"Where do you live?"

He put his hand into the big leather bag he was carrying; Hilda presumed that it held the money he had collected and his payment book. He drew out a wallet and handed her a business card with his name and an address on Nelson Road. *Good!* she thought. *Not too far to go.*

"When would it be convenient for you to come down? I gather your daughter doesn't get home much before half six."

"No," agreed Hilda. "And she has to have her tea. Would tomorrow night be suitable?"

"Yes, yes. That will be fine."

Ina, having caught threads of the conversation through the hallway and into the living room, now came to the door.

"Ah!" Mr Johnson exclaimed. "This is the young lady, is it?"

"Yes," said Ina.

"Well. We don't have a lot of choices these days, but I'm sure we can fix you up with something."

"We'll see you tomorrow night then?" said Hilda.

***

Mr Johnson's "shop" was his front room. There were clothes on rails or draped across the furniture. Piles of boxes rested on a small table. In spite of a centre light, the room was rather gloomy.

"I've put out some raincoats for you," he told Ina.

There were four in her size, draped over a chair. The first one she tried on was a light beige trench coat.

"It's a bit light," Hilda remarked. "Not really serviceable, Ina."

"No," Ina agreed reluctantly. She had rather liked it. It was like an army officer's, but more feminine.

Hilda looked at the price ticket. "It's nearly £4.0s.0d, anyway. I don't think we can go to that."

Ina picked out a navy blue with mock leather buttons. She tried it on.

"That's all right," Hilda said. "Much more like it. What do you think?"

"Yes," Ina agreed. A mac was a mac. And it was quite smart.

Again, Hilda looked at the price ticket. "Well £2.12s.6d that will be all right." She turned to Mr Johnson. "What will that be a week?"

"It will be 2s.6d. The odd amount will be adjusted on the last payment."

"We'll take it," Hilda said, handing him the raincoat.

"Er . . . I do ask for a small deposit of 1s.0d on the pound. Half a crown in this case. That takes care of the interest."

He gave her a form to sign agreeing to the terms and also a payment book. He wrapped the garment, and Ina and Hilda made their way home.

***

Jim looked up as they walked into the living room. "You've got it then?"

"Yes," Hilda replied.

"How much?"

"It was £2.12s.6d."

Ina took the raincoat out of its wrapping. Jim looked at it. "Looks all right," he said. "Glad you didn't go in for some fancy thing that wouldn't last five minutes. Don't forget," he went on, stabbing a finger at Ina, "you pay your share of it."

"Yes. I will, Dad."

He took his wallet out of his back pocket. Taking out a ten shilling note, he handed it to Hilda.

"Here you are," he said, "there's something towards it. That leaves you £2 to pay. And don't think this is an easy way of getting things. Just make it the first and last time."

"Can you afford it, Jim?"

"No!" he answered. "That's my beer and 'baccy down the pan for a week."

Ina had caught the faint smile around the corners of his mouth. "You aren't a bad old dad, are you?" she said.

***

Friday morning was fine, so there was no need for Ina to wear her new raincoat. She told Stella about it when she met her off the bus.

"Funny, that," said Stella. "My mum told me she'd ordered me a coat from our Doreen's club book."

"Didn't you know anything about it?"

"No. She didn't say anything at first, in case they'd sold out of my size. Doreen said it should be here either today or tomorrow."

"Hope it comes before we go to Tidworth," Ina said.

"We haven't heard anything, have we? I don't suppose it's any good to go to the bridge tomorrow night in case they're back."

"David said we wouldn't see them before Sunday, as they probably wouldn't be back from exercise. They might not even be back then."

"If we don't hear, shall we take a chance and go to Tidworth anyway?"

"They won't know what bus we'll be on," said Ina.

"There's bound to be a timetable they can get hold of. The buses don't run all that often on a Sunday. We could chance it, and if they don't turn up, we'll just have to mooch around Tidworth by ourselves."

***

Ina was undecided on what to wear. The day was fine and warm. There was no sign of rain clouds. In the end, she settled for her pink dress, navy suede shoes, and the jacket of her blue costume.

"Don't make a habit of wearing that jacket on its own, or it will fade and won't match the skirt," Hilda warned her. "You'd better get a move on, or you'll miss the bus and your connection at the bus station. Have a nice time at Stella's, and don't leave it too late coming back."

Ina felt a little guilty at having deceived her mother into thinking she was going to spend the day at Stella's. She hoped it wouldn't always be like this and one day soon she could summon up enough courage to tell her parents about David.

***

When Ina got to the bus station, the bus was already in. She boarded and sat by the window in the left-hand side. From there, she would be able to see Stella at the bus stop. She had only been to Stella's once before and was still a bit uncertain of exactly where she was. It was a nuisance not having adequate signposts. She hoped Stella would be waiting at her bus stop, or she didn't know where she would go from there. She hated the thought of going to Tidworth by herself.

When she had told her mother she was spending the day at Stella's, Hilda had said, "You certainly don't get invited over there very often." Hilda could have commented before about her lack of visits to the Auden's, considering the number of times Stella had stayed at the Welland's.

When the bus reached Amesbury bus station, there were three American soldiers waiting for the Salisbury bus. Sometimes, passengers had to change here, but not her bus today, thank goodness. She could not help noticing the flash of the 2nd Armoured Division on their sleeves. Good! They were back. She settled back in her seat and relaxed.

To Ina's relief, Stella was at her bus stop and wearing her new coat! It was emerald green with a tie belt. The colour suited her fairness. She stood there with her hands in her pockets and her handbag over one wrist. *She doesn't deserve new clothes*, Ina thought. *She'll have the pockets baggy in no time.*

Stella came up the aisle and sat beside Ina.

"Your new coat looks very nice," Ina told her.

Stella's hair was loose. Hanging slightly over one eye, it reached just above her shoulders and curled up at the ends into a page boy bob. "Do you think my hair's okay?" she asked.

"It looks fine," Ina said. And then she grinned and added, "You look like Veronica Lake."

The bus trundled its way to Tidworth.

"You haven't been to Tidworth before, have you?" Ina asked.

"No. I haven't."

"We shan't know where to get off."

"I'll ask the conductress when she comes to collect my fare," replied Stella.

The conductress, when Stella asked her, told them that the bus terminated in the town centre.

"You'll know when to get off because everyone else will," she said.

Ina looked out of the window at the unfamiliar landscape. The fields were already carpeted green with the shooting corn. Lambs, now nearly grown, grazed a little apart from the ewes, leaving a discreet space between themselves and the later born lambs that were nuzzling their mothers. There was bloom on the hedgerows and new leaves on the trees. Soon she settled down and let herself enjoy the ride. Besides making some small comment now and then, she and Stella did not converse much but made most of the journey in silence.

As the bus drew into Tidworth town, their eager eyes searched through the window, scanning the people waiting to catch the bus back to Salisbury. Among them were quite a few American soldiers. Then Stella spotted them. "There they are!" she cried.

A feeling of relief swept over Ina. The little voice in the back of her mind that had been telling her David would not be there had been wrong. There he stood, holding a paper bag. She and Stella got up from their seats and made their way towards the back of the bus to join the boys on the pavement. David held his hand out to her. She reached it with her own. Suddenly she felt a little shy.

"Miss me?" he asked, a wide smile on his face.

She nodded.

"I sure missed you," he went on.

Joe told them there was a café open farther down the road. "I guess you girls are dying for a cup of tea," he remarked, teasingly.

"Dying for something," Stella replied and, catching hold of Ina's coat sleeve, dragged her off to the nearby "ladies".

"Won't be long," she called over her shoulder.

"It's all that tea they drink," said Joe.

***

The café was small but welcoming. A row of booths ran along either side with long narrow tables and padded benches.

"Will we squeeze into these seats?" Stella asked.

"Your little figure will fit anywhere!" Joe told her.

When they were seated, Ina and Stella one side and the two boys the other, David put the paper bag on the table. "Got you a little present," he said.

Ina reached into the paper bag and drew out a box of chocolate candies. There was something else inside. This time, she found a pair of nylon stockings. "Oh!" she exclaimed.

There were other people in the café, and some turned to look in her direction. She did not miss the derisory look on the face of one woman.

"Thank you, David," she said quietly.

"You like your gifts?"

"Not half!" she answered, her face shining with pleasure.

"What does that mean, not half?"

"It means ever so much."

"I must remember that," he said. "They told us when we were coming to England that we wouldn't have any problem with the language, but I get confused at some of the things you people over here say."

"All you have to do is ask me, and I'll try and translate!" Ina smiled.

Joe broke in. "Here's a present for you," he told Stella, putting a package, also containing a pair of nylons on the table.

"Thank you," she murmured.

Ina glanced in her direction. If she was put out by having less than Ina, she gave no sign. The waitress brought the tea and coffee.

Ina turned to David. "You haven't told us how your exercises went."

David hesitated and glanced at Joe. There was a slight frown on Joe's face.

"There's not much to tell really," said David.

"You shouldn't ask," Stella said. "It's probably secret."

A silence fell around the table. Then Joe said, "It was the usual thing—a bit of scrambling up cliffs and practicing getting in and out of landing craft. Not much to excite anybody."

"Did you do any swimming?" asked Ina.

"Well," said David, "maybe accidentally."

"What did you do? Fall in the water with your clothes on?" Ina laughed.

"Maybe," said David, "but you don't want to hear about all that."

His face took on a solemn expression. Something warned her not to pursue the subject further.

"We had a thunderstorm in Salisbury Monday." Stella put in. "Did you get it where you were?"

"No," Joe said. "But it rained some."

"Anyway," Stella went on, "what are we doing for the rest of today?"

"Do you want to see a football game?" Joe asked.

"American football? Like they play in the films?"

"Well . . . I guess it's like they have in the films."

"All right," said Stella breezily. "Try anything once, me."

Ina asked where the game was being played.

"In the camp grounds. It's ground they have set up as a sports area for us. Football and ball games."

"Will they let us in?" Ina asked.

"Don't see why not. There's always someone watching the game."

"What, civilians too?"

"Yeah. Some of your people work around the camp."

"Do you play football, David?"

"No. Not football. Used to play some ball back home—you know, baseball, but not good enough for serious games. Never had the chance to practice much."

They had finished their tea and coffee. Joe went up to the cash desk and paid the bill.

"It's a bit of a walk up to the camp," David said.

"Paying us back for all the walking we've made you do." Ina smiled.

She put her arm through his, and he held her hand. They walked along the road some distance; other American soldiers were going in the same direction, some in small groups, some with girls beside them. Ina thought they were probably Tidworth girls. From time to time, jeeps and trucks passed them on the road, filled with GIs in combat clothes. They turned into a side road, and Ina could see the tops of the trucks above the high hedgerows. They followed the course of the vehicles turning down the same side road and saw them pass through a gate. There were two military policemen on the gate, but they made no attempt to apprehend the girls as they passed through. Soldiers were getting out of the trucks, which had drawn up at the far side of the field; they were carrying rifles.

"Makes you feel as though you were in an American war movie, doesn't it?" whispered Stella.

***

There was quite a crowd around the pitch. Joe led them to a place behind a wire fence, where they could get a good view of the game, which had just started. Ina found it was more or less as she had expected, the players dressed in padded kit, with big wide shoulders and helmets on their heads. It made them look like something out of a Popeye cartoon that she had once seen. It was not like English football. The Americans played the game very much like rugby, dodging and weaving, going into a scrum, tackling the man with the ball. Now and then, a player would be knocked to the ground. Men with a stretcher would run onto the pitch, put the injured "hero" on to it, and then run off the pitch with him. Ina tried to keep some interest in the game but found her attention wandering.

Stella said, "Any of your friends playing, Joe?"

"Yeah. A couple," Joe answered. "But looks like they ain't doing so good."

"What team are they?"

"The ones dressed in blue."

"Come on the blues!" shouted Stella.

But her shout of encouragement was lost in the roar of the spectators as the red team scored. The game seemed to come, at last, to an end, the blues loosing. Ina felt a surge of relief as the crowd began to drift away. Her back ached, and her legs felt stiff from standing still for so long.

"You girls hungry?" asked Joe.

"I am," Stella told him.

"We'll go up to the camp, see if we can get some chow," he replied.

***

The camp was a conglomeration of wooden and brick buildings. At the main gate were more military policemen.

"These ladies with you?" one asked.

"Yeah. Sure. They're with us," Joe answered.

"Guess it's okay for you to go in then."

The MP stood to one side, and the four followed other couples who passed through. Inside the mess hall, they stood in line with the rest of the diners, in front of a long table on which were deep trays of steaming food. David pushed Ina in front of him and handed her a tray. Ina looked at the tray in some surprise. It seemed to be made of aluminium and had different shaped sections. She noticed that the servers behind the table were ladling food into the sections of the trays.

Behind her, Stella said, "No plates!"

And Joe said, "What's a plate?"

Ina looked down at her tray as the servers put items of food into each of the sections—mashed potato, diced carrot, peas, some funny little pea-sized yellow pellets that she later realized was sweet corn. A large helping of what looked like a very big faggot was the meat dish. There was one section left in the tray, and that was filled with two peach halves and, to Ina's surprise, real whipped cream. At the end of the line, she stood back a little until David's tray was filled.

"Can you manage that?" he asked.

"I think so," she told him, feeling a little uncertain all the same.

"I'll go and find us a table," said David.

The tables were long, but he managed to find one with four places and made a beeline towards it. Joe and Stella were close behind. David put his tray on the table and turned towards Ina, taking her tray from her and putting it next to his. The seats were at one end of the table, and Ina slid along the bench, leaving room for David; Joe and Stella sat opposite them. Joe passed paper napkins and forks over to them. Ina felt she'd dare not ask for a knife. She had seen enough American films to know that they were only used to cut the food, which was then conveyed to the mouth with the right hand holding the fork. She gave a discreet glance around and saw the girls who had accompanied the other soldiers were managing quite well. She looked across at Stella who had put her fork into the meat concoction.

Stella caught her eye and mouthed, voicelessly, *When in Rome.*

Ina grinned back. The meat, she found out, was meatloaf. Of course, she'd heard of it but couldn't remember her mother ever making it. When they had finished, David and Joe picked up the trays and took them back to the counter. The girls got up and followed them.

Joe said, "We're gonna pay a call. Do you want us to show you the ladies' powder room?"

They both knew by now what the powder room was.

***

The toilets here were even more luxurious than those at the Red Cross. Over each hand basin, was liquid soap in a dispenser and a large mirror with a shelf underneath. There were also two full-length mirrors, one at each end of the room. A container of disposable paper towels and a bin to put the used one in were placed at intervals on the walls, and the whole room was furnished with four small gilded chairs with a little white table placed between each couple.

"No expense spared," muttered Stella.

"Bet it's an eye-opener when they go into our public lavs," said Ina

"Or in the pubs," said Stella.

Outside the boys were waiting for them.

"Thought we'd take a stroll into town," said Joe, "across the fields. You don't mind going across the fields, do you?"

"Seeing as we do it all the time"—Stella grinned—"no."

David and Ina fell in step behind the other two. They went through the gate and along the lane. In the hedgerows, the blackberry bushes sported their small white flowers, matching the tight buds of the may blossom. Buttercups, wild hyacinths, and vetch peered out from the cow parsley. They left the lane and climbed over a style and into a field. The sun was now quite warm. They walked the narrow path beside the hedge and then veered away, travelling across the grass. They had walked for about ten minutes when Stella and Joe flopped to the ground.

"We're gonna take five," said Joe, "soak up some sun. Haven't seen so much sun since I got to the UK."

David and Ina walked on until David said, "Do you want to sit a while?"

"Yes. All right," she said.

They had come to a dip in the grass.

"Careful how you get down," David warned. "This grass is a mite slippery. Don't want you falling on your face."

***

He went down the slope and held his hand out to her. Once down, they both sat with their backs leaning against the incline. Ina struggled out of her jacket, folded it carefully, and laid it down beside her. David turned and watched her. He lay on his side, his elbow digging into the rise, his chin in his hand.

"I'm glad you wore your pink dress," he said.

She turned to him. "Are you? Why?"

"I have another present for you." He sat up, put his hand into one of his outside pockets, drew out a small package wrapped in blue tissue paper, and placed it in her lap.

"You've already given me presents," she said, "the chocolates and the nylons."

"This is an extra one. Sorry it isn't gift-wrapped."

She did not quite know what he meant; she smiled at him anyway and said, "Thank you."

She opened the layer of tissue paper. Inside was a necklet. She held it up and gasped. "It's lovely, David."

It was a chain of pink enamel daisies linked together, with a hook and eye fastening at the end of the chain.

"Here," said David, "let me put it on for you."

She bent her head forward and lifted her hair away from her neck.

"There," he said when the clasp was done up. "It looks fine."

She turned to him and, on an impulse, threw her arms around his neck and kissed him. "I'm so lucky!" she exclaimed.

"Why? Because I've given you a few little gifts? I wish the chain had been more valuable, but they don't have that sort of stuff at the PX. Something to do with excise duty."

"It doesn't matter. It's what it means to me that counts." Then she added without thinking, "As it is, my dad will wonder where it came from."

She realized, straight away, that she had been indiscreet.

David said, quietly, "He knows you have a boyfriend, doesn't he?"

She answered, with equal quietness, "In a way."

"In a way!" he repeated. "What do you mean 'in a way'? Doesn't he know we're going steady? Is there some reason I shouldn't meet your folks?"

She could feel herself getting flustered and hoped it wasn't all too obvious to him. She sat up and looked at her hands, fingering the tissue paper.

He looked at her intently and then said, "It's because I'm a GI isn't it?"

She didn't answer, so he pressed the subject.

"Is it, Ina? Look at me."

She turned her gaze towards him with a look of sheer misery. "You don't understand," she said, quietly.

"Too darn right I don't understand! I'm well aware of what some folks here say about us, but surely he knows you well enough to know you wouldn't do anything wrong."

"It isn't you personally; it's just that the girls who go with American soldiers seem to get a bad name. Some of them are cheap and common, and people think we're all the same, even though we aren't . . . bad girls, that is."

"Is that what your folks would worry about? What the neighbours would say?"

"No . . . I don't know . . . but people can be nasty and rude and sarcastic and horrible. There are two girls down our road, sisters. They're a bit older than me, and they both had babies."

"Americans' babies?"

She nodded. "People are always talking about them and they aren't very nice to their mother—not my mum, but some of the neighbours . . . It's . . ." She broke off.

"Don't people know you're not like that?"

"I don't think it will make any difference. They'd think it just the same."

He gave an exasperated gasp. He sat with his arms resting on his hunched up knees, his hands held loosely together. "It's not going to happen to you Ina, least ways not while you're with me. I'm no angel; soldiers aren't expected to be, but I was brung up to know a decent girl when I met one and to treat her right."

"I know, David, and I trust myself anywhere with you. I've made you cross with me again, haven't I?

"No. I'm not cross. I just feel—"

He didn't say anymore, and she went on. "With my dad, I think he would worry about me ending up like my auntie Nell. He told me that once and said that if I ever bought a Yank home, he would show him the door."

"What's you auntie Nell go to do with anything?"

"You know I told you about my cousin, Teddy—the one in the Jap POW camp?" She hesitated.

"Go on." he prompted.

"Well, my uncle Sid isn't Teddy's dad. She met an Australian soldier during the last war. They got engaged, and then he went to France where he was killed. Then she found out she was going to have Teddy. People gave her a hard time—not my gran or granddad and not my mum either because they were friends, although my mum is a lot younger. And some of the girls she worked with were nice to her and were on her side. Not my dad, though. I don't know why . . . My dad wouldn't have anything to do with her or the baby. He said she'd betrayed all the British boys who had fought in the war by having a foreigner's baby. My granddad died in the flu epidemic in 1919, and my dad told her it was the scandal she'd caused that played a part in his death. I don't know why he said all that, although things settled down after a while, but I don't think he has ever forgiven her."

"Your pa sounds like one mean man."

"No. He isn't really. He just doesn't want . . ." She trailed off.

"He doesn't want you to end up like your auntie Nell," he finished.

She looked at him. His face was expressionless, but there was a look in his eyes that was between hurt and anger. Instinctively, she put her hand out and covered his.

He said, "What am I suppose to do here? Say so long, Ina, it's been nice knowing you. Have a good journey home?"

She felt a surge of panic clutch at her. "No! Please no! I'll tell him tonight."

"I thought maybe you had feelings for me like I got for you. Do you have feelings for me, Ina?"

"Yes, of course I do!" Her face was aflame with embarrassment and a little guilt. "I'm sorry," she whispered. "I went about this the wrong way, didn't I?"

"Hell! I don't know if there's a wrong way or a right way for a girl to tell a guy he's not welcome in her father's house. I kinda thought we were doing some real courting, and I wanted to come back to the UK some time and pick up where we left off and make a go of it."

She thought, *Is he asking me to marry him? Why doesn't he come straight out with it and ask me properly?* To David, she said "I'll tell him tomorrow. I promise. I really will tell him tomorrow."

"Not tonight?"

"He'll be in bed. He's on at two in the morning. I shan't see him till I get home from work tomorrow evening."

"I want things settled, and I can write to my mom. She knows I'm dating an English girl, but I haven't told her we're maybe past being friends."

He lay back against the rise and pulled her down beside him. She lay with her cheek against his, relieved that the bad moment seemed to have passed.

"I'll remember all this when I'm over in France," he said.

"Don't talk about going away," she murmured.

"Okay. I won't."

"Sing me your song."

"You and that song!"

"It's your song, David's song. I'll always think of it as your song."

"Thought you didn't want me to talk about going away."

He sang, but when he got to the chorus sang, "Goodbye, Ina," and stopped abruptly.

She just smiled at him. After a while, Joe and Stella came up to them.

"You ready to go to town?" Joe asked.

Chapter 10

Just before they reached town, they turned in at a pub that lay a little off the road. Going round the rear of the pub, they found a small garden that boasted four long trestle tables with benches on either side.

"This is all right, isn't it?" Stella said.

"Yes," Ina agreed. "It's nice to be able to sit outside."

"Don't you have any pubs with gardens in Salisbury?" Joe asked.

"Yes. The Rose and Crown round Harnham, and I expect there are a few more."

"Never had the chance to find out, did we—not going into pubs?" Stella explained.

"What are you girls going to have? Some of that fizzy stuff?"

Stella looked at him with wide open eyes "You mean . . . champagne?"

"No! I don't mean champagne. That stuff you call lemonade," Joe replied.

"Oh. All right then." She paused for a moment, considering, and then said: "I'll be a devil and have a shandy."

"A shandy," Joe repeated. He looked at her intently. "What's a shandy?"

"Lemonade—with beer in it."

"How much beer?"

"They'll know. Just ask for a beer shandy."

"And for me as well, please," Ina put in.

Joe and David walked across the grass to the entrance of the pub. Stella suddenly turned to Ina.

"Where did you get that necklace from? I don't remember seeing it before."

"David gave it to me this afternoon, when we were sat down in the field."

"Aren't you the lucky one?" There was a slight edge in Stella's voice.

Ina flushed a little.

"Two pairs of nylons, box of chocolates," Stella went on, "and a necklace!"

Ina didn't answer. She found it difficult to comment. She placed the paper bag on the table. Stella watched her: "Have you opened the chocolates yet?" she asked.

Ina shook her head.

"I should think they'd be beginning to melt by now."

"Do you want one, then?"

"Could try one, I suppose, see if they're any different from ours."

"I don't think I'd know," Ina told her. "It's such a long time since I had a box of chocolates." She took the chocolates out of the bag and lifted the lid. "They look the same to me," she said, removing the covering. "They're dark chocolate."

Stella edged closer. "What does it say on the lid?"

"Nougat, taffy (I think that's toffee), praline (whatever that is), coffee cream, fudge—all the same as we have, I think."

They each took one chocolate, savouring the taste.

"Not bad," Stella remarked.

"I thought it was a bit sickly," Ina said.

"Yes, it was a bit, I suppose. It's probably because we're not used to chocolate."

"Do you want another one?

"Don't think so. Not just now."

"I'll leave them out in case the boys want one."

Ina put the lid back on and pushed the box along the table. The men returned with the drinks and set them down.

"Never thought to ask," Joe said. "You girls want potato chips?"

They both shook their heads and said, "No. Thank you."

"Do you want a chocolate?" Ina asked.

"Not for me, thanks," was Joe's reply.

"Keep them for when you are on the bus," David suggested.

"What are your shandies like? Got enough beer?" Joe grinned.

Stella grinned back. "Very nice," she said, "but it would have been nicer with champagne!"

***

The May sky was beginning to take on its evening glow as they left the pub and walked backed towards the town centre. Sunset sent rosy ribbons across the darkening sky. The air had cooled, and Ina felt a slight shiver run through her body.

"Here," David said at her side. "Put your coat on." He held it out for her while she fitted herself into it.

"Better?"

"Yes, thanks."

Several people were waiting at the bus stop. Somewhere, a clock boomed out a half hour chime. Half past nine. It was still early, Ina thought. But she would have another bus to catch at Salisbury to get her home. As though reading her thoughts, David pushed two half crowns into her hand.

"I don't need that," she told him. "We have return tickets."

"It's for a cab home."

"Well, I—"

"You do as you're told."

"Thanks," she whispered.

***

There seemed to be quite a few people out and about. Across the other side of the road, Ina watched two girls, each on the arm of an American walking two abreast. Lucky girls! They didn't have to catch buses home. She was not prepared for what happened next. From their side of the street, a woman suddenly darted across the road into the path of the front couple and started to pummel the American soldier on the chest. Even in the dim light, Ina could see the girl's contorted features. The soldier put up his hand, trying to catch hold of her.

"Get off, you goddamn bitch!" he cried. "What in hell's name are you playing at!?"

A string of foul language issued from the girl's mouth, word's that Ina had never heard of before. She clamped her hands over her mouth and leaned towards David. He put both arms around her and pulled her to his side. Stella had gone pale; she backed away a step and clung onto Joe's arm.

"It's okay, honey. They can't hurt you none," Joe soothed.

The other soldier went to the aid of his buddy and was caught in the face by a flying fist.

"You two-timing bastard!" the girl screamed. "You cheating sod! You got all you could out of me and chucked me for that floozy!"

"I took nothing you didn't throw at me!" said the soldier. "I told you we were finished."

Two British policemen arrived on the scene; obviously they had been alerted.

"All right!" said one. "What's going on?"

"Get this crazy dame out of here, will you, buddy, before she does me some real harm?"

"Come on then, Miss. Come quietly now, or we'll have to cuff you."

The fight seemed to have gone out of the girl, and she let the policemen lead her away.

"Did you want to make any charge?" asked one of the policemen.

"No," the American said. "Just get her out of my sight."

"She's nothing but a common little tart," came a voice behind Joe.

"Do you know her? Joe asked.

"Know her? Yes, I know her! Have anyone in trousers, that one. She's got two kids at home, and her old man's soldiering up in the Orkneys. Asking for trouble, she were. These girls go out with you blokes for what they can get out of you. Don't like it when they get chucked."

David turned and caught the man's eye. The man continued, hastily, "Present company excepted, of course. Can see you two girls aren't like it. Frightened you, did they?"

Ina didn't answer.

Stella said, quietly, "I can't believe I saw all that."

***

The bus came in, the queue moved forward.

"You see what I mean?" Ina asked David.

"Yeah. I guess so. But that's not you, is it?"

Ina shook her head.

"Then you tell your folks."

"Yes."

"Promise?"

"Promise."

"I don't like the idea you keep things from them."

"Fair enough, David. I'll tell them."

Getting on the bus, Ina sat on an inside seat. Stella would be getting off first. The boys stood alongside until the bus moved—out of Tidworth and into suburbia and then into the countryside. The two girls sat side by side, each with her own thoughts, until Ina broke the spell by asking if Stella wanted more chocolate.

"Oh . . . All right. Go on," Stella answered.

Ina withdrew the box and lifted the lid; Stella took a chocolate and put it in her mouth.

"Take some more," urged Ina.

"Don't you want to take them home?"

Ina looked uncomfortable. "I don't know how I'm going to explain them away."

"Oh, yes . . . and what about the nylons and necklace?"

"I can keep them in my shoulder bag."

"Can't you put some chocolates into the bag the nylons are in?"

"I could do, I suppose. Could you put some in your bag?"

"All right then."

Both girls took the nylons out of their paper bags and put chocolates in.

"Oh, crumbs!" said Ina. "There's another layer underneath!"

"Well. I haven't got any more room. If I cram more chocolates in, I shall have a horrible mess at the bottom of my handbag."

"I'll just have to hide the box somewhere."

"Can't you just throw it away?"

"I don't want to do that. It's such a pretty box, all those mountains and that."

"Oh. What a tangled web we weave," quoted Stella.

"Don't you start! I've already had a lecture from David about keeping secrets from my mum and dad."

"Is that because they don't know about him?"

Ina nodded.

"So you reckon it's getting serious then?"

"I think so."

"Has he said anything about marrying you?"

"Not in so many words. He hasn't actually said he loved me, but he doesn't just like me, he said."

"Well. Joe reckons he's serious about you. I couldn't say anything in case Joe had got the wrong end of the stick. So, are you going to tell them?"

"Dad will be in bed when I get home. I'll tell him when I get home from work tomorrow."

"You're not going to tell your mum first, then, sort of prepare the way?"

"I can't let her in for the roasting, can I? I'll have to tell him myself."

"Good luck, then."

"Do your mum and dad know about Joe?"

"I haven't said anything, but I suppose I'd tell them if they asked."

"What do you think they'd say?"

Stella shrugged. "Don't know," she answered. "Don't know if they'd say anything."

"Lucky you."

"Perhaps your dad won't say anything about David."

"You don't really believe that, do you?"

"Suppose not."

The bus was slowing down.

"Well. Here's my stop." Stella said. She got up out of her seat and tried to look out the window. "Darn this blackout. I'm going to end up in Amesbury one of these days."

The bus came to a halt.

"This is it, then. Hope you find somewhere safe to hide the loot!"

She started to walk towards the platform. "See you in the morning,"

Ina turned in her seat. "By the way," she called. "What did Joe say about your hair?"

Stella called back, "He said I looked like Veronica Lake! Night!"

"Goodnight."

The bus stopped again in Amesbury, and Ina was glad that no one came to sit in Stella's place. Through Amesbury, up the hill and onto a dark, grey road fringed with black hedges and topped by a navy blue sky.

***

134

Ina put her key in the front door and opened it. As she stepped into the hall, she could see a light under the sitting room door. Was her father still up? Or was it just her mother? She closed the door gently and walked to the foot of the stairs. The living room door opened, and her mother whispered, "Is that you, Ina?"

Who did she think it was?

"Yes, Mum. I'm going on up. I'm dying to spend a penny."

"All right. Had a nice time?"

"Yes, Mum. Goodnight."

She crept upstairs and, for authenticity's sake, went into the bathroom and found she really did need to "spend a penny". All she wanted now was for Hilda to come to bed just as she came out and ask her what was in the bag! As it was, she got safely into her bedroom just as she heard footsteps coming up the stairs. She opened her wardrobe door and put the bag at the bottom under a spare blanket.

Chapter 11

Ina tried hard to concentrate on her work the next day. It was not very busy. She would have preferred it to be so. Her mind kept going back to the ordeal ahead of her. It was like knowing you had to go to the dentist and not seeing beyond that point. Rehearsing what she was going to say to her father got her nowhere. At lunchtime Stella asked her if they were going to walk around town.

"I thought it might take your mind off your cares and woes," she said.

"It'd take a journey to the moon to do that," Ina replied.

"You'll have to make do with Salisbury. Coming or not?"

"Go on then."

They walked towards Silver Street.

"Let's walk around Woolworth's," suggested Stella.

"Do you want anything in there?" asked Ina.

"Not particularly; just a walk around."

They looked at every counter, even the china and cutlery.

"I thought you might get some ideas for your bottom drawer," Stella said.

"My bottom drawer? That's pushing it a bit, isn't it?"

"It's never too soon. You might get married by the end of the year."

"Some hopes."

***

The anxiety hit Ina directly she put her bicycle in the shed. They were all sat at the table when she went into the living room. No one seemed to notice that she was quiet as she took her place at the table. Hilda put her meal in front of her, and she picked up her knife and fork.

She had only swallowed one mouthful when she blurted out suddenly:

"I've got something to tell you."

"Tell who?" That was Clive.

"Tell Dad . . . Mum and Dad."

Three heads turned in her direction. Three pairs of eyes focused on her face.

"It's about my boyfriend . . ."

Jim was looking at her intently. "What about your boyfriend? If you've got something to tell us, you'd better spit it out, and it had better not be something I'd rather not hear."

Hilda was looking anxiously at her. Ina put down her knife and fork, put her hands underneath the table, and clenched them tightly. "He's an American soldier."

There! She'd said it! For a moment there was a deadly silence, and then Jim's face darkened.

He leaned towards her. "What was that you said?" His eyes had narrowed, and his voice was quiet and low. It changed to an angrier tone when he said, "Did you say an American soldier? What the hell did I tell you, girl? I'm not having any daughter of mine going out with a bloody Yank! Do you hear me?"

"You're being unfair. You don't know him."

"No! And I don't want to either, so you can knock it right on the head. I'm not having this family talked about—saying that all my girl is good for is going out with Yanks. How long has this been going on?"

"Since the beginning of March."

"March? We're into May! So you've been lying to me and your mother all these weeks—going out with farm boys! Is Stella in on this?"

"She goes out with his friend."

"Do her parents know?"

Ina shook her head and said, quietly, "I don't think so, I don't think she's said one way or the other."

"So they don't care! Well. I do. Do you want your mother talked about in the shops and the whist drive like Mrs Purdy? Don't you think your grandmother had her share with Auntie Nell?"

"It isn't like that!" Ina protested. "David isn't like that!"

"They're all like that! Out for what they can get! Tell you he's got a big ranch, did he? Got oil wells in Texas? Going to take you to Hollywood and make you a film star?"

"No! Of course he didn't. His family is poor. His dad died during the Depression. He and his brother had to leave school and find work to help his mum."

"Well. That's a new line anyway."

"It's true!"

"How far has it gone, this 'romance' of yours, then? When are you going to come home and tell me you're in trouble?"

"I won't, I shan't be, I told you, he's not like that. He respects me!"

"Well. He won't get a chance to prove it one way or another because you won't be seeing him again."

"You can't stop me seeing him!"

"Oh, can't I? While you're under my roof, you'll do as I say! You're underage, and you will be for a few more years yet! You don't go out anymore evenings or weekends until you've come to your senses."

"I've gone seventeen, and I'm old enough to know my own mind. You can't keep us apart. We're fond of each other."

"Fond, Fond! What kind of word is that to use? You don't know the meaning of the word, a kid your age."

"I'm old enough to know how I feel and you aren't going to keep us apart."

Jim thumped the table with a ferocity that bounced the dishes. "All right! Have it your way, you know where the door is. Take your sluttish ways somewhere else!"

"Jim!" Hilda cried in protest. "You can't turn her away."

"Keep out of this, Hilda."

Clive cried, "Don't talk to Mum like that!"

"And that goes for you as well," Jim said angrily. "I don't want any lip from you. You're not too old for a thick ear."

Clive got up from the table. "If our Ina goes, I'm going too."

"*Sit down!*" Jim bellowed.

Clive sat down, hardly able to hold back his tears.

Jim turned to Ina and said, coldly, "You see what you've done? You upset your mother and your brother. Satisfied now?"

Ina got up from the table, walked out of the sitting room, and sped out of the house, slamming the door behind her.

"Jim!" Hilda cried. "Go after her. You don't know where she might end up."

"She'll be back. She knows which side of her bread's buttered. Now if you don't mind, I'll finish my meal in peace."

***

Ina rushed out of the house and across the road, heedless of the car that swerved to avoid her. She ran until she reached the top of Ashley Road. Almost out of breath, she slowed her pace.

They were in the living room when she opened the door and walked in. Her grandmother was sat in her armchair listening to the radio. Nell was ironing at the table. Ina had rehearsed what she had intended to say. Now, that went by the board. She stood by the table and sobbed like she hadn't done since she was a tiny child.

"For goodness' sake, Ina, what's the matter with you?"

Ina gasped out her sorry story between the sobs.

"Sit down, Ina, opposite me and let's get some sense out of you."

She sat down in the chair opposite and laid her head back. Her sobbing had ceased, and with a dull voice, she recounted everything that had happened. She told them about David, that he wanted to meet her family.

"He wouldn't have asked me that if he didn't think something of me, Gran, would he?"

"Well, dear. It couldn't have been very nice for your dad to think you'd been going out with this young man behind his back."

"It wasn't serious then."

"And now it is?"

"I don't know" replied Ina "He hasn't actually said that he's more than fond of me, but . . . All I wanted Dad to do was meet him. He could have done that. He needn't have gone off the deep end like he did."

Nell had finished the ironing. The ironing cloth was folded up and put away in the cupboard, and the iron was unplugged and put out on the kitchen windowsill to cool. She came back in and said to Ina, "You'd better stay here with us tonight."

"I'll fix up the chair bed," said her grandmother. "You can sleep on that."

"Do you think your mum and dad will guess you're down here, Ina?"

Ina shook her head. "I don't know," she said. "I don't think Dad will be bothered one way or the other."

"Don't say that, Ina," Nell said as she patted Ina's shoulder. "I'll take a stroll up there and let them know you're staying with us tonight. Don't worry, Ina. He'll come round. Everything will work out."

***

These days, no one asked Nell if she had heard from Teddy. The pain in her eyes as she had answered in the negative was more than they could cope with. She had left school at thirteen and had been apprenticed to a dressmaker. Fully qualified to work on her own initiative, she had nevertheless gone to work at the milk factory in 1915, in answer to the call for women to do more towards the "war effort".

The girls at the milk factory had been invited to a few army camps for dances and social evenings. It was at an Australian camp that she had met Eddy, a fair-haired young soldier whose accent had completely fascinated her. After several meetings, she had taken him home to meet her parents. Her younger brother, Jim, was already in France, and the Wellands welcomed the Australian into their home. When Eddy had first asked for permission to marry Nell, Mr Welland had, at first, had reservations, but the young man would soon be going to war. As his wife told him, wistfully, they were all mothers' sons. They were engaged on Nell's twentieth birthday.

They had another month together, and then he was gone. Two months later, there was a knock on the door. Eddy's friend, Barney, stood there, in his hospital blues, a crutch under each arm and the bottom half of one trouser leg pinned up. Eddy had been killed.

Another month went by, and Nell realised she was pregnant. Most of the women at the milk factory were sympathetic. Hilda, who had gone to the factory straight from school, was her best champion, knitting endless bootees for the baby-to-be with the dedication of her fifteen years.

When Teddy was born in the last months of 1918, it was Hilda who had gone to the Welland household and taken the baby out in his perambulator at weekends while Nell, no longer able to work at the factory, took in alterations. Most of her customers never bothered about her being the mother of an illegitimate child. Indeed, some of them even made a fuss of him, but there were others who looked meaningfully at the gurgling babe in the cradle and haggled over the price.

As time went by, Teddy had become accepted. Nell and her mother were no longer the subject of veiled caustic remarks. Teddy grew strong and healthy, a handsome little boy.

He was nearly eighteen months old when Jim finally came home, and as far as he was concerned, his sister and her brat did not exist. His parents tried to soften his attitude towards Nell and their adored little grandson but to no avail. Nell was spoken to only when necessary, and Teddy was completely ignored. Nell was hurt but bowed to the inevitable.

A flu epidemic hit the country. One day, Will Welland came home from work, flushed, aching, and running a temperature. Two weeks later, he had died. On the day of his funeral, Jim had said to Nell, "If it wasn't for the worry and scandal you caused, he might have gotten over it."

To Nell, the unwarranted jibe was like a knife through her soul. For her mother's sake, she kept quiet, but she would never come to terms with her brother's rejection of her son.

Jim received a letter one day from an old army pal. "You remember, Mum. I told you about him. He can't get a job up north—wants to try his luck down here, wants to know if we can put him up."

And so, Sid came into her life. Sid, who always made time for Teddy, who played with him, made him laugh, and even helped to feed him. Sid, who in time she gave her heart to and married in a quiet little ceremony in St Paul's church. If Jim had any objections, he did not voice them. It was when Terry was born a year later that her brother's preference for his younger nephew caused hurt to Nell all over again.

Hilda had kept in touch with Nell and had gone to see her often. Soon Jim, although he was few years older than Hilda, began to show a marked interest in her. He proposed and was accepted. Nell made her bridal gown and dresses for the two young bridesmaids. When Avril came along, Nell hoped that, now Jim had a child of his own, he would feel more kindly disposed towards Teddy. It had not worked out like that.

***

When Ina had gone, Jim turned to Hilda and said, "I blame you for all this."

"Why me?" Hilda retorted, angrily.

141

"You should have kept an eye on her, found out where she was going."

"She's seventeen. I can't tell her who she can go out with and who she can't."

"Can't you? You mean you don't care about her cavorting with damned Yanks. Yanks for God's sake!"

"She's not contorting with them. It's only one."

"And that's not bad enough!"

"You could have shown her a bit of trust instead of jumping down her throat."

"Trust, trust! When she didn't even tell us what she was up to?"

"Perhaps she didn't know him well enough to tell us. Besides, she probably knew what you reaction would be."

"Too damned right she did. So why did she carry on seeing him then? Did you know what was going on?"

"Of course I didn't," protested Hilda.

"I bet young Stella's behind this. I always thought she seemed a bit fast."

"She told us about him when she realised she liked him. Don't you have enough faith in her to trust her judgement?"

"It's no use making excuses for her."

"It's better than driving her out of the house!" Hilda was close to tears.

What Jim's answer to that statement would have been, Hilda would never know. There came a loud and persistent knock on the back door.

"What now?" Jim asked irritably.

Hilda opened the door to find her sister-in-law on the back doorstep. Jim looked up as Nell came into the room. He turned his head away, got out his tobacco tin, and rolled a cigarette.

"I came to tell you Ina's down our house. Mum's putting her up for the night."

"Thanks Nell," murmured Hilda.

Nell turned to Jim. "You needn't ignore me, Jim. It's you I've come to talk to."

"And what gives you the right to poke your nose into my family's business?"

"Because I don't want you putting your own daughter through the same hell as you put me and my son through."

"What are you talking about?"

"You know full well what I'm talking about—your rejection of us both. All these years, and you are still punishing me."

"What about what you put Mum and Dad through? Don't forget, if it wasn't for you—"

"Don't make Dad's death an excuse for your reason. There's a lot I've never forgiven you for, brother or no brother, and that's the way you treated Teddy. I could take what you doled out to me but not what you did to him."

"You're talking out the back of your head. What was it I did to him?"

"You ignored him right from the time you came home from France. It didn't matter when he was tiny. But I saw the hurt look in his eyes when he was old enough to understand that you had no time for him. You never made the same fuss over him as you did Terry. You never even listened to him when he tried to speak to you. Once, he drew a picture of you standing by an engine. When you thought no one was looking, you screwed it up and threw it in the litter bin. I saw you, Jim, and so did he. He was eight years old. Thank God he had Sid!"

"Have you finished?" Jim's face had a sullen look, and his tone was harsh.

"No. I haven't!" Nell replied. "Because I know where all this comes from."

"Oh! You do, do you?"

"Yes! I know all about that Belgian girl you met. You went out with her—any chance you got! You were nineteen, a year younger than Ina's young man, and the girl was seventeen, the age Ina is now. And you wanted to marry her. You met her family, and they made you welcome. Then you went back to the war. When the ceasefire was given, you went back to her. You'd been away for six weeks, and when you met her again, she was all set to marry an Australian soldier. That was it, wasn't it, Jim? She threw you over for an Aussie, a 'foreign' soldier! What a shock to come home and find your sister had an Aussie's bastard son! Didn't matter that we were engaged to be married and that he'd been killed before he knew I had fallen for his baby. It isn't what people will say, is it?

"As far as you're concerned, it doesn't matter that Ina's bloke is a Yank; he's 'foreign', so he is not acceptable to you. If you're not careful, you'll drive Ina away like you did Teddy. You made an excuse not to come to his twenty-first, and you didn't even bother to say goodbye or wish him luck before he went to Singapore! He wrote letters to Sid and me, to Terry and Mum. In our letters, he sent his love to Hilda, the girls, and Clive. Not to you, Jim. He'd given up on you."

"Well, you certainly have the gift of the gab! Funny you never mentioned all this before."

"I could have, Jim, but I didn't want to upset Mum. I didn't know if Sid told me about the Belgian girl in confidence, but I couldn't keep it back any longer. I don't know if my son is still alive, but if he is, and one day he comes home, I know you won't be among the welcoming committee."

Jim's face had taken on a beaten look. "Don't accuse me of being so hard-hearted." It was not a completely defensive statement.

"Well!" replied Nell. "That's the impression you've given me over the years."

There was a break in her voice, but she could not give in now. "Don't forget, Jim. Ina will be eighteen next year and will probably go into one of the services. There's an old saying—once you leave home, you never return. She'll become independent, leading a new life."

"She'll still be under my control until she's twenty-one," Jim cut in.

"Maybe, but she won't tolerate a lot of interference in her life, and—just think of this—if she wants to get married without your consent, there's always Gretna Green!"

"Now you're being stupid!"

"Well, maybe, but I've said what I came to say. I'll see myself out."

"Nevertheless," Hilda said, "Go out the front way, Nell," and walked with her to the front door.

"I'm sorry you heard all that, Hilda."

Hilda shrugged. "You had every right to speak your mind. Is Ina all right?"

"Yes. She'll be back tomorrow."

Hilda closed the front door and pulled the bolts across. She went back into the sitting room. Jim was standing in front of the mantelshelf, winding up the chiming clock.

"She had a lot to say for herself," he muttered.

"It was right what she said. You did ignore Teddy. I noticed it, especially when Terry and our kids came along. However you played with them, Teddy was always left out. They're all still around—safe, out of danger. But God alone knows how that boy is being treated by those Japs! Can't you spare a bit of pity for your own sister? And just think of Ina's boy's mother, all those thousands of miles away. They're boys, just boys. They probably haven't seen their families for a couple of years. He may get killed over in France, and Ina would never forgive you."

Jim shut the glass door of the clock and turned to her. "All right. All right! She can bring him home. But if I don't take to him, he's out. Don't expect me to kiss him on both cheeks."

"He's American, Jim, not Belgian."

He glared at her for a second and then said, "Oh to hell with it. I'm going to bed!"

"Why did you never say anything about that Belgian girl?"

"There was nothing to tell."

"Not even when it affected things between you and Nell? What was it, nearly thirty years ago?"

She saw his face change, and his head bowed a little. In a quiet voice he said, "Do you really think I don't care about the boy?"

"You haven't shown otherwise."

"Well. You know me. I'm not the sloppy type."

"I don't call answering a kid when he speaks to you and asks a question being sloppy."

"No. I suppose not. I do care, Hilda."

"Then tell Nell, not just me."

Jim nodded and left the room.

***

"How did you get on?" Stella was eager to know when Ina met her off the bus the next morning.

"I didn't."

"You did tell your dad?"

"Oh, I told him all right! He went up the wall!"

"What did he say?"

"What didn't he say? I slept down my gran's last night. I shall have to go home tonight; I haven't got any clothes. These are what I was wearing yesterday."

"Wondered why you still had them on. Did you just run off then?"

"He told me I knew where the door was . . . He said I had sluttish ways."

"I can't imagine your dad saying that."

"He threw Auntie Nell up at me."

"What's it got to do with her?"

"You know. The baby she had in the last war, our Teddy."

"What? He's still harping on about it after all this time?"

"He thinks I'll go the same way and be the talk of the neighbourhood."

Stella was surprised at the sarcasm in Ina's voice. It was so unusual for her to adopt that tone.

***

Ina's thoughts as she worked that morning travelled in all directions. Her emotions encompassed anger, self-pity, and desire to get some sort of revenge on her father. She would not go home again. She would go and collect her things, and that would be that. She'd ask her gran if she could stay with her . . . But where? On Gran's chair bed? She could ask Stella if she could stay with her. Was there enough room? Perhaps she could go to Tidworth. Get a job on the camp. David said they had civvies working there. Perhaps she could find somewhere to live in Tidworth. Wouldn't that put the cat among the pigeons!

Oh, Lord. Help me! she said to herself. By the time lunchtime had arrived, she had a thumping headache.

"Have you an Aspro in your bag?" she asked Stella. "I've got a splitting headache."

"I'm not surprised—the state you've got yourself into."

Stella reached into her handbag and brought out a small bottle of pills.

"Here, try one of these."

"What are they?"

Stella looked at the label. "They're . . . er . . . Don't know. I can't pronounce it. They're what the doctor gave my sister for her whatsits."

"Are they all right for bad heads?"

"Well, they're for pain."

Ina sounded doubtful. "I'll just take one."

"Why don't we go for a walk round? A bit of fresh air might do you good?"

"Oh. Yes. Good idea."

***

Ina got off the bus at her stop and waited for it to go on its way before she crossed the road. She had her front door key in her bag but walked around the back—slowly. She knew she was playing for time, and she felt rather silly and childish. What kind of reception was she going to get? Somehow, her legs carried her to the back door and her hands lifted the latch. Her father and Clive were seated at the table, her father reading the paper. Her mother was getting cutlery from the sideboard. Each of them looked up; only her mother spoke.

"I thought I heard the bus go up," she said. She held the cutlery out to her. "Put this round for me, please.

Ina took the cutlery. Her father had gone back to his paper. He lifted it up as she put his knife, fork, and spoon in front of him. She noticed that Clive's hands were under the table, clasped between his knees. He looked at her and his father in turn. Whatever was going through his mind, he was not going to put into words. Hilda came in with two plates of food and put them one before Jim and one before Clive. Ina followed her back into the kitchen and returned with her own meal and her mother's. She sat down at the table. Clive gave her a faint, self-conscious grin. Hilda came back in with a dish of cold stewed apple and "mock" cream.

They ate in silence. *It's as if nothing has changed*, Ina thought. Everything was going on as normal, as if yesterday had never happened. She looked at her father, eating his tea and listening to the remainder of the six o'clock news. He thinks I've come home because I have backed down. He thinks I won't see David anymore. She fell into some kind of reverie so that she jumped when Hilda said, "Ina, eat your tea."

Ina looked down. She held her knife and fork but she had not taken one bite of food. Without looking up, she slowly ate her meal. When the meal was over, Jim got up and sat in his chair by the fireplace, rolled up a cigarette, and picked up the evening paper. Clive fetched his school satchel and went into the front room to do his homework. Ina collected the crockery.

Hilda met her at the kitchen door and took it from her. "Your father has something to say to you, she said."

What more could he find to say? Ina stood before him.

"Sit down," he said, pointing to his recently vacated chair.

She sat down sideways on the chair, facing him.

147

"You can bring this boyfriend of yours home and we can meet him—"

Ina's eyes and mouth opened wide, but before she could make a comment, Jim went on, "I'll tell you the same as I told your mother. If I don't like the look of him"—he gestured towards the door—"he's out. Do you get it? You can bring him home for Sunday dinner."

"Oh, Dad . . . Thanks, Dad. You will like him. Everyone likes him!"

She fell to her knees by the side of his chair, put her arms around his neck, and started to kiss him.

"All right! All right! There's no need to act daft! Go and help your mother to wash up."

***

Dressed in her poppy frock, Ina left the house on Wednesday just before six o'clock and made her way, not to the bridge, but Castle Street. She would be early, but she could no longer contain her impatience to see David as soon as possible. Walking along, casting glances behind her to see if the trucks from Tidworth were in sight, she kept walking until she came to the road that led to the parking area. There were already girls waiting there, some of the usual ones, chewing gum, over made up, and smoking. Some were probably there as an arranged "date"; others were taking the chance of meeting a "companion" for the evening.

Ina crossed the road. On the pretext of looking in the shop windows, she walked a short distance up and down. The shops, of course, were all closed.

She heard the trucks arriving and turned. It was not long before the first of the soldiers appeared down the road into Castle Street. The girls who had arranged meetings linked up with their partners while the "hopefuls" waited to be chosen.

It's like a slave market, Ina thought to herself.

A voice near her called "Hiya." She turned and saw Stella.

"Why aren't you at the bridge?" Stella asked.

"I was early so I came on down. Thought I might as well wait here."

"The trucks are in then," Stella remarked. "They should be coming into Castle Street soon."

As she spoke, the boys came into view. They turned to go towards the bridge. Stella called after them. They waved, crossed the road, and headed towards the girls.

"Saving us a walk?" Joe asked.

"Ina was early, or eager—one of the two, so she decided to wait for you here," Stella answered.

"Well away from the reception committee!" Joe laughed.

"I thought we would be less conspicuous over this side of the road" replied Ina

"So you were," Joe agreed.

Stella put her arm through his and then started to walk towards town.

David crooked his arm for Ina to slip hers through and held her hand. "You're looking real pretty tonight."

"It's because I'm happy."

"Has it got anything to do with me?"

She placed her other hand over his. "It's got everything to do with you!"

He smiled down at her. "And what have I done to make you so happy?" he asked.

"It isn't what you've done; it's because I am going to take you home."

"To your home?

"Yes. My parents have invited you for dinner next Sunday."

"To dinner?"

"What you call lunch. We call it dinner."

"You told your dad!"

"Yes!"

"How did he take it?"

"He blew up at first, but he came round."

Ina felt there was no need to tell David about her spending the night at her grandmother's.

"You sure he's okay with it?"

"Yes, really."

"So, I'm meeting your folks at last!"

He called out to Joe, and both he and Stella stopped walking and waited for the other two to catch up.

"Yeah? What is it?"

"I'm going to Ina's home to meet her folk next Sunday."

Ina had told Stella at work that morning, but it was doubtful that Stella had told Joe. A small frown appeared between Joe's eyes, just briefly. Ina wondered in that moment if David had spoken too openly. Did Joe wonder why Stella had never mentioned taking him to meet her parents? Perhaps it didn't matter if they weren't serious. Perhaps Joe thought she, Ina, was coming between himself and David—all that comrades in arms, buddy-buddy stuff.

The moment had passed. Joe said, "Well! That's good news. Just you be on your best behaviour, boy, d'you hear me?"

"Yes, Sarge," David laughed.

Stella's face was impassive. "Are we going to the Red Cross?" she asked.

Ina could almost see her feet tapping. Ina, herself, didn't really want to go. She would rather do what she wanted to for a change.

"It's too nice to be stuck in," she said. "Why don't we go up to the Greencroft and sit down there for a while?"

"What's this Greencroft?" David asked.

"It's like a small park," Ina explained.

"It's where kids play," Stella said.

"Well, we'll give it a try," said Joe.

They walked to the end of Castle Street, along the Blue Boar Row and Winchester Street. They walked up the steps of the Greencroft and along the tree-lined path. The late evening sun shone through the branches and dappled the ground. They sat down on one of the seats. There were small children playing there, on the swings and see-saw, twirling themselves around the chains of the maypole or going on the carousel.

"All those little houses around," David said, "they're quite old, aren't they?"

"They are Olde Worlde, boy!" put in Joe.

Ina was not sure if Joe was laughing a little. She had the impression sometimes that he wasn't all that taken with England. Maybe he was just homesick.

"I wouldn't mind living in a little house like those," David said, "looking out the door and seeing kids play."

"Don't you think you're getting a bit sentimental for your age?" Joe laughed.

"Yeah, maybe," David replied. He turned to Ina. "Those little buildings up there, are they air raid shelters?"

"Yes, they are."

"Did you ever go in one?"

"Not those ones but some like them."

"They wouldn't stop a bomb exploding would they?"

"Not if it were a direct hit. They were more for saving people from the blast."

"Can we go see inside one?"

He got up, and Ina followed. When they reached the shelter, she said, "It's probably not very nice in there. It hasn't been used for ages because we don't get air raids like we used to."

Inside the shelter, it was fairly dark. It smelt of wet concrete and dampness. There was a considerable amount of litter on the floor.

"They're not very nice places at all, are they? What did you do with yourselves in them?"

"We sang songs mostly."

David began to back out. "C'mon," he said." Let's get out of here. This place gives me the creeps!"

Joe and Stella stood up as David and Ina walked back towards them.

"Like what you saw?" Joe asked.

"I was not impressed," David replied. "I'd rather have a foxhole."

"Guess we move on then."

Ina sighed. Next stop—the Red Cross.

***

The Red Cross was warm and stuffy. The band was in full swing, and Stella's toes were tapping before they'd found a place to sit.

"What do you want?" asked Joe, making his way to the bar.

"Aren't we going to dance first?" Stella wanted to know.

"Beer first; dance second," Joe replied.

"Just get me a small beer," David told him.

"Shandies for you girls?"

They both agreed.

"Do you want a hand there?" David asked.

"No. I'm okay. Go find a seat."

Joe came back with the drinks on a tray and set them down on the table. He and Stella sat side by side making small talk with the occasional giggle from Stella.

David appeared very quiet. Ina stole a glance at him now and then, but his face gave nothing away. Joe and Stella got up and made their way to the dance floor. Ina turned to David "Are you all right?" she asked.

"Yeah, sure. Why shouldn't I be?"

"I wondered if you might be a little worried about meeting my dad."

"No. I'm not worried. A little anxious maybe, but I'm not worried about meeting him. He'll either take to me or he won't, and if he doesn't, I guess there's not much I can do about it."

"I'd still go on seeing you," she said.

He smiled at her and said, "Why don't we go for a stroll?"

They both stood up and made their way towards the door.

"I'll just tell Joe we're leaving."

David strolled across the dance floor. "We're taking a walk," he told Joe.

"Okay," Joe said. "Meet up with you later?"

"What time will you be back?" Stella asked over Joe's shoulder.

"We shan't be long. We'll come back here."

Outside on the pavement, David looked up and down High Street. "Where can we go?"

"Back up to the Greencroft?"

"No. I don't think so.

"Back to the bridge?"

"It's a bit of a way. We don't have the time to walk all the way and come back. It won't give us time for talking. How about if we go sit in the cathedral grounds?"

"I'm not sure what time they close the gates." She caught hold of his arm. "Come on," she said. "I know where we'll go."

David was propelled along until they came to a river that ran a course through the water meadows, with the cathedral in view. Between the green and the riverbank, a few benches were placed here and there. Ina stopped by one of these, sat down, and drew David down by her side.

"Why haven't we seen this before? I don't remember that we were this close to the cathedral or these seats being here when we walked along the river before."

"It's a different river."

"You have more than one river?"

"Five, actually."

"Five? Why does a little town like Salisbury want five rivers?"

"It's to impress visitors who only have one," she smiled.

He smiled back at her. "It's okay," he said. "I know you're having me on."

He leaned against the seat, stretching his arms across the back and his legs in front of him. The water was flowing gently by. Now and then, a ripple broke the surface as a fish caught a floating fly. Presently, she broke the silence. "I'm sorry I took us up the Greencroft. You didn't like that shelter at all, did you?"

"No. I did not."

"Did you imagine being in there during a raid."

"No. I was glad to dive in anywhere when we were going through Italy. It was what was in there. I didn't want you to see it."

"What was it, a dead rat or something?"

He took his arms away from the back of the seat, drew his legs up, and sat up straight. "No. It wasn't; it was something else. People had been there and left things behind. There were some johnnies on the floor."

"Oh!" she said, "um . . . thingies."

"Thingies," he repeated. "Is that what you call them?"

"Well . . . there is another name. But we see them all the time, David, especially after the weekend—in shop doorways and in the gutters, even in passageways."

"Well, I didn't want you to see them—not while you are with me. I'd have been mighty embarrassed."

She slipped her arm through his. "I'm lucky to have you, aren't I?"

"You reckon?" He put an arm around her. "What would your pa say if I asked him if we could get engaged?"

For a moment, she was completely stunned. He had said he had "feelings" for her but had never said he loved her or wanted to marry her. She swallowed hard and said, "I don't know . . . Perhaps that we were too young or hadn't known each other long enough. But he couldn't stop us from getting engaged because I'm over sixteen."

"Not twenty-one?"

"That's only marriage."

"And that's different?"

"Yes. It seems like it."

"I don't get it."

"I don't know why it is."

"Does this age thing go for boys as well?"

"Yes, it goes for boys as well."

"But they can be drafted into the army when they aren't much older than you and fight—maybe get killed."

She shrugged. "I'm afraid so," she replied.

"We gotta wait all that time to get married."

"You really want to marry me?"

"Sure I do, or I wouldn't be asking."

"But you haven't actually asked me," she told him

"Well. Maybe not, but you know how I feel. You know I want you to come to the States after the war."

"As long as you love me, I'll follow you anywhere."

"Sure I do. You must know I do." His face was slightly flushed. "Look, sweet pea, where I come from, we're not that good with words. I never asked a girl to marry me before, and I guess maybe I'm no good at it. Back home, you meet a girl and you walk out. After a time, you get hitched. I guess it's not very romantic. I'm not much good at romancing."

"Did you ever meet a girl before you thought you'd marry?"

"No. Never did."

***

If Ina ever imagined David proposing to her, it was always in a romantic setting. The war would suddenly be over. They would be in a garden somewhere. There would be a big house in the background with light streaming through a French window, mixing with the moonlight that was bathing them. Somewhere, an orchestra would be playing Glen Miller's "Moonlight Serenade". Somehow, she would have come into some money . . . and coupons, of course . . . and she'd be wearing a long, flowing gown. And here they were—by the side of a river, where people were walking along the path and children were playing in the grass, where dogs roamed, making use of every tree they passed. Swans sailed by and, every so often, rose out of the water, flapping their wings noisily before sinking back into the river. Ducks dived deeply to the bottom of the riverbed, sticking their tail ends ungraciously into the air. Come to that, he hadn't actually asked her to marry him, just that as they were going out together, he'd like them both to get hitched. He was a soldier who had been in action and, probably, would soon be fighting once more. Yet he had a certain coyness about him. He had never asked a girl to marry him before.

Yet . . . he'd sort of told her that he'd—had he? Not that it mattered what he had done before she met him.

I'm going to get engaged, she told herself.

One day, she would go to America and marry him. Tomorrow, she would have to confront her father, this time, with a sequel.

David's voice broke through her thoughts. "Guess we'd better be heading back. Don't want you to miss your bus."

They stood up and began to retrace their steps.

"Ina?" he said presently "Don't say anything about us getting engaged. I don't want it spreading around until I've told Joe when I get him alone, just in case you know. I'd feel one hell of a fool if your dad told me there was nothing doing . . ."

"Perhaps it's just as well," she agreed. "I'll tell Stella not to say anything."

***

At breakfast the next morning, Ina wondered if she should tell her mother of David's intention of asking her father to let them become engaged. Perhaps now was not the best time to broach the subject, not while she was bustling round from kitchen to living room setting their meal before them and making the best she could of filling their lunch boxes with something satisfying, if not original. No. Better to wait till tonight when her father would be there. Whichever way it went, Ina hoped that no one would tell the Daleys until it was all official, not that it would bring many congratulations from Cissie.

Ina could imagine her reaction. "That Ina Welland!" she could hear Cissie say. "She's got herself engaged to one of those Yanks! Be hearing the patter of tiny feet soon, I expect."

At work, she was hardly able to contain herself, although her emotions were somewhat mixed; there was the thought of being engaged to David and anxiety at the prospect of telling her father. She would tell Stella lunchtime; she would warn her not to say anything to anyone at work. If things went wrong and ended like they had when she told her parents she was going out with David, it could be much worse, and she would feel so stupid. She understood David's reluctance to tell Joe until they were alone for the same reason.

Nevertheless, when they were sat down in the staffroom and she was about to broach the subject, Stella said, suddenly, "Did you enjoy your moonlight stroll by the river last night?"

She jumped and went a little red.

Stella looked at her. "Didn't do anything I wouldn't do, did you?"

"No! I did not!" she replied hotly.

"All right. Keep your hair on! I'm only kidding."

"Yes . . . well . . . it's not funny."

"No. It isn't. Sorry."

"David wants us to get engaged. He's going to ask my dad when he comes Sunday."

Stella looked at her. "Well! There's a turn up for the book!" She said after a brief pause, "What do you think your dad will say?"

"I don't know. Look . . . don't say anything about it in the shop, just in case something goes wrong . . ."

"Like your dad chucking you out and cutting you off without a shilling?"

"Don't even joke about it!"

***

The afternoon passed, and Ina's bike ride home seemed to take less time than it usually did. She made up her mind that if her dad said no, they would get engaged anyway. He couldn't stop her seeing David. He couldn't keep her locked up! She had to go to work, and it wouldn't be worth his while to make her stay at home. Hilda, unwittingly, gave Ina her cue.

"Did you tell this young man of yours he could come to Sunday dinner?"

"Yes. He was very pleased about it. He wants to ask you something."

Jim paused in the act of putting a forkful of food into his mouth. He lowered the fork and looked at her. He did not speak, and Ina took this as a sign to carry on.

"He wants to ask you if we can get engaged."

The fork was laid down on Jim's plate. His eyebrows rose high above his eyes and then lowered into a small frown. When he spoke, it was with a resigned tone. "Give you an inch and you take a yard," he said.

Ina looked at him anxiously. He spoke again "We'll talk about it Sunday when he's here. I want to get to see this bloke of yours before I make any decisions."

He hadn't said no. *He hadn't said no!* Ina was hugging herself. "Thanks, Dad. You'll like him!"

"So you said before."

"But you will." She was almost jumping up and down in her chair.

"Don't get excited then," he said, "and don't come round here slobbering all over me. Leave it till Sunday and let me finish my tea in peace."

157

Chapter 12

Stella was not at work the next day. Ina went to the bus station as usual, but Stella was not on the bus. Ina knew there wouldn't be another bus for an hour. She rode her bicycle to the shop, looking behind her now and then to see if she'd missed her in anyway. She arrived at the shop alone.

"Miss Auden not with you?" asked Mr Phillips.

"No. I'm afraid not, Mr Phillips."

"Have you any idea where she might have got to?"

"Not really. She was all right when I left her last night."

"Oh, well. We shall hear sooner or later. Thanks, Miss Welland."

But the puzzle remained in Ina's mind. It was so unlike Stella not to turn up for work. She was, like Ina, bursting with good health in spite of wartime rationing. What could have happened to her? Vera did venture to say she hoped that Stella was all right. Mrs Gray, however, used the situation to make acid comments.

"You girls of today! Go out on the razzle last night? Perhaps she's got a hangover."

"She doesn't drink," Ina replied. "We're not old enough to go into pubs."

"What? When some girls of fifteen or sixteen go into pubs getting Yanks to buy them drinks!"

"You've seen them in there, have you?" Ina asked.

Mrs Gray flushed. "No! But my Ern could tell you something of the goings on in Castle Street when he's on the nightshift."

"Well. That's them. Not me and not Miss Auden, right?"

Mrs Gray said no more but walked hurriedly away.

***

Lunchtime came with still no word from Stella. Ina sat on the table eating her sandwiches, wondering if she'd ever have salmon ones again, even if it was out of a tin. Somehow, the room looked shabby and gloomy. In the winter, the girls sat by the gas fire, toasting their sandwiches and chatting. The room was cosy then.

She decided to go out round town. Even if she had no money to spend, she could still look round the shops. She'd go into Woolworth's and have a walk round the counters. She might see something in there. Tomorrow was payday; she could pick out something—some nail varnish perhaps clear, of course. She could go in tomorrow and buy it.

When she got back to the shop, Mr Phillips was standing just inside the doorway talking to a middle-aged woman. She didn't seem to have bought anything. Ina gave her glance and went on through to the staff room. Mr Phillips came through as she was combing her hair.

"That lady came in to tell me Miss Auden's sister has met with an accident. Apparently she was just going to a neighbour's house when a car came around the corner and knocked her down."

"Was she badly hurt?"

"Not too badly. They took her to hospital; seems as though she is badly bruised and shaken up. Miss Auden is looking after her sister's children until her husband can come. Miss Auden should be in tomorrow."

It left Ina wondering how Stella's sister got off so lightly. Having gone to Stella's once, she knew the unpaved roads could be treacherous.

"One of those great Yankee army lorries I bet," was Mrs Gray's comment. "Just because they drive on the wrong side of the road over there, they think they can do it over here

"Mr Phillips said it was a car," Ina replied coldly.

"Well, it must have been one of those jeep things, then."

"You really have got it in for the Americans, haven't you?" Vera put in.

Mrs Gray looked at her. It was unusual for Vera to comment on conversations they had. Mrs Gray snorted "Can you blame me?" she asked. "All you see going on round Salisbury—those girls hanging around the Red Cross and up Castle Street where the trucks come in. My Ern says it's disgusting outside the pub on a Saturday night."

"I thought your husband worked inside the factory, not on the pavement," Ina said.

"You can be very cheeky sometimes, Miss Welland. I should have thought your parents would have brought you up different."

At one time, Ina would probably have apologised, but Mrs Gray could be so annoying. She wanted to say, *Did your mother give you a good hiding every time you were nice to someone?* But she didn't, of course.

***

Stella was on the bus the next morning. As they walked along, Ina asked what actually happened to her sister.

"It was her own fault. She's knows that's a bad corner; that's why everyone goes the back way round."

"Good job she wasn't badly hurt."

"The car didn't actually hit her. It came round the corner, and she didn't step back onto the grass in time. The side of the car just knocked her, and she fell backwards. One of the neighbours came and got Mum. I was all ready to catch the bus. I went with Mum to bring the kids back to our house, and Mum went to the hospital with her. She's coming home today."

"Thank goodness for that. Mrs Gray had a field day. First it was an American truck that knocked her down and then a jeep."

"Didn't Mr Phillips tell you it was a car?"

"Yes. That's when she decided it must have been a jeep."

Later on that day, when Mrs Gray came in and asked Stella what it was that knocked her sister down, Stella answered, with no hesitation, "It was a little boy on a trike."

***

Ina managed to keep her impending engagement to David between Stella and herself but was still relieved when it was home time. Saturday was so busy they hardly had time to draw breath. At lunchtime, they went round the market. There, too, it was busy. People thronged the paths between the stalls. Two women were having a verbal set-to because one had told the other she had no business bringing a pram full of kids through the market on a Saturday. It was almost impossible to get to the stalls.

"Where have they all come from?!" Stella exclaimed.

"I don't know, "Ina said, "but I've had enough."

They went to a little café on Queen Street and had an ice cream.

After a busy afternoon, trying to avoid the sea of shoes that was beginning to swamp the floor, Mr Phillips said, "We'll cash up earlier tonight, Miss Jenner."

They cashed up just after five thirty. By the time they had finished, the floor was clear of shoes. He went over to the door, turned the sign round to "closed", and said, "Sufficient unto the day is the evil thereof."

At ten to six, Ina and Stella were walking along Market Street.

"I'm glad we're a bit earlier tonight," Stella commented, "even if it's only fifteen minutes. It means I can catch the bus before the one I usually do. I don't have to hang about."

"You don't stay at our place like you used to," Ina told her.

"It's a bit awkward," Stella answered. "My mum hinted that I wasn't spending enough time at home. I suppose I didn't. Not getting home till late at night and then coming in Wednesday and staying weekends."

"I suppose I can see her point," Ina agreed

"Besides," Stella continued, "if David's coming to your house, I don't want to play gooseberry."

"Okay," Ina said.

"What time's he coming in?"

"He's going to find out the times of the buses and let me know tonight. We can work out what time the bus gets in, and I can meet him. I shall tell him to get off on Castle Street, just before the railway bridge."

"Are you nervous about him meeting your mum and dad?"

"A bit, especially as he's going to ask Dad if we can get engaged."

***

Saturday evening, she walked to the bridge and saw the boys waiting there. Stella had not arrived, so she walked along Castle Street between them. She felt a bit awkward, as if she was keeping some dark secret to herself. She wanted to ask David if he had found the bus times and when he would be in. She did not know if Joe knew about the engagement. They had crossed the road and were walking towards the post office when Joe said, "I reckon we ought to have met up with Stella by now."

Ina suddenly remembered the accident and told them about it. "It was Thursday when it happened. She was in work Friday and today."

Stella suddenly come flying round the corner, nearly bumping into them. Joe put his hand out. "Steady on!" he said. "What's the hurry?"

"Is everything all right at home?" Ina asked.

"Yes. The bus was late. We got held up as we came out of Amesbury. There'd been an accident of some kind, and we got in a traffic jam."

She fell into step beside Joe. "Was it bad?" he asked.

"Don't think so. As we got moving, we saw one of your army trucks by the side of the road and some skid marks. There was one of your MP jeeps there and some of our civvy police. There wasn't anything else. I don't think there could have been another vehicle involved. I think the driver must have forgotten he was supposed to drive on the left."

"It could be," Joe agreed. "It takes some getting used to."

It started to rain. None of them had a raincoat.

"Let's get on up here," Joe said. "We can go to the movies."

"There's a queue," warned Stella.

They could see there was a column of people forming along Chipper Lane. Nevertheless, they went up to the Regal. The billboard outside the entrance had most of the seat prices with "full" signs on them.

"Only 3s.6ds," bawled the commissionaire.

Joe and David went through the doors, the girls trailing uncertainly behind them. Inside Ina whispered, "3s.6d, David, 3s.6d! That's 7s.0d."

"Sweet pea, don't embarrass me. I can afford 7s.0d. We went upstairs before remember."

"Sorry," she murmured.

He put his arm around her and gave her a quick hug. "That's okay," he answered. "I guess it's a lot of money to you."

"Yes. It is." She didn't tell him that it was not much less than British troops got in a week.

In the interval, she asked him what time he would get into Salisbury in the morning.

"I've got a lift in. One of the guys has to go to the Red Cross for something. Where do I get out?"

"Just before the railway bridge you go under to get to the lorry park."

"Okay. I got it."

"About what time will you get there?"

"Say eleven o'clock to a quarter after?"

"That's fine. I'll wait for you on the other side of the road."

***

They came out into the foyer. The girls went to the cloakroom. David and Joe leaned against a wall waiting for them.

"So," said Joe, "you're going to ask her pa for her hand in marriage?"

"Yep!"

"Think he'll agree?"

"Like I told her, he'll either take to me or chuck me out!"

"You think you're going to be okay with this?"

"Are you trying to put me off?"

"No. No, but Ina's a bit young. I know it's no big deal back home, but I don't somehow think it goes down so well in England."

"What about Stella?" David asked "Do you think about her? You know, serious?"

"Stella? No. Don't get me wrong; she's a nice girl, and we have fun, but get hitched? Not for me. I don't aim to settle down yet. Get this war over, and I've still got some living to do."

"How do you think she feels about you?"

"She's given me no reason to think she's any more serious than I am."

David was quiet for a moment and then said, "Do you ever think of that girl you had in Italy?"

"Nita? Maybe . . . sometimes. Maybe if we'd stayed there longer . . . I don't know. We were good together, you know? What do they say in the song? It was too hot not to cool down? Couldn't understand a word she said half the time, but I must have given her the right answers."

The girls came back. Stella came up to David, reached up to him, and kissed him on the cheek.

"What was that for?" he asked.

"For making Ina happy."

They walked down the stairs and out into the night.

***

Ina figured out it must have been about five to eleven when she reached Castle Street bridge. She had started to cross the road when she saw the jeep heading along Castle Road. She crossed over quickly and had just reached the other side when the jeep pulled alongside her. David jumped out; the driver saluted and drove off.

163

"Right," David said, "which way do we go?"

"We cross over and go along the road in front of us."

They walked along, David peering both left and right. "There's a lot of houses like those over here in England," he remarked.

"Yes. They were all built at the end of the last century, mostly for working class families. What's yours like?"

"Well it's made of wood, and we have a porch going along the front. I guess you've seen houses like it in the movies. It's quite ordinary."

"Yes. I have," Ina answered. They came to St Paul's Church. "That's where my mum and dad got married," she told him, "and Auntie Nell and Uncle Sid. We were all christened there, Avril, me and Clive, Teddy and Terry."

"What is your religion?" he asked.

"Church of England." She stopped and pointed. "You see that flag on top there? That's the flag of St George, our patron saint. All the Churches of England fly that flag."

"How did you get to know all this?"

"At school, when we learned about the Reformation."

"What was that?"

"When King Henry the Eighth broke from the Roman Catholic Church and made himself head of the English church."

"Now you're getting in too deep for me. All I know about your Henry the Eighth was that he was a big fat guy who had a habit of chopping his wives' heads off!"

"It was only two of them." Ina laughed. "What is your religion?"

"Same as most folks in the Southern states—Baptist. We get baptised."

"I'm learning about you all the time, aren't I?"

"You've only got to ask." He smiled at her. "I'll tell you my life story if you've got time to listen."

They reached her house. "This is it!" she said.

There was no going round the back today. She walked up to the front door, put her key in the lock, and walked into the hallway, David following her. He saw he was in the hallway with the stairs going up on the right-hand side, a door on his left that was ajar, and another at the end of the hall. Ina pushed the nearest door open wider, caught hold of his hand, and led him into the room.

Jim was sat in an armchair by the fireplace and Clive opposite him.

"Dad," Ina announced, "this is David."

Jim had looked up as the door had opened. He saw a fairly tall young man, lean and fair, who looked him straight in the eye without flinching, an open and honest look. The thought that went through Jim's head was, *Oh, my God. You look so young!* He stood up, aloud he said, "Come in, David." He turned to Clive and nodded his head towards the door. Clive got up and, with a grin to David, who smiled back, left the room.

"Ina, take David's jacket and hang it up and then go and help your mother," Jim said.

Ina, dismissed, went too.

"Sit down, son," Jim said, indicating the chair that Clive had vacated.

David sat down and Jim sat down again in the opposite chair. "Now then, lad. What's all this about you and Ina wanting to get engaged?"

David was taken aback a little. He hadn't thought the question would come so soon. "Er . . . Yes . . . That's right, sir."

"You do know that Ina cannot get married without my permission?"

"Yes. I'm aware of that."

"Things are different in America, I take it?"

"Yes. It varies from state to state. Once, a girl could get married at fifteen. I think it's sixteen she doesn't need permission. I know things are different here, and I'm willing to go along with them. I'll wait for her"

"Four years is a long time."

"I'll stick it out if she can."

"I'm not going to beat about the bush, David. I can't say I approve of wartime romances, but I was young myself, believe it or not. I think you and Ina are too young and you haven't known each other for long. What do you intend doing after the war?"

"I want to go to college and get some qualifications. I don't mean reading and writing and all that, just something that will help me get a decent job. I was brung up to know if you didn't work then you didn't eat."

"True enough. Ina said something about a turkey farm."

"I've been thinking about it. But I know it's not just a matter of chucking a few handfuls of corn at them. I want to get in on the business side of things. Do it properly."

"Well. You seem to have your head screwed on the right way. Do you have any idea where the two of you will live?"

"I'll get a job while I'm at college and maybe rent us some place until I settle to something. Don't worry about Ina. My mom will look out for her."

"You lost your father then?"

"Yes. He died in '38. I was fifteen, and my brother, Todd, was seventeen. Mom married again in '41, and we moved to his spread. It wasn't a big place, but he made a living out of it. Todd went into the Navy in '41. I was drafted in '42."

"Was your brother at Pearl Harbour?"

"No. He went soon after. Said it was quite a mess. Guess the Germans did the same to your harbours?"

"Yes. They did. All the docks copped it. We had one of our blokes killed just before they reached Southampton docks."

"Was the train bombed?"

"No. But the line had been, and the train went into a crater before anyone could stop it."

"Were any passengers hurt?"

"No. It was a goods train."

Jim looked reflective, and David did not question him any further.

Jim spoke again. "You've been in action already, I take it?"

"Yes—Italy."

Jim put a hand up and rubbed it across his forehead. Then he said, "I can't stop you and Ina getting engaged—"

"I'd rather it was with your approval."

"Ah, well. What can I say? Get engaged, and we'll take it from there."

"Thank you, sir."

"The name's Jim."

"Okay, then. Thanks, Jim."

There was a gentle tap on the door, and Hilda's head came into view.

"Couldn't hold onto her curiosity any longer!" said Jim.

"I just came to see if you wanted anything," she said.

"Come in and meet the boy properly then."

Hilda came into the room, and David stood up out of his chair.

"This is Ina's mother," Jim said.

David walked towards her and held out his hand. "I'm pleased to meet you, ma'am."

Hilda took his hand in both of hers. "Not ma'am; I'm Hilda," she said, "and it's nice to meet you, David."

"We shan't want anything," Jim went on. "We're going down the legion. That's if you want to come, David."

"Yeah . . . Sure . . . I'd like to come."

"Right, then. Let's see if Alb's coming."

Hilda went back into the living room, and they followed. Jim went out the back and called out to Alb.

Ina looked at David. "Well?" she whispered.

"Okay," he whispered back. "Who's Alb?"

"He lives next door, Mr Daley. His name is Albert, but he got called Alb one time, and it stuck. We usually call Albert's Bert."

"I think we just call them Al."

Jim came back. "He's going to catch us up."

"Can I come too, Dad?" Clive piped up.

"Yes, just as long as you don't make a nuisance of yourself. We'll go out the front way," he added to David. "You can get your coat on the way out."

Alb caught them up, and Jim introduced him to David. Already primed by Jim, Alb showed no sign of surprise to see that this boyfriend of Ina's was American. He shook hands with him, patted his shoulder, and said he was pleased to meet him.

***

At the legion door, Jim 'booked' David in. "Have to do this," he explained. "Shows you're with a member."

If David was a little lost at this procedure, he gave no comment. Alb found them a seat and went to the bar to get some drinks in.

"Here. Let me get those," David said, beginning to rise from his seat.

"No," Jim told him. "You stay where you are. They can't serve you anyway because you're not a paid-up member. A club is different from a pub. Find it a bit strange?"

"Guess I do a bit." David smiled.

"What do you think of our beer?" Alb asked.

"Well . . . It's okay as far as taste. Some ways I like it better, but it took me some while to get used to drinking it warm."

Alb chuckled. "I expect it did."

Clive asked if it was hot were David came from.

"Alabama? Yeah, it can be."

"They're sensible in America," Alb said. "They have air conditioning and fridges to keep things cool; isn't that right, David?"

"Yeah, mostly. But I recall a time when we didn't have it in our house, and believe me, it could get mighty hot!"

Clive glanced towards the door. "There's Uncle Sid!" he exclaimed.

Sid saw them, waved, and came over to them.

"This is David," was Clive's introduction, "our Ina's boyfriend."

David stood up and shook the proffered hand.

"Good to meet you, David," Sid smiled.

David returned the greeting.

"Are you in for the weekend?" Sid asked.

"No. Only came in for today."

Sid nodded. "See you again presently; just going over to see Jim."

Jim was stood at the bar waiting to be served. He turned as Sid approached him. "Hello, Sid."

"I've just met your Ina's bloke."

"Yes," Jim said slowly, "he doesn't seem too bad."

"Nice-looking lad."

"His clobber's better than our boys'; that's for sure."

"What do you think then, Jim, him being a Yank and all that?"

"Can't say I was over the moon about it, but what can I do, Sid? I can't risk her clearing off somewhere. He's going to war. He's been in action in Italy, so he knows what it's all about. She doesn't. If I forbid her seeing him and anything happens to him . . ." Jim's voice trailed off.

He gave his order with an extra drink for Sid. "Besides, as Nell told me under no uncertain terms, she'll be called up next year and become her own person."

"But she still can't get married until she's twenty-one."

"She's too young to know her own mind. She's only known him five minutes. I know what you're thinking . . . about the Belgian girl and me. She didn't know her own mind from one minute to the next, did she?"

"Seems a bit rough though, Jim. Kids in this country can't even get the vote until they're twenty-one, but they can get sent to war by a government they weren't even allowed to vote for."

"Well. Maybe it'll change one day. Anyway, I don't particularly want her to get married while the war is on. If she's eighteen when it ends, I'll think about it then. All the same, Sid, a lot of water is going under the bridge before that happens. I don't really want that kid to go off thinking

I felt he is not good enough for her. He's in a strange land, miles from home. This is a different war. In our time, we disembarked, got ashore, and went straight up the line. There weren't any Germans waiting for us; these poor little sods don't know what they're going to meet with when they land."

Chapter 13

There was no strict protocol in the Welland family. Although Jim was, in no doubt, the head of the family, his seat at the table was not at the head but at one end of the side with his back to the fireplace. Hilda sat beside him, Clive at the end, and Ina, opposite her father. How this arrangement had come to be was unknown. It always had been in Ina's memory, and no one had ever changed it. The empty space opposite Clive was deemed to be Avril's. When David took his seat at the table, it was beside Ina. If he thought it strange, he gave no sign.

"Good crowd down there?" Hilda asked.

"Not too bad, the usual Sunday morning lot," Jim replied.

"Didn't you get tipsy then David?" Ina asked.

"No. I reckon I can hold my liquor—up to a point, that is." He smiled.

Hilda and Ina put the food round and had taken their seats when David said, "You'll have to excuse the way I eat. I'm not much good at holding my fork in my left hand."

"You do whatever you want, David," Hilda told him. "We shan't mind a bit."

"It's nice of you to invite me to your house for a meal. I know how hard it must be with the rationing."

"We don't get all that hard up that we can't stretch things a bit."

"Hilda can make a banquet out of a tin of baked beans!" put in Jim.

"They come from Boston, don't they?" Clive piped up. "Boston baked beans."

"You learn that at school?"

"Yes. We were doing about the Boston Tea Party. All that tea. Going in the water. Those fishes must have got fed up with drinking it. We've learned lots about America; did you ever learn anything about us?"

"Clive." admonished Hilda. "Stop chattering and let David eat his dinner in peace!"

"Sorry." He grinned at David ruefully.

"That's okay. Tell you about it some other time."

The plates were taken, and Hilda brought in apple pie and a jug of Ideal milk.

"That smells good," David declared. "I've not had home cooked apple pie since I left home. They make it in the cookhouse, but it doesn't taste the same."

After they had finished eating, Ina helped Hilda clear the dishes away.

"Can I help with the dishes?" David asked.

"No, David. You go and talk to Jim."

"If you're sure . . ."

"Jim, take David in the front room. I'll make a cup of tea in a minute."

They both got up. Clive, with a "man of the world" look on his face, got up to follow them.

"You can go and help put away," Jim told him.

Jim sat in a chair by the fireplace and motioned David to sit in the one opposite. He took his tobacco tin off the shelf and opened it.

"Can't offer you a fag, son, but you're welcome to a roll up."

"No. I don't smoke. Thanks."

Jim nodded and carried on. "When do you reckon on getting engaged then?"

"Before I go over, I hope."

"Any sign of when that will be?"

"Don't exactly know. There are plenty of rumours buzzing around camp—like where and when. But I guess we won't know until the last minute."

"What are you doing about a ring?"

"I guess that's something we'll have to figure out between us. Shopping's a bit difficult. The shops are shut before I get into Salisbury, unless I can get in next Saturday morning and take Ina round in her lunch hour."

"True. That sounds a good idea. Are you going to be all right for the cash?"

"I can get the money out of my bank anytime, so I've no problem there."

Hilda came in with a tray of tea and put it down on the small table.

"I'm sorry I can't offer you coffee, David. I'm afraid we've run out until my next allowance."

"Tea will suit me fine! No sugar—" He stopped and then added, "Sorry, your sugar's rationed anyway, isn't it?"

"That's all right, David. If you wanted sugar we could have given you some." Hilda laughed.

David turned to Ina. "Your dad wanted to know when we are getting engaged. I thought we could maybe get the ring Saturday."

"The shops are closed when I leave work," Ina said.

"We're usually finished by lunchtime Saturdays. I could get a lift or a bus in early and see you when you have your lunch break. How about it? You could have a stroll round during the week and see if there's a ring that catches your eye."

"Yes. We'll do that. I can choose something. I could see if it fits."

"Okay. That's settled then."

"Would you like a little party? Say next Sunday?"

"Oh. Mum! Can you manage it?"

"I expect so. We could ask Gran and Auntie Nell. Is Sid working next Sunday, Jim?"

"Err . . . No . . . I don't think so. I'm on six to two, so I'll be free."

"Good! Stella and her boyfriend can come as well."

Ina glanced at her mother and father. This was going all too well. What were they thinking?

"We'll ask them tonight when we see them," she said.

"What time do you have to meet them?"

"About half past six."

"I'd like you to go down Gran's on the way."

"Yes. We'll do that, Mum."

"Look at all the presents you'll get," Clive said.

"Clive!" said Ina severely. "We're not getting engaged for the presents."

"If you don't behave yourself, there'll be no party for you, my lad!" scolded Hilda.

***

Ina and David left at quarter past five. Neither wanted tea. At old Mrs Welland's, they went round to the back door and found it open. Ina called through the doorway and then walked in. Nell had gotten up to meet them.

"I've brought David to see you," Ina said.

"Come in, both of you," Nell told them.

Going into the living room, Ina found her grandmother in her chair, drinking tea and eating a sandwich. The table was laid with their tea.

"I've not long made a pot," Nell said. "Do you want a cup?"

"Have we disturbed your tea, ma'am?" David asked.

"No, of course you haven't. It's nice to see you both."

"Come right in," said the old lady, "and let me see this young man of yours."

"This is David, and that's my auntie Nell."

He shook hands with Nell and then the old lady.

"Sit yourself down," she said, pointing to the chair opposite.

David sat down.

"You've come all the way from America," said old Mrs Welland.

"Yes, ma'am."

"Where are you from?"

"Alabama."

"How long have you been in the army?"

"Two years, well, just over. I was drafted in February 1942, when I was eighteen."

"My son—Ina's dad, was in the last war. So was my son-in-law, Sid."

"I met him this morning down the legion."

"He's gone to work now. You've missed him. Never mind if you've already met him."

"Where's Terry?" Ina asked.

"He's gone on some jaunt or other down on the New Forest," Nell told her. "About a dozen of them have gone down by coach. I don't know where they got the petrol from."

David looked at Nell. "Is this the New Forest where Robin Hood was supposed to hang out?"

"No," Nell told him with a smile. "It was Sherwood Forest where he was. That's up in the north."

"I don't know a lot about English geography," David said, returning the smile.

Ina thought it was time to interrupt. "Gran, Auntie Nell" she looked at David "We've something to tell you."

"Yes? Go on then," said Nell.

"We're getting engaged—next week. Mum's giving us a party—Sunday. You will come, won't you?"

"Well! Ina. This is a surprise!" her grandmother said. "Your dad never said anything to me yesterday."

"David only asked him today."

"And he gave his consent?"

Nell kept quiet. She had a faint smile hovering around her mouth.

"Yes, Gran," Ina replied.

"You're both very young."

"I'm nearly eighteen, and David's twenty-one—nearly."

"We don't aim to get married yet, ma'am," David told her. "It won't be until the war's over and I'm back home in the States. I'll either send for her or come and get her. It's all in the future right now."

"Yes. I suppose it has to be. And, David, don't call me ma'am, my dear. You can call me Gran."

"Okay, Gran." David laughed and then, on a more serious note, added, "I'll take good care of her, I promise."

"Well, from the little I have seen of you, I think you probably will."

"You'll come then, Gran?" Ina asked.

"If I can get up that hill!"

Nell said, "We'll do the same as we did at Easter, Mum. We'll catch the bus."

She turned to Ina. "Uncle Sid will be able to come. I doubt if Terry will be back in time. If he does, he can come up later."

"That's all right then!" Ina's sigh of relief was audible.

"Congratulations then," said Nell, "and good luck."

"Yes. Good luck to you both," put in the old lady.

"We shall have to go," Ina said. "We have to meet Stella and Joe."

"Joe's Stella's friend, I take it?"

"Yes, Auntie."

"Will they be at the party?" her grandmother asked.

"Yes. Hope so."

***

"Well?" Stella wanted to know. "How did it go?"

"Dad said we could get engaged."

"So, when will it be?"

"Next Saturday we get the ring, and we're having a tea party at our house on Sunday. You're both invited."

"A tea party!" said Joe. "I've never been to a tea party."

"Are you poking fun, Joe Smith?" Ina asked.

"No, no, honey. I'd love to come to your tea party."

He leaned towards her and planted a kiss on her cheek. He turned to David and held out his hand. "Congratulations, Dave."

David took his hand and shook it. "Don't I get a kiss on the cheek?"

"No. I haven't known you long enough," answered Joe.

Joe and Stella made their way towards Castle Street; Ina and David followed.

"Are you going to look for a ring?" David asked.

"Yes. I can have a good look round during my dinner break all this week and let you know which one I've picked on Wednesday."

"Okay. Make sure you pick one you really like."

"There's just one thing," she said.

"What's that?"

"You haven't told me how much you can afford."

"I don't know. Just pick one you like, as I said. Er . . . maybe not go into three figures."

***

Monday, after they'd finished their lunch, Ina and Stella made a beeline for the jewellers' shops.

"Where do you want to go first?" Stella asked.

"If we start on Queen Street, we can work our way round."

"How much can you go to?"

"David said not to go into three figures."

"Well. There you are then. You can pick something for £99.0s.0d."

"Stella! I wouldn't choose one for that much!"

They wandered up and down, looking in the windows for something to catch Ina's eye.

"I like that one," she exclaimed, after they'd looked in several shops.

It was a three-stone ring, square-cut diamonds in a platinum setting.

"Do you like it, Stella? It's neat, isn't it? It's not ostentatious."

"No. It's not a bit . . . ostentatious. How much is it?"

"£12.10s.0d"

"Not quite £99.0s.0d!" was Stella's remark.

"I shan't have time to try it on now, shall I?"

"You'll have to come back tomorrow."

"What if it's gone?"

"That's a chance you'll have to take. You should have asked Mr Phillips for a bit of extra time."

"Yes, and that's another thing I suppose I'll have to do."

"What?"

"Tell him I'm getting engaged to a Yank."

***

Tuesday morning the ring was still there.

"Are you going to try it on then?" Stella asked.

"Yes." Ina pushed the shop door open. "Here goes!" she said.

There was a young couple being served and a man behind the counter putting trays of bracelets away on the glass-fronted shelves underneath. He stood up. "Yes, Miss. What can I do for you?"

"I'd like to try a ring on, please. It's in the window, tray twenty-three."

He took some keys out of his pocket, unlocked the window door, and fetched out the tray.

Please let it fit, Ina prayed. She pointed to the ring, and the man lifted it from the tray.

"Do you know your ring size?" he asked.

"No. I don't."

"Well try it on, and if it doesn't fit, I'll measure your finger, and we'll see what else we have in your size."

He gave her the ring. With hands that trembled a little, she tried it on. The ring slipped over her finger as if it were custom-made.

"Look, Stella! It fits!"

"Relief all round," said Stella.

"It's a very pretty ring," commented the man. "Nine carat gold, of course—utility. But it is a good ring. The shank is platinum."

Ina took the ring off. "Do you think you could put it by for me until Saturday?"

"I'm afraid I will have to ask for a deposit, in this case, £2.0s.0d"

"Oh, crumbs!" Ina said. "I haven't got that much on me."

"How much have you got?" Stella asked.

"About five bob."

"Afraid I can't help you there," sighed Stella.

"I could have got it out of my post office, but they'll be closed now and all day tomorrow, and I shan't see my boyfriend till tomorrow night."

The pitiful look on Ina's face must have touched the man's heart. "Where do you work?" he asked.

"In Burtons."

"Oh, I know Mr Phillips. We meet at the local traders' committees meetings. I'll tell you what I'll do. I'll put the ring aside until Saturday with no deposit. I'll tell my staff."

"Thank you, very much." Ina said.

"I'll just take you name."

Ina gave him her details.

"That's fine. We'll see you Saturday, then, Miss Welland.

***

Wednesday evening, when Ina met David, the first thing he asked her was if she had chosen a ring. She told him she had and described it in detail to him. "It's quite a nice ring, isn't it, Stella?"

"Yes," Stella replied, "fits nicely too. And it's not ostentatious."

"Oh, you!" said Ina. "You won't let me forget that, will you?"

Stella laughed. "No, really, David, it is nice."

"What happens now?" David asked.

"The man in the shop put it by for me till Saturday."

"Then we go buy it?"

"Yes. What time can you get in? I can meet you around half past twelve."

"Twelve thirty? Yeah. I can be here by then."

"You can meet me by the Poultry Cross."

"The Poultry Cross," he repeated. "That's the big archway through to the market square."

"Yes. You haven't asked me how much."

"Okay, then. Let's hear the worst."

"It was £12.10s.0d. What's that in dollars?"

"I don't rightly know. The exchange rate is going up and down like a yo-yo. I'd say . . . about thirty dollars, something like that." He looked at her. "That's cheap," he said. "Sure that's the one you want?"

"Yes, really. What is this exchange rate thing?"

"It's how many dollars you get to the pound."

"Oh. I see. So you think the ring is quite cheap?"

"I reckoned on paying more."

"There you are." Stella grinned. "I said you could go to £99.0s.0d!"

"Hey! Don't give her big ideas." David laughed back.

***

Mr Phillips was on his morning break. Ina knocked the door and went into the staffroom.

"Yes, Miss?"

"Mr Phillips, could I have a bit of time over my dinner time please?"

"How much time? It's Saturday. Is there a particular reason?"

"Yes, I'm getting engaged. Saturday is the only time my boyfriend can get off."

Mr Phillips eyes opened wide. "Really, Miss? I had no idea you were courting a young man."

"We've known each other a while now. It wasn't serious at first. Now we want to get engaged before he goes to France."

"He's in the forces, then."

"Yes, the army actually" She looked down at the floor "He's" She paused. "He's an American soldier."

"Mr Phillips looked a little stunned.

"I know you don't approve of our girls going with Americans, but it's respectable. He respects me. He wouldn't do anything to hurt me—" Ina went on. She knew she was floundering and stopped talking.

"I take it your parents approve?"

"Yes. They do. They like him."

"Well. If your parents approve, then there's little I can say. I've always found you a sensible and trustworthy young lady. I don't have any fears about you acting in a way to bring the shop into disrespect. I can only wish you the very best. You can take some extra time, but try not to be too long."

"Thank you, Mr Phillips."

***

Ina's place in the staffroom was taken by Mrs Phillips.

"Miss Welland looked very pink cheeked. You haven't been scolding her, have you?" she asked.

"No. Not at all. She's getting engaged, apparently. She needed a bit of time off to get the ring."

"Well, I never!" Mrs Phillips exclaimed. "She's a little young to be getting engaged, isn't she?"

Her husband shrugged. "What's young these days? Her young man's American."

"Good grief! Did you know?"

"I didn't even know she was courting, Anyway, I can't see her doing anything that will reflect on the shop. Her parents approve, so I don't see any reason why I shouldn't. Besides, this time next year, she'll be miles from here—her and Miss Auden. Goodness knows how I am going to replace them—girls with a few years' experience in the shoe trade." He chuckled. "I bet Mrs Gray will have a few comments to make when she gets to hear about it!"

***

David was standing in the Poultry Cross. Ina hadn't told him which direction she would be coming from. He was looking left and right. She caught his eye as she came through by Clarke and Lonnen's. He came forward to meet her. "Where to now?" he asked.

"Just along here."

They walked together to the shop and went in. The woman behind the counter looked in their direction. "Can I help you?" she asked.

"Yes,'" Ina told her. "I came in Tuesday and tried on a ring. The man who served me said he would put it by for me until today."

"I see. Have you got the receipt for the deposit?"

Ina looked at the woman. "I didn't pay a deposit," she said. "He told me he wouldn't take one. He knows the manager of the shop where I work."

"Just excuse me a minute then. I'll just go to the back and see what I can find for you."

"What's this deposit all about?" David wanted to know.

"He wanted £2.0s.0d, but I didn't have that much money on me. I didn't have much at all."

"Why didn't you say they'd want something down? I could have given you some money?"

"It's all right. He put it by anyway."

The woman came back into the shop. "Here we are then, Miss Welland." She put a small box on the counter. "Did you want to try it on again?

"Yes, please," Ina said.

The woman opened the lid of the box. Ina took out the ring and slipped it over her finger and then held out her hand for David's inspection.

"Well? Do you like it?" she asked.

"Yeah" he said staring at her ring finger. "Yeah. It's pretty. Are you happy with it?"

"Yes, I am," she answered.

"Then that's all that matters."

He extracted three white five pound notes from his wallet. As he handed them over, he looked into the glass top of the showcase. "Those bracelets you have there—how much are they?"

"They're 17s.6d each, sir."

"Can I see them?"

"They are actually rolled gold, sir. The stones are imitation."

"Well, I guess that's okay. Do you like them?" he asked Ina.

"Yes . . ." she replied, uncertainly

"Want to pick one?"

"Me? Oh . . ."

"I'm not going to wear it!"

She gave him a quick smile, put her hand out, and chose one of small filigree links with a coloured stone in the centre of each.

"How much do you want?" David asked the woman.

"That'll be £4.7s.6d, please, sir."

David handed over the money. The woman rang in the amount on the till and gave him his change.

"I'll just put your purchases in a bag for you," she said.

Once outside the shop, David asked Ina if she wanted to wear the ring there and then.

"No. Keep it until tomorrow and make it official."

"Heck, Ina, right in front of everybody?"

"Well, it is our engagement party."

David sighed. "Okay then . . . if that's how you want it."

"What are you going to do now?"

"Head on back to camp."

"What, and then come all the way back in?"

"I got a few things to do. I'll see you tonight."

***

When Ina got back to the shop, she had five minutes to spare and was hungry. She walked into the staffroom to find Stella getting ready to go back into the shop.

"Where is it then?"

"David's keeping it till tomorrow."

"So we have to wait till then!"

"You've already seen it anyway."

Stella grinned and went out the room. Ina opened her lunch and took a bite out of a sandwich while struggling to put on her overall at the same time.

As Stella went through the door into the shop, Vera was on her way to the staffroom. "Did Ina get her ring?"

"Yes, but David's keeping it until tomorrow."

Mrs Gray was standing within earshot. "Stood her up, more like," she said, sourly. "They're all the same, these Yanks. Full of promises till they get—" She broke off.

Stella was glaring at her. "Get what? Mrs Gray?"

"I was going to say cold feet," she muttered and pushed past them both to go through the door and into the lavatory. Vera went on through. and Ina joined Stella in the shop.

Chapter 14

Ina didn't mind so much going to the Red Cross that evening because she was going to have David all day tomorrow. It had begun to rain anyway, and she was not wearing her raincoat. The sky looked menacing.

"Reckon we're in for a rainstorm," Joe commented.

"You could be right at that," David replied.

They hurried along Castle Street, just reaching the club doors when a large streak of lightning flashed across the sky, followed by a loud clap of thunder and a downpour of rain.

"Crikey!" Stella exclaimed. "Hope it clears up before going home time."

Inside, the place was beginning to fill up. The evening had brought in the usual bunch of "gum chewers"; it was this that Ina was not so keen on. She was glad that David and Joe didn't chew gum, or Stella for that matter.

As the boys went up to the bar, something crossed Ina's mind. She had been wondering about it off and on all day but had not liked to broach the subject with Stella at work. Now they were here she could ask her.

"Stella?"

"Yes?"

"What was going on when I came back into the shop this afternoon?"

"Going on? Nothing was, as far as I know."

"It looked as if you and Vera had some sort of set-to with Mrs Gray. You were both looking daggers at her."

"Oh. That. Well it wasn't much."

"Not for you to look at her like you did?"

"Well" she paused "If you must know, she said something sarcastic about David not turning up when you came back without the ring." Stella thought it prudent not to say more.

"Oh. Well she would. I wonder what she'd say if she saw us here now."

"She would have to be here, wouldn't she? And that would make her no better than us." Stella paused and then said, "Come to think of it, though, I wouldn't mind seeing her in here, plonking herself down on some GI's lap, skirt up to her long-knicker legs, chewing gum, and holding a fag in one hand and a pint of Guinness in the other."

The boys came back with the drinks. "No shandies," said Joe, "no lemonade, so we got you coke. Is that okay?" He didn't wait for an answer but said, "I have to go and talk to a guy. I'll be right back."

They watched him go up to an American soldier who was carrying a white canvas bag.

"Who's that?" Stella wanted to know.

"No idea," David said with a smile.

Joe came back with the bag and put it down between Ina and David.

"What is it?" Ina asked

"Never you mind," Joe said. "Take it home tonight."

Ina bent down and put her hand on the bag.

"Don't open it here!" Joe hissed.

Ina drew her hand back as if she had been stung.

"Ooooops!" she said. "Did I nearly drop a clanger?"

"Could be you nearly did," Joe said.

Virgil came in and walked up to their table.

"Where's Bob tonight?" Joe asked.

"He's up at the bar," Virgil said.

"Is it still raining outside?" Stella asked.

"No. I think the storm's passed over."

Bob came back with the drinks.

"Only small ones?" commented David.

"Not stopping long." Explained Bob. "We've got a couple of girls to meet."

"I don't know," Virgil said. "I reckon I'd just as soon stay here."

"What about the girls?" Bob wanted to know.

"They'll soon latch onto somebody else."

"Okay. If that's what you want."

"You don't seem too bothered about it," David told him.

"What if the girls won't have any more to do with you?" Ina asked.

Virgil spread his hands expressively.

"It's not likely to worry him," said Bob nodding towards Virgil. "He won't be without a girl for long. Old Casanova there only has to raise his eyebrows at dames, and they drop like flies!"

"Can I help it if I've got what they want?"

"Make the most of it, boy," Joe put in. "This war ain't gonna last forever."

Stella tried to peer over towards the dance floor. "What's it like in there?" she asked Bob.

"From what I could see, pretty crowded."

She turned to Joe. "Is there room for us two?"

"If you say so," Joe replied and got up from his chair. Stella followed him to the ballroom.

***

"Thinks a lot of himself that Virgil, doesn't he?" Stella said.

"Virge? No, he's okay. Most of it's just his way."

"But those two girls, what if they got wet waiting for them?"

Joe led her onto the floor. "Don't lose any sleep over those two, honey. They're a couple of good-timers anyhow."

"You've met them?" Stella asked him.

"Yeah, I've met them, that time they were with two other guys."

"Talk of the devil," Stella said

"What?"

"Virgil's just come in with Ina," she answered.

"I expect he asked Dave's permission." Joe grinned.

"Well, as long as he doesn't raise an eyebrow and expect her to drop like a fly!"

***

Virgil and Ina managed to find a spot on the dance floor, but it meant all they were doing was gliding around in a circle.

"Bob was right. It is crowded," Virgil said.

"They've all come in to get out of the rain." Ina laughed.

184

"Like the animals in Noah's ark." Virgil smiled back.

"We've had some bad floods in Salisbury, not recently but some time ago," Ina went on.

"Floods are bad things," Virgil said. "We've had some pretty bad ones in the States."

"I suppose we're lucky in a way. We don't have earthquakes and things like that."

"Tornadoes—they're the worst, especially if they blow in straight from the sea. They can do a lot of damage to homes, and many people lose their lives. They're mainly on the east coast, Florida and that. They can come right inland. If one hit England, it'd blow half of it away."

"That's what Hitler tried to do."

"I guess he did. But he didn't succeed, did he?"

"He had a darned good try!" Ina said.

Virgil tilted his head back a little and looked into her face. "You're looking pretty perky tonight," he said.

"It's because I'm happy."

"Why are you happy?"

"David and I are getting engaged tomorrow."

There was a silence from Virgil. She looked into his eyes. They showed no expression. She smiled at him, and he seemed to find his voice. "You and Dave are getting engaged?"

"Yes."

"I didn't know it was that serious."

"He asked me two weeks ago."

"Oh, I see . . . You and Dave. Well, I'd better congratulate him, hadn't I?"

"We're having a small family party tomorrow at my home; then I get my ring, and it's official."

"You've . . . got the ring then?"

"Yes. We got it today—at my dinner . . . lunch hour. David came in earlier this morning and went back to camp afterwards."

Virgil nodded but made no comment. Someone bumped into them.

"It's getting mighty crowded in here," he said.

"It's getting hot, too." Ina replied.

"What say we call it a day?"

"Yes. All right," she agreed

They walked off the dance floor. Ina wasn't surprised to see Stella and Joe close behind them.

***

Back at the table, David was in deep conversation with Bob. Whatever it was they were talking about, they both laughed.

Virgil butted in. He held his hand out towards David. "Congratulations, Dave."

David shook his hand. Bob sad nothing, so Ina presumed he knew.

Virgil turned to Bob and said, "C'mon, then, buddy, if we're going to meet these dames."

"Thought you'd changed your mind?"

"We might as well go," Virgil answered, "see what's on offer."

"They're probably gone by now," Bob told him.

"So what? We can find a place and have a few beers."

Bob got up. "So long, folks. Sorry we have to leave. See you some other time." He followed Virgil, and they were both went out of the club.

"I guess we'd better be making tracks if we're gonna eat before the girls get their buses," Joe said.

"You'd better let me carry the bag," David told Ina as they stood up to leave. "Better get a cab home tonight."

For once, Ina didn't argue. The bag looked heavy.

***

That night, when Ina walked into the living room, Hilda's eyebrows were raised when she saw the bag.

"What on earth have you got there?"

"I don't know," answered Ina, "but it's blooming heavy!"

"Put it on the table then. Let's see what's in there."

Ina lifted it onto the table and opened it.

"Crummy!" she withdrew a large tin. "It's butter, Mum! A tin of butter!"

Hilda took the tin from her. "Good grief! It's a pound—a whole pound of butter!"

Ina took out a packet, unwrapped it, and found that it contained some sliced cold meat. "Is this ham, Mum?"

"Yes. It's ham all right. There must be over half a pound there."

"I think there's another tin in here," Ina said. She folded the bag back and revealed a large tin of fruit salad.

"Where did all this come from?" Hilda asked.

"Joe brought it in tonight. It's to help with the party."

Hilda looked worried. "Where did he get it from?"

"I don't know. The stores I suppose."

"He was taking a risk, wasn't he? What if he'd got caught?"

"He must have thought he'd be able to get it all right. You are going to use it, aren't you?

"Too right I am! I'm not looking any gift horse in the mouth. Don't, for goodness sake, tell Clive, or it will be all round the school and we'll have our police, the American police, and Uncle Tom Cobleigh and all on our doorstep."

***

Stella and Joe found their way up about four o'clock. Ina, Hilda, and Nell, who had volunteered to come up and help, were in the kitchen making sandwiches when Stella and Joe arrived. Clive had answered the front doorbell and brought them through to the kitchen.

Stella introduced Joe. Hilda took his hand and said, "Very pleased to meet you, Joe." Then she whispered, "Thank you."

Joe shook her hand and smiled at her. "Pleasure's all mine, ma'am." Then whispered to her, "Anytime, ma'am."

Hilda turned to Ina. "Take Joe and Stella into the front room and you can keep them company."

"Are you sure?"

"Yes. Go on."

"We can manage, Ina," Nell told her.

***

"Hasn't Joe got some lovely blue eyes!" Nell exclaimed when Ina had taken Joe and Stella through to the front room.

"Yes, he has," agreed Hilda.

"And was it him who gave you the stuff for tea?"

"Yes, it was. You haven't said anything to anyone, have you?"

187

"Good Lord, no! Mother wouldn't know anyhow. She gets very vague about things these days, and Sid wouldn't notice anything. What about Jim?"

"I had to tell him, but he just laughed."

***

In the sitting room, Stella looked at David. "When are you going to give Ina her ring?" she asked.

"At teatime," David replied

"Are you going down on one knee?" Joe asked.

"No, sir! Not me. In front of all those folks?"

"Spoilsport!" Stella said.

The other guests arrived, at least Old Mrs Welland and Sid. Terry had not come back from his trip.

David and Joe stood up when the old lady came into the room.

"Here," said David, "sit in this chair."

"No. It's all right, David, thank you. I'm going in the other room to see how the girls are getting on. She looked at Joe. "You're Stella's young man then?"

"Yes, ma'am.

"You are David's friend?"

"Yeah, we're buddies."

"Good to have friends in the army." She turned to Stella. "That's a pretty dress you have on, Stella."

"Thank you, Mrs Welland." Stella smiled.

The old lady departed into the living room. Ina, who was near to Stella, said, under her breath, "Never seen you in that dress before."

"My sister never said I could borrow it before," Stella whispered back.

Ina looked around the front room. Her father was sitting in an armchair by the fireplace. Uncle Sid sat opposite, David, Joe, and Stella on the sofa. Clive was sitting on the pouffe between Stella and Joe, and she, Ina, squatted at David's feet.

I can't believe it, she thought. *The four of us, actually sitting here in our front room! And Dad with a smile all over his face!*

She caught Stella's eye. Stella grinned at her and, behind Joe's back, gave her the thumbs up sign. Ina grinned back.

188

Jim, a smile still on his face, took out his tobacco pouch.

"Neither of you boys smoke, I take it?"

They both shook their heads.

He proffered the pouch to Sid, who said, "Ta, Jim."

"Best Virginian, that is," Jim told Sid. "David brought it in for me this morning."

"He brought me some bars of chocolate and Mum a big box," Clive chipped in.

"Did he now?" Sid said. "Well, aren't you the lucky one!"

"I'm going over there one day and help with the turkey farm," Clive continued.

"Are you?" Sid answered. "That's your future taken care of then!"

Clive turned to David. "Why don't you farm cows instead of turkeys? I could soon learn how to use a lasso."

"Could you now?" David replied. "I guess you'd be a darned sight better at it than I'd be an' all."

"Don't you think you'd be any good then?"

"If it's all the same to you, fella, I'll stick to my turkeys. Me and cows just wouldn't get along together. I'll leave that to the boys out west."

Nell came in. "All right you lot, tea's ready. Bring some chairs in, will you?"

They all trooped into the living room. Hilda and Nell, as usual, had done wonders.

"Strewth!" exclaimed Sid when he saw the table. "What a sight for sore eyes!"

"A cake!" cried Ina. "Oh, Mum! You made a cake!"

"No. That's what your gran brought up for you."

"It's only a baker's one, Ina, and it's only sponge with some icing on it. But a celebration is no good without a cake."

Ina went over to her gran and kissed her on the cheek. "Thanks, Gran."

Joe sat as his appointed place. "Well," he remarked, "no one told me I'd be sitting in an English house having a real old-fashioned English tea." He looked at Hilda. "Do you know, ma'am, what it means to us, being invited to your home and sitting at your table having tea with you?"

"I don't suppose you have teatimes in America, do you?" asked old Mrs Welland.

"Some people in the south—especially those who have English ancestors—take tea. Old habits die hard! But not a spread like this! With all this rationing you folks have and all."

"We don't have this every Sunday," Clive told him.

"And she did have a bit of help," put in Jim, with a slight wink at Joe.

Ham sandwiches; sandwiches of cucumber, lettuce, tomato and grated cheese; sausage rolls; small fancy cakes, besides the iced cake and a dish of fruit salad with a jug of evaporated milk.

At the end of the meal, Stella looked down the table at David. "When do we get the ceremony then?" she asked.

"C'mon, Dave. Now's as good a time as any," Joe told him.

David, slightly flushed, stood up. He put his hand in his pocket and drew out the box. Opening the lid, he took out the ring.

"I'm . . . not much good at speechifying," he began.

"Aren't you going down on one knee?" asked Sid.

"No! Not even if you twist my arm!" David said with a smile. "But I guess I should say a few words of thanks to Ina's mom and dad for letting us get engaged and for having us here and giving us this party. So, thanks . . . thanks a lot."

He looked down at Ina. Taking her cue from him, she rose from her chair and stood beside him.

David said, self-consciously, "Ina, will you marry me and wait for me till the war is over and come to the States?"

Ina held her hand out and said, "Yes, please."

David took her hand in his. In the other hand, he held the ring between thumb and finger. Conscious of all eyes on him, he wavered a little. Ina wiggled her ring finger; he looked at her gratefully and slipped the ring over it. They both sat down to a round of applause.

Jim stood up. "Well, I think this calls for a celebration," he said. He went to the sideboard and came back with a bottle of sherry.

"Get the glasses, gal," he said to Hilda. Hilda fetched the glasses and put them round the table, hesitating in front of Clive.

"Yes—him and all," Jim said. He opened the bottle and carefully filled the glasses. He went back to his place at the table but remained standing. "Sorry Avril could not be with us today. She was on duty and could not swap with anyone. I'm not going to make a long speech," he declared. "David and I have already had a good long talk. He's a good lad who can look me straight in the eye. I like that in him. So, all that remains for me to do is to ask you all to join me in wishing them both luck and, please, God, let this damned war be over soon."

The company stood up and drank the toast.

"Are we going down the legion later, Dad?" Clive wanted to know.

"No. Not tonight, son. This is a family party, and we're going to party here."

"Don't worry about the drinks," Hilda said. "Dad, David, and Uncle Sid brought enough from the legion this morning to open their own club!"

Chapter 15

Monday morning seemed a bit of an anticlimax as Ina cycled along the quiet streets. Coming to the bus station, she saw that Stella's bus was in. Stella jumped off onto the pavement just as Ina approached.

"Well?" was her greeting. "What does it feel like to be an engaged woman?"

"Don't know," answered Ina. "It feels funny having a ring on my finger. I want to keep turning it around."

"You'll wear it out," Stella commented dryly.

They made their way towards the shop.

"I shan't know what to say when I get inside," Ina said.

"Don't tell me you're shy! Just wave it about and say, 'Look everybody. Look at my ring!'"

She opened the door for Ina to push her bicycle through. Mr Phillips stood by the cash desk.

"Ah. Miss Welland. I trust everything went off well?"

"Yes, thank you, Mr Phillips."

"And, you're wearing your ring, I see."

Ina held out her hand.

"Yes, Miss. Very nice—good setting; not a bit ostentatious."

Stella dived through the door into the workroom, leaving Ina to follow, pink cheeked and trying to compose her face.

***

As Ina wheeled her bicycle into the shed after work, she heard a voice call her name. She came out of the shed to see Harold Daley in his garden.

She returned his greeting. "Hello, Harold. Home on leave?"

"Yes, just for a few days. I've finished my basic; now I'll be on to another camp to do some more training—the tough stuff. Ready for the big push."

She looked at him closely. This was not the Harold she knew. He seemed to have grown in stature. There was no sign of acne on his face now, just a faint trace of what would soon be whiskers. He looked quite nice in his uniform. He must be all of nineteen now.

"I hear you got yourself engaged," he went on.

"Yes."

"A Yank."

"That's right." She looked for the usual sardonic expression on his face, but his smile seemed genuine.

"Well. Good luck to you both," he said.

"Thanks."

Cissie came out of her back door. "Tea's ready, Harold."

Harold walked towards his mother. "I'm just congratulating Ina," he said.

"Oh. Yes. Congratulations Ina." There was no warmth in Cissie's voice

"Thanks, Mrs Daley."

"Tell your mother I'll be around later."

"Yes. I will."

Ina and the Daley's disappeared through their respective back doors.

***

"Well?" Hilda asked as Ina walked into the living room. "What did they think of your engagement ring?"

"They liked it."

"It's a pretty ring. Make sure you take care of it. Don't go putting it down any old where."

"No, Mum. I'll look after it. Mrs Daley said she'll be round later."

"Coming to have a gawp, I expect," said Clive.

"Well. At least I've got something Maureen hasn't got." Ina grinned. Then she went on. "I saw Harold outside. I didn't recognise him. He seems different, no spots. He says he going on a course, more commando training."

Jim looked up from his evening paper. "Reckon it's making a man of him. It's knocking a bit of discipline into him."

As good as her word, Cissie gave her "Cooooeeee" just after Ina and Hilda had finished the washing up and putting away. Jim, with his newspaper and tobacco pouch, beat a hasty retreat to the front room, followed by Clive.

"I just called round," Cissie said, "to see if everyone was all right."

"Yes. We're all fine," Hilda assured her.

Cissie had other avenues to explore. "I was a bit concerned as you didn't go down the club last night. I would have called round, but I knew you were having a family get-together. Ina's boyfriend here, I gather."

"Yes," Hilda told her. "It was a small party for her engagement. We wanted the rest of the family to meet him. We didn't go down the club because David is rather a shy young man and didn't want a fuss."

"Oh. I see. I thought it was because he's . . . umm . . ."

"An American?" Hilda finished for her. "He's already been to the club with Jim, you know."

"Yes. I know. It's. Well I want you to know that it makes no difference to us."

"Thank you, Cissie; that's very generous of you." Hilda gave her a smile that didn't quite match her voice.

"Oh. No! I didn't mean . . . I'm sure he's a very nice respectable person, or I know you and Jim would not have agreed to let Ina go out with him. I expect we will meet him sooner or later."

"Your Alb already has. They seemed to get on together," Hilda said. "And our family has taken to him."

"That's all right, then, as long as the family approves."

Hilda set Cissie off on another course. "Show Mrs Daley your ring, Ina."

Ina, who had been watching the discourse between the two women with mixed feelings of anger and amusement, went over to Cissie with her left hand extended.

Cissie bent her head over the ring. "Ye-e-e-s," she drawled, slightly grudgingly. "Very nice—nine carat, of course . . ."

Ina flushed slightly. "Yes," she said. "It's nine carat. Eighteen carat isn't available unless you buy second-hand. I didn't want a ring that someone else had worn."

"No. No. Of course you didn't," agreed Cissie.

"Maureen didn't get engaged at Easter after all, then," Hilda put in.

It was Cissie's turn to have pink cheeks. She was silent for a while and then said, "No. They decided to wait until the war's over, when things are more plentiful and there's more choice. Maureen will have a solitaire, of course."

"Of course!" Hilda replied through gritted teeth.

***

In the morning, there was a letter from David.

We've been stopped from coming into Salisbury as from now. We cannot go outside Tidworth. Don't know what it's all about. No one's telling us. Can you come over here, Wednesday? Should be a bus in about six. Will meet you off. Joe's writing to Stella. Say hi to your folks. Thank them for the party. It was great. Can't stop, someone's waiting on me to post this for me. See you.

Love David
P.S. Oh, Yes. xxxxxxxxxxxxxx

***

The boys were there to meet them when the girls got off the bus.

"Have you found out what it's all about, yet?" asked Stella.

"No," Joe responded. "And I don't think we're going to find out."

"Perhaps there's been a fight in Salisbury, though I haven't heard of one," Ina added.

"We'd have heard of it as well. Anyway," Joe finished, "we've not been confined to camp, so let's make the best of it. Are you girls hungry?"

"I'm always hungry," Stella told him.

They made their way to the café they had been to before.

"I wonder if they do fish and chips here?" Stella mused.

"I don't think I could go your fish and chips right now," said Joe.

"What's wrong with good old British fish and chips?"

"Not a thing, honey! We ate before we came out."

"All right then, coffee and cookies."

"I'm with you there!"

"And we'll get some fish and chips before we go home," Stella said, "and we'll eat them walking along the road."

"What's that?" asked David. "Some sort of ceremony?"

"Kind of. They have to be eaten from newspaper while you're walking along . . ."

"On a cold, dark night," Ina finished.

"Out of a newspaper?" David asked

"Tell me," Joe asked, "isn't that a little unhygienic?"

"Why?"

"Don't the print come off onto the grub?"

"All goes down the same way," Ina explained.

"Guess I've heard of 'eating your own words' but not somebody else's."

***

There was still warmth in the air. They decided to go to the little pub with the garden, as the girls were still not keen about going inside public houses. There was a trestle table under a tree. Four other people already occupied it. Virgil and Bob with two girls. They went up to the table.

"Mind if we join you?" asked Joe.

"No!" Virgil told him, smilingly. "Sit down and make yourselves at home. There's plenty of room."

Ina and Stella sat opposite the others. David and Joe remained standing.

"Can we get you some drinks?"

"No, thanks," Bob replied. "We just got some in."

Virgil looked across at Ina. "So your party went off okay, did it?"

"Yes. Very well, thanks. Mum did us proud."

"Can't be easy with the way you're rationed."

"No, but she managed." It was best not to mention the food parcel from Joe.

"What was it—a birthday party?" asked one of the girls.

"Dave and Ina got themselves engaged," Virgil told her.

"Oh. Congratulations. Can we see the ring?"

Obligingly, Ina held out her left hand. The two girls leaned forward.

"Oh, yes. That's pretty, isn't it, Joan?"

"Yes. It is. It's something like the one you had, Rita."

196

Bob, sitting at the other end of the table, turned to Rita, who was obviously his girlfriend, and said, "You were engaged one time?"

"Yes, once," Rita replied, "sometime ago."

"What happened to your ring?"

"He chucked me, so I flogged it. Mingy sod in the jeweller's shop only gave me three quid for it, and it cost seven."

"What did you spend the money on?"

"I bought my new boyfriend a watch."

"Well. They say it's an ill wind," said Bob.

David and Joe came back with trays of drinks and crisps.

"Here," said Joe and put a bag of crisps in front of each of them.

"Potato chips!" exclaimed Bob. "Thanks."

"Crisps, boy, crisps," said Virgil.

"Sure. I keep forgetting."

"Potato chips are what you have with your battered fish," said the other girl, Joan.

"And you have to eat them out of newspaper while you're walking along the street on a cold, dark night." Joe grinned.

"Out of newspaper!" asked Bob. "Why newspaper?"

"If you didn't have them in newspaper," Stella said, solemnly, "you'd get salt and vinegar all over your hands."

"Hey. C'mon." Bob protested. "You're having me on!"

"No. It's true," Ina put in. "But we were pulling your leg. They're put in greaseproof paper first and then newspaper."

"Well. I'll take your word for it. You were pulling my leg? I'll have you know my leg can be pretty sensitive in places!"

There was a sudden flurry of flying fur as a squirrel jumped from a nearby tree and landed at the end of the table where Ina was sitting. She gave a squeal.

Virgil, who was sat opposite her, pushed it away. "Get out of here, little fella," he said. "You aren't wanted."

The squirrel hopped in front of David.

"He's after your crisps," Ina said.

David held a crisp out to it.

"Don't let it bite your finger!" Ina warned. "They're pests. They're full of disease!"

"Aw!" Bob grinned. "And he's such a cute little fella."

The squirrel ran along to the other end of the table. Bob shooed it away. It jumped down and ran up another tree.

"Don't you have squirrels in America?" Joan asked.

"Sure," Bob told her, "but what we mostly get is chipmunks."

"Chipmunks?"

"They're like squirrels but sort of grey and black and white, all mixed up."

"Like skunks?"

"Er . . . Not exactly; they're smaller."

"Do they pong?"

"Pong?"

"You know—smell, like a skunk does."

"No. They don't smell. You'd soon know the difference if you got near a skunk."

"Why do they do it?"

"Some say it's because they've been disturbed. Some say because they're angry. I reckon they do it because they're just plain ornery cusses."

When the squirrel had jumped onto the table, Ina had crept closer to David, leaning against his arm. She had not moved back again. She now became aware of him stiffening. She looked up at his face. His eyes had narrowed and were focussed on the far end of the pub garden. She followed his line of vision and saw, coming towards them, Sharkey and his friend. Stella had seen them as well.

"Oh, no!" she cried, "it's blooming Pudding Face!"

"What the hell does he want?!" Joe exclaimed. "The guy bugs me everywhere I go!"

Whether he was unaware of his reception or didn't care, Sharkey approached the group. He came up to the table and stood by Ina. She could see sweat on his brow and upper lip. She could also smell the drink on his breath as he breathed in and out of his flabby mouth.

"Well. Well. Well. Now looky here! Four pretty soldier boys and four pretty little Limey dolls."

"What do you want, Sharkey?" Joe's voice was low.

"Why! I just came to see how you all are; just paying a friendly call."

"You've paid it. Now you can go."

"Hey! Now, c'mon, Smitty. Just wanted to know if these girls here were showing you a good time—"

"Watch your mouth, Sharkey," Joe hissed.

Sharkey blundered on. "Just wanna make sure they're showing their appreciation to you guys real good, you know? Coming all the way over here to fight the Brits' goddamn war for them 'cuz they're too yaller to fight it for themselves?"

There was a deadly hush all around the table. Joe half rose from his seat.

Before anyone knew what she was going to do, Ina was on her feet, her face alive with anger. "Don't you dare say we're cowards! We were fighting this war long before you came in. We've had our cities and towns bombed and our people killed. Your people back home don't know what war is. None of them know what it's like to sit in an air raid shelter night after night for two whole years listening to bombs dropping around you and wondering when one's going to blow you to bits! No one was with us in those days. We had to go it alone. And we didn't give in like the rest of Europe did. Your people haven't been rationed up to the eyeballs. They can go into a shop and buy all the food they need. They can buy clothes whenever they want to; we can't. And when you're spouting your big mouth off about fighting someone else's war, when my cousin joined up, he thought he was going to fight the Germans but he went to Burma instead and was taken prisoner by the Japs. Remember the Japs, Pudding Face? They're the one's who bombed your Pearl Harbour. My auntie hasn't heard from my cousin for two years. She doesn't know if he's dead or alive, and all because our boys and the Australians were helping you fight the Japs. We were in North Africa, and we went all through Italy with you. And when you go to France, we shall be there too. Germany declared war on you, and they sunk some of your ships before you even came into the war. So it's not just our war, you great tub of lard, it's your bloody war as well!"

She picked up her glass and threw it; it caught him in the chest and the dregs at the bottom spilled down his tunic. The glass, unbroken, fell back onto the table, rolling towards Virgil. He stopped it before it fell to the ground.

Ina pushed her way past Sharkey and, half walking, half running, made her way across the green.

David muttered, "Jesus," got up and followed her.

Sharkey looked around at the group. "What did I say?" he asked.

"You know darned well what you said," Virgil told him.

Joe leant across the table. In a voice that was low and harsh, he said, "Beat it, Sharkey. Get the hell out of here, or so help me, I'll push your goddamn teeth right down your goddamn throat."

"Okay! Okay! I'm going!" Sharkey turned to his friend "You comin'?" he said and strode off across the green.

His friend looked ruefully at them and shrugged. "Sorry," he said and followed Sharkey.

Joe sat down. Looking at Stella, he saw that she had paled and her mouth was set in a hard line. She faced Bob and Virgil across the table.

"Is that what all you Americans think," she asked, "that you have to fight our war for us because we're cowards?"

"Hell. No, honey." Bob exclaimed. "We all know what you folks have been through!"

"Don't let Sharkey get under your skin," Virgil told her." He's a loud-mouthed baboon. He shouldn't have said what he did. He had no call to rile Ina like he did."

"He got what he deserved," Joan put in. "I lost a cousin like that girl did. He was in the navy. He was on the *Hood* when she was sunk. He was just eighteen, and my auntie's only child."

The air seemed to have suddenly chilled. The light-hearted banter between them had gone.

Joe put a hand on Stella's arm. "You want we should catch up with Dave and Ina?"

"Yes." She slipped off the bench and, with Joe, prepared to leave. They said their goodbyes to the others and started to walk away.

"Tell Ina we're on her side," Virgil said.

She smiled at him and nodded. "Yes. I will," she answered.

As they walked away, Virgil said: "Some day . . . real soon, someone's going to find Sharkey flat on his face with a bullet in his fat neck, and I'm betting on it not being from a Kraut gun."

***

David caught up with Ina just before she reached the gate. He put his hand on her shoulder. She shrugged it away.

"Hey. C'mon, now, sweet pea; it was Sharkey saying those things."

"Sorry," she murmured.

"He's got a big fat mouth," David went on. "Guys like him cause trouble for everybody."

"Why do they have horrible blokes like him in the army?" Ina asked hotly.

"It's wartime. They got to have good and bad."

"But why make him a sergeant over someone's head?"

"Because they reckon he's a good soldier. He's tough, and he's mean. He's the type of man that gives no quarter."

"But if he upsets people!"

"Don't make no difference to the army. They don't judge soldiers on their personalities."

"Will you get into trouble with him?"

"Why would I be in trouble with him?"

"Because of what I said, what I did . . ."

"No. He can't do anything to me. Do you want to go back to the others?"

"No. I feel stupid."

"Why do you feel stupid?"

"They'll laugh at me because I lost my temper."

"They'll do no such thing. They got no time for Sharkey, especially Virgil. He had Virgil busted down to private for something he did himself."

"Didn't Virgil say it wasn't his fault?"

"No. It's not something you do in the army."

"It's not fair."

"Maybe not, but that's the way of things. Anyhow, looks like Joe and Stella are heading our way."

When Stella and Joe reached them, Stella said, "Message from Virgil. Tell Ina we're on her side."

Ina smiled. "That was nice of him."

"Told you, didn't I?" David said.

"Are we going for these fish and chips then?" asked Joe.

"I have to pay a call first," Stella told him.

"Okay. You girls go and powder your noses, and we'll wait up here."

Together, Ina and Stella made their way to the pub.

***

"Ina okay?" Joe showed concern.

"Yeah. I guess."

"She sure gave Sharkey the works!"

"Didn't know she had it in her, Joe."

"They've all had enough. What she said—having her people killed and all the rationing—she was right. Folks back home don't know what it's like. I guess something had to give. And no better guy than Sharkey to take it."

"Is this my last day with her, Joe?"

"I don't know."

"How long you reckon we got?"

"Hell! I don't know any more than you do. Nobody tells us anything."

"Thought there might be some rumours."

"There's always rumours. Best to keep your ears shut. You'll know soon enough. You know the routine, 'Get your gear together ready to move out. Write your letters home. Make sure your will's in order!' They'll see you're all prepared to fight and all prepared if you get blown away."

Chapter 16

June 1944

Hilda called to Ina, "Come on. Hurry up. There's a letter for you. Looks like it's from David."

Ina came bounding down the stairs and walked into the living room.

"I wonder what he's got to say this time. Not very much by the look of it."

The letter was less than half a page and the text was brief.

Confined to camp. Can't get into Salisbury, not even Tidworth. Can you get over here Sunday, say about three? Go up the road towards camp until you see a church. Go past there into the next field. We'll meet you there.

***

"I know what you're going to ask me," Stella said as she stepped off the bus. "Yes, I've had a letter from Joe."

"What do you think is going on?" Ina asked.

"I don't know, and we shan't know until we see them. Perhaps they've been naughty boys."

"No, seriously, Stella."

"Maybe they're on the move."

Ina felt a coldness creep around her heart. "Do you think they're getting ready for France then?"

"Wait till we see them. We'll find out then."

***

This time, there was no one to meet them at the bus stop. There were no military uniforms to be seen, except for a few British and American MPs either walking in twos or riding in vehicles. What civilians there were, were going about their Sunday afternoon business.

"What if someone stops us and asks us where we're going?" Ina asked anxiously.

"We'll sort that out if we come to it," Stella replied.

They crossed the road and made their way towards the camp. Soon, the houses and shops gave way to hedges, beyond which were fields. They came to a wide gap in the hedges, through which a rough track ran, flanked on either side by banks of cow parsley, ragged robin, and an assortment of other wild flowers. The hedges here were mostly of dog roses.

Stella, without warning, darted up the track.

"Where are you going? That's not the way!" Ina shouted in alarm.

"Come on," Stella said. "I've got an idea."

Ina caught up with her.

"Got any scissors?" Stella asked.

"Only nail scissors. What are you going to do?"

"They'll do."

Ina took her manicure set out of her handbag.

"Good!" Stella said. "Two pairs."

"You're not going to cut those roses!"

"We both are."

"They're prickly!" Ina protested.

"We'll put some dock leaves around them."

"What are we going to do with them?"

"If anyone stops us, we can say we are going to the church to put them on a grave."

"But they're dog roses!"

Stella looked at Ina and, without blinking an eyelid, said, "Well! There *is* a war on, you know!"

They found the church. It was a little way off the road, with a lychgate and a gravel path running up to the porch. Beyond the church was a high hedge.

They put the roses on the first grave they came to, although by now, most of the petals were gone.

"They look pretty sorry for themselves," Ina remarked.

"Whoever's under there isn't likely to pop up to smell them," Stella answered.

They managed to find an entry point into the field and hoped it was the correct meeting place. The field rose gently into a low hill. Opposite where they had emerged from the hedge, a spinney ran the length of the field. Here, they stood patiently, waiting for David and Joe.

When they came, it was out of the spinney. As they drew nearer, Ina could only stare at them. Instead of their usual uniforms, they were dressed in khaki cotton jackets; their trouser legs were tucked into their boots and bound round with webbing, which made the whole thing come halfway up their calves. They were wearing helmets with the straps hanging either side of their faces. They were dressed as those soldiers were who had climbed out of those trucks the day she and Stella had gone to watch the football match. Had they been on exercise and not had time to change? She had seen American soldiers dressed like that on the newsreels, storming up the beach of some Pacific island. *They're dressed ready for war*, she thought.

Stella had not seemed to notice. She put her arm through Joe's and, laughing up at him, walked with him up field.

David stood looking at Ina, questioningly. "Cat got your tongue?" he asked.

"No . . . no," she said, composing herself.

"Been waiting long?"

"No. Just got here. We stopped on the way to pick some roses."

"Pick . . . roses?"

"Yes. Well, it was a brainwave of Stella's. She thought that, if we got stopped, we could say we were going to the church to put them on a grave."

"You didn't pick them from a garden, did you?"

"No, of course we didn't. We picked them from the hedge. They were dog roses." She pointed to the hedgerow near to them. "Like those," she explained. "Only by the time we got there, most of the petals had fallen off."

"What did you do with what was left?"

"We put them on a grave anyway."

"I bet that pleased them up in heaven."

***

205

They started to walk up the field. David removed his helmet and carried it by one strap.

"Better keep close to the hedge," he said.

"You're not taking a big risk getting out of camp are you?" Ina asked.

"Some, maybe. Don't worry. We'll be okay."

"Have you seen anymore of Sharkey?"

"No. He's keeping pretty much out the way. He knows he went too far."

"Is he married?"

"I don't rightly know. Don't think he gets many letters. He usually creeps away when we get our mail."

"Perhaps that's what's wrong with him." Ina laughed. "He feels lonely and unloved."

"He could do at that. Anyway, let's not talk about Sharkey. We haven't much time. We have to get back in before we get missed."

They passed the spinney, which had now given way to the high hedges bordering the field.

"Shall we sit here awhile?" David asked.

"Yes, all right."

They sat themselves down and looked back at the way they had come.

"It looks like the field we were in when we went to see the football match," Ina remarked.

"It's pretty much the same, I should think. The camp's way over behind the wood we came through."

He looked at her and gave a little chuckle.

"What are you laughing at?" Ina asked.

"I was thinking of you girls picking those flowers. What was it you called them, dog roses?"

"What do you call them, then?"

"I don't know that we have them at home. Maybe we do. I just don't remember seeing them."

"What kind of flowers do you have?"

"Oh . . . all kinds. Just don't know what they're all called. Seems like they just grow."

She was going to say, *Like Topsy*, but paused, remembering the "spat" they had had on Harnham Hill. Best not to quote from *Uncle Tom's Cabin*. She changed the subject entirely.

"Sing your song to me," she said.

"Thought you said it made you sad."

"Just the chorus then."

He sang the chorus to her and, when he'd finished, said, "It's about time I heard a song from you."

"I can't sing."

"I reckon you can sing well enough to get by."

"You flatter me."

"I'm not flattering you. You have a pretty speaking voice, so you should be able to sing pretty."

She laughed and said, "No one ever told me that before. It must be my Wiltshire accent, though I'm not as broad as my dad."

"Could be. When we first came over here, a lot of the guys thought the people in the pubs were trying to take the rise out of us, you know? The British movies we get back home, folk speak different, sort of . . . well, I don't know . . . maybe like your David Niven."

"Posh."

"Is that it? Posh?"

"Like Oooooh! Ay say Ahmandah. Ay daw lake yaw driss!"

David laughed "I guess that's it!" he said. "What about the London folk. They don't all speak like that."

"You mean the cockneys."

"Yeah. I think maybe I do."

"They'd say something like . . . umm . . . like Wotcher, me ole china. Ah's the trouble and strife?"

"What the heck does that mean?"

"Hello, mate. How's your wife?"

"I'd never have guessed!"

"England's full of different accents. My dad's cousin came down from the northeast—Gateshead—I couldn't understand a word he said." And then she added the word "S'now."

"What's that? Snow?"

"It's Wiltshire for 'you know'."

"Okay! You've got me confused. Just sing me a song in Salisbury English, Ina style."

"There's one I learnt at school. It's about a girl who had to say goodbye to her soldier boyfriend, like Mary did."

"Okay. Let's hear it, then."

She started off, shyly at first, and then, as she sang a few bars, her confidence grew.

As sweet Polly Oliver lay musing in bed,
A comical fancy came into her head.
Nor father, nor mother shall make me
False prove.
I'll 'list for a soldier and follow my love.

"That's all I can remember," she said.

"I said you could sing." He picked up her hand and kissed it. "Is that what you'd like to do, sweet pea? Follow me to war?"

"Women used to years ago. They used to do the cooking and washing and that."

"I guess there was plenty of 'and that'!"

"You're laughing at me."

"No. I'm not. I did hear some women went with their men folk during the Civil War."

"There were even women aboard HMS *Victory* when we won the battle of Trafalgar."

"Oh, for a life on the ocean wave!" David laughed.

He lay back against the bank, one arm behind his head, the other across his chest, and one leg drawn up.

She turned on her side, leaning on one elbow and holding her head in her hand. She looked down on him. His eyes were half closed, his skin, lightly tanned, was clear. He was twenty. Surely he shaved? There was a faint mark along his brow where his helmet had been. She looked at his helmet, lying on the grass beside him—part of this uniform he was wearing. These unfamiliar things he had on—no collar, no tie, his trousers tucked into those boots. Where was David—the handsome young man who had put that ring on her finger, the smart young man who wore a smart uniform, a shirt, a tie, and a jacket with shiny brass buttons and the US insignia and the "crossed rifles"?

This was a different David, who was soon going to war. This uniform would be what he'd be wearing when he scrambled up some French beach carrying his gun. His gun! She tried to visualise it but couldn't. He wasn't her David. He belonged to the army, and the army belonged to America. He had already been in action, carrying his gun. Had he shot anyone?

Had he killed anyone? Was he at all scared? She looked at his hand, lying so innocently across his chest. The fingers were long and slim; his forefinger—wasn't that what they called the "trigger finger"? She put her own forefinger alongside his. He trapped it between his thumb and the side of his hand.

He looked up at her, his eyes wide open now. "What are you thinking about, sweet pea?"

"I just wondered how you felt . . . if you were . . . you know . . . scared."

"About what?"

"Going over to France. About going into battle again, now the time's near?"

"I guess we're all a bit scared. We don't know what's waiting for us. Hanging around doesn't help. It was nearly all over in Italy when we got there. This time, it's going to take a bit longer. Anyhow, you don't have much time to get scared. There's someone shouting orders at you, telling you where to go and what to do. Were you scared when the blitz was on . . . when Salisbury was bombed?"

"We only got bombed a couple of times. I don't think I was so much scared. I thought it was a nuisance. It was stopping me from doing what I wanted to do. But I was scared in 1939 when everyone was wondering if there was going to be a war. I thought that if there was, my dad would have to go and he might not come back."

"He was in the last war, so you thought he'd have to go again?"

"Yes. It was the last summer holiday before the war. We went on a railway outing to the seaside. It was nearly time to go home, and I went down to get some water in my bucket to wash the sand off my feet before I put my socks and sandals on. Dad was there too, getting water for Clive. The tide was out, and the sand was very wet. Dad told me not to be long, and as he walked up the beach, I saw his footprints gradually disappear. I took it as a sign that there was going to be a war and he would go and I'd never see him again."

"But he didn't go."

"No. We went down Gran's for some reason later on that week. She, Mum, and Auntie Nell were sitting out the back. Dad and Uncle Sid were up the garden. Gran had a little table against the wall, and I was sitting on that. There were some seashells there—big ones, you know? Clive was putting them to his ear to see if he could hear the sea. It reminded me of

Dad's footprints going like they did, and I cried because I didn't want him taken away from me. Gran called me a daft turmot—"

"A what!"

"Turmot. It's what we call a turnip."

David shook his head slightly and said, "Go on."

"Well, I wasn't worried anymore because she told me that Dad wouldn't get called up, as railwaymen would be needed to take troops about and that he was probably too old anyway. Now I think of how Auntie Nell must have felt. She doesn't know if Teddy will ever come home."

"C'mon, sweet pea. Don't think about it. We'll get the Japs sooner or later."

He put his arm around her shoulders and pulled her down towards him. She lay with her face against his shoulder. He bent his head and kissed her brow.

"I love you, Ina," he said.

At last, he'd said it! "I love you, too, David," she replied, but it sounded silly and childish, like one of those simpering phrases in the women's magazines her mother read.

***

They lay silently. The clouds were low, and Ina hoped it wasn't going to rain. She could hear, faintly, the sound of the traffic moving along the main road. A bumblebee danced around a head of clover, darting in among the petals and then flying off, only to come back. Perhaps it thought there was more nectar to be had, or perhaps it didn't realise it was the same clover head. It was quiet, so quiet. Ina felt a sense of unreality. It didn't seem possible that she was here, in this field, with David.

This is me, she thought, *here and now.* She felt the slightest move on her part would crack open time itself. She would find herself back in the world she knew before she had even met him. She wanted, suddenly, to be closer to him—so close that she became part of him. A thought went through her mind so alien to her that it caught her breath. She could feel the warmth of his hands, one on her shoulder and the other on the top of her arm. His breathing was regular and deep and his heartbeats, steady.

If he asks me to "go somewhere" with him, I shall go!

The very thought made the colour rise in her cheeks. She waited for him to say something, but when he did speak, he said, "I think maybe we'd better take a stroll again."

Not knowing if she felt disappointed or relieved, she stood up and brushed herself down. She took her comb from her shoulder bag, and David, now standing with her, took it from her and gently drew it through her hair. She let herself revel in this act of intimacy. When he had finished he said, "There. Now you're fit for parade."

She smiled and put the comb back in her bag.

David picked up his helmet and crooked his arm for her to put hers through. Together, they walked the perimeter again, slowly. He bent down suddenly and picked a flower from the hedgerow.

"I know what this flower is," he said. "It's a buttercup. Hold up your chin; let's see if you like butter."

She laughed. "So you know that one. Do you make daisy chains as well?"

"Sure. We make daisy chains, not that I've made any lately." He smiled down at her. "We're not so very different, are we?" he said.

As they made their way towards the spinney, Ina noticed a gap in the hedge. Why hadn't she seen it before? She paused and looked through. In the field beyond, there were rows and rows of tanks. She gazed wide-eyed at them. The sight disturbed her. This afternoon she had been forcibly reminded of David's participation in the forthcoming invasion of France. Now these armoured monsters would be playing their part. The clouds passing over the sun cast wavering shadows across them. It looked as though they were already moving.

She heard David's voice at her side. "Looks like they're ready to roll," he said.

She pushed a fist hard against her mouth; nevertheless, a sob was wrenched from her throat. Her eyes started to burn and prickle. A tear ran freely down her cheek.

"Ina . . . Don't cry. I don't know what to do when girls cry. It makes me feel kind of awkward, like . . . maybe I'm gonna cry too!"

"I'm all right."

"It'll all be over before you know it. I'll be writing to tell you to pack your trunk and get aboard the ship to the States. Hey! I'll tell you what. I'm going to take you to the city and buy you pretty dresses and silk lingerie and a pair of nylons for every day of the week and high-heeled shoes—"

"And all the turkey I can eat, because I've never tasted it."

"Sure, and all the turkey you can eat."

"Where's all the money coming from?" she asked

"Don't you worry about that. I'll find it from somewhere."

She heard Stella's laugh and knew that, for her and David, their time together was over.

As Stella and Joe reached them, Joe put his hand on David's shoulder.

"Time to go, boy," he said.

One more kiss before we part, thought Ina.

She had her last kiss; they said their goodbyes, and she watched as the two men made their way towards the spinney.

Once, David looked back and gave a slight wave of hand, and then they were both gone; the spinney had closed behind them. Ina recalled her father's footprints in the sand. She felt now as she had then.

Tonelessly, she said, "I am never going to see him again."

Chapter 17

Monday morning, the skies were overcast.

"Better wear your mac," Hilda warned Ina. "It looks like rain before the day's out."

"Yes. All right, Mum."

"I could do with a new gab," Clive said.

"You'll be getting a new one to go back to school with in September," his mother told him. "You've not long had a new school uniform, so you'll have to hold on to the one you've got now for a bit longer."

"He only had that one last year," protested Jim

"Two years ago, Jim. He's grown a bit since then."

Jim grunted and went back to his newspaper. Ina was glad that no one asked her why David had been confined to camp. Hilda had other things on her mind, and if her father had any notion why, he did not put his thought into words, although he had looked at her a few times as though he was going to speak. She'd tried not to engage his eye and had managed to avoid searching questions. She got up from the table and went into the hall to fetch her raincoat.

Coming back, she heard a knocking on the front door. Opening it, she saw a railway call boy on the doorstep. He handed her a piece of paper. She went back into the living room and handed it to Jim. "Call boy, Dad."

"What do they want?!" He unfolded the piece of paper. "They want me to go back in."

"When, now!?" Hilda said, holding a tray ready to clear the breakfast things.

"I'll have to go and get dressed," Jim said.

"Your clean railway things are in the cupboard on the landing. I'd better do you some sandwiches."

"No. Don't bother; I'll get something in the canteen."

Ina put her own sandwiches into her bag, said goodbye, and went into the back garden.

She had just reached the shed when Hilda called to her from the back door. "Bring Dad's bike out, will you, Ina? Bring it round to the side, please."

Ina brought her father's bike out and then her own. Precariously, she wheeled both along the garden path and left Jim's leaning against the side wall.

Cissie's back door opened; she called to Hilda. "Do you know what's going on, Hilda? We've just had the call boy. Alb has to go in. He was rest day today and all."

"No, Cissie, I don't. Jim was called in as well. He wasn't on till two."

"I don't know," grumbled Cissie. "We were going out this afternoon. Now I don't even know what time he'll be home."

"Jim's going to get some dinner at the canteen."

"I suppose Alb could as well. Who'd be married to a railway man?"

***

Ina and Stella were in the staffroom when Vera walked in.

"Did you see your George?" Stella asked to Vera's reflection in the mirror.

"No." Vera replied quietly. "He's confined to barracks. He phoned our neighbour with a message."

"Didn't say why, I suppose?"

Vera did not answer, just shook her head. Stella finished combing her hair and put the comb back into her handbag.

"Did you see yours?" Vera asked them both.

"Ours were confined to barracks as well," Ina told her. Best not to say they had broken camp.

"Don't worry too much, Vera," Ina said. "They may get a stand-down."

Vera shrugged. "I don't know what we're going to do if he's over in France in August, and we can't get married. My dress is nearly finished, and we've booked the church and the hall. My mum's got all the invitation cards . . ." She looked close to tears.

There was nothing Ina or Stella could say. When Mrs Gray came in later, she remarked how quiet everything seemed coming through town. "Ern said it was a real treat last night not to have any trouble in Castle Street," she said.

"There's nothing to report then," Stella said.

Mrs Gray looked at her searchingly, but Stella's face gave nothing away.

Ina felt she now had something in common with Vera. Stella seemed to have accepted the fact that this was the prelude to Joe and David going to France, and there was no change to her usual cheery self. Ina, on the other hand, felt downcast. She wondered how she would cope with not seeing David for a long while . . . or never meeting him again.

***

Ina, putting her bicycle in the shed, noticed her father's wasn't there.

"No Dad?" she asked her mother as she went into the kitchen.

"No," Hilda replied, "and I don't know when he'll be home."

"Why do you think he was called in, Mum?"

"Lord knows. I don't know whether to put a dinner up for him or not."

"A boy at school said he'd seen a train loaded up with tanks," put in Clive.

"When did he see them?" Ina asked.

"This morning, on his way to school. He said they weren't actually moving, but a man on the bus told him they were probably going to Southampton or Portsmouth or somewhere on the coast. Do you reckon Dad and Mr Daley will have to drive them down?"

"I've no idea," his mother told him. "All I know is it seems to be so hush hush they can't tell drivers' wives what time their husbands will be home for their tea."

"What about the soldiers, Mum? Do you think Dad'll be taking them down?" Clive went on. Then, without waiting for an answer, he turned to Ina. "Perhaps David will be among 'em, Ina. Just think, he's going to France to fight the Germans—"

"For heaven's sake!" cried Ina. She got out of her chair and went into the front room.

Hilda turned to Clive. "You're supposed to be an intelligent boy. Sometimes I wonder . . . It's all those stupid comics you read. Go into the front room and apologise to her."

Clive looked at Hilda. "I didn't think," he muttered.

"Well! Do as I ask."

Clive went into the front room. Ina was stood looking out the window.

"Sorry," he said. "I didn't mean to upset you. David will be all right. He'll come back."

Ina said nothing, just turned to face him and nodded. Together they went back into the living room.

***

It was nearly midnight when Jim finally got home. Hilda sat in an armchair wearing her nightdress.

"Haven't you gone to bed, then?"

"I thought you might want something to eat."

"No. There was a Red Cross stall down on the docks, and the WVS was there so we could get a cuppa and some sandwiches. I had some cottage pie in the canteen."

"Was it Southampton Docks?"

"Yes. And we went to Portsmouth Harbour. A lot of Yank stuff went to Weymouth."

"Was it tanks you took down?"

"Them and some field guns and limbers . . . other stuff . . . It was all, I don't know, sort of unreal, if you get what I mean."

"Did you take any troops down?"

"No. No men. I expect they'll go by road transport; either that, or they'll be taken by train later. There may have been some down there already."

"Do you think it's the start then, Jim?"

"Could be, could be. There was a lot of gear already down there. Tell you one thing, if it is, they're not going to have good weather for it."

***

Ina was in the field at Tidworth. It didn't look quite the same. She couldn't see the church, and she knew it was here she was meeting David. Where was Stella? Had she missed the bus? Suddenly, she was back in town, by the bus stop. All these buses were coming in. People were getting off but no Stella. She thought she saw her as one of the buses pulled out. Why hadn't she gotten off? There were two soldiers with her, American soldiers? Was it David and Joe? Why were they still on the bus? They were laughing and waving to her. There was a buzzing in her ear—like the bee in the clover. It became louder and louder. Far away, she could hear her name being called.

Through the haze of sleepiness, Clive's face came to her; he was bending over her. The haze cleared. She was awake, but the buzzing continued.

"What is it?" she asked.

"Look out the window!"

Ina knelt up on her bed and drew the curtains back. Wave after wave of aircraft filled the sky, some towing gliders. The sky was black with them.

"It's the invasion, Ina," Clive said, quietly and gently. He did not want to upset his sister again.

Ina just looked. Whatever feelings of fear and apprehension she might have had were overwhelmed by the greater feeling of awe. Reaction would come later.

***

Stella looked a little pale.

"Are you all right?" asked Ina as they walked along Endless Street.

"Yes. I'm all right. Didn't get much sleep last night."

As they reached Queen Street, Stella looked in the direction of the newspaper man standing on the corner of the Blue Boar Row.

"Didn't take long for the news to break."

"Invasion Latest," screamed the news board.

"I don't suppose the newsmen got much sleep last night either," Ina commented.

"It's funny, isn't it? We've become part of it."

"How?" Ina asked.

"Well, we've got our boyfriends in it."

"I wonder what they're doing now," mused Ina.

"Probably wishing they were somewhere else," Stella replied.

***

If Ina thought Stella pale, Vera looked like a ghost. Dark rings were under her eyes, it was obvious she had been crying. She said nothing, so Ina and Stella kept their thoughts to themselves. Mr Phillips' only comment was to hope the sea was not too rough for the crossing and asking them to keep things low-key if customers were to engage in any conversations.

For Ina's part, she wanted to keep off the subject of the invasion anyway.

Not so Mrs Gray. The temptation to air her views was more than she could resist and, dying to get a dig in about the Yanks and their behaviour was so paramount that the fact she would also let some of her barbs fall in Vera's direction did not occur to her. It being Tuesday and a market day, she could not get an edge in until the middle of the afternoon when trade had slackened off.

One of her customers had remarked on the quietness of the town in spite of it being market day. "I expect it will seem very quiet in Salisbury tonight," she had said. "It's a pretty anxious time for those whose men folk have gone."

"Yes," was Mrs Gray's response, "but look how nice it will be without all those soldiers, especially those Yanks, and we're able to walk the streets of Salisbury without bumping into them and the common tarts they go with."

The woman looked at her and raised her eyebrows but said nothing. Mrs Gray set her lips tight. She had been expecting agreement.

"Look," the woman said, "I haven't got as much time as I thought." She took off the shoe she had been trying on. "Perhaps I can get in later in the week." She put her own shoes on and left the shop.

Stella, who had overheard the conversation, said, "Lost a sale, Mrs Gray?"

Mrs Gray coloured. "She didn't have as much time as she thought."

"You embarrassed her more like. How do you know she didn't have a daughter going out with a soldier?"

"More fool her."

"And what about Miss Welland?"

"And more fool her too."

"Haven't you got a little bit of sympathy?"

"Why? All you girls who go out with soldiers, whether they're Yanks or British, knew they would be going to war, so you've only got yourselves to blame if you're on your own."

Mr Phillips who had been in the staffroom for a late break came through the door at that moment and overheard Mrs Gray's comments. So did Vera, and with a sob, she ran through the door to the staffroom.

"That's an unfortunate remark you made, Mrs Gray," Mr Phillips told her.

Ina said, "Shall I go after her?"

"Yes. Go on, Miss Welland."

Ina, herself looking pale and near to tears, went after Vera.

"I really don't know what all the fuss is about," said Mrs Gray petulantly.

Stella faced her. "Those boys that are going over there are going to fight. You've never had any kids so you've got no one to go. You're all nice and safe here, and your Ern's in a good job in a factory so some other poor bloke can fight your war. A lot of them won't come back, so it looks like you'll have Salisbury to yourself for a good long time."

Stella was only just keeping her temper under control.

Mr Phillips who had let the confrontation run its course, now said, "All right, ladies. I think that's enough for now. We'll have the customers thinking the invasion's taking place in the shop."

After a while, Ina came back, followed by a white-faced Vera. As Vera walked through the shop, a customer came in. Being first sales, she immediately went forward and asked if she could help.

"That," hissed Stella to Mrs Gray, "is what I call guts!"

***

Hilda looked at Ina anxiously as her daughter came into the living room.

"You look a little pale."

"I'm all right. Don't put me up a lot to eat. I don't feel very hungry."

"You must eat."

219

"Yes. But not too much, Mum, please."

"I'll have her share," Clive said.

"No, you won't, she may feel hungry later on."

"Dad back to normal now?" Ina asked.

"Yes. If you can call what's going on normal." Hilda gave a small sigh.

"He looked done in when he went to work."

"They landed at Normandy," Clive chirped.

"Normandy?" Hilda's answer was vague.

"Yes, Mum, you know, where King William I came from—the king who conquered us in 1066. Our history master said we're right in the middle of making history now."

"In that case," Ina told him, "I hope we stop making it—the sooner, the better."

Clive went on into the front room to do his homework.

"You'll have to be a little patient with Clive, Ina. He doesn't understand much about the war. It's all a big adventure to him, like something out of those blessed comics he reads. He's very proud of Avril being in the WAAF and Brian in the RAF. Now that he knows David is part of what's going on—" She added, quietly, "He's a kid who likes to boast a bit to his school chums, like the ones who have probably got fathers and brothers fighting."

"Yes. I know. We had a bit of trouble with Mrs Gray today."

"What's she been up to?"

"She upset Vera and me too. Going on about how nice it was to have all the troops gone and how she could have Salisbury to herself and it was the girls' own fault they'd been left on their own. They shouldn't go out with soldiers. She dragged the Yanks into it as well. Why are some people so nasty? Mrs Daley might be a bit sarcastic at times; it's because she's a snob. But I don't think she'd go that far."

"No. Cissie has Harold in the army now. That's the last thing she'd say."

***

Friday morning, a letter came. Ina picked it up from the doormat.

"It's from David!" she cried

"I don't know if you've got time to read it now, Ina. It's twenty to nine."

But Ina had already torn open the envelope.

Hello, Sweet pea.

We've been told to write our letters before we leave. Can't say a lot, as the post is waiting on us. Just want to say thanks for the good times we've had together, and I shall miss you like hell. Seems funny to think I shan't be making anymore trips to Salisbury to see you or have you coming out here. I'll remember our times together all the while I'm in Europe. I've written to my mom. Can you write her a few lines? Tell her I'm okay, will you? Give my regards to your folks. Tell them thanks again for the party. Don't worry if you don't hear from me for a while. Somehow I think we're going to be kind of busy.

Take care of yourself.

Love,
David

***

She asked Stella if there had been a letter from Joe.

"No. Should there have been?"

"Well. I thought . . . as David had written—"

"He'll write when he wants to," she said.

"I wonder why I only got the letter this morning. He must have written it Monday."

"Perhaps he missed the post. Isn't there a date on the letter?"

"No."

"You got a letter anyway, so what's the problem?"

***

That night, Ina wrote to David and his mother. She had bought some picture postcards on her lunch hour to send to her mother-in-law-to-be, one each of the cathedral, the Poultry Cross, and Stonehenge. On the back of the cathedral card, she had written, "This is where we went when we first met." On the Poultry Cross, "This is where we met when we bought my ring." And on the back of Stonehenge, she'd penned, "I went here once on a school trip. Haven't been there since. It's very old but, really, just a heap of stones."

Chapter 18

Towards the end of June, Ina still felt the strangeness of being without David. Going to the cinema, she could hardly wait for the newsreels to begin, and when they did—showing the progress of the Allied advance—she clung to her seat and stared at the figures on the screen, willing David to appear. He never did. But there could always be another time. Walking around town during the lunch hour, Ina paused in front of a photographer's window.

"I'd like to get my photo taken for David," she said.

Stella pointed to a sign on the door.

"They close from twelve to two and all day Wednesday. Unless you get time off work, I don't know when you will get it done."

"We could go to Fordingbridge; their half day is Thursday," suggested Ina, "You'd like yours taken, wouldn't you?"

"I don't mind; I suppose I could." Stella didn't seem to be at all enthusiastic.

"It'll be a change to go somewhere different. We could go straight from work and get something to eat over there."

"All right, if you say so," Stella replied.

"Joe would like a photo of you, wouldn't he?"

"I suppose I could send him one," Stella conceded.

"So, it's on, then?" Ina persisted.

"Anything for a quiet life," Sighed Stella.

***

The next Wednesday, they boarded the bus at the bus station and were well on their way when Stella asked, "Have you ever been to Fordingbridge before?"

"No," Ina said. "I've been through it on the way to the New Forest."

"How will we know when to get off?"

"It's the first big place we come to. Anyway, we can ask the conductress, like we did the first time we went to Tidworth."

They were set down in what looked like the town centre.

"Which way do we go now?" Stella was peering up and down the road.

"Let's just stroll around," Ina suggested.

"It'll be a change looking at different shops. Oh, look!" she exclaimed "There's a shoe shop!"

"Is that what you've come all this way for, then, to look at shoe shops?"

They stood looking in the window.

"I rather like those blue suede court shoes," Stella remarked. "I wonder if we will ever get anything like that in Burton's?"

They wandered along the street, first up one side and then down the other. They found the photographer's wedged between an optician's and a hairdresser's.

"Handy, that," remarked Stella. "You can get your hair done and then pop next door to get your photo taken."

Inside the shop was a long counter. At one end was a display of cameras—old, mostly, and probably second-hand; at the other were cardboard cut-outs of happy smiling faces, advertising films. There was no sign of any rolls of film. Around the walls hung photographs of wedding groups, children, single portraits, and men and women in uniform. Some were obviously not recent.

A woman stood behind the counter. She smiled at them as they approached. "Can I help you?"

"We'd like our photos taken, please," Ina said.

"I'll just get Mr Stone for you," replied the woman. She turned and knocked on a door behind the counter and called through, "There are two young ladies here who would like to have their photographs taken."

The door opened, and Mr Stone stepped through into the shop. He was a tall, lean man with shock of untidy grey hair and a large bushy moustache. He wore a black alpaca coat and mittens, and his fingers were stained brown.

"Yes ladies," he said, breezily. "Perhaps you'd like to step inside."

He stood to one side, and they entered the room beyond. It was quite dark inside, and for a while, they had a job to see exactly where they were. Mr Stone followed them in and switched on a light.

"Right," he said, "singly or together?"

"Singularly, please," Ina told him

"Right," he said again "Who's first?"

"She is," said Stella, giving Ina a little push. "It was her idea."

In front of a backdrop of branches of cherry blossom was a white, upholstered dressing stool. Mr Stone motioned Ina to sit down and then walked across the room and switched off the light. He turned on an arc lamp and disappeared under a cloth over the camera.

"Very still, now," he said. "Nice smile."

After a while, he emerged from under the cover.

"There. That's fine," he said.

***

Ina got up from the stool, and Stella took her place.

When the session was over, Mr Stone led them back into the shop. From somewhere underneath the counter, he produced a large book, which he opened and, picking up a pencil, asked them how many prints they wanted.

"Three for me," Ina answered.

"I'll just have two," was Stella's reply.

He wrote in the book. "They'll be ready by next Wednesday," he said.

"Could you post them to us please?" Ina asked him.

"Yes, but I'm afraid I'll have to charge you postage."

"That's all right." Ina told him.

He entered their details in the book. "You've come from Salisbury then?"

"Yes. It's early closing this afternoon, and we don't have time to go to the photographer's on our break."

The transaction completed, the girls left the shop.

"I could do with a cup of tea and something to eat," Ina remarked as they walked along the street.

"I won't be able to afford much," said Stella, "not after paying for the photographs."

"We need only have a sandwich or something," Ina told her, "just a snack."

They found a small café in a side road. A bell over the doorway jangled as they opened it and walked in. There was no one else inside and no sign of anyone serving. They sat down and waited. On the counter at the end of the café were two large urns beside covered plates of sandwiches and teacakes but nothing else in view. Stella got up, went over to the door, and opened it; the bell jangled once more.

This time, a woman came through a curtained archway behind the counter. She wore a crossover pinafore, carpet slippers, and round her head, a turban that obviously hid an array of Dinkie hair curlers. "Yes?" she asked, ungraciously.

"Two teas, please," said Stella.

The woman poured the tea from one of the urns. "Milk?" she asked.

"Yes, please."

"Sugar?"

"No, thank you."

She brought the teas over and put them down in front of the girls.

"Have you anything to eat?" asked Stella.

The woman nodded her head towards the counter. "Egg sandwiches or toasted teacakes, that's all."

"I'll have a toasted teacake," Stella said.

"I'll have the same," Ina added.

The woman went back to the counter, put two teacakes onto a plate, and took them through the curtain into the kitchen.

"I didn't fancy those egg sandwiches," Stella whispered. "From where I'm sat, it looks like the corners are turning up on them. It's probably reconstituted dried egg powder anyway—horrible muck!"

"Not a bit like our nice little café behind the bus station."

"No," Stella agreed, "nor the Bib and Tucker."

Stella took a sip of her tea and pulled a face. "Strewth! This tea is nearly cold!"

"It tastes stewed to me. What do you think?"

"Reconstituted eggs and reconstituted tea leaves," Stella answered.

The woman came back with their teacakes.

"I'll take the money now, if you don't mind. It's sixpence each, thruppence for the tea and thruppence for the teacake."

The girls looked at each other. Tuppence for a cup of tea was the general charge anywhere else, and teacakes were only a penny each in any baker's shop; even allowing for the toasting and buttering, it was over the odds. What was more, the cakes were only toasted one side and burnt on the other. Nevertheless, they handed over the coins, which the woman hastily put in her pocket. Before she went through the curtain again she called over her shoulder, "Don't forget to shut the door behind you when you leave."

"Funny woman!" Stella remarked.

"She obviously trusts us not to rob the till," Ina said.

"It's probably empty anyway." Stella pushed her teacake to one side. "With her prices, I doubt if she has many customers."

"Only mugs like us!" Ina grinned.

"Come on. Let's go." Stella got up from her chair.

Leaving the unfinished teacakes, they left the café. As she went through the door, Stella turned the "open" sign to "closed."

***

Once back in the street, they continued to amble along gazing through the shop windows. The day was warm but there was a breeze blowing. They came to a bridge and stood looking over it into the water.

"David told me once," remarked Ina, "that if you looked at the water long enough, it would feel as if you were moving."

Swans were drifting along the river. The girls watched them as they floated down stream.

"We should have brought the teacakes to give them," Ina remarked.

"Why?" asked Stella. "What have they done to you?"

They heard a rumbling behind them and, turning round, noticed a truck coming towards them. As it drew closer, they could make out the American white star on the side of the vehicle. It was carrying a passenger load of GIs. There were wolf howls and whistles as the truck passed by and the girls were spotted.

"Hi, there, girls!" one of them called. "Want some chocolate?"

227

He threw something from the truck, and it landed on the pavement a little way from them. Ina bent forward to retrieve it. She picked up a small paper bag.

"It's four bars of chocolate and two packets of gum," She said.

They both waved their arms to the soldiers, who waved back until the truck was out of sight.

***

The next letter to come from David caused Ina a little concern. When she thought of David, she saw him as they portrayed the troops on the cinema newsreels, marching along a road, waving to the cameras, or squatting down somewhere in groups reading their mail. Now she saw him as a soldier fighting a war in a foreign country. He had written.

Dearest Ina

We are holed up here at the moment. I can't tell you where. We've been in action but are not hurt any. We haven't moved much since we stopped fighting, so I am writing this while I have the chance. Glad you wrote Mom. I heard from her. She got your letter and will write back. I don't rightly know how I feel about this place, not much I guess. Lots of ruined buildings that must have been folks' homes. I reckon there must be plenty of places like this in the UK. Thought about what you said to Sharkey. You were right. I sure could do with a good meal right now, roast beef and Yorkshire pudding. K rations aren't so hot.

Well, it looks as though we are getting ready to move out. Guess I'll have to close.

So long, sweet pea.

Love,
David

Chapter 19

July 1944

Ina came home from work and flopped down in the nearest chair.

"It's so hot!" she moaned. "I have had a rotten day; stupid women who can't make up their minds and stupid kids who just won't sit still while you're trying to get their feet into a pair of shoes."

Hilda took a letter down from the mantelshelf and handed it to her. "Here," she said. "This will cheer you up. It's from America; it came by the afternoon post."

Ina took the envelope and turned it over. "It's from David's mother," she said.

She read.

My dear Ina

Thank you for writing to me. It is so good to hear from someone who has been close to David. He has told me all about you and your nice family. I am pleased he has met a nice English girl. Did he ever tell you that his great-grandmother on my side of the family was English? She came from a place called Manchester. Is it anywhere near to you? I liked the picture cards you sent. Your cathedral is so grand and so big! We have nothing like it here. In the big cities maybe, but they wouldn't be so old. Your Poultry Cross must be very old too. I can see all the people long ago with their crates of hens. I guess they don't do that anymore. Where we live is not a big place, but we have a nice house and neighbours we call on. We have to drive a way into town to get our supplies.

I've heard from David since he got to Europe, but I don't hear from him or my son, Todd, as often as I wish. I try to understand they have a job to do, but I do worry so.

We hear what you have all been through in the UK with the bombing. It must have been dreadful for you all; you have been at war so long. I don't know how families have coped with all the rationing. We are lucky not to have been through all that I guess. I hope this war is over soon and we get our boys home. I look forward to the time when you can get over to the States. Write me again soon, Ina; give my regards to your folks.

Affectionately yours,
Olivia McKinley

***

The photographs came the next Thursday morning. Stella had received hers also.

"Well? What do you think of yours?" asked Ina as they studied them during the morning break.

"They're not bad," Stella answered. "What are you going to do with yours?"

"I'll send one to David and one to his mother. Mum can have the other one."

"What about your gran?"

Ina pondered for a while. "I suppose I ought to give her one really, shouldn't I?"

She put her photographs into her handbag. "I'll go to the phone box and phone the photographer and order two more. He put his phone number on the receipt. I can send a postal order for them and the postage."

***

It was two weeks before she heard from David again. The letter was a little lengthier than usual. Reinforcements had come up the line, and they were having a little respite. There hadn't been many people around but the few they had seen seemed pleased to see them. He and the other soldiers couldn't speak any French, and none of the French people could speak any English. There was a lot of handshaking and pecks on the cheek. One old lady took him by the hand, leading him through an open door into the kitchen. He wrote.

> *It scared the hell out of me. We're told that we mustn't go into their houses, just in case it's a trap and there are Germans in there. The other guys were hooting and hollering, "Your lucky day, Easton." I gathered she wanted me to take off my helmet. When I did, they called, "Don't forget to take your boots off!" I tell you, honey, I was really embarrassed. She took my helmet, and do you know what she did? She went to a cupboard, took six eggs out of a bowl, and put them in my helmet. The others were standing just outside the door. You should have seen their faces when they saw the eggs. We took them back to base and scrambled them in our mess tins over the fire. I sure think a lot of your photograph; I keep it in my wallet next to my heart. Some of the guys are saying when we get to Germany, if all goes well, we will get furloughs to the UK. If it happens, do you think your folks would let us get married?*

***

Later, Ina sounded her father about David's suggestion.

"No, Ina!" was Jim's reaction. "You're not getting married until the war is over."

"It may be by then!" she persisted.

"I'd rather you waited until he's back in America and settled in a job."

"Well, I still won't be able to go to America until the war's over."

"What's the rush? You've got all of your lives in front of you yet"

"If we're already married, the American government will pay my fare."

"Where did you get that idea from?"

"It was on the wireless. They were on about all the girls who had married American soldiers—GI brides they called them. They said they would get free passage over."

"Sounds a bit far-fetched to me."

"Honestly, Dad. If I get married before I go, you won't have to pay my fare. Please?"

"Let's just see what happens, shall we? He's not through France yet, let alone Germany."

"Will you think about it then?"

"Like I said, let's just wait and see what happens."

***

Ina and Stella had gone to the pictures Saturday night and Stella had stayed over at the Welland's. They had just finished Sunday lunch and were now helping Hilda to wash up. Jim sat at his chair in the living room reading his Sunday newspaper.

"Blooming newspapers," he muttered. "Can't even get a decent read on a Sunday. Six pages! I ask you, six pages! What news can you get on that?"

"They've been like that a long time, Jim," Hilda told him.

Clive chipped in. "There's a war on, Dad," he said.

"Is there any news about France?" Ina called.

"They reckon to be in Paris by the end of next month. Whether they will or not remains to be seen."

"Not very optimistic, is he," Ina said quietly.

"He's tired," said Hilda equally as quietly. "They're having problems. Some of the young firemen don't turn up for work, and it delays the trains."

"Aren't the fireman afraid of getting the sack?" asked Stella.

"That's just it," Hilda said. "They are in a government reserved occupation, and there is a shortage of manpower."

"But if they keep on doing it—" persisted Stella.

Hilda shrugged her shoulders.

"Don't they realise," Ina put in, "that there's young men their age and even younger fighting a war for them."

"Perhaps they just don't care," said Stella. "The railway ought to threaten them with the sack and tell them the army will get them and send them to France or Burma."

"What are you girls going to do this afternoon?" Hilda asked, changing the subject.

"We thought we would go down and see Gran," said Ina. "Stella wants to catch the five o'clock bus home, so we can't go far."

"You won't be here for tea then, Stella?"

"No, thanks. I promised my sister that I would babysit," Stella explained.

***

When Ina and Stella reached old Mrs Welland's house, they went along the passage that ran between the terraced houses to the back of the house. The passage led to the path that ran in both directions along the rear of the terrace and separated the residents from their gardens. They paused for a while at the Welland's garden, although it was Sid and Nell who kept it up these days. There was an archway over the gate into the garden, which was covered in honeysuckle. Irises, lupins, lilies, and gladioli flanked the fence between the garden and its neighbour on one side, and a sprawling mass of rambling roses the other. At the top of the garden, runner beans were climbing up their sticks. The frothy fronds of carrots grew beneath them, and a bush of ripening tomatoes was growing against the small garden shed.

"There's certainly a lot in there for a small garden," Stella remarked.

"Uncle Sid has an allotment down the meads near my dad's. They grow most of the vegetables there."

A voice behind them said, "Hello, you two. I thought I heard footsteps coming along the passage." It was Nell. She turned to go back inside the house, and the girls followed her. "We're in the front room," said Nell.

It was an old-fashioned room, just as Ina had always known it. Once, when she was small, she had asked Nell, "Why don't you have some modern furniture?"

"I don't think your gran would like it," Nell had replied. "Besides, she has had this furniture from when she was married. She wouldn't want to change it."

Perhaps, Ina had thought, *Auntie Nell and Sid will change it when Gran died.*

She recalled this to mind as she and Stella sat on the old horse hair sofa, her gran sitting in one of the matching armchairs and Uncle Sid sitting in the other.

"I'll make some tea." Nell went out to the kitchen.

"Everyone at home all right then, Ina?" asked her grandmother.

"Fine, thanks, Gran," answered Ina.

"Avril's coming home soon, isn't she?" the old lady continued.

"Yes," Ina replied, "early next month."

"Is Brian coming as well?" Sid asked.

"No. They can't get leave at the same time."

"That's a shame," said her grandmother. "That's the trouble with both of them being in the forces."

Nell came in with a tray of tea. "Have you heard from David lately?" she asked Ina.

"Yes, but he doesn't write very often," Ina replied.

"Bit awkward when they are on the move," answered Sid. "They never know when or where they are going to stop or for how long."

"Was it a bit like that in the last war, Uncle?"

"A bit. But it was a different sort of war. We were either stuck in the trenches or going over the top, and we never seemed to make much ground. Sometimes, we got a bit of respite and might visit a village if we were lucky. We weren't as mechanised as they are today, and we didn't have the equipment. I don't remember getting much air bombardment. We didn't have the planes. And, of course, we didn't have the airborne troops then."

"It said in Dad's newspaper that they reckon to be in Paris by the end of next month," Ina told him.

"Well," Sid replied, "they're not making bad headway at the moment."

The conversation fell into desultory talk, bringing Stella into it. Ina looked at the framed portraits on the wall, enlargements of photographs, old-fashioned and clouded around the edges after the fashion of the day. One was of Jim and Nell as children, sitting on a lawn either side of a big black dog. There was one of her grandparents on their wedding day. Her grandfather sat in a high-backed chair holding a trilby hat on his knees; her grandmother was standing to the side of him with her hand on his shoulder. Slim-wasted and high-bosomed, she was dressed in a bead-embroidered gown and had her hair piled up on her head. Then there was "Bertie-Who-Died". He had been their first and had died when he was two. On the rare occasions when her grandmother had spoken of him she always referred to him as "Bertie-Who-Died", and that is how Ina thought of him.

Once, as a small child, she had gone to Devizes Road cemetery with her grandmother to put flowers on the graves of her grandfather and the uncle who had died many years before she had been born. She had looked around her at the various monuments over the graves—tablets, angels, open books. Most of the graves had vases of flowers on them, some, white plaster lilies and doves under a large glass dome. She had taken it all in and thought to herself, *They are all dead people under there.* That night, she had lain in bed and the knowledge that she, too, would some day die had terrified her. She had tossed and turned to the degree that she had disturbed Avril, who had then gone to fetch their mother to comfort Ina.

She, Ina, had refused to consider anymore visits to the cemetery, and her grandmother, having been told, said to her, "You have far more to fear from the living than the dead."

***

It was time for Stella to be on her way to the bus station.

"There's a bus due up at the top," Nell informed her. "You should just about make it."

They reached the top of Ashley Road and saw the bus to town coming along Devizes Road. Ina saw Stella board the bus and then went home.

Hilda was laying the table for tea when Ina arrived. She got the cutlery out of the sideboard drawer and placed it on the table alongside the plates. Hilda went out and came back with a plate of bread and butter. No one had butter during the week; the week's ration was saved until Sunday. Ina looked at the bread first. She had almost forgotten the taste of prewar bread. She remembered the different loaves her mother used to get from the baker—cottage loaves, barrel loaves, farmhouse, and Cobergs. There was no telling what colour this bread was supposed to be; it was a sort of greyish brown. It was supposed to be healthy, having more wheat germ in it than white bread. Hilda brought in salad and a plate of sliced Spam. Ina went into the kitchen and fetched a Victoria sponge. *We don't do so badly, really*, she thought.

The family were sitting at the table when the clock on the mantle shelf struck six. Jim got up and turned the radio on.

"This is the BBC Home Service. Here is the six o'clock news, and this is Alvar Liddel reading it," came the voice from the radio.

Everyone was quiet while Jim listened to the news. The tea over, Jim left the table and sat down in his armchair. Quietly, Hilda stacked the tea things on a tray and took them out to the kitchen. Ina took what was left of the salad, covered it up, and put it on the marble slab in the larder. The remains of the sponge she put into a tin. Hilda turned on the Ascot, and hot water trickled into the washing up bowl; she sprinkled a handful of soda crystals into the water and swished them around until they dissolved.

"Have you thought about when you are going to have your week's holiday?" she asked Ina.

"Not really," Ina replied. "I know Vera is having hers in September. I don't know when Stella wants hers. We can't have them at the same time. Why do you want to know?"

"I just thought it would be rather nice to have some time with Avril. She's bound to be at a loss without Brian. Would you like to go to Guildford?"

"Both of us?"

"Yes. I can write a few lines to Grace. It would do you good to go away. I can write to Avril as well."

"I'll see Mr Phillips in the morning and tell him."

***

When Ina saw Stella the next morning, she asked her when she was taking her holiday.

"I don't know," Stella told her. "I shan't be going anywhere, why? When do you want yours?"

"The first week in August, if I can. Avril will be home for fourteen days, and I would like to spend some time with her. Mum suggested we could go to my auntie Grace's."

"That's all right. I'll have the week after. We'll have to okay it with the boss."

Mr Phillips was quite agreeable. It didn't matter about the short notice, he told them. It wasn't as though he had large amounts of staff with conflicting holiday requests.

***

Ina told her mother that she had arranged to take the first week in August off.

"Oh," Hilda said.

"What's the matter?" Ina asked.

"I should have thought the week after would have been better?"

"Why?"

"I wrote to auntie Grace to ask if it was all right for you and Avril to go to Guildford for the week. She has often said that she and Uncle George would like to see you both."

"I suppose it is a bit short notice, isn't it?"

"It means that no sooner than Avril gets here she will be off again. Oh, well, I don't suppose it will matter. I asked Grace to let us know as soon as she could."

"I can't change it now, Mum. Stella has put in for the week after."

"You'll have to let me know what you will be taking with you so I can get it all up together."

"It won't be much," murmured Ina.

Hilda wrote again to Guildford, telling Grace when the girls would like to come, and to Avril to tell her of the arrangement. Thursday morning, two letters arrived—one from Grace saying they would love to have the girls and, if Hilda told she and George what train they were catching, George would meet them. The other was from Avril to say that she would like to go to Guildford. "I shall be bringing all clean clothes with me," she wrote, "so you won't have to do any washing for me."

"Thank goodness for that!" commented Hilda

***

Friday morning, a letter came from David.

We are still plodding on towards Paris. Don't know how long it will take. I'm looking forward to it. See if it's all it's cracked up to be. I'll buy you something nice: some pretty undies or some perfume, both if you're lucky. I promise I won't get fresh with any Parisian girls.

Chapter 20

August 1944

Avril was there when Ina reached home Saturday night.

"Everything's all settled," she told Ina. "Mum and Dad have got it well organised. Dad's given us the times of the trains, and Mum's written to Auntie to let her know when to expect us. There's a fast train to London Waterloo about half ten Monday morning, and we should get to Woking about twelve."

"That's the only thing wrong with going to Guildford," Ina said, "changing trains at Woking."

"It won't take long," said Hilda. "At least you won't have to change at Basingstoke as well."

***

Monday morning, their suitcases were packed and standing in the hall. Sunday they had gone down their grandmother's to say goodbye to her and their aunt and uncle. Now they were waiting for the taxi that would take them to the station. Ina sat on the bottom stair, and Avril stood just inside the open front door. Outside on the path, by the garden gate, Jim stood with his pocket watch in his hand. When the taxi came into view, he called out, "It's here."

The taxi drew up, and the driver helped Jim to put the cases in the boot. The girls got in the back, and Jim sat beside the driver. At the station entrance, they saw Alb. He came over to the taxi.

"You're off then, girls. Catching the 10.32?" he asked.

They alighted from the taxi; the driver helped Jim take the suitcases from the boot of the car. Jim picked up one case and Alb the other.

"Are you driving our train up?" Ina asked Alb.

"No," he replied. "I'm just on the way home. I thought I would hang on and help your dad see you on the train."

"You'd better get on over to the ticket office," warned Jim. "Get there before there's a queue."

The girls moved over to the ticket office. Ina took out her purse and handed her money over to the clerk. Avril got her station card out with her money; she had already shown her warrant for her journey home, but her card would allow her to travel at a reduced fare, especially as she was wearing her uniform. Down the subway they went and then up the other side to the platform. There were, surprisingly, very few people waiting for the London train.

"Looks like you'll be lucky and get a seat," said Alb.

"What if there are a lot of passengers already on it?" asked Ina.

"There'll be plenty of people getting off here," Jim told her.

A dull clanging of a bell could be heard.

"She's on her way," said Jim.

***

The train could be seen coming around the bend. It came roaring along with plumes of smoke issuing from the chimney stack and stopped at the platform with a long drawn out *hiss* and a cloud of steam. Carriage doors opened all along the train, and as Jim had said, a stream of passengers stepped out of the train and disappeared down the subway. Jim ushered the girls into the nearest carriage and then climbed in himself and put their suitcases up on the luggage rack. Having satisfied himself they were settled, he rejoined Alb on the platform. The guard's voice drifted down the platform.

"Close all doors, please. Close all doors."

The sound of doors being slammed resounded along the platform. The guard blew his whistle, waved his flag, and got into the guard's van, and with a snort and a belch of steam, they were off. Both girls had a window seat opposite each other. At the corridor end on Ina's side sat an elderly man reading a newspaper; opposite him on Avril's side were two middle-aged women each reading a book. Avril stood up and removed her jacket; she folded it carefully and, sitting back down in her seat, laid it across her lap. She took off her cap and placed it on top of her jacket.

The elderly man looked up from his newspaper. "Would you like me to put your coat and hat on top of your suitcase?" he asked.

"Oh, yes, please," she answered. She lifted up her jacket and hat; he took them from her and very gently laid them on top of her case.

"Thank you very much." she said. "That's very kind of you."

"Not at all" he replied. He sat down again and went on reading his paper.

The two women cast a cursory glance in Avril's direction and then, they too, resumed their reading.

"We ought to have bought some magazines from Smith's bookstall," remarked Ina.

"I suppose so," Avril replied. "Never mind; we must remember to get some for the journey back."

She leaned her head back against the upholstery. Ina looked out of the window. She watched the fields and hedgerows as they flashed by, the woods and the backs of people's houses. Some people were sitting in deckchairs in their back gardens; in some, children played. At the back of the little terraced houses, zinc baths were hung up on a nail driven into the wall. As a child, she had looked from a train window at the scenery flashing by in fascination. It had seemed to her that it was all fixed to a massive roundabout as she could still see things in the distance even when those in front had gone by. She watched now as the telegraph lines seemed to dip low, only to be jerked up again when they met the next telegraph pole. They passed through several stations, stopping at Basingstoke. The man with the newspaper got out here, but the two middle-aged woman stayed where they were. No one else got into their carriage. As the train was running into Woking, it slowed down and ran along the track at a moderate speed.

Avril stood up. "We're here," she said.

She put on her jacket and cap and took down her suitcase. Ina reached for her own suitcase and rested it upon the seat. The train stopped with a jerk. Avril stepped past the two women, with Ina following, out into the corridor through the door and onto the platform.

A porter was passing by. "Let me have those," he said, picking up both cases as though they were empty. "Where are you going?" he asked.

"Guildford," replied Avril.

"Right, follow me."

He took them up the steps, along the covered way, and down another flight of steps to the platform where the Guildford train was standing.

"Here you are." He opened a carriage door, and the girls climbed in.

Being the only occupants, they left their cases on the carriage floor. The train moved off with a *whirling* sound, strange to the ear after the *chuff, chuff* of the steam train.

"Does Uncle George drive one of these electric trains?" asked Ina.

"I don't think so," Avril answered.

***

The journey was short. The unfinished structure of Guildford Cathedral came into view.

"Come on. We're here," Avril said.

Ina looked out the window as the train pulled into the station. "I can see Uncle George!" she cried, pointing to two figures that stood on the platform talking to each other.

"Oh, yes, I see," Avril confirmed.

The train stopped. George looked around and saw Ina waving from the window. He paused for a moment and then waved back.

"I don't think he recognised me at first," said Ina "What's the betting, the first thing he says to us is 'Haven't you grown.'"

They stepped out onto the platform. George and the other man came towards them.

"This is Arthur," George said indicating the other man. "He's staying with us for a while until he can get a house in Guildford."

Arthur was dressed in a uniform different from those usually worn by footplate men or other station staff, although it bore the Southern Railway insignia.

"These are the two girls from Salisbury who are staying with us," George explained to Arthur, "Avril and Ina. "We haven't seen them for some time. I hardly recognised them."

Arthur nodded at the girls and smiled but did not attempt to shake their hands. He picked up one of the suitcases and said, "I'm going to give George a hand getting you indoors."

The girls followed the men along the platform and up the steps to the passé meter. Once there, they turned left and went along to the exit.

Ina took a peek from the windows as she passed them. Avril turned and looked at her.

"I had to stand on tiptoe to do that last time," Ina said.

***

They came out into Guildford Park Road and took another turn to the left. Walking beside the iron railings edging the pavement, Ina looked through them down the steep bank onto the railway lines below.

"We used to look down there, didn't we? And watch the men hosing out the cattle trucks," remarked Ina.

"The things you remember!" answered Avril.

They crossed the road and arrived outside the gate. Grace must have seen them; by the time they reached the front door, it was open and she was standing just inside. She was of average height, slim, and angular. Her greying hair was in a roll around her head, the same way Stella often wore hers at work.

"Oh! Look at you both!" she cried. "All grown up! Did you have a good journey? How are your mum and dad and Clive? I expect you would like to freshen up, wouldn't you? George, take the girls cases up, will you? You must be hot in that uniform, Avril; I must say, though, it's very smart. Do you have to wear it all the time?"

"We have to wear uniform to and from the RAF Station, especially when we travel. I have my photo in uniform on my station card, and I have to show it when I use my travel warrant. I have brought some summer dresses with me. I shall be glad to get out of uniform."

"You go on upstairs and put your stuff away. Uncle George will bring you up a jug of hot water. There are clean towels on the washstand. I'll have the dinner all ready for you when you come back down."

They went upstairs and into the bedroom. George came up behind them with a large china jug filled with hot water, which he poured into the wash bowl on the washstand.

"Sorry you'll have to share the same water," he said. "Tomorrow when I'm out of the way, you can wash downstairs in the back kitchen; that's what Auntie Grace calls the scullery. I prefer to wash downstairs myself. I can splash about more. If you girls want a bath any time, just let me know, and I'll get the bungalow bath out of the shed and your aunt can light up the gas copper." He turned to go." Don't worry about the water," he said over his shoulder. "I'll empty the bowl later on."

***

With their clothes hung up in the wardrobe or placed in the chest of drawers and their toiletries arranged on the washstand, the girls, standing in their knickers and bras, proceeded to wash as carefully as they could without making a mess with the water. They washed their faces and arms and ran a flannel under their feet.

"We'll do the private bits tomorrow." Avril grinned.

"I've just thought of something," said Ina.

"What's that?"

"There's only a downstairs toilet here, isn't there? It means if we want to go during the night we'll have to go downstairs and outside."

Avril bent down and lifted up the bedspread. She put her hand under the bed and pulled out a chamber pot.

"We will just have to use the po," she said.

Wearing cotton dresses, stockingless and with their feet in sandals, their hair combed and make-up restored, the girls went down to the living room. The table was covered in a snowy white cloth with a blue patterned border. In the middle stood an EPNS cruet set, the condiments enclosed in small glass pots with a very small spoon protruding from the lid of the mustard pot. A glass dish of salad was nearby with a small dish of beetroot beside it. All this was accompanied by a bottle of sauce, a bottle of salad cream, a jar of chutney, and a jar of pickled onions. Grace came through from the back kitchen with a dish of steaming new potatoes, closely followed by George carrying a plate of cold, sliced bacon.

"Ah. There you are. Sit down," Grace said.

The girls took their place at the table alongside their hosts.

"Tuck in, girls," said George. "Help yourselves."

There was the clink of cutlery against china and the passing of dishes. Plates were filled, and the meal began.

"Oh, Auntie," said Avril "I nearly forgot, I've got my ration card with me and Ina's got her book."

"Oh, have you, dear? Give them to me later on. I shan't do any shopping until tomorrow."

"Isn't Arthur going to join us?" asked Ina.

"No. He was on an hour's break. He had to take a train to Portsmouth," George explained.

"Is he a driver?"

"He's a motorman. That's what they call drivers on the juice."

"Juice? What's the juice?" Ina wanted to know.

"The electric trains."

"Like the one we came from Woking to Guildford on?"

"I think you must have been on them before," put in Grace. "We've had electric lines in Guildford for a long time."

"Long before the war," said George.

"I suppose we must have been then," Avril agreed.

"This is a nice spread you have put on for us, Auntie," said Ina. "That joint of bacon must have been your ration for a month."

"Well, it was," said Grace with a smile. "We don't have bacon during the week, so that's what I do, save the ration and then get a joint. Sometimes we have it for Sunday roast, as it helps with the meat ration."

"Mum does that sometimes," Ina said.

"All the salad came from my allotment," George explained. "All accept the cucumber."

"We do very well on the whole," said Grace.

"I grow what I can in the garden," George went on. "We've got a few runners and broad beans. We've pulled some carrots and the beetroot we've got here. Not much room for anything else. Auntie Grace likes a few flowers and a bit of lawn, so I didn't dig it all up. I grew the spuds in the allotment."

"Don't forget the rhubarb, George."

"Oh, yes, the rhubarb. I grew that on the allotment too. Hope to get some bushes in later on—gooseberry and currant."

"We've got some of the rhubarb for afters," Grace told them. "I made a pie. It is warming up in the oven now. If everyone's had enough, I'll dish it up." She stood up and started to collect the plates. The girls made to rise. "No. You stay there. It won't take me long."

They heard the oven door open and then close again. Soon, Grace came back in bearing a large enamel pie dish and set it onto the table. She returned to the kitchen and, this time, came back with four desert dishes in one hand and a milk jug in the other.

"I managed to get a big tin of evaporated milk," she said. "I thought we could have it over the pie."

As Grace broke the crust, the aroma of hot rhubarb wafted over them. She cut through the pastry and spooned pie into the individual dishes, passed them around, and told everyone to help themselves to the evaporated milk.

When she sat down, she asked Avril how her boyfriend was. "Brian, isn't it?"

"Yes, Brian. His family lives at Harnham."

"I think I remember your mum telling me. He's not on leave with you, then?"

"No. We don't get together very often. The last leave we had at the same time was last Easter. We haven't seen each other since then. If we do get a forty-eight hour pass, by the time we've reached home, it's time to turn around and go back again."

Grace turned to Ina. "And what about your boyfriend, Ina? He's American, your mum tells me."

"Yes."

"Whereabouts in America does he come from?" asked George.

"Alabama. But he wants to go to Florida when the war's over."

"That's where all the rich people go—film stars and that, isn't it?" George smiled.

"Well." Ina smiled back. "If I'm going with him, there'll be two people who won't be rich."

"He hasn't got a big ranch in Alabama, then?"

"No. His people have a small farm, and I don't think it brings in a lot of money."

"I suppose he's in France, isn't he?" asked Grace.

"He went over on D-Day."

"Do you hear from him often?"

"He writes when he can. Dad says you can't fight a war and write letters every five minutes as well."

"No. I don't suppose he can."

I wish she wouldn't keep asking me all these questions, Ina thought to herself.

And immediately she felt mean and ungrateful.

As if Grace had read her thoughts, she said, "We didn't have any Americans here; we had Canadians. The girl two doors away is engaged to one. Nice boy. He's in France. There's still one or two of them around."

The meal was over. Grace got up and, this time, didn't demur when the girls rose also. Together, they cleared the table of cutlery, plates, and food. George got up and, taking the tablecloth off, took it outside the back door and shook it. Bringing it back inside, he carefully folded it and put it in the sideboard drawer. A very large kettle was simmering on a low gas. Grace bent down and took an enamel bowl from under the sink. Putting some cold water into the bowl, she put her hand in and then poured in the hot water from the kettle.

After the washing up was done and everything put away, the girls went into the living room while Grace made tea. She brought it in on a tray with the milk, cups, and saucers. A green tapestry cloth with a tasselled fringe round the edge covered the table now. Onto this, Grace put down the tray. She poured milk into the cups and poured the tea in through a strainer.

"Here we are then," she said as she handed the cups round. She sat down. "What are you two going to do this afternoon?"

"I don't think we have really thought about it," Avril answered.

"Well, you must feel free to come and go as you wish; it's your holiday. I have all this week off from the hospital. I don't have to go until next Monday. I only work part-time, ten to four, and no weekends. I don't think I could stand the heat in those kitchens for longer, especially this weather. Why don't you have a walk into town? I won't go in with you now, but if you want me to go anywhere with you, you only have to ask."

"Perhaps that's what we'll do, then," said Avril.

"Yes, all right," agreed Ina. Her head was spinning a little. Auntie Grace dodged from one subject to another and then back again. Ina found it difficult to keep track of what she was saying.

***

They followed Grace's instructions on how to get to town. They crossed the railway bridge and followed the road until they came to a flight of stone steps to the road below; walked on until they came to the bridge over the river Wey; continued until they reached the end of the road, where they turned right; and then went left past the Friary brewery and onto North Street.

"There doesn't seem to be a lot up here," Ina remarked.

"Auntie said the big shops were on High Street," Avril told her. "I think there's some little alley ways we go up."

"Do you remember any of this?" asked Ina.

"Vaguely," admitted Avril.

They crossed over the road and took a turn to the right.

"Oh look!" cried Ina, "a Market Street."

"I wonder if they've got a Burton's shoe shop?" smiled her sister.

At the top of Market Street, they came out to High Street.

"I remember that archway," Avril said, pointing to Tunns Gate. "I seem to remember going through there and up a steep hill. We went to some sort of ruined castle."

"I remember that as well. It was high up on a steep mound, and a path wound round it like a spiral staircase. I wanted to climb up there and go inside. Dad wouldn't let me, and I cried. He gave me tuppence for an ice cream to shut me up."

"Didn't I get an ice cream?"

"Don't think you cried."

"Spoilt brat!" hissed Avril.

Chapter 21

They caught the bus back. It stopped on Guildford Park Road quite near the house. Grace was in the back kitchen. "Ah, there you are!" she cried.

"We're not late, are we?" enquired Avril anxiously.

"No. No. Not a bit. We'll have a bit of tea, and then we can go outside and sit in the garden for a while. That'll leave the table free for Arthur when he comes in."

The white cloth went back out on the table and plates were put around. Grace went into the back kitchen and started to cut slices of bread. Ina offered to spread the margarine on.

"Yes please, dear. I just hope it isn't too soft. This weather melts it in no time, even though it's kept in an earthenware dish on the cold slab. And as for the butter . . . well, it just goes nowhere. It's not as if we have a lot to start with. Put the bread on that blue and white plate, will you, Ina? In the cupboard up there"—she pointed to the kitchen cabinet standing against a wall—"you'll find a pot of blackcurrant jam and a jar of Betox."

Betox! thought Ina and remembered the day that she and Stella had first met David and Joe.

"Is there anything I can do, Auntie?" asked Avril.

"Yes, there's a biscuit tin in the other cupboard with an iced sponge in it. I got it from the co-op this morning, so it's nice and fresh."

While the trio sat at the table, Grace asked the girls what they had done in town.

"We just mooched around looking at the shops," said Avril. "We fancied going to that ruined castle. I know we went there with Mum and Dad, but I couldn't remember exactly where we went after going through that archway."

"Tunns Gate," said Grace.

"Yes, Tunns Gate. I know we went up a steep hill . . ."

"Pewley Hill," said Grace.

"Yes. Then I didn't know where we went from there."

"I remember something," put in Ina. "On the corner where the two roads met there was a joke shop—had all sorts of things in the window, like rubber spiders and itching powder and false beards. I remember the shop door had a big poster on it with a woman's face, smiling. Over the top, it had 'Laugh like' and underneath, 'Helen B. Merry'."

They all looked at her.

"Well," she finished lamely. "That's what I remember."

"If you want to see the ruins, we could go up in the week," Grace told them. "It's not actually a castle it's the 'keep' of a castle that was once there. The grounds are nicely kept. The garden should be looking lovely now."

After the tea things had been cleared away, George took the girls into the garden. A wooden seat stood against the dividing wall between them and the garden next door.

"I made that seat myself," George informed them.

"Did you?" Ina asked.

"Yes. It was an old sofa. I stripped it down to the frame, and then I put the slats across."

The girls looked at the seat. It did not look very comfortable.

Grace came out. "You'll want some cushions on that," she commented and went back inside.

George fetched two deckchairs from the shed and erected them. "Here you are, girls; you have these. Auntie doesn't like them. She has a job to get out of them."

Grace came out with two large cushions. She put them on the seat, and she and George sat down. Ina leaned back in the deck chair and studied the garden. It was not as large as the one at home, but there seemed to be space for everything it contained, although the two deck chairs did not leave a lot of room for manoeuvre. George's runner beans were sprouting out long green fingers, and the broad beans were in flower. There was not a profusion of flowers but enough to give colour to the borders. Clumps of iris, lilies, lupins, and wispy golden rod fringed the opposite wall. A begonia was in full bloom.

The thing that really caught her attention was the low half-submerged structure on top of which earth had been thrown and that was now crowned with an assortment of small, spreading annuals. It was an air raid shelter. Suddenly, she was jerked back to the reality of war still going on around them. At home, they did not have a shelter. Dad said they'd be just as safe under the stairs. Here, there was no "under the stairs"; the stairs went up between the living room and front room, like they did at Gran's. Gran had a shelter, right down at the bottom of the garden. It was between them and the Coopers next door. Mr Cooper, Jim, and Sid had dug out the ground between them. If they were all together, they would be company for each other, and Gran would be looked out for if the siren went when she was on her own.

***

There had been a raid on Salisbury in 1942. Ina didn't know if Gran's shelter had been used then; it certainly hadn't been used of late and was now, like so many others, waterlogged. Here she was, in this garden, with the scent of flowers in the air, the hum of conversation around her and the sound of the trains coming into and going out of the station. Threads of cloud scarcely moved across the sky—the same sky that David was fighting under, far away. She could see him in his tunic, his trouser legs tucked into the high-laced gaiters, his helmet with the straps hanging loose on either side of his face, that big pack on his back, and his rifle over his shoulder. Yet it seemed so far away . . . hazy and unreal . . . since the last time she had seen him. Was it all fading away from her?

***

Her reverie was broken by Arthur coming around the back into the garden. He smiled and said hello to them all, and the women smiled and said hello back.

"I've got you a kettle on," said Grace, getting up. "Your dinner is all laid; by the time you have gotten washed and changed, it will be ready. I've just got to fry up some new potatoes. You've got rhubarb pie for afters."

She disappeared into the house with Arthur following behind her.

"Uncle?"

"Yes, Ina"

"What was Guildford like during the blitz?"

George stretched his legs and pondered a bit before he answered. Then he said, "Well, we didn't know much about it here—the bombing that is, considering how near we are to London. We did have a couple of raids; that was '41, I think. Most of the bombs fell on the Hog's Back. Some fell near to some houses in Onslow Village and blew the fronts off. Then they had some the other end of town. I believe someone was killed. Our trouble was that, when London had their raids, we usually got the siren too.

"Then there are the buzz bombs. They are some devils, mind. If you hear the motor stop, that is your lot! I don't think we'll get much more now—one or two maybe. But I reckon Hitler will be too busy trying to stop the Allies getting out of France and Belgium and into Germany."

Grace had come back and joined the company. "There," she said. "I'll sit down for a few minutes."

"How long have you had Arthur staying with you, Auntie?" asked Avril.

"Oh," replied Grace. "It must be getting on for four months now. He came up from Havant, Portsmouth, way. His wife and children are still down there. He's looking round for a house. We're all keeping a look out for him, but finding a house in Guildford is like looking for gold dust. There are so many refugees from London and some from Croydon."

"We have a lot from Portsmouth," said Ina, "school children, mostly."

"We have some kids from Woking—the railway orphanage," put in George. "That wooden building across the road—that's run by ASLEF, the footplate men's union. They call it Orphanage Hall. We've a committee that organises functions there—whist drives, wedding parties, birthday parties. We have a party for the railway kids at Christmas and one for the grown-ups to. We used to have daytrips to the seaside, but the war put a stop to all that. Most men on the southern region pay a sub towards the upkeep of the orphanage, and all the profit the hall makes goes towards it as well. It was one of the first places that the government confiscated at the beginning of the war. They wanted it for an army hospital, but I don't think it's ever been used for that. All the kids were shoved out, and railway men around the region took them in. We had two boys, had them for ages. They grew up, left school, and went home."

"We didn't have anymore," said Grace. "I got myself a job in the kitchens at the Surrey County Hospital, and there I am, still."

Arthur came out into the garden carrying a dining chair.

"You all right with that chair?" asked George.

"Yes. I'm fine. Don't worry about me," Arthur replied. He took a tobacco tin out of his pocket and held it out towards George. "Want a roll-up, mate?"

"Ah. Ta. I don't mind if I do." George took the tin.

Ina watched the men as they settled back with their roll-ups. They reminded her of her father and Uncle Sid . . . Alb Daley, too. Did all railwaymen roll their own?"

Grace gave an audible sigh. "You meet a lot of people during the war that you wouldn't have met normally," she said philosophically, "and you say goodbye to a lot too. I wonder where we shall all be this time next year?"

I want to be in America, thought Ina. *Please, God, let me be in America.*

***

The next morning, the girls went shopping with Grace.

"I'm not going far," she told them, "just to the co-op to get your rations. That's where we're registered. I thought, if you like, we could have a walk up to the cathedral. It isn't finished yet, so there's not much to see, but you can say you've been there."

The girls agreed, and they set off towards the shops. They walked along the road, past the brickworks, and turned right at Ridge Mount and into the road running along the backs of the houses between the estate and the cathedral precincts. The steps up to the cathedral from here were wide but steep.

"I suppose it was built on high ground so that it could be seen from a long way off," said Avril. "Will it have a spire?"

"No, I don't think so," said Grace. "It will be taller than it is now when it is finished . . . whenever that will be."

Ina looked around the surrounding grounds. The grass was long and unkempt. Dandelions and clover spread across the green, and nettles, ragged robin, cow parsley, and other weeds grew among the bordering hedges. Grace caught her look.

"Not much like Salisbury cathedral, is it?"

Ina shook her head.

"It will be all right when it is finished," went on Grace. "They do try to keep the grass down, but this time of year, it grows too fast. The manpower shortage doesn't help."

They walked around the perimeter.

"Can anyone go inside?" asked Avril.

"I don't think so," Grace answered. "Kids used to go down into the crypt, but it became waterlogged down there, so the entrances were boarded up, just in case one of them drowned."

They made their way down the grassy slope until they came to the road, which they followed round into the chase.

"This road goes through the estate," Grace told them.

"They're nice houses," commented Avril.

"Yes. They're nice inside too, quite roomy. There are a few railway families living here."

"The road's very wide," said Ina, "and the pavements, too. It looks open."

"A nice place to bring children up," said Grace.

They walked down the chase until they reached the co-op. Grace went in, and the girls followed. Grace took Ina's ration book and Avril's card and handed them over the counter.

"Just the rations," she said.

These were portioned out; wrapped; and, with the book and card, handed back over the counter.

"Next door now," said Grace.

Next door was the butchery department. Grace went up to the man standing behind the counter. "Any liver?" she asked.

"I'm afraid not, Mrs Bradley. Expectant mothers only and there's a lot of them around these days. They had the lot. No offal at all right now."

"How about faggots?"

"Nope. We hope to be making some towards the weekend."

She looked through the glass front; there were some "savoury sausages" on an enamel tray.

"What's in those besides bread and suet?"

"Savouries," he said with a grin.

"Oh. Go on, then. Give me a pound and a half, and I'll make a Toad in the Hole; I've got some dried egg."

"I've got some rabbits out in the cold store; I couldn't put them out because of the heat."

"Are they paunched?"

"Yes."

"Can I have a couple?"

"Certainly. Want me to skin them for you?"

"Yes, please."

"And chop them up?"

"If you would."

He took the sausages from behind the counter, cut off a dozen, weighed them, wrapped them, and gave them to Grace. He picked up an empty tray, took it through a door at the other end of the shop, and came back with the chopped rabbits.

"What do you want with your meat ration?"

"What can I have?" she asked.

"A couple of mutton chops?"

"Yes," Grace said. "That'll do."

***

The women were walking along Madrid Road when Grace paused.

"I must go in Dolly Dray's and get George's tobacco," she said.

This time, the girls stayed outside looking into the shop window. The shop was obviously a newsagent's, tobacconist's, and confectioner's. The window Ina and Avril were looking into had an array of chocolate boxes on show, Top Hat, Carefree, and Dairy Box among others. Bars of Fry's, Cadburys and Nestles chocolate were arranged on the base. One pyramid of chocolate bars had fallen over, revealing the lettering stamped on the back—"Dummy." They both grinned.

"I shan't be spending any sweet coupons on those," laughed Avril.

The girls had taken turns carrying Grace's wicker basket back, not that it was heavy; but as it contained their rations and dinner for two days, it seemed the proper thing to do. They reached the house, and the shopping basket was put on the small kitchen table and unpacked.

"Would you like to go to the Castle Keep this afternoon?" Grace asked.

They said they would.

"I'll put the rabbits in a stew in the oven on a low gas, and it will be cooking while we are gone," Grace said.

She lit the gas oven and got an enamel oval roaster out of a cupboard. The chopped rabbits were rinsed under the tap and wiped dry and then sprinkled with flour and put on a plate. The girls peeled swedes and parsnips, scraped carrots, and chopped onions. Into the roaster went pearl barley, yellow split peas, and red lentils; on top of this, the chopped rabbits.

"What won't feed will fatten," Grace remarked as she poured on water and put the roaster in the oven.

Chapter 22

Ina thought she had never seen such an abundance of flowers and shrubs in one place. The grounds of the keep were certainly well kept. As they walked along the pathways, they breathed in the fragrance. Men and women, all middle-aged people, were playing bowls on the green,. The keep towered above it all on its sloping hill. A path, bordered by a rustic fence, ran round it like the helter-skelter at a fairground.

"I'd like to go up there this time," said Ina.

"Better let her go up, Auntie," laughed Avril. "Otherwise, she'll start crying, and we will have to buy her an ice cream."

Grace looked at them, blankly, and then smiled. "Oh. I remember," she said. "That time when you came up when you were little, Jim bought Ina an ice cream to stop her crying in the street because she couldn't go up to the top."

"I never did know why they wouldn't let me," Ina complained.

"They did tell you, but you must have been too young to understand."

"Why was it then?"

"They were doing some building work up there. It wouldn't have been safe. The public were stopped from going inside."

"I didn't have an ice cream," Avril said.

"No," Grace replied. "You said ice cream made your tooth hurt so you had a comic instead."

Grace declined to go up to the keep.

"I've climbed enough hills today," she said. "I'm going to sit on one of these benches and have a breather."

Inside the keep, there was nothing much to see; it was like an empty shell. They climbed the steps, which took them to the top, and looked over the wall onto the scenery laid out beneath them. There was much of it they did not know, but Avril, pointing, said, "See that ribbon of road, right over there? That's the hill we came down this morning when we went to the co-op, isn't it?"

"Yes," agreed Ina, following Avril's line of vision. "That must be the cathedral to the right. You can just make it out."

They spent a little time gazing at the unfamiliar landscape.

"Guildford's a nice place, isn't it?" Avril remarked.

"You haven't seen it all yet."

"I know, but I like what I've seen so far, and there's lots of places just outside of Guildford—the Silent Pool, Jacob's Well—"

"How do you know all these places?"

"I don't know. Some of those bits of information you pick up from here and there. Perhaps we have been there and forgotten about it." Avril sighed. "I think I would like to come here with Brian, on our honeymoon."

"I don't suppose I'll ever come here with David for our honeymoon."

There was a slight edge to Ina's voice, and Avril realised she had trodden on sensitive ground. Hastily, she tried to make amends. "Of course you could! He might get some leave later on if things are going well, and Dad might let you get married."

Ina shook her head. "No. he won't," she said. "He's told me I can't get married until David's out of the army and settled in a job. That could be years."

"Isn't there any chance that he could come over here to you?"

"I don't think so. He wouldn't be able to afford it."

"You really love him don't you?"

"I suppose you think I'm too young to know my own mind, like everyone else does."

"No. Not really. I was only sixteen when I started going out with Brian, remember. I knew then that I didn't want anyone else."

"But he wasn't in the RAF then, was he?"

"No, but the war was on and we knew it was only a matter of time before he was called up. I wasn't much older than you when we got engaged."

"David's not here. He's in France."

"Brian had to go to Egypt."

"It's not the same. Brian came back to this country; he will get a job in this country. You will have him here with you in this country!" Ina cried, vehemently. "Brian's English. He's not American!"

A heavy silence hung between the two of them. Avril could think of nothing to say to her sister. She suddenly realised the tension that Ina must feel. She, herself, had worried about Brian being in Egypt, but she had never had the added feeling that Brian would not come back to her.

It was Ina who broke the silence. "Sorry," she murmured

"That's all right," said Avril, in what she hoped was a comforting voice.

"Let's go back down to Auntie." Ina turned away from the wall. They wound their way down the spiral path and re-joined Grace.

"What did you think of the view?" was her greeting.

"Lovely, isn't it? Avril replied.

Grace stood up. "Time we were getting back," she said. "I thought we could go back a different way."

The girls followed Grace along the pathway and through a gate at the bottom end of the grounds. They found themselves going down a steep hill between two high walls. It led to another road, which they crossed, walking until they reached a flight of steep narrow steps between two rows of terraced houses.

"Gosh," commented Avril. "You can knock two doors at once."

They passed the watermill, went over a bridge, walked along by the river, and came to Mill Mead. Ina saw the bridge in front of them, and thought for a minute that it was the same one they had crossed Monday afternoon, and then she realised they had come out at the bottom of High Street.

"Do we have to get to North Street for the bus?" asked Avril.

"Actually," Grace said, "we're not that far from home. By the time we walked there and waited for the bus, we could be home."

When the railway bridge came into view, the girls knew where they were. As they crossed the bridge on the left-hand side, Grace nodded her head in the direction of the wall. "That's the 'Loco' sheds down there." And as they crossed into Guildford Park Road, she pointed up the Farnham Road "And that's where the hospital is."

"Guilford," remarked Avril, "seems to be all hills."

They went round the back way.

George was in the garden. "Hello," he called. "Had a good day?"

They told him they had.

"I opened the back kitchen door and the window. It was like an oven in there. You got something in the oven?"

"Yes; your dinner," Grace told him.

"Do you want us to do anything, Auntie?" Avril asked.

"Well, one of you can lay the table, and if someone scrapes the potatoes, I'll get on making the dumplings."

"I'll lay the table," said Ina, going into the living room.

"I'll do the potatoes then, shall I?" Avril said to Ina's retreating back.

Avril went to the cupboard where the vegetables were kept and put some potatoes into the bowl. Grace placed a mixing bowl onto the draining board and made the dumplings.

Ina came into the kitchen. "Anything else I can do? Do you want me to help you scrape the potatoes?"

"We can't all get round the sink," replied Grace. "Why don't you go out into the garden and keep Uncle George company?"

***

Out in the garden, Uncle George was talking over the fence to a neighbour. Ina hesitated. George turned his head in her direction.

"Come over here and meet Fred," he called to her.

She walked towards him.

"Fred wants to hear all about Salisbury," George said.

What was she supposed to tell him?

***

Grace made the dumplings, took the roaster out of the oven, and put the dumplings in the gravy. When she had put them back in the oven and shut the door, she said to Avril, "Is there anything wrong with Ina?"

"Umm" Avril paused "I don't know. Why do you ask?"

"She was very quiet all the way home. I wondered if anything had upset her." Grace had picked up a knife and started to help Avril scrape the remaining potatoes.

"It might have been something I said," Avril confessed.

"You haven't had a falling out, have you?"

"Not exactly, Auntie. It was while we were looking at the view across Guildford from the top of the keep; I said something stupid without thinking. I happened to say I would like to come here with Brian for our honeymoon. I could have bitten off my tongue."

"Why would that have upset her?"

"Because she thinks she will never be able to bring David here, nor anywhere else for that matter. If they do get married, it will be in America, away from it all."

"What if he gets leave? He can come over from Europe and marry her, can't he?"

"Dad won't let her get married until David's out of the army and in a steady job."

"Surely he can come over here from America and they can get married here?"

"I don't know if he could afford it. Anyway, Auntie, it's all in the future, and I think it's telling on her sometimes."

"Poor little mite," sympathised Grace. "She is so young to have all this on her shoulders. At her age, she should be out enjoying herself. Is it really so serious between them?"

"I think she really feels for him. His mother writes to her."

"Has he got a job to go back to?"

"I don't think so. I think he worked in the orange groves in Florida before he was called up. His family have a farm, but I don't think they make a lot of money out of it."

The potatoes finished, Grace put them into a saucepan on the stove.

"Who is going to pay for her to go to America when the time comes?"

"Dad's hinted that he'll pay for her passage over there, but David will have to pay her fare from wherever she lands to Alabama. That is where he lives."

"What does Jim really think about it all, Avril?"

"I think he and Mum are hoping that as time goes on it will all fizzle out."

Avril caught her breath, and a tear ran down her cheek. "I feel so sorry for her."

"Don't upset yourself, Avril. I know it's hard to stand by when she's hurting. She's being torn all ways. Don't let her see you've been crying. It might upset her even more."

Avril took her handkerchief from her pocket and dabbed her eyes. "It'll all come right in the end," Grace told her. "You wait and see." "Does it look as though I've been crying?" "We'll say you've got something in your eye."

Chapter 23

"Is the Lido open, Auntie?"

They were having breakfast the next morning. Ina looked more like her old self, and nothing about her manner suggested that the sadness that had enveloped her yesterday remained today. Grace, for one, was glad to see that Ina was still eager to enjoy her holiday.

"Yes, Ina," she answered, "I think it must be. They take parties of school children; we've seen them pass by here from the school in Onslow village, with their towels rolled up and tucked under their arms. Were the two of you thinking of going?"

"Yes," Avril said. "Mum wasn't sure if it had been kept open or not. We brought our cossies and bathing caps just in case, and Mum packed a couple of towels for us."

"Oh. She needn't have done that. I've plenty of towels."

"You don't mind if we go, then?"

"No. You go by all means."

They passed the morning helping Grace around the house, wrote some cards, and walked along the road to the letter box and posted them.

"Do you remember going to the Lido before?" Ina asked.

"No. I remember going to the paddling pool. I think there was some sort of small lake there with a little bridge going over it and children sailing boats. Don't you remember any of it?"

Ina shook her head. "I can't say I do. Was it where the Lido is then?"

"I've got a feeling it is."

Asking Grace later, she confirmed that the Lido was in part of the grounds where the paddling pool was.

"It's a fair old step from where you get off the bus, mind," Grace warned.

After lunch, the girls made ready to set off. Grace took a shopping bag off the back of the larder door. It was made from some sort of mackintosh material.

"Here," she said. "Put your towels and that into this. You won't make your clothes wet when you bring your things home."

***

Grace had told the girls to go up to the very top of North Street when they got off the bus and take the turning left. They seemed to have been walking some distance when Ina remarked that they must have been going forever. "We are on the right road, I suppose?"

"Well, this is the way Auntie told us," Avril said. "She said Stoke Road, and this is Stoke Road."

"Those poor little school kids!" Ina said. "Fancy having to walk in a crocodile all this way."

There were two people walking towards them. Avril asked them if they were going in the right direction for the Lido. Yes, they were, they were informed. They were to keep walking until they came to the railway bridge, go under it, and the Lido was a little farther along on the right. As they approached, they could hear music playing, obviously records transmitted through a tannoy system. Following the sound, they came to the complex that housed the Lido. They paid their entrance fee and walked through the turnstile. On their left were the changing huts and lockers.

A woman was in attendance. "When you've changed," she said, "I'll put your things away in a locker. If you take my advice, you'll put your handbags in as well if you're going in to the water together."

She pushed open the doors of two adjacent cubicles. When they were ready, the attendant showed them to the lockers. They put away their clothes, handbags, and the shopping bag Grace had given them. The woman handed them each a disc with a thin cord threaded through. Ina looked at it.

"They go on your wrists," explained the woman. "Don't lose them. They have your locker number on them."

"What happens if we want anything out of the lockers?" Avril asked.

"Come to me, and I'll open them for you."

***

They made their way to the pool. It seemed to be quite full of bobbing heads, children's and adults'. The pool itself was large and rectangular. There was a shallow end at both ends of the pool, the deepest part being in the centre. At one side was a structure of diving boards of varying heights and a springboard. There were two water chutes, one high and the other lower, and at either end fountains played.

"I wouldn't mind having a go down that high water chute," Avril said as they passed by.

The paving stones around the pool were patterned with wet footprints. People were sitting on the low wall around the perimeter of the pool or on the sloping bank behind.

"Where shall we go?" Ina asked.

Avril pointed in front of her. "Let's go up that other bank. There's some sort of cafeteria right up there. We can get a drink and something to eat later on."

They went up steps to the other bank and settled between the cafeteria and the pool. There were quite a few people here, some lying in the sun, some sitting. The girls spread their towels out and sat down on them.

"I hope we don't get our towels pinched," said Ina. "Mum won't be very happy if we do."

"There's plenty lying about with nobody on them," Avril remarked. "Anyway, some are more posh than ours."

Ina looked at some of the gaily coloured towels that had seemingly been left while the owners were in the water. Theirs were more commonplace—coloured stripes with fringes at both ends. Avril put on her bathing cap and fastened it. "Coming?" she asked.

She stood up and Ina followed, putting on her own cap as she walked along. They went down the steps that led into the water. It was mostly children who were here, some being held under the chin by grown-ups trying to teach them the basics of swimming, small arms and legs flailing in all directions; others, more independent, safely harnessed in inflatable runner rings, tried to bring uncoordinated limbs into some semblance of recognisable swimming strokes. The girls waded through the water until they came to the deeper part of the pool. Here again, swimming was not made easy by the other people trying to find enough room to manoeuvre. They found themselves caught up in a game of beach ball between two

265

young men and two or three girls. It became obvious after a while that Ina
and Avril were being favoured by the young men whenever they returned
the ball. This continued until one of the girls managed to intercept the
ball and left the pool with it firmly within her grasp. The two young men
shrugged their shoulders.

"Guess that's game over," said one.

Ina felt her stomach churn. That accent! It wasn't the same sort of
drawl that David's was, but it was distinctively "Americanised".

Ina had not swum for a long time, and now her limbs felt heavy and
dragging. "I'm getting out for a while," she told Avril.

"Aren't we going down the water chute?" Avril asked.

"All right then," Ina replied.

It was when Ina was halfway up the steps behind Avril that she heard
the accent again and realised the two young men were coming up behind
them. She hit the water with speed at the end of the chute. The water went
up her nose and into her mouth, making her cough and splutter.

"Hey! Are you okay?" One of the young men was holding her upper
arms.

"Yes," she replied. "Yes. I'm all right. I wasn't expecting to reach the
bottom so quickly."

Avril came over to her.

"What happened?"

"I wasn't prepared when I hit the water."

"Do you still want to get out of the water?"

"I think I will. There's no need for you to come with me."

"That's all right. I think I've had enough anyway."

They climbed out of the water; made their way back to the green; and,
once there, stretched out on their towels.

"Time for a bit of sunbathing," said Avril.

Ina lay on her stomach, her head resting on folded arms. She could
see the two young men standing by the water chute. Tall, well built and
muscular, their bodies suntanned—what were they doing here? Why
weren't they in France? She closed her eyes.

Sounds came to her. The shouts and screams of those in the pool, the
music coming through the tannoy, the murmur of conversation from the
people around her. Suddenly, there was a cry from Avril.

Ina turned to see what had caused her sister's distress. Avril was on her feet, brushing off her towel. "Ants!" she shouted. "Blooming ants! Blasted things have bitten me all over. Haven't you felt them?"

"No," replied Ina, getting to her feet.

"Shall we go and get dressed and come back for a cup of tea?" asked Avril.

"Might as well," agreed Ina.

Together, they walked back to the cubicles, Ina noticing on the way that there was no sign of the two young men.

***

There were tables and chairs placed in front of the cafeteria. Avril went up to the counter. "I'll get the teas," she said. "You get us a table."

Ina sat down and placed Auntie Graces' bag, which now contained their wet things, beside her.

"Do you want anything to eat?" Avril called.

"What have they got?"

"They've got packets of biscuits or crisps."

"I'll have crisps, then, please."

Avril put two cups of tea onto the table and then two packets of crisps. Ina opened her packet, took out the twist of salt, and sprinkled it over her crisps. She was vaguely aware of two soldiers standing by the counter of the cafeteria and when one of them said, "Do you mind if we join you, girls?" she was startled to hear once more what she had presumed was an American accent. To her, they looked like ordinary British soldiers, until she noticed the flash at the top of their sleeves—"Canada". Of course! Auntie Grace had said the Canadians had been in Guildford, as had the Americans in Salisbury. Now she recognised them as the two young men from the pool.

Avril looked up. "No," she said. "Help yourself to a seat."

They pulled up two chairs and sat at the table. One of them turned to Ina. "Are you okay now?" he asked.

"Yes, thank you," she replied, a little shyly.

"So, you're from Canada?" Avril said.

"Yep. That's us! We've come from right across the ocean blue."

"Where in Canada are you from?" Avril asked.

"I'm from Alberta," he answered, "and Bill, here"—he pointed to Bill—"he's from Vancouver."

"How long have you been in England?"

"Oh. Sometime."

Bill spoke up. "In case you were wondering," he said, "we've been to Europe and come back again."

"Didn't you like it?" Avril asked teasingly.

"No, sir! Too noisy! Thunder and lightning and firecrackers going off all the time! Couldn't get a wink of sleep some nights, could we, Roy?"

"We've got to go back sometime soon, though," Roy said. "I guess they have something special lined up for us."

Ina had noticed the "airborne" insignia on their sleeves and the red berets folded and pushed through the lapels on their shoulders.

"We have airborne troops in Salisbury," she said. "At least we did have. I think a lot of them went over on D-Day. A girl who works with me is engaged to one. She was supposed to be getting married this month."

"That's tough," said Roy.

"Salisbury? Is that where you come from?" asked Bill.

"Yes," Avril told them. "We're on holiday. We go back Saturday."

Roy nodded his head in the direction of the girl's hands.

"I see you are both spoken for," he commented.

"Yes," agreed Avril, "we're both engaged."

"And are your boys overseas?"

"Mine is," said Ina. "My sister's boy is in England. He's in the RAF."

"He's not been back long from Egypt," Avril added.

The sky darkened suddenly. The light faded.

"I reckon we're in for a storm," said Roy

"Anytime now it's going to pour down." Bill got up from his chair. "Come on and get under this awning, girls, or you'll get drenched."

They and Roy joined him under the awning that fringed the outside of the cafeteria, getting as close to the counter as they could. As the heavens opened and the rain pelted down, more people joined them. Those who were lying on the grass simply jumped back into the water; others, who could find no immediate shelter, made for the cubicle and locker area, which was under cover. Rain lashed down on the paved walkways and into the pool with a force that sent up spurts of water. It filled up the cups and saucers they had left on the table and, in spite of their shelter, sent up muddy jets off the grass onto their legs. The rain was followed by a loud clap of thunder and, almost immediately, a streak of lightening flashed across the pool. There were shrieks and screams from the children as parents dragged them from the water and followed the crowd going to the covered area. Several people remained in the water in spite of the lightning.

"It's the worst thing they could do," remarked Bill.

The next clap of thunder was not so loud, and the lightning flash, a while after, not so near.

"I think it's tailing off now," Bill remarked.

"It's all that thunder and lightning you had in France." Avril smiled. "You brought it back with you."

Bill smiled back. "Firecrackers anytime now," he said.

When the last of the rain had fallen and the thunder and lightning had faded away, the girls decided to leave the Lido and go home.

"No good asking you girls if you'd like to come out with us this evening, I suppose?" asked Roy.

"No, not really," said Avril. "Thanks for asking anyway."

"That's okay. We understand."

"It's been nice knowing you, if only for a short time," Bill said.

Ina held out her hand. "Goodbye then," she said.

They shook hands all round.

"Don't suppose we'll meet again," Roy said.

"I shouldn't think so," answered Avril, "in spite of Vera Lynn's song!"

***

By the time Ina and Avril were walking once more along Stoke Road, the sun was shining again.

"We're in for a nice long walk to the bus now," Avril remarked "I just hope it doesn't rain again. My feet are squelching in my sandals."

Chapter 24

Ina, to the best of her knowledge, had never been to London, so that when Grace suggested that she take the girls there Friday as a last treat before they went home, Ina was full of enthusiasm.

Avril's only sight of the big city had been through the window of a train coming into or going out of Waterloo station when she travelled between the RAF bases and home. Being at Waterloo did not affect her in the same way as it did her sister. Ina could only stare around in complete amazement. She looked up into the high roof space, the scrolled iron girders, and the thick pillars that supported them. There were so many people! It seemed as though many different nations were represented judging by the variety of uniforms. Everyone was in a hurry, dashing about the platforms to the exits or down to the subways.

"Where do you want to go?" Grace's voice broke into her thoughts.

Without thinking, she said, "Piccadilly."

"Piccadilly?" echoed Avril. "What do you want to go there for?"

Ina shrugged her shoulders and half wished she'd said, "Buckingham Palace."

"Come on then," said Grace. "Follow me and keep up. I don't want to lose either of you. There isn't much to see in Piccadilly. Might be a few shops open. Avril, just keep a watch out for Ina on the escalator. I expect you're used to the underground. Keep to the side and don't let anyone push in."

By the time Grace had finished giving out her instructions, they had reached the top of the escalator.

"Let Auntie go first," Avril said. "You go next, and I'll come behind."

Ina put her foot forward and stepped onto a stair. At first, the motion unsettled her and she thought she would lose her balance.

"You're all right," Avril assured her. "Keep a bit of a distance between you and Auntie and keep your eye on the stairs until they level out."

People were running down the stairs beside her and up the stairs on the other escalator. The ride down seemed interminable, but when she saw, at last, the stairs levelling out, she was prepared and, following Grace, stepped off with an ease that surprised herself. They followed a hurrying Grace to the ticket barriers, along the subway, and onto the platform; here they stood with the crowd waiting for the train. To Ina, it was cold and unwelcoming. There was a smell about the place that she couldn't identify. Also, it was claustrophobic. The headlights of the train came through the tunnel like the eyes of a monster, followed by a clattering whine. It stopped in front of them, Grace caught hold of her hand, and Avril pushed her gently from behind.

She was on the train, squashed into a seat between Avril and Grace. People clambered in after them; those who couldn't find seats were strap-hanging. There was a treading on toes and a banging of legs with briefcases. The doors closed, and the train whirred on its way.

***

Ina was glad when they stopped at Piccadilly Circus and got out of the train. Up another escalator and onto another platform, soon they were out on the street. Ina gave an audible sigh; the others turned around to look at her.

"You look pale, Ina. Are you feeling all right?" Grace asked her.

"She's not used to all the hustle and bustle of crossing London," said Avril.

"I don't think I like the underground much," Ina explained. "Did people really stay down there during the blitz, Auntie?"

"Yes. They did," Grace told her. "There's a woman at work who came to Guildford from here during the blitz. She said it was cold and damp and smelled to high heaven."

Ina felt a little better now that she was in the fresh air. As they walked along, she took an interest in her surroundings. Bomb damaged buildings stuck out like broken teeth; already weeds were growing amongst the ruins. Occasionally, she would spot children playing on the bomb sites. She wondered at this.

"A lot of the kids who were evacuated were brought home again when the worst of the raids tailed off, fatal for some because the bombing wasn't entirely over. When I came up here last . . . it must have been three years ago . . . they'd had had a raid the night before. There was rubble all over the place."

"Where are we now?" Ina asked.

"Piccadilly Circus."

"I suppose they call it that because the road goes around that monument thing in the middle, like a circus ring."

"That's where the statue of Eros was. They took it away for safekeeping. There's not a lot to see really, just the shops that stay open. Uncle George and I used to come up here sometimes and go home on a late train just so we could see London all lit up."

***

Ina was suddenly aware of American soldiers walking along on the opposite side of the road. They were accompanied by an assortment of girls of varying ages, shapes, and sizes. The familiarity of the uniform struck her for a moment. All the same, she hoped that she and Stella never looked like these girls. Over made up, peroxided hair . . .

Grace said, "This is Rainbow Corner. Not a nice place to come to now, especially at night. No decent girl would be seen here. The American Red Cross Club is here. That's why those women congregate here; it's to 'get off' with Yanks for their money."

Ina felt herself flush. Avril looked at her and half smiled. Auntie Grace didn't seem to realise that she might have said anything to offend Ina as she wandered on, the two girls following her. They looked into the shop windows and went inside some of the larger stores, browsing around. One had a cafeteria, so they stopped for a cup of tea.

"Well. Is there anything else you want to see?" Grace asked when they were once more out onto the street.

"I suppose all the places like Madame Tussauds are closed, aren't they?" asked Avril.

"Yes. I think they are."

They ended up going to Westminster and Buckingham Palace. Ina, who had dreaded any further journey by tube, now found she could take them in her stride. Nevertheless, she was still relieved when they had caught the last tube train, gone up the last escalator, and were on the Waterloo platform waiting for the train back to Guildford.

***

It was time to go home. The girls' cases were packed and brought downstairs. This time, they would be managing without the help of George and Arthur, but Grace would see them off on the train.

They waved goodbye to Grace as the train pulled out of the station and trundled passed a few landmarks that had become familiar to them. At Woking, they found their platform and settled to wait for the Salisbury train. A bell rang, and a voice announced the impending arrival of the train. As it came into the station, the voice made another announcement:

"This train is the eleven forty-five from Waterloo and will be calling at—"

"Crikey!" exclaimed Avril. "It's stopping at every station. Uncle George didn't tell us it was a 'slow'."

"Listen," warned Ina.

The voice continued. "Passengers for Salisbury and Exeter change at Basingstoke—"

"Oh! No! What else!" cried Avril.

Their troubles were not over. The train was packed. There were no seats available. In the corridor, people were either standing or sitting on their upturned cases. The girls followed suit and propped their own cases against the wooden wall of the compartment alongside three sailors similarly seated. The train moved off with a lurch, and Ina stopped herself from pitching off her case.

"You all right?" asked the sailor nearest to her.

"We didn't expect this," she said.

"What? A crowded train? It's state normal these days."

"Where are you going?" asked another sailor.

"Salisbury," Avril replied.

"You have to change at Basingstoke, too, then?"

"Yes. We didn't know that until we got to Woking."

"We've been travelling since early this morning," the first sailor said. "We had to get to King's Cross and then over to Waterloo to pick this train up. It was packed when we got on it there. Now we've got to change at flipping Basingstoke to get the train to Exeter, and then we have to change again at Exeter for the Plymouth train."

***

The train had only just gathered speed, it seemed, when it slowed down and stopped at the first of the many stations it would halt at before it reached Basingstoke. Every time it started off again, it would jerk and shudder, making Ina feel insecure perched on top of her case. People got off, and more people got on. No one in the seats moved. Passengers were walking along the corridors looking for a seat. Every so often, the ticket collector would inch his way, crablike, between the windows on one side and the bodies and luggage on the other. People scrabbled to get their tickets out to show him.

***

Basingstoke at last! The sailors waited for the girls to get out and handed their cases to them before they got down to the platform themselves.

"We shall have to find which platform we get the Salisbury train from," said Avril.

"The sailors seem to know where to go," Ina told her. "We'll just follow them."

They picked up their cases and made to go after the three sailors, who promptly disappeared through a door with "Gentlemen" written across the top.

"Oh, well," sighed Avril. "This is one time we don't follow the fleet."

Finally, they asked a porter, who gave them the platform number and told them they would have twenty minutes' wait. On the platform, only a few people were waiting, most occupying the seats.

On one seat, however, sat a man and woman. The rest of the seat was taken up with their luggage. Avril went over to them. "Excuse me," she said, "would you mind removing your luggage so that my sister and I can sit down?"

The woman glared at her. The man got up and put the cases down by the side of the seat. The girls sat down.

"I don't know," the woman said, "put them in a uniform and they think they own the place."

Avril turned to her, "Oh really?" she said, loftily. "By the way you had commandeered the whole seat, it looked as though you thought you did."

The train came in, and this time, they found seats. Ina was glad to see the sailors had boarded a little further along and hoped they too had found seats.

"I didn't hear the announcer call out any stations before Salisbury," Ina said. "Maybe this is a fast train."

Familiar small stations flashed by, and when Andover had been overtaken, they knew they were nearly home.

Jim was waiting on the platform. He came over as the train stopped and took their cases as they stepped onto the platform.

"For heaven's sake, where have you been?" he greeted them. "I've been up and down this platform nearly two hours. Your mother will be tearing her hair out."

"The train was a 'slow'," explained Avril, "and we had to change at Basingstoke."

"I bet you caught the eleven forty-five from Waterloo. Didn't George tell you it was a 'slow' and you had to change?"

"Perhaps he didn't know. He just told us the time for Woking."

Jim grabbed both suitcases, and the girls followed him out of the station.

"Grab that taxi," he said, nodding towards the rank.

The taxi driver put the two cases in the boot. The girls got into the back of the cab, and Jim climbed in beside the driver.

"It'll be a long time before I go travelling again," Ina said.

"It's all right for you," replied Avril. "I've got to get back to High Wycombe."

"Never mind. You'll have a week to recover before you do."

"There's only one thing I want," sighed Avril, "and that's a nice hot bath."

"You're out of luck," said Jim, over his shoulder. "The Ascot's on the blink, and the bloke can't come to fix it until Tuesday. If you want a bath, you will have to boil the copper up and take the water upstairs in a bucket."

***

"I expect you thought I had gone to Guildford to fetch them, didn't you?" Jim said to Hilda as he walked through the door.

"No. Alb called in and said he thought they must have caught a later train as he didn't see them get off the earlier one."

"I'm darned if I saw him up the station," Jim muttered.

"You didn't have a very good journey back then?" Hilda turned to the girls.

"No, Mum."

"Good Lord, Avril! The state of your uniform! It looks as though you've slept in it for a week."

"I know, Mum. I'll have to see if I can get it dry-cleaned before I go back."

"There's some letters for you both. They came yesterday. I didn't think it was worth sending them on. There are two for you, Avril, and one for Ina. Take your cases on upstairs. I'll make some tea and get something to eat. Spam fritters and chips all right?"

"Yes, Mum."

Upstairs, they unpacked and sorted out their clothes. Ina's letter was from David. He hoped she would have a good holiday and not to forget to send him a card. She looked at the date. It had been written a week before. Avril was sat on her bed, a letter in each hand. Beside her were the two envelopes—one, obviously, had contained a letter from Brian; the other was a brown manila one with OHMS stamped on it.

Avril looked across at her sister and said, "Do you want to hear the good news or the bad news?"

"What's wrong?"

Avril held up one of the letters. "This one says I've got a posting to Upavon—"

"And?" Ina prompted.

Avril held up the other letter. "This one is saying Brian is going over to France."

Chapter 25

The time seemed to pass slowly for Ina the week following her holiday. There was no Stella to discuss her stay at Guildford or exchange snippets of news with. Dialogue with Mr Phillips, Mrs Gray, and Vera had been confined to asking if she had enjoyed herself and what the weather had been like. Avril had gone to Brian's parents for a few days, and Ina, having been in her sister's company twenty-four hours for seven days, felt alone and bored. Vera, who was not very communicative at the best of times, now seemed to have withdrawn completely into her shell and only spoke when she needed to. Ina, out of habit more than need, still walked around the town during her lunch hour.

***

Hilda felt torn two ways. She was glad about Avril's position in Upavon but, at the same time, was acutely aware of her elder daughter's anxiety over Brian's departure to France.

"I didn't think Brian would be going over," she confided to Jim.

"They're bound to have the RAF there once they've established a base. It probably won't be the big stuff—the long-range bombers and all that. We might have bombed the French airfields, and the runways might not be in operation over there. Maybe that's why the RAF's going over—to build them up. They're bound to have some sort of set-up, I suppose. It's a question of saving fuel for light aircraft. They don't need to refuel so much if they don't have to cross the channel. Leastways that's how I see it."

"It will be nice having Avril home more often. She can get here and back in a weekend."

"By the time she's done the rounds here and gone over to Harnham, she won't have much of a weekend left," said Jim.

"Trust you to pour cold water on," Hilda retorted.

***

On Wednesday, Avril came back home.

"I'm glad you're back," her mother told her." Ina's been mooching around like a lost soul. I expect she's missing young Stella."

"Oh, yes, of course. Stella's on holiday, isn't she? When Ina gets home, I'll ask her if she wants to go to the pictures later on this afternoon."

It was after two o'clock when Ina got home from work.

"You're late," commented Avril.

"I know," said Ina. "We were 10s.0d out in the till, and Mr Phillips got quite upset about it. He thought he might have given someone the change for a pound by mistake. We went all through the receipt books. He thought he'd have to put the money in himself."

"Oh, dear! I bet that hurt!"

"He's not mean, but I think Mrs Phillips keeps a tight rein on the finances. Anyway, he found it. He took the till drawer out, and it had gone down the back."

"I thought we might go to the pictures this afternoon."

"It's a bit late now, isn't it?"

"Not if we go soon. Mum left some cheese sandwiches. Directly you've had something to eat, we'll get on."

"I don't feel hungry. Have you had something?"

"Yes."

"I'll go upstairs then and freshen up." Ina paused at the door. "Any letters?"

"No. I'm afraid not."

***

The show had already started went they arrived at the cinema. The usherette showed them to their seats. The film was a B rating and, as they had no idea what it was all about, they could not make head or tail of it and soon lost interest.

278

It was only when the newsreels started that Ina gave the screen any attention. It concerned mostly Montgomery, Eisenhower, or Churchill directing and controlling the war. There were some shots of British soldiers walking along, waving and cheering, and then some of American troops. Ina leaned forward, her eyes narrowed, hoping she would see them better. She looked at the men on the screen hoping to see a shoulder flash of the 2nd Armoured Division but failed to spot any. There were news items on the Royal Family, people who were doing strange things for the war effort, and the latest tips put out by the ministry of food.

The feature film was about an RAF station that had participated in the Battle of Britain. Avril watched this avidly.

It was hot and stuffy in the cinema. Ina could feel the roughness of the seat upholstery prickling her legs through the skirt of her dress. When the film was over, Avril asked her if she wanted to wait and see what they'd missed. She shook her head. "I just want to get out and get some fresh air," she said.

***

Hilda was laying out the evening meal when the girls walked in.

"I've made some salad," she said. "I wasn't sure what time you'd be home. I've cooked some new potatoes to go with it."

She called Clive in from the front room, and they all took their places at the table. Although Jim was at work, Hilda told Clive to put the radio on for the news, a matter of habit more than anything else. None of them was particularly interested until they heard Paris mentioned.

"Hush!" said Hilda.

Reports are coming in that there seems to be some sort of civil unrest in a certain quarter of Paris. The Germans have reinforced their security network around the city. It looks likely that there could be signs of small pockets of rebellion in some areas of the city . . . We will be broadcasting further bulletins as news becomes available . . .

"Good old Froggies!" Clive cried. "Let the Jerries have it!"

***

When Jim came home at 10 o'clock, the radio was still on.

"Did you hear the news?" he asked Hilda.

"Yes, but there's been nothing more since six o'clock."

There was a knock on the back door, and a voice called, "Only me!"

Alb came into the living room. "What do you think of the news then, Jim?"

"Don't know what to make of it, Alb. Hilda says there haven't been any further reports."

"Flash in the pan, would you say?"

"The Jerries might have put a stop to it."

"Can't be that far off Paris, now, can we?"

"I shouldn't have thought so, but you know what it's like with the news—blow hot one day, cold the next."

Avril announced she was going to bed, and Ina did likewise.

Ina's bed was alongside the window. She stood in her nightdress, looking through, past the garden to the fields beyond.

"What are you doing?" asked Avril.

"I'm just looking over Stratford."

"Oh, well. Goodnight, then."

"Goodnight."

Ina could see the outline of the castle rings. Along there, somewhere, the river ran between its banks towards the little bridge. She had walked along there so many times with David. She leaned her head against the coolness of the glass.

"David," she whispered softly. "Oh, please!" she begged silently. "Please let them get to Paris soon. Let them get leave and come back to Tidworth. Let me see him again!"

Usually, when she wished for something with all her being, a warm glow would suffuse her body. Somehow, this time, she felt nothing inside herself but cold.

***

Along a dusty French road, fringed by briar hedgerows separating it from the fields beyond, moved a column of tanks. Each side of the tanks, in single file, walked the men, hot in the August sun, helmets pushed back on their heads with the chinstraps hanging loosely either side, no longer marching but striding out at a leisurely pace. Some were calling out to others, some silent in their own thoughts, and some singing the songs soldiers sing. Birds flew among the hedgerows, their chirping mixing with the grinding and rattling of the tank tracks on their bogey wheels. From a field nearby came the lowing of a cow, and a voice called out, "Anyone here wanna glass of milk?"

There came an explosion. The leading tank reared and bucked and then tilted at an angle, fire and smoke pouring from its belly. Men were screaming, calling for medical aid. For a while, panic and confusion reigned. Then silence fell. And on the ground lay the dead and the dying . . . and the injured—who would bear the scars of their wounds for the rest of their days.

***

Ina had spent a restless night, and getting out of bed was a hard task. In the bathroom, she washed her face in near cold water. The plumber had still not been to fix the gas geyser. Coming downstairs, she walked into the living room. Clive was already seated at the breakfast table.

"Has the post been?" she asked Hilda.

"Yes. I'm sorry there was nothing for you today."

Ina sat at her place at the table. "I don't want much to eat, Mum. Can I just have some toast?"

"Are you all right, Ina? You look a bit peaky."

"I didn't sleep very well last night."

Avril came in and sat down. "Want me to meet your dinner time and have a stroll around the town? We can go and have something to eat and a cup of tea somewhere."

"Yes, all right. I won't take any sandwiches in that case, Mum."

"It'll save me a job," Hilda replied.

***

Mr Phillips was pulling the blinds out over the pavement with the aid of a long hook-ended pole. Ina got off her bicycle and hauled it onto the pavement.

"Morning, Mr Phillips."

"Good morning, Miss. I hope head office realises that we're conforming to their rules that the blinds are meant to keep the sun off the windows and not the rain off the pavements."

"No sign of rain," she said, smiling.

She pushed her bicycle on into the shop. Vera was in the staffroom putting on her overall. They exchanged good mornings, and Ina asked if she had heard from her boyfriend.

"Yes," was Vera's reply. "I had a letter this morning."

"No mention of him getting any leave then?"

"No. Too late now anyway. We've cancelled everything."

"I am sorry," Ina said.

Vera nodded.

As she turned to go out the door, Ina said, "He never mentioned any trouble in Paris, did he?"

"No," Vera answered. "But they're not allowed to say anything that won't get past the censor, are they?"

Ina put the bicycle out in the yard, came back into the staffroom, and put her overall on. She gave a quick glance in the mirror and went into the shop. The morning passed by uneventfully. Avril came into the shop just before it was time for Ina's lunch break. She passed a few pleasantries with Mr Phillips, and as there were no customers waiting, he told Ina she could go on.

Outside, Avril said, "I thought perhaps we could go to the Bib & Tucker."

"No!" Ina said, sharply.

"Why not?"

"It's too far away."

Avril looked at Ina questioningly but, as no further comment was forthcoming, shrugged her shoulders and suggested going along the canal.

✯✯✯

The café they approached was more of a transport café. It was mostly used by taxi drivers or bus crews changing shifts or the coach drivers who brought people in from the villages. The trade was a quick turnover, so it was not surprising that the seating consisted mostly of high stools and narrow counters set by the wall on either side of the café, with just a few tables and chairs in the centre. Perched on a high stool, with used crockery and overflowing ashtrays taking up most of the counter space, Ina began to wish that they had, after all, gone to the Bib & Tucker.

As Avril placed the tea and two sandwiches on the counter and sat down, Ina asked, "Does Brian have any idea of when he's going over to France?"

"In a week or two, as far as he knows."

"Will he get leave before he goes?"

"Lord knows. He might get in a weekend, if he's lucky. It's come at the wrong time for us. If I hadn't had my leave already, I might have been able to swing it and go to his station. I could have put up at the mess, and it would have given us a bit of time together. Now, I don't know."

"But if you're at Upavon and they let him have leave to see his parents before he goes—"

Avril sighed. "We'll just have to wait and see."

***

Back at work, Ina felt a headache coming on. From her handbag she took a packet of Aspro. She pulled the strip out of the packet, peeled a tablet from the waxy paper, swallowed it down with a drink of water, and went into the shop.

She had served several customers, when, towards the end of the afternoon, Mr Phillips asked her to go to the post office for some stamps. The headache had lifted, and she walked sprightly along to the post office, which was at the end of Market Street on the opposite side of the road. Her errand done, she came out of the post office and stood on the pavement, waiting to cross the road. There was not much in the way of traffic, except for a brewery dray passing by. The horse lumbered along, its hooves clopping on the cobbles and the harness bells jangling. Ina looked in both directions to make sure the road was clear. As she glanced to the right, she thought she saw a figure, an American soldier dressed in combat gear. Even as she watched, the figure, tall and slim, disappeared around the corner into the canal. Her heart began to race. She ran across the road and along the pavement, past the shop and towards the canal. Once there, she looked up and down both sides of the canal towards High Street but could see no sign of the figure.

I must be seeing things, she thought to herself. *It's the sun getting in my eyes.*

***

Mr Phillips was talking to a customer by the gents' department. Ina stood by the cash desk with the stamps and the change from the money he had given her. A strange feeling came over her, and she felt light-headed. She heard Mrs Gray say, "Are you all right, Miss Welland?"

She pulled herself together. "Oh. Yes . . . I'm all right. I just felt . . . you know . . . like . . . someone was walking over my grave."

Mrs Gray looked searchingly at her. "As long as you're sure . . ."

Ina thought to herself, *She thinks I'm pregnant.*

Mr Phillips came over to the cash desk. "Thank you, Miss," he said, taking the change and stamps from her.

He opened the desk drawer and took out the petty cash tin and a small ledger. Putting the stamps and cash in the tin, he opened the ledger and began writing in it. "Better keep the records straight."

***

On Saturday, Avril went back to her RAF station. She and Ina had said their goodbyes in the morning, and now she was in the carriage of the Waterloo train, looking out of the window. Her parents were standing on the platform. This was a moment Avril hated, waiting for the train to pull out and trying to find something to say to fill in the waiting time.

"Write to let us know you got back all right," Hilda said. It was what Hilda always said.

"Yes, Mum."

"Are you all right for money?" Jim asked.

"Yes, thanks, Dad."

The guard walked along the platform. "Hello, there, Jim."

Jim turned. "Oh, hello, Jack. Are you taking this train up?"

"Yes. Seeing the girl off then?"

"Yes," Hilda replied. "She's going to Upavon soon after she gets back."

"Ah? She won't have so far to come home."

Avril smiled at him.

He turned to Jim. "Looks like they've got a foot in the door in Paris then, Jim. Lots of heavy fighting going on, and the Froggies are fighting in the streets."

"Where did you hear that?"

"On the wireless, earlier on."

"Damned if I heard anything."

"Dick Bishop got hold of a wet battery wireless from somewhere and fixed it up in the guards' room. Well, I must get on."

Jack walked on up the platform and threw his bag into the guards' van. "Close all doors" he called.

He waved his flag and blew his whistle, and the train moved slowly out of the station.

***

Avril took off her jacket and sat down. Into Paris! Once in there, they would soon be in Germany. She wondered if there was any real need for Brian to go over now. This time next year, the war would be over. It had to be! She could start planning her wedding. Next September. That would give her a year. They'd be at peace. No more rationing. No more clothes coupons. She'd be able to buy as many dresses as she could afford. She'd have a gorgeous white wedding dress . . . satin . . . with a long train, four bridesmaids dressed in pink, and a three-tiered cake. She would be able to buy lots of frilly underwear for her trousseau. She leaned back and gave herself up to the wonderful life she imagined to be in front of her.

Chapter 26

On Monday morning, Ina stood at the bus station waiting for Stella's bus to arrive. The first thing she noticed when Stella stepped onto the path was her new hairstyle, swept up from the back and piled on top of her head.

"What happened to you?" Ina said in surprise.

"Don't you like it?" Stella asked

"Yes. It looks quite nice. Do you think it will stay like that?"

"Yes. It should do, just as long as I don't nod my head too much. Anyhow, how was your holiday? Thanks for the card by the way."

"It was all right. Saw the cathedral; went swimming; went to London one day."

"What was London like?"

Ina shrugged. "To tell the truth . . . I didn't think much of it. It was horrible on the tube and on those moving staircases."

She didn't mention Rainbow Corner or the two Canadian soldiers. Her holiday seemed far away now, and it was somewhat irrelevant. "What did you do?" she asked.

"Not much. I went to the pictures and a dance in Amesbury ballroom."

They reached the corner of Endless Street and Winchester Street when Stella stopped and pointed across the road. Ina's eyes followed; on the opposite corner, on the Blue Boar Row, stood an elderly man selling papers at a brisk rate. Ina read the billboard:

Allied Troops Converging on Paris.
Fierce Fighting in the City between German Troops and French Resistance
"Well!" said Stella "What do you know!"

***

Vera was in the staff room when they reached the shop.

"What do you think of the news then, Vera?" Ina asked.

"Good, isn't it? I heard it on the radio."

"You never know," Ina went on. "They might give your boyfriend leave, after all."

"It'll be too late for us now." Vera said flatly.

"Oh . . . Yes. I'm sorry. I didn't think. You'd have been married by now."

Vera gave Ina a rueful smile and went into the shop.

"Me and my big mouth," Ina said.

When Mrs Gray came in, she could hardly wait to get into her overall and get back into the shop.

"She's got something to tell us," Stella muttered.

"Probably the news about Paris," Ina suggested.

Mrs Gray's news wasn't about Paris, and it was relatively trivial. "Did you come down Fisherton Street this morning?" she asked Ina.

"No," Ina told her. "I went down St Paul's Road and along Castle Street. Why?"

"Well! You never saw nothing like it! There were those American soldiers that wear the white helmets."

"Snow drops," said Stella

"Yes . . . well. They were all stood outside the bank on the corner of High Street. Some more soldiers were taking boxes inside the bank. And the ones outside had Tommy guns—"

"I doubt if they were Tommy guns," put in Mr Phillips.

"Well. They looked like Tommy guns to me. Talk about turning Salisbury into Chicago. It was just like something out of the pictures."

"I expect they were putting money into the bank," Mr Phillips said.

"Money!" huffed Mrs Gray. "I wonder they have any to put in a bank the way they toss it around!"

"All good for trade, Mrs Gray," Stella said. "Ask the breweries."

***

News from France filtered through during the week, sometimes conflicting from paper to paper. Rumours flew everywhere. Jim stayed with the radio, the BBC being the only believable reporting.

***

Wednesday evening, Ina came home and asked if there was any mail.

"No. Sorry," Hilda said. "Perhaps you'll hear tomorrow."

"I haven't heard since I came back from Guildford, and that letter he'd written nearly a week before I got it," Ina said petulantly.

"It wasn't all that long ago,'" Jim told her. "I've told you before. The boy can't just drop everything and write a letter. Once they've finally got the Jerries out of France, they can rest up before they push their way towards Berlin. Then you'll hear more often. Now, be quiet and let me hear the rest of the blinking news."

The only consolation Ina was left with was that Stella had not heard from Joe either. News came through that the Allies were finding little opposition to their progress into Paris. The Parisians had formed their own militia, and the resistance movement had been fighting with them. There were signs that the Germans were fleeing the city, and on 25 August, Paris was liberated. Led by General De Gaulle and the Free French Army, the Allies marched in.

***

On Saturday, Stella arranged to stay the night with the Wellands, and she and Ina went to the cinema in the evening. The newsreels showed British and American tanks moving along the streets of Paris. People were crowding around, some climbing on top of the tanks. Young girls were throwing flowers and hugging and kissing the soldiers, who were walking alongside the tanks. French, British, and American flags were waved in front of the newsreel cameras.

"I wonder what the boys are doing?" Ina mused.

"Flirting with the French girls, I expect," Stella replied.

***

Monday morning, Mr Phillips regarded the summer over and decided to change the window displays to reflect the coming of autumn. Sandals would be taken off sale, those in the windows and those in the shop, and slippers put in their place.

***

August gradually drew to a close. Soon, the evenings would be drawing in. Already the leaves were changing to red and gold, and the earlier summer flowers were dying off. The roses would be left to bloom alone until they were joined by Michaelmass daisies, chrysanthemums, and autumn lilies. September heralded its arrival with heavy rain. And still no word came from David or Joe.

Chapter 27

September 1944

"I've had a letter from Joe," Stella said as she stepped off the bus. "He's in the military hospital at Tidworth; he's been wounded."

"Oh, heavens; is he badly hurt?"

"I don't know . . . He didn't say."

"Did he say how long he's been back in England?"

"No. But he wants me to go over there, and he wants me to take you with me."

Ina felt a chill creep over her. "Is it something to do with David?"

"Yes, I think so."

"Did he say what it was?"

"I'm sure it's nothing serious, or he would have said so. Don't panic, Ina. David probably gave him something to give to you."

"No," said Ina. "Something's wrong, I know it."

"I'm sure everything is all right. We won't know anything until we've seen Joe."

"When can we go over to Tidworth?"

"How about going tomorrow afternoon, straight from work?"

"Yes, that's all right," Ina agreed.

Somehow, Ina got through the day. But by the time she had reached home, the strain told on her. She had only just gotten into the living room when she burst into tears.

Alarmed, Hilda went to her. "What is it, Ina? Whatever is the matter?"

"It's David," she sobbed. "There's something wrong, and Joe hasn't said what it is."

"Joe? What's it got to do with Joe?"

She told her mother about the letter Stella had received from Joe.

"You'll have to calm down," Hilda warned, "or you'll make yourself ill. If there was anything wrong, David's mother would have told you."

"Perhaps it's only just happened. Perhaps she doesn't know."

"What are you going to do?"

"Go to Tidworth with Stella tomorrow afternoon. We thought we'd go after work."

"Will you have enough for your bus fare?" Hilda took her purse from her handbag. "You'd better have some money to get yourself something to eat."

***

The Tidworth bus stopped at every little village it went through. Yet, when at last, it reached Tidworth town, Ina felt reluctant to get off.

"I'm dreading getting there," she said to Stella. "What am I going to find out?"

"We've got to find the place first," Stella told her. "I haven't a clue where to go. It could be near the camp. We went up this road, didn't we?"

Several American soldiers, obviously from the hospital, were walking about. All showed signs of having been wounded. Some were on crutches; others had an arm in a sling; one had the arm of his jacket pinned halfway up his arm. Ina thought about Jack in David's song. Stella approached one of them and asked the way to the hospital.

"Just keep going along this road," he told her. "Take the first turn on the left; go up that road, and it's about halfway up."

"You can't miss it," another one put in with a grin.

In spite of how she felt, Ina could not help smiling at this; it was an American take-off.

***

The American flag, flying from a standard in the grounds, was the first thing they saw.

As they neared the main gate, two military policemen came towards them.

"I've come to see my boyfriend," Stella told them. "He's in this hospital. He was wounded in France." She took Joe's letter from her handbag and passed it to one of the MPs.

He took it, glanced at it, and handed it back to her. "Got any identification?" he asked.

The girls fished out their identity cards.

The MP looked closely at them but did not take them. "Keep hold of them," he told the girls. "You may have to show them to the guy at the reception. Go to the main entrance door; reception is just inside."

Holding the identity cards, and, Stella, Joe's letter, they walked through the door. A sergeant was sitting behind the desk. Stella walked up to him.

He looked at her enquiringly. "Yes, young ladies, what can I do for you?"

"We've come to see Sergeant Joe Smith," Stella told him. She held out her card, but he did not take it. "Can you tell us where he is?"

"Don't rightly know offhand," he replied, "but I can look it up for you."

He pulled a large book towards him and turned a few pages, running his finger down them as he did so. "Yeah. Here he is. I'll get someone to take you so you don't get lost."

He picked up the telephone receiver and pressed a button. "That you, Red?" he called into the mouthpiece. "I have a job for you."

He turned to the girls. "Red'll take you to where your boy is. Best get somebody to take you; got to make sure they're all in a fit state for visitors, if you get my meaning."

A door along the corridor opened, and a young man wearing a white short-sleeved jacket and white trousers walked through.

"This is Red," the sergeant informed them. "He'll show you the way."

Red was a nice-looking boy, tall and slim with a mop of ginger hair.

"Which of you is Sergeant Smith's girl?" he asked.

"I am," Stella said.

He turned to Ina. "You come along for the ride?"

"Yes. Something like that," she answered.

"We'll soon have you there," he went on. "Just follow me."

He led them along the corridor and then down another, at the end of which were double doors. They came to a halt here, and Red peered through the glass inset at the top.

"Guess it's okay for you to go in," he said.

The girls found themselves in a long ward with a row of beds either side. Red walked in front of them, stopping at one of the beds. "Got some visitors for you, Joe."

Joe was propped up in his bed with pillows; a cradle was over his legs. He smiled at them and held his hand out to Stella.

Red got a chair each for the girls and said, "If everyone's okay, I'll be on my way."

They thanked him, and he left the ward.

"Nice guy," Joe murmured.

They sat down, Stella holding Joe's hand.

He turned to Ina. "Ina, honey . . . Dave . . . I hardly know how to tell you."

"What is it Joe? Has he been killed?"

"No. No. Ina . . . He got wounded, pretty bad."

Ina put her hands to her face. "How bad? What happened?"

Joe was silent for a while, and then he said, "The tank he was walking behind hit an anti-tank mine and blew up. A lot of the guys were hurt. Some were killed outright. Dave caught it all down his right side . . . hurt his hand. I'm so sorry, Ina, but he lost his right eye."

Ina sat stunned. She felt as though she should be screaming and that it was only because she was in this hospital ward, surrounded by bed after bed of wounded soldiers, that she didn't. Joe was still talking: she had a job to concentrate on what he was saying.

"I wasn't there when it happened," he went on. "Heard the noise and saw the smoke and the flames. I ran back to see if he was okay. They were taking him to the field hospital when I reached him. They told me what had happened to him. I tried to talk to him, but he was all morphined up and wasn't making sense. Next day, I made some enquiries, but he'd been taken from the field hospital and shipped back to the UK."

"Do you know where he is now?" Ina's voice was quiet and it quivered a little.

"No, honey, I don't. I've tried to find out, but no one of that name had been brought in. I guess him and the other guys who were with him went someplace else."

Silence fell around Joe's bed, until Stella broke it. "What happened to you?" she asked.

"Some of us were out scouting around, about a couple of days after Dave got hit. We ran into a machine gun post. They caught us by surprise. Two of my boys were killed. We got told before that there were no Germans in the area. Someone forgot to tell the ginks that fired on us."

"Are you badly hurt, Joe?" Stella asked.

"No. Not too bad. Took a few bullets in the leg, but they didn't get to the bone. It'll soon heal. I just have to rest up a while."

"What happened to the Germans?" Stella wanted to know.

"We all lobbed hand grenades at them. We wiped them out but not before they'd fired a few shots and wounded a few more of us." Joe eased himself up a little. "Can you pour me some water please, honey?" he asked Stella.

Stella picked up the carafe of water, which was standing on Joe's bedside table; poured some into the glass that stood beside it; and passed it to him. He took a large swig and put the glass back onto the table. He leaned back on his pillows. Joe and Stella resorted to small talk with the occasional ringing outburst of Stella's laughter. She hadn't even expressed her regret for what had happened to David. Ina felt alone and shut off.

I'm in the way, she thought. *I really don't want to be here.*

It didn't matter how hard she tried; she couldn't help her eyes straying in the direction of the wounded men. Some, like Joe, had cradles over their legs. Some were sitting up, the top half of their bodies swathed in bandages, others with an arm in a sling. One had the side of his face covered with a dressing and a bandage around his head to keep it in place, and there was one with the bound stump of an arm. She thought of David's song and Jack, who had been told by his friends that he could still hold his girl with one arm, and . . . David—half blinded . . . If she loved him, it wouldn't make any difference, would it? Ina felt suddenly faint and got up out of her chair.

"If you don't mind," she said, "I think I'll go outside for a bit of fresh air."

"You don't have to go," Stella told her.

"No. Of course not," added Joe.

"I think I will, just the same," she said.

"Okay, honey. If you're sure that's what you want. Take care of yourself, now. Don't go getting lost."

***

She found her way along the corridors and came to the reception desk. The sergeant was there, talking to Red and another medic. They turned as they saw her approach.

"Going already?" asked Red

"No. I'm just going out for some air," she replied.

"You look a little pale," Red observed. "Are you feeling okay?"

"Yes. I'm fine," she answered. In spite of her steady reply, she was near tears.

"Tell me to mind my own business," he said, "but you look a little upset to me."

He had followed her to the door and now held it open for her. "Mind if I take a walk with you?"

He fell into step beside her as she walked through the door. "It's a big place out there. You could get lost. Besides, there are a lot of wolves around, dressed in soldiers' clothing."

She looked up at him, he smiled down at her, and she smiled back.

"That's more like it," he said and then, "Something wrong?"

"I've had some bad news. I'm having a bit of a job to take it in."

"Your boyfriend?"

"He's been wounded, Joe told me. He and Joe are friends. We all went around together before they went to France."

"So, you were going steady then?"

"Yes. We got engaged, and we're going to get married after the war."

"Was he badly hurt?"

"He's lost his right eye."

"That's real tough," Red sympathised. "Do you know where he's at?"

"No. Joe tried to find out, but no one has seen him."

"You could always try the American Red Cross."

"Will they tell me what hospital he's at?"

"They may not tell you where he is, but they would probably give you an army post office number, so you could write to him."

"Do you know where the Red Cross is?" Ina was beginning to have hope.

"They are in London." He had seen the hope in her eyes. "Do you want me to give you the address?"

"Yes, please, if you can."

"Come on back inside" he said, "and I'll root it out for you."

There was another medic in Red's room, sitting at one of the two desks, typing. It was the same medic who had been talking to the sergeant earlier. He looked up as they walked in.

"This young lady wants the Red Cross address," Red told him. He turned to Ina, "I'm sorry, honey, I never caught your name."

"It's Ina," she replied.

"Ina," Red repeated. "Well, Ina, this here is Chuck. Chuck, this is Ina. She's a friend of Joe Smith's."

Red pulled a spare chair up to the desk and placed it opposite his own. "Sit down and make yourself comfortable," he said.

He went to a filing cabinet, opened a drawer, and took out a folder. He put the folder on the desk. "Won't be long," he told her.

Chuck looked over at her. "Wanna coffee?" he asked.

"Yes please," she said, gratefully.

Chuck got up and lifted a coffee pot from a hotplate.

"Make that two, will you?" put in Red.

Chuck poured the coffee into two cups. "Cream?" he asked Ina.

Cream! She remembered the day she and Stella had gone into the mess at Tidworth. The only cream Ina had been familiar with was tinned, and she now had visions of big blobs of it floating on top of her cup. Nevertheless she said, again, "Yes please."

"Sugar?"

"No, thank you."

"Sweet enough, eh?" Chuck grinned.

"My family gave up sugar in their tea when rationing came in. My mum told us if we didn't give up sugar, we wouldn't have Christmas puddings or cakes."

"You people have been rationed a long time," Chuck said gravely.

"A few months after the war started, I think," Ina told him and then added, equally gravely, "We've been at war five years since the third of this month."

Chuck shook his head as he sat down again and resumed his typing. Red, meanwhile, had extracted a letter from the file.

"I have it," he said. "I'll write it down for you."

He pulled a notepad towards him, tore off a sheet, wrote something down, and passed it to her. She glanced at it and then placed it in her handbag. They sat there, drinking their coffee.

Red asked her "Where do you and Joe's girl come from?"

"Salisbury," Ina replied, "at least I do. Stella comes from just outside Amesbury."

"I know Salisbury," said Red. "I've been there a couple of times, but I don't know this Amesbury, though I think I've heard of it."

"The Tidworth bus passes through it on the way to Salisbury," she said. "Where do you come from?"

"Virginia," he answered. "A place called Norfolk."

"We have a Norfolk," Ina told him.

"So I've been told. We have a lot of places in the States that are named after places in England. Our state was named after your Queen Elizabeth."

"What did you do before you joined the army?" she asked.

"I'd just finished college and was aiming to go to medical school. I wanted to be a doctor like my dad."

"Your dad's a doctor?"

"Yes. He's an army doctor, but he's back home in the States. When are you coming over to see Joe again?"

"Sunday, I expect."

"Well, I don't think you'll have heard anything by then, but maybe by the Wednesday after."

There came a knock at the door, and a young soldier came into the room. He was in bandages from the waist up to under his arms. From one shoulder, the bandaged stump of an arm protruded. He saw Ina sitting there and seemed to be confused. "I'm sorry, ma'am," he said. "I didn't realise there was a young lady in here, or I would have covered up."

"Don't worry," Ina told him. "It's all right."

"I came to see Chuck," the young soldier went on.

"What is it?" Chuck asked him.

"Can I see you outside for a minute? It's kind of personal."

"Okay," said Chuck. He got up, walked to the door, and went outside with the boy.

"Oh, dear!" Ina said. "I don't suppose I should be in here, should I?"

"You're okay here," Red assured her. "I wouldn't have asked you in otherwise."

She stood up. "I ought to be going," she said. "The others will wonder where I've got to."

Red got up out of his chair and came round her side of the desk. "I'll walk you along the corridor," he said. "And by the way, when you get your letter from the Red Cross, bring it in when you come to see Joe. I won't promise anything, but I may be able to tell you from the post office number where the hospital is."

"Oh, could you? If it's not too far away, I can go and see him."

They walked along the corridor. The young badly wounded soldier who had come into see Chuck was walking along towards them. As he passed, Ina gave him a smile, and he smiled shyly back. When he had gone by, she said to Red, "I suppose you get used to seeing these wounded boys coming back from France."

"No. Not really," Red answered. "But you do what you can for them. We try to make things a little easier for them. It's what we've been trained for. It's our job."

"David told me once he'd rather be killed outright than be badly disabled."

"A lot of guys say that," Red replied. "But when the time comes, all they want to do is live."

Chapter 28

When Ina arrived home, her parents and Clive were in the front room; she went through and joined them. Hilda looked up as her daughter came into the room. One look at Ina's pale face told her all was not well. "Did you see Joe?" she asked.

Ina nodded.

"Did he tell you what it was he wanted to see you about?"

"David's been wounded." Her voice was just above a whisper.

"Do you know how badly?"

Ina clasped her hands together until her knuckles were white. "He was hit by shrapnel when a tank went over a mine and blew up. It caught him down his right side. His right hand was hurt and . . ." She paused.

"What is it, Ina? What else happened to him?"

"He's lost his right eye."

"Dear God, no! Oh, God. I'm so sorry!" Hilda was visibly shaken.

"Is he in the same hospital as Joe?" asked Jim.

"No. Joe doesn't know where he went. He asked around, but none of the others in the ward have seen David. Joe supposed that he and the others who were wounded with him must have been taken to some other hospital. Joe wasn't with him when it happened. When he heard about it, he managed to find him just before they took him to the field hospital. He said David had been given morphine and couldn't talk properly. As far as Joe knew, they took him to a hospital ship to bring him back over here. One of the medics at Tidworth Hospital said I could write to the American Red Cross; they might give me an army post office number. He said he would try and find out from that where the hospital is."

"Well, said Jim, "that's something."

"Dad, do you think his mother knows?"

"She's bound to know by now. She's his next of kin, so she'd be the first to know."

"I feel I ought to write to her, but I don't know what to say. I wonder how long she's known."

"If you think you should have heard from her, don't forget she must be as shocked as you were, and she probably doesn't feel much like writing letters. As for writing to her, I should wait until you hear from the Red Cross. If it isn't too far away, you can go and visit him; then at least you'll be able to let her know you have seen him," said Hilda.

Hilda got up from her chair. "I'm going to make some tea," she announced. "I'll make some cheese and tomato sandwiches, unless anyone prefers Spam."

"Cheese will do for me," said Jim.

"And me," put in Clive and added, "Could I have brown sauce on mine, please, Mum?"

"You and your brown sauce!" Hilda retorted. "You can come and put it on yourself."

"I want it on my sandwich, not on myself," Clive answered with a grin.

"Not so much of your cheek," warned Hilda.

"I'll cut the sandwiches for you if you like."

"No thanks. We want sandwiches, not doorsteps."

Clive got up off the sofa and followed his mother out into the kitchen. Jim leaned back in his chair and reached for his tobacco pouch. Ina followed his movements; it was such a normal everyday thing for him to do. She had bought the pouch last Christmas with an ounce of his favourite tobacco and a packet of cigarette papers. Clive had given him a Zippo lighter.

Normal. What was normal? Was it that everything went on in the same way, no matter what? David had been wounded . . . seriously. He was in some hospital somewhere. She didn't know where; she couldn't be with him; neither could his mum . . . And here was Dad; rolling a fag, and Mum making tea . . . It was as though nothing had happened.

Jim rolled his cigarette between his fingers. He looked at Ina. "How was Joe wounded?"

"His patrol ran into a machine gun post. He had bullets in his legs. They wiped the Germans out. Joe reckoned that had he been nearer the post, he would probably have lost his leg. As it was, the bullets lodged in his calf and didn't go through to the bone."

"I'd say he was very lucky," Jim remarked. "They're very vicious things, machine guns."

He was about to say that he'd seen men nearly cut in half by bullets fired from them at close range but thought better of it. Ina had been well acquainted already with the horrors of war. Being in that hospital ward at Tidworth had most likely given her some idea. There had probably been bandaged heads and trunks plus a few amputees, let alone her thoughts on the tragedy of David's wounds.

Hilda came back into the room bringing a tray of tea. Clive brought up the rear carrying a plate piled high with sandwiches. The tea and food, along with four tea plates, were deposited on the low table in front of the sofa. Clive handed his father a plate, took one for himself, put a sandwich on it, and sat down.

"Mind you don't get crumbs all over the sofa," Hilda told him. She handed a plate to Ina.

"No thanks, Mum. I don't want anything to eat."

"You must have something. You can't go without your food. You haven't been all day without anything inside you I hope."

"No. We went to a café in Tidworth before we caught the bus home."

"Did you have something substantial?"

"Hamburgers, chips, and peas."

"Hamburgers?" said Jim. "That's what they have back in America, isn't it?"

"Yes, Dad," Clive piped up. "It's what Wimpy eats in the Popeye cartoons. He eats great stacks of them."

"I suppose they're after the American trade in Tidworth," said Hilda.

"They have them in our cafés, too." Ina didn't tell her mother that she had not finished her meal.

"Are you sure you don't want anything, Ina?" Hilda persisted.

"No, Mum. Honestly. I'm not hungry."

"If there's something else you fancy besides—"

Jim held his hand up. "Hilda," he said. "Don't press the girl."

Hilda sighed and sat down in her chair. "I won't say anymore, but you know how I worry."

"There's no need to, Mum. I'm all right."

"Why don't you stay home tomorrow? I have to pop into town in the morning. I can call into the shop and tell Mr Phillips you won't be in."

"I'd rather be at work, Mum. I don't want to be here all day on my own."

Ina got up and put her empty cup on the tray. "Do you mind if I go on up to bed?"

"No, of course I don't. An early night will do you good." Hilda turned to Clive. "It's time you were on your way, young man. It's school tomorrow."

Clive followed Ina up the stairs. He paused at his bedroom door. "Sorry about David," he said.

She smiled at him and went into her own room. She undressed and put her nightclothes on. She did not get into bed straight away. Instead, she went to her dressing table drawer, took out her writing case, and wrote to the Red Cross. She tried to give them as many details as she could. Having addressed the envelope, she stuck on a postage stamp and slipped the letter into her handbag, ready to post in the morning.

***

For a while, she lay there in the darkening room, sleep far away, listening to the sound of the traffic going along Devizes Road. Some nights, in the stillness, she could hear wagons being shunted in Fisherton yard. Where was David? Why hadn't he written? He had been wounded on 22 August, and *Joe two days later. But Stella had heard from Joe.*

He's been badly injured, she told herself, *worse even than Joe. His right hand was hurt and he'd lost his eye. He couldn't write, could he?*

Why couldn't she cry? She wanted to, but there weren't any tears; there was just this cold feeling inside her. Something bad had happened, and there was nothing she or anyone else could do about it.

Her mind suddenly went back to that day at Tidworth when they had said their last goodbyes and she had watched him as he walked across the field towards the barracks. She had turned to Stella and said, "I'm never going to see him again, am I?" Had it been a premonition? She told herself that that was stupid. That day at the seaside, when she had thought her father would be going to war. Well? He hadn't, had he?

In spite of herself, she slept, and in the morning, there was a letter from Olivia. It was brief. She had heard that David had been wounded.

The army had not told her where or how badly, just that it was not life-threatening and as soon as the hospital was satisfied he was able to travel, he would be transported back to the USA. They hadn't told her which hospital, except that it was in the UK. Had Ina heard from him? If so did she know where he was and had she been able to visit him?

"She obviously hasn't heard from him herself," Hilda commented when Ina told her the gist of the letter. "She must be a very worried woman, poor soul."

***

Ina cycled straight along Devizes Road, posting her letter at the sorting office when she reached Fisherton Street. From there, she made her way to the bus station via the town centre.

"Are you all right? You look ever so pale," Stella remarked when they met up.

"I didn't have a very good night," Ina told her.

"No. I don't expect you did," Stella sympathised. "Have you managed to write to the Red Cross?"

"Yes. I wrote last night. I'll write to Olivia at break time, though what I am going to say to her I don't know. I had a letter from her this morning. She knows he's been wounded but doesn't know how badly. I can't tell her, can I? She will probably get to hear officially. I'll have to tell her that I've found out he's been wounded but not go into detail. I'll tell her I've written to the Red Cross and say I'll let her know as soon as I find something out myself."

Mr Phillips had been put in the picture about the summons to Tidworth. He was sympathetic and hoped Ina would hear something soon. She said nothing to Mrs Gray, but Vera knew. Still upset about the cancellation of her wedding, she nevertheless put a hand on Ina's arm and told her how sorry she was. Ina felt that, in a way, she and Vera had something in common, in both being concerned about their fiancés. Vera was also waiting for a letter from France that was a long time in coming. In spite of the anxieties of his staff, to Mr Phillip's gratification, neither girl let it affect her work.

One thing that concerned him though. Towards the end of the morning, he said, "I don't know what to do about these American officers' shoes. We haven't sold many, and I don't expect we shall get many officers in now."

"I think there are still a few in town," said Ina.

"There's the American hospital at Odstock," Vera put in. "I expect the army doctors there would be interested if they knew about them."

"I could try putting them all in the window," Mr Phillips mused.

Having decided on this, he opened the door, which gave him access into the window. Ina, meanwhile, was standing stock still as though in a trance.

"Buck up, Ina," Stella nudged her elbow. "You look as though you've turned to stone."

"Did you hear what Vera said?" asked Ina.

"What did Vera say?" replied Stella.

"She said Odstock! The American hospital . . . at Odstock!"

"Don't get your hopes up, Ina," Stella warned her.

"No," said Ina, deflated. "It would be too good to be true."

***

Ina and Stella went over to Tidworth Sunday afternoon. Joe was sitting in an armchair next to his bed. His leg was still in plaster, and crutches were leaning against the wall.

"Been doing some walking," he said. "Thought I'd wait for you to turn up and get you to come outside with me."

"Are you sure you're up to it?" asked Stella anxiously.

"Sure, I'll manage fine."

It was slow going, but Joe made his way along the corridor.

Red appeared out of his office. "Just take it easy, there," he said to Joe. "Don't get out of your depth."

"Promise." Joe grinned.

They walked a little way through the grounds of the hospital until it became obvious that Joe was tiring. There were seats here and there around the green areas of grass.

"Think maybe I'll sit awhile," he said.

They sat down on one of the seats, and Stella propped Joe's crutches against a nearby tree. It was pleasant in the grounds. The mid-September sun felt warm, and a gentle breeze was blowing. Ina did not notice any flower beds but some late flowering shrubs had been planted here and there and were now in bloom. Birds flew into the sky and then soared back down into the already yellowing leaves of the trees. Some patients were being wheeled along the gravel pathways, their legs covered in blankets. Ina could tell that a few of them had lost a leg, and in one case, a young man, probably no older than David, had lost them both. A group was sitting on a low wall by the hospital building, listening to a soldier playing a guitar. The notes of the music drifted across the air with the breeze. It wasn't a song Ina recognised. Perhaps it was a folk song, like David's song. She wondered if he knew the song. She would have liked to go and ask him, but he might take it the wrong way and think she was after him.

Stella wouldn't mind if it was her, but she didn't have Stella's self-confidence, or was it cheek? She realised that, until she'd met David, she had more or less walked in Stella's shadow. Even now, sitting here with Stella laughing up into Joe's face and punching him playfully on his arm, she felt awkward and self-conscious. She was playing gooseberry, and she wished she were somewhere else.

When Joe said, "Come on, then. I'm ready to go," she could only sense a feeling of relief.

Stella protested. "We haven't been here very long!"

"I feel like a stroll," he said. "My butt is getting numb. I sit on it nearly all day."

He started to rise. Ina fetched the crutches and handed them to him. Together she and Stella managed to get him to his feet. He took hold of the crutches and put one under each arm.

A voice behind them called, "Do you need some help, there?"

They turned to see Red coming across the green.

"I think I'm okay now I'm on my feet, Red," Joe answered.

He took a few steps and then, getting his confidence, started to walk more easily along the path.

"I'd reckoned to take the girls for a cup of coffee," he said.

"Mind if I tag along? I can fetch them for you," Red told him.

"Sure," Joe said.

"Where did you figure on going?"

"To the canteen."

"Reckon that you will make it?"

"Yeah, sure I'll make it!"

The going was slow, but they finally made it to the canteen. They found an empty table and sat down, Red hovering over Joe to make sure he was comfortably settled.

"You all want coffee? Or would you girls prefer tea?"

"I'll have tea if that is all right," Stella said.

"I'll have tea as well," Ina told him.

"Two teas and two coffees it is then."

Red walked towards the counter. Ina looked around her. It was just as it had been at the barracks, when David and Joe had taken them there. There were women sitting at the tables, only this time the women were nurses. Some were sitting with the men and some on their own. She and Stella were the only two civilians. There were a few soldiers dressed like Red, but mostly they were patients, some in wheelchairs, others wearing plaster casts.

Even as Ina was taking it all in, two medics came into the room, each giving an arm to a young soldier, not more than a boy. A bandage across both eyes was keeping two cotton pads in place. Ina suddenly felt near tears. David had lost one eye; this boy appeared to have lost both. Red returned with a tray of coffee, tea, and a jug of what the girls took to be milk and put it down on the table. He handed the cups around, put the jug down, and lodged the tray against the table. Ina and Stella looked into their cups and then at each other. The cups contained hot water, and in each saucer was a small bag with a tiny length of fine twine attached.

Joe caught their look. "They don't run to teapots here." He grinned.

"Hey!" exclaimed Red "I never thought about that!"

"It's all right," Ina said. "It'll be good practise for when I go to America; all I have to do now is learn to eat my dinner holding my fork in my right hand instead of my left."

The milk turned out to be single cream, but they made no comment. They put the teabags into their cups with the twine hanging over the edge and spooned them around until the water resembled the colour of tea.

"How about some doughnuts?" asked Joe. "You girls want doughnuts?"

"Yes, please," replied Stella "We don't see them very often these days."

"I'll get them," offered Red, getting up from his chair.

Joe put his hand in his pocket and drew out some coins. "Here," he said.

Red took the coins. "Okay," he said, "seeing as how you get paid more than I do."

He grinned at the girls and, picking up the tray, went back to the counter. He came back with six doughnuts and three plates.

"Only six doughnuts?" queried Joe.

"None for me," Red answered. "I had a big lunch."

Joe and the girls helped themselves.

Stella suddenly cried out, "Joe Smith! What are you doing?"

Joe had picked up a doughnut between a finger and thumb and was dipping it into his coffee.

"I'm dunking my doughnut, what do you think? Don't you dunk yours at home?"

"I'd get my hand slapped if I did," she retorted.

"It doesn't taste the same if it hasn't been dunked," he answered.

"Our doughnuts are big and round. I don't think they'd fit in a cup," Stella explained to him. "Anyway, they're filled with jam—not so much now as they used to be but enough to make a mess of your coffee."

"You don't have ring doughnuts?" asked Red.

"Not that I know of; at least I don't remember seeing any."

"I have," said Ina. "I've seen them being made."

"Where was that then?"

"When Avril and I went to Guildford."

"What? When you went up to see your aunty and uncle in August?"

"No; it was before the war. Avril and I stayed a week with them. We usually went with Mum and Dad, but this time we went on our own. Actually, they're not a real aunt and uncle; they're friends of Mum and Dad. We have always called them our aunt and uncle since we were little. Uncle George was on the railway with my dad; when they passed out as drivers, Dad stayed here, and Uncle went to Guildford. That was in 1935. We went up there on our own in 1938. I was eleven years old. Avril was about fourteen. She'd just left school."

"What has all this got to do with ring doughnuts?" Stella asked.

Ina continued, "One day, we went into town with Auntie Grace to do some shopping. We went to this bakery. Auntie went inside, but we stayed outside looking in the window. There was a kind of round vat, with oil in it, going round in a circle. Hanging over it was a cylinder. A man was standing behind it, and he poured some kind of batter into the cylinder.

The batter came out of a spout at the bottom, like flat blobs with holes in the middle—*plop*—into the hot oil."

All the time Ina had been talking she had, unconsciously, been using her hands to illustrate her narrative. "Halfway round, a sort of paddle thing turned them over. They went on until they reached the man who scooped them up by putting a little white stick through the holes. He shook sugar over them and then put them into a paper bag and gave them to Auntie Grace."

There was a short silence when Ina had finished her tale, and then a bout of clapping broke out. The applause came from the table next to them, where four soldiers were sat.

One of them leaned across. "That was a swell story, honey. You know? I might have gone through the rest of my life not knowing how doughnuts were made!"

Chapter 29

The Wellands were sat at the table when Cissie opened the back door and, "coo-e-e-d."

"Come in Cissie," called Hilda.

Jim sighed.

Cissie walked into the living room. "I haven't seen you all day to tell you the good news."

"What is it then, Cissie?" asked Jim.

"Harold's passed out with top marks, and he's volunteered for commando training."

"You must be very pleased," Hilda said graciously. "Where will they be sending him?"

"I don't know. He didn't say. He probably isn't allowed to. I only got his letter this morning. He didn't say much at all, really, except that he'd passed out and he was getting his gear up together ready to move. Directly he gets there, he'll send me his new address." She turned to Ina. "Your young man's been wounded then, Ina. I'm so sorry. Do you know where he is?"

"No. I've written to the American Red Cross in London."

"Will they tell you?"

"I'm hoping they'll give me an army post office number; at least I can find out from that, I should think."

"Yes. Your mum told me you had written to them. Well, I must go. I just had to tell you the good news about Harold. I mustn't keep you from your tea."

"Well at least," said Ina when Cissie had departed, "there were no sarky comments."

"Now that Harold is in the army, she'll probably get a different view of things. It might make her a bit more sensitive. I know she's over the moon about Harold, but I expect underneath she's as anxious as any mother for her son, for all that boasting."

"I can't say I've ever been all that stuck on the boy," Jim remarked. "All the same, I'm glad he's done well, for Alb's sake as much as anything. He's got a lot of hard training in front of him. I wish him luck and hope he makes it."

***

The letter from the Red Cross arrived on Friday morning. It told her that David George Easton was hospitalised in an American military hospital and gave her the army post office number.

"All I have to do now is find out where it is." Ina felt as if a weight had been lifted from her shoulders.

"You reckon that bloke at Tidworth can find out?" asked Jim.

"I hope so, Dad. In any case, I can write to David."

***

When they reached the reception desk at Tidworth, Ina glanced around hoping that Red would be there, but there was no sign of him. In the ward, Joe stood by one of the beds talking to the occupant. He no longer had his leg in plaster but still leant on one crutch.

"Your plaster's off!" cried Stella.

"You noticed!" he said. "I aim to throw away this crutch in a few more days."

"What'll happen? Will they send you home?"

"I doubt it, honey. Once I'm all patched up, I'll go back to Europe I guess."

Ina was horrified. "Back to the fighting?"

"Honey, as long as you can walk and wave both arms in the air, you're reckoned to be fighting fit. Now, have you heard from the Red Cross?"

Ina took the letter out of her handbag and passed it to Joe. He read it and handed it back to her.

"I don't know much about these post office numbers," he told her.

"Red said he might be able to find out when he told me to write to them." Ina looked at Joe anxiously.

"Well, I reckon he could tell if anyone can. Don't know if it is classified information. Guess we could find Red and ask him."

Together, the trio walked along the corridor. When they reached the desk, Joe asked the sergeant if he knew where Red was.

"In his office, as far as I know," was the reply.

The girls followed Joe as he led them down the corridor. He stopped outside Red's office door, knocked, and opened it.

"You gotta minute, Red?"

"Sure, Joe. What can I do for you?"

"You remember young Ina here? She's heard from the Red Cross, got a post office number. Figures you may be able to find where her boy is."

"I'll sure try. Come on in."

He held the door open wider, and all three trooped into his office. Red motioned to then to sit down. He then walked over to a large metal cabinet, took a bunch of keys from his pocket, and opened the lock. He took a binder out, placed it on the desk, and leafed through the pages.

"Here we are," he said." It's in Northern Ireland".

"Northern Ireland!" cried Ina in dismay. "I'll never be able to visit him over there!"

Red looked at her crestfallen face and said gently: "Look. I can't promise anything, but with a bit of luck, I may be able to get a phone number."

He got up and, this time, went to a filing cabinet. He shuffled about in one of the drawers until he drew out a file. Putting it on the desk next to the binder, he flicked through the papers. There was complete silence in the room. Joe and Stella were looking intently at Red, while Ina, her hands gripped together in an effort to stop them trembling, concentrated on a pot of chrysanthemums in the window.

When Red said, "I've got one," her heart was beating so fast she thought it would burst. Her eyes were now on Red as he pulled the phone towards him and dialled the number.

After what seemed an age, he spoke into the mouthpiece. "Do you think you can help me? . . . I'm calling from Tidworth—Tidworth, Hampshire, England . . . . Yes . . . It's an American military hospital. My name is Red Baker. I'm a medic here. I'm trying to trace a Private First Class David George Easton . . . come to you from France . . . Facial injuries . . . Okay, I'll hold the line." He looked at Ina. "They have to find out which ward he's in."

The waiting was interminable.

At last, Red said, "Yes," to the phone. There was another silence and then, "Yes, that's right, Private First Class David George Easton. What? When? Oh. I see . . . Well, thanks anyway."

He put the phone down and looked at Ina. "Honey, I'm so sorry. They shipped him out yesterday. He's on his way back home."

Chapter 30

OCTOBER 1944

It was a little while before the letter came. Ina slit the envelope open and drew out the letter. She read.

My dearest Ina,

When you get this letter, I shall be home. I have been wounded. I have lost my right eye and my face has been cut about some. No matter how they patch me up, I shall be scarred. What I am telling you is, if you change your mind about us, I shall understand. You haven't seen me yet. I am disfigured. I feel I can't tie you to me for life. You are young and can find some other guy. I still love you, sweet pea, but I don't want you should come over to the States and find you can't handle it. If you write to me, send it to my home. So that's where I'll be. I wrote my mom. She knows the score. My hand got hurt, so someone else is writing this letter for me.

Love,
David

***

She met Stella at the bus station and told her she had heard from David. "Oh, good," said Stella. "What did he have to say?"

313

"He only confirmed what Joe had told us, except how he was wounded."

Ina did not tell Stella that David had offered to release her. Between yesterday evening and now, doubts about how this information would be received by others had crept into her mind. Would they see it as his excuse to break with her? She, herself, was sure it wasn't. After all, he was home. He need not have written to her at all. She wrote a hurried letter to him, telling him she still loved him, whatever had happened to him.

Lunchtime, she went along Market Street to the post office to send the letter by airmail to David. As she stood on the pavement to cross the road on her way back to the shop, she had a sudden flash of memory. She had stood here before, waiting for that horse and cart to go by and she had seen . . . No! She *thought* she had seen a tall figure in combat uniform. That had been last August . . . When?

Could it have been the day David had been wounded? No. It couldn't have been. Or could it? Would he have been trying to tell her? Those things were only supposed to happen if the person had died, and David was alive! It had been a hot day. The sun had gotten into her eyes.

She became aware that people passing by were looking at her standing on the edge of the pavement when there was no traffic in sight. She crossed the road hurriedly and made her way back to work.

She had never told anyone about what she thought she might have seen in Market Street that day. If she said anything now, they would think she was making it up. By the time she had walked into the staffroom, Stella had finished eating her lunch.

"Sorry about that," Ina apologised. "But I had to get David's letter off."

"That's all right. Don't worry about it," Stella replied.

"It'll be too late to go anywhere after I have eaten my sandwiches," Ina said.

Stella shrugged. "I'm not bothered about going out; looks like it's going to rain anyway."

Ina glanced out of the window just as the first drops hit the glass and ran down the panes.

***

The shop was very busy that afternoon, and it was quite late before Mr Phillips was able to go on his tea break. On the occasions he left the shop, Mr Phillips would hand the desk keys over to Vera; this was such a time. Ina had just served a customer and Vera was about to shut the desk drawer when Ina said to her, "Before you shut the drawer, Vera, do you think I could have a look at the petty cash book?"

Vera looked at her in mild surprise. Although there was nothing sacred about the book, it was, nevertheless, a strange request.

"I purchased something for the shop from outside a while back, and I'm not sure whether Mr Phillips entered it in or not."

Even to Ina, the reason seemed lame, but Vera handed over the book without question. Ina flicked the pages back until she found the August entries. She studied the page for a while.

"It's all right; he did." She gave the book back to Vera.

As Ina walked towards a waiting customer, Vera, who had seen the date that Ina had turned to, opened the book to the page that Ina had wanted to read.

21 August

Silks	*Win. St*	*Dubbin*	*9d*
PO	*Mk. St*	*1 doz. stamps*	*2/6*

Vera closed the book, a puzzled look on her face. What had been on that page for 21 August that had made Ina turn so pale?

Chapter 31

The girls were still going to Tidworth on Sunday afternoons. Ina had elected not to go on Wednesdays anymore. Stella understood. There was not much for Ina to do while she and Joe were together, and once a week was quite enough. They went over the Sunday after David's letter had arrived. Joe was now able to walk without any support, although he limped a little. Joe was pleased that Ina had heard from David.

"Really, Ina, he's one of the lucky ones—he's going home—if you can see it that way."

"Yes. I suppose so," she agreed. "All the same, I should have liked the chance to see him just once more."

"Sure, honey, I know." He put his arms around each of them. "What say we have a walk into town?"

"Do you think you can manage it?" asked Stella doubtfully.

"It's a long walk, Joe," Ina warned.

"I'll manage fine."

When they went to reception with Joe to get his going out pass, Red was talking to the sergeant.

"You reckoning on going to town, Joe?" he asked as the sergeant handed out the pass.

"Yep! Gonna take a stroll."

"Sure you will be okay?"

"I've been practicing."

"Maybe I'll come with you. Then if the going gets tough, I can organise some transport. Wait till I change my clothes."

"Okay. Just as you say!" Joe answered.

The journey to town took a while, but Joe didn't falter; the others slowed their pace to match his. It seemed natural for Ina and Red to fall into step behind Joe and Stella. Once they reached the town centre, they entered a park and decided to sit down and relax for a while. They were near a bowling green and became interested in the game in progress.

"You ever play bowls back home, Joe?" asked Stella

They sat in the early October sun; Joe and Red reminisced about the things they did back home before America came into the war.

Ina found her attention wandering. She sat gazing at the scenery—the people playing bowls, the well-kept green, other spectators sitting on deck chairs on the veranda of the pavilion. One wouldn't think there was a war on and, not that far away, a hospital with men, some of them not much more than boys, who were lying, wounded, far from their homes and families. She had a sudden flashback and saw once more the American soldier who she had seen at the bus station and had felt such pity for. Was he unharmed? Was he in France still? Would he go back home to his wife and family, or would they never see him again? A breeze lifted leaves from the trees bordering the green. Some fluttered gently to the ground. When leaves begin to fall . . .

She was stirred from her reverie by Red's voice addressing her. "You heard from your boy, Ina?"

"Yes. I had a letter last Tuesday. He wrote it from home."

"That's good that you've heard. I guess you'll be sorting out your trousseau ready to go to the States."

"I shall have to wait until I am eighteen," she said. "My dad won't let me go over until then. I hope the war's over by that time."

"Once we get to Berlin, it'll be a piece of cake." Red told her.

Joe, who had overheard their conversation, said: "They told us that, once we were across the Rhine, the game was ours. Trouble was nobody knew where the Rhine was . . . or how long it took to get there."

***

On Monday morning, Vera failed to show up for work.

"Can't think what could have happened to her," Mr Phillips remarked. "So unusual for her not to let me know. It's nearly ten o'clock, so she can't have overslept."

"Perhaps she's unwell," suggested Ina. "I think she's been under a bit of a strain, what with having to cancel her wedding and not hearing from her boyfriend."

It was later on in the afternoon when a middle-aged man came into the shop. Mr Phillips went forward to serve him.

"I'm Mr Jenner, Vera's father," he explained. "I'm sorry Vera isn't in today. I'm afraid she's had some bad news. We've heard that her fiancé has been killed in action. He was badly wounded and died on the hospital ship bringing him home."

For a moment, Mr Phillips was speechless. Ina and Stella looked at each other, horrified. Then Mr Phillips said, "I am so sorry, Mr Jenner. This is dreadful news. Please convey our deepest sympathy to her. She must have as long as it takes until she feels able to come back to work."

"That's very kind of you. At the moment, she doesn't seem to know whether she's coming or going. It's hard for us, me and her mum, not being able to do anything for her."

"I'm sure it must be."

"Well. I must get on. Thank you for your condolences."

"Not at all," Mr Phillips replied. "I only wish there was something we could do."

"Give her our love," Stella called as Mr Jenner turned to leave.

Ina had been serving a woman who had been trying on shoes and was now looking at them in the foot mirror. She had obviously heard the conversation between Mr Jenner and Mr Phillips. She turned to Ina and said, "Workmate of yours, was she, the young girl whose boyfriend has been killed?"

"Yes." Ina's voice was subdued. "She was getting married last August. He couldn't get leave from France."

"Such a shame," the woman sighed. "All those young men losing their lives. My daughter lost her husband in North Africa. She was left with three little kids, all because some maniac wanted to rule the world."

She sat down, took off the shoes, and handed them to Ina. "Do you have a boyfriend in the army?"

"Yes," Ina replied.

"Where is he?"

"He was wounded in France, and he's gone home, back to America."

"Oh," the woman said. "Oh. I see. Do you think you will ever see him again?"

"I hope to go over there and marry him."

Ina felt her cheeks burning at the woman's obvious scepticism.

"I'll take these," the woman said.

Ina found it difficult to smile at her and say, "Thank you." Stung and a little bitter, Ina still managed to get through the morning.

"We must get Miss Jenner a nice card—let her know we're thinking of her," said Mr Phillips. "Can one of you get her a card then?"

"We'll go," Ina volunteered.

"We'll all put towards it and get her a really nice one," Stella said.

"I'll take it home with me," Mr Phillips told them. "I'm sure Mrs Phillips will wish to sign it."

The girls went to a greeting card shop at lunchtime and looked for a card of condolence; there was not much choice.

"We sell out of them so quickly," explained the girl who served them. "It's the war. We don't get many in, and then we have a run on them."

They chose a card, paid for it, and left the shop.

"She was a cheerful soul," remarked Stella as they made their way back to work.

During the day, they all signed Vera's card. Mrs Gray had shown very little emotion when they had told her. Her only comment had been, "Well . . . It happens." She had, nevertheless, signed the card. Mr Phillips took a postage stamp from the desk drawer and stuck it on the envelope.

"There's not much we can do for Miss Jenner," he said. "Perhaps the card will show we are thinking of her."

***

When Ina reached home that night and told Hilda of Vera's tragedy, she could not keep her tears back.

"Don't upset yourself, Ina," Hilda said, consoling her.

"I can't help it, Mum. I feel so sorry for her."

Jim came into the kitchen from the living room. "What's going on?" he asked.

"She had some bad news today," Hilda explained. "Young Vera, one of the girls who works at the shop, her boyfriend's been killed. You remember, he went to France and they had to cancel the wedding?"

"Oh, ah! I remember. Poor kid!"

He took his place at the table, saying to Ina, "Come on and eat your tea; it'll make you feel better."

"I'll just go and wipe my face over."

"Don't let your tea go cold," Hilda said.

"Let her go," Jim told her. "Give her chance to get herself together. She'll come down as soon as she's ready."

Hilda sighed. "I don't understand why she's taking it so badly. I didn't think she was that close to the girl."

"No. I don't think it's all to do with this young Vera; this has been coming on for some time. She's been under a lot of strain, what with David getting wounded and going home before she got another chance to see him. She's too young to be going through all this. At her age, she should be out enjoying herself, not worrying about when she's going to hear from him."

***

Ina was at the top of the stairs when the post came. By the time she reached the bottom, Hilda was picking up the mail. She shuffled through the envelopes and handed Ina a letter.

"Is this what you want?" she asked with a smile.

Ina took the letter.

"The post was early," Hilda remarked. "You've plenty of time to read it before you go to work."

Ina sat at the table and opened the letter. A twinge of disappointment came over her. The letter did not seem very long. She opened it up and noticed it was in his own handwriting, although the words were a little shaky. She immediately felt guilty; here she was, thinking he could have written a longer letter, and he probably had a job to write with his bad hand anyway. She read,

My dearest Ina,

Everything here seems different; guess it's because I've been away for so long. I seem to have a job settling down. I am in my old room that I used to share with Todd. Your picture is on my dresser. I keep looking at it and wondering how you are and what you're doing. I'm glad you caught up with Joe. Give him my regards when you go over to Tidworth next time. Glad he wasn't hurt too bad. I have to report to the army hospital; it's a distance away, and I have to catch a train. But I have a travel warrant, and my mom drives me to the rail station. I don't know how much longer I shall be in the Army. I'm

320

going to Florida for a couple of days, so I'll get my picture taken and send it to you. Mom is glad to have me back, but she cries over me. I wish she wouldn't. Sorry my writing isn't so hot. My hand is taking a while healing, but the tendons weren't damaged so I guess I'm lucky in that respect. When the socket has healed up I'm going to be fixed up with a glass eye.

I wish you were here with me. I guess your dad won't let you come out to me while the war's still on. Please don't get fed up with waiting. I know I shan't. Write me again soon.

Love,
David

***

The next Sunday when the girls went to Tidworth, they found Red waiting for them outside the reception area.

"Stella," he said walking towards them. "I'm so sorry. Joe's been shipped out back to France. He left a letter for you."

She took the letter from him. "Why didn't he say something Wednesday?" she asked plaintively.

"It was sudden," explained Red. "They found him fit for duty, and that was that."

Stella read the letter and put it in her handbag.

"He'll write when he gets there," she said flatly.

Ina looked at her friend, but Stella's face was expressionless.

"I'm sorry you've come all this way for nothing," Red said. "There was just no way of letting you know."

"Well, then, Ina, we might as well go back home. We shan't be coming here anymore," Stella said.

"I shall miss seeing you girls." Red smiled. He held out his hand and each, in turn, shook it.

"Thank you for what you did for me, Red." Ina smiled back at him.

"Glad to be of help, honey. I just hope all goes well for you and you get to be with your boy real soon."

***

They found a small café in town that was still open. The smell of cooking food greeted them as they walked in. The café was quite full, but they managed to find a table for two in a corner. There was not an awful lot of choice on the menu; they settled for beans on toast.

"We shall have to find something else to do on a Sunday," Stella said.

"We're back to where we were when they first went over."

Stella shrugged. "Suppose it will be the pictures then."

The beans on toast arrived, and they ate in silence.

A group of British soldiers sat near them. One of them turned to the girls. "Doing anything after? Want to come out with us?"

"No. Thank you," Ina replied. "We're going home."

"Don't you want to come to the flicks?"

"No, thanks," Stella told them.

"Where's home?" asked another.

"Salisbury," Stella replied.

"We'll come with you and go to the flicks in Salisbury," the first soldier persisted.

Ina thought quickly. "My parents are having company, and I promised to be home."

"What have you been doing here today then?"

"We've been visiting a friend who's in hospital, if you must know," Stella answered, tartly.

"The Yankee hospital?" a third soldier put in. "You're wasting your time, Tommo. They're over here looking for Yanks. They haven't got any in Salisbury."

Ina felt her cheeks burning. The meal was finished and she got up from the table.

"Coming?" she asked Stella.

She picked up the bill. Stella got up and followed her to the cash desk.

As they went out, one of the soldiers called after them. "Good luck, girls. Hope you find some big fat Yanks with plenty of money!"

"I just hope the bus is in, and we don't have to hang about here," Stella said as they walked along the road.

"It is!" Ina cried. "Come on."

They scrambled onto the bus and clambered up the stairs, sitting in their seats just as the conductress rang the bell. Just before they reached Amesbury, Stella got off the bus.

"See you in the morning," she said.

Ina continued the journey alone, she gazed out of the window as they passed fields of stubble left by the harvest, small cottages, and village greens. She wondered what the scenery was like in Alabama. Were there green fields with rivers running through them? Somehow she had the idea that it might be dusty with the houses miles apart from each other, like in the Western films.

She thought about the soldiers in the café. Did all British soldiers feel like that if they were turned down? Why had she fallen in love with an American soldier? She had nothing but months—maybe years—of loneliness in front of her. How was she going to fill the time? There would be other occasions when the events of that afternoon would be repeated in some form or another, when instead of accepting an invitation to go out with someone else, she would decline, as graciously as she could, but still manage to bring down a level of bad feeling upon her head. Well, she would have to grin and bear it. There were others far worse off—Vera, for instance, who'd had all her plans and dreams shattered.

***

She got off the bus in Castle Street just before the railway bridge. She faced a long walk home, all uphill, but she wanted to avoid the town. As she turned into the gate, she decided that if her parents were going to the legion that evening, she would go with them.

Chapter 32

There were three items of mail waiting for her when she arrived home on Monday evening.

"They came by the afternoon post," said Hilda.

There were two letters and a pull-out folder of picture postcards showing views of Florida. It showed her the sandy beaches, the palm trees, and the blazing colours of formal gardens and exotic wildlife. She handed it to her mother.

"It looks a lovely place," said Hilda. "No wonder he wants to go there to live. Who are the letters from?"

"One's from David and the other from his mother."

She picked up David's letter. From the feel of it, it contained something fairly rigid.

It was a photograph of David in his uniform, head and shoulders. She studied his smiling face carefully. He was wearing his cap, and the peak cast a faint shadow over his face, but even so, she could make out the scar that went from his eye to his chin on the right side of his face, and he had obviously been fitted with his glass eye. *He's still good looking*, she thought, *still my lovely David*. She passed the photo to Hilda.

"That's a lovely photo of him!" her mother exclaimed. "You'd hardly tell he was scarred if you didn't know it."

She gave it back to Ina and said, "We shall have to see if we can find a nice frame for it."

Ina opened Olivia's letter. At first, she wrote about things in general, and then the mood of the letter seemed to change. Ina read on with a sense of foreboding. Olivia had written.

He doesn't seem to be able to settle, he goes off to places, and we don't know where he is or how long he's going to be gone. He took his car. We told him not to, and he crashed it. He wasn't hurt, but he could have been. There was no need for him to drive. I can take him where he wants to go. He calls out in his sleep some nights. He worries me. I'm sure he'd be all right if you were over here.

Ina put the letter down. Hilda caught sight of the frown on her face. "Not bad, news is it?" she asked anxiously.
"No . . . I don't know."
Hilda sat down at the table opposite Ina and held her hand out.
Ina passed the letter to her. "It's the second page."
Hilda read without comment for a while, and then she put the letter down.
"I don't know what to make of this," she said. "It sounds to me as though he's going through all the time he spent in France. He's reliving it."
"Do you think it's serious, Mum?"
"I think it's something to do with his nerves. I really don't know, but I shouldn't worry too much. They would have put him in a hospital if it was really serious. I expect by the time you get another letter, things will have settled down."

***

Tuesday morning, she told Stella about the letter from David's mother.
"Don't they call it shell shock or something?" Stella asked.
"I don't know, but I do know that, whatever it is, it won't make any difference as to how I feel about him. I'm still going over there." Ina was defiant.
"Well, I shan't be going to America; that's a sure thing," Stella said.
"Would you like to have?"
"Only if I'd met the right Yank."
"And that Isn't Joe?"
"No. We never were serious, Ina. You knew that."
"Are you going to keep up writing to him?"
"I suppose so, until one of us stops."
"So what do you do in the meantime? Find someone else?"

Stella was quiet for a while, and then she answered. "I might have already found someone else."

Ina was shocked at Stella's disclosure.

"Why haven't you said anything before?"

"There wasn't much to it at first," Stella answered.

"Who is he then? Where did you meet him?"

"I went to a dance at Amesbury. There was a girl there who I used to go to school with, Iris. She was with a couple of soldiers. One of them asked me to dance, and I spent most of the evening with him. I didn't think much of it at the time. He seemed quite nice, but it was not long after Joe and David went on D-Day. I forgot all about him until I saw Iris with him and the other one, waiting for a bus at the bus stop down our road. Iris said they were going to Amesbury Ballroom Friday night and why didn't I make up a foursome. She said Jeff had asked her about me; that's his name, Jeff."

"Where's he stationed then?"

"Larkhill."

"Artillery?"

"Yes. He's a lance bombardier."

"Did you tell him about Joe?"

"No. We went to Amesbury pictures some Sunday nights."

"Are you still seeing him?"

"No. They've been posted to somewhere along the south coast. I don't know where. They went just before I heard that Joe was in Tidworth."

"So, you weren't going out with him while we were going to the hospital then?"

"No. We're writing to each other now."

"Why didn't you tell me about all this? I thought we were friends and didn't keep any secrets from each other. All this time, you've been going out with this Jeff of yours, and I knew nothing about it. I would have understood. I wouldn't expect you to not go out with other blokes if you weren't serious about Joe and you were fed up with not going dancing. You should have told me."

"I know. I'm sorry. I thought you'd think badly of me if you knew."

There was a pause for a second or two, and then Ina asked, "You really like him?"

"Yes. I do."

***

Stella's revelation had disturbed Ina somewhat. She had already felt a subtle change between her and her dear friend. She supposed Stella was in a slightly awkward position. There was this Jeff fellow who had come into her life—who seemed to catch her affection like no one else had ever done—and her continuing relationship with Joe. Ina knew Stella well enough to know that she would not send Joe a "Dear John" letter all the while he was in Europe. The Allies were now in Belgium, racing towards the Ardennes, aiming to soon be on German soil. The war could be over at any time. What would Stella do if Joe had leave and came back to England?

***

The next letter from David brought better news.

I'm glad you got my picture okay. As you could see from it, I've been fixed up with a glass eye. It took some getting used to, made my eye water some, but I don't have to go to the military hospital again. The next thing is my discharge from the army, could be any day now. I've been granted a 75 per cent disability allowance. It will help towards my studying at college

From that letter on, there seemed to be a period of silence. He had not mentioned her going to America.

"Be patient," Hilda had told her. "It's still early days."

***

Work seemed to be one long grind, relieved only by a consignment of shoes that, for a while, commanded Ina's attention. Although the delivery contained mostly repeats of the shoes already stocked, there was a new line in ladies fur-lined ankle boots.

"I'd like to get my mum a pair of those for Christmas," Ina told Stella.

"Have you seen the price of them?" Stella asked

"Yes," Ina answered, "£2.9s.11d; they might just as well call it £2.10s.0d."

"Won't your Avril go halves with you?"

"It's still a lot. I have to make my club money stretch out, and I have David and his mother and stepfather extra this year."

Vera had come back to work, a little wan and with a faint air of tragedy about her. She seemed to have drawn even further back into her shell.

"Do you like these boots?" Stella asked her.

"They're very nice," Vera replied dispassionately. "I don't seem to have much interest in clothes these days. There doesn't seem to be anything worth dressing up for."

"Oh, dear!" remarked Stella as Vera turned away.

"I think I know how she feels," Ina said.

"Do you think it's not worth dressing up anymore because David's not here to see you?"

"It sometimes seems to be a waste of time."

"I think you're getting yourself into the doldrums," Stella said. "Why don't you change your mind and go dancing one night?"

"I told you why. Look. I don't blame you for taking up with your Jeff, especially when there was nothing serious between you and Joe, but it's different with me—"

"I know, I know. 'No love, no nothing'," Stella sang the first bars of the song.

***

October ended in mornings of swirling mists. The evenings darkened early. It was the time to start thinking of winter drawing in. Jim spent most of his spare time either on his allotment or in the garden getting rid of the summer debris and planning for the next season. Bean and pea sticks were pulled up, dried off, and put away for the next year's crop. He dug and raked and, Saturday afternoons when he wasn't working, lit bonfires to dispose of the rubbish, making sure there were no signs of burning when it was lighting up time.

***

A letter came from David that brought the reality of Ina's future with him sharply into focus:

I am now out of the army. I am a civilian. I always thought I'd be glad to be out. Now, I'm not so sure. I'm not being told what to do anymore. It is all so strange. People seem different, and I don't seem to be able to talk any sense to them. They ask me what it was like in France. What can I tell them . . . that it was a tea party? I mustn't get too impatient, must I?

He wrote a few more lines and then closed in his usual style.

Chapter 33

November 1944

Ina met Stella at the bus station and noticed immediately the look of concern on her friend's face.

"I've had a letter I wrote to Joe come back," Stella said.

"Do you know why?"

Stella shrugged. "No, I don't."

"There's nothing on the envelope to give you a clue?"

"No. It just has 'Return to sender. See over' and an arrow pointing to my address on the back."

"And you really don't know what it means?"

"I have no idea. The only thing I can think of is that he doesn't want to write to me anymore."

"I can't see Joe doing that. He'd write if he wanted to break it off," Ina said, frowning. In her own mind was the thought that something bad had happened to Joe, but she wouldn't say that to Stella. Instead she added, "Perhaps they have moved him to another unit or he's been wounded again."

"They wouldn't have sent his letter back. They didn't with David's, did they? My letter would have followed him. After all, all it needs on the envelope is his name, rank, and army number; as long as the army post office number is on it, it shouldn't matter."

"That's true," Ina agreed. "I didn't think."

It was a mystery that would probably remain unsolved.

***

Jim was on a late shift that week, so was home at teatime. They were all sat at the table when Ina told him about Stella getting Joe's letter back.

"Sounds to me he might have been killed," Jim said gravely.

"I suppose I had the same idea at the back of my mind," Ina agreed.

"Wouldn't they have told Stella?" asked Hilda.

"Not necessarily," Jim replied. "They are only obliged to tell next of kin. I take it Joe had a family back home."

Ina hesitated for a moment. "I honestly don't know. I don't remember Stella ever saying anything about Joe's family. I've never thought about it before. I used to tell her about David's family. He might have told her, but she wasn't interested enough to tell me. It was never serious between them."

"Maybe just as well in that case then," Jim said. "I'm sure that must be the reason."

"Are you going to say anything to Stella?" asked Hilda.

"No. No, Mum. Not unless she mentions it to me."

After the evening meal was over, Jim said, "Ina, I want a serious word with you."

"What about, Dad?"

"This letter you've had from David, wanting you to go over to America soon."

"Mum told you about it then?"

"Your mother doesn't keep anything from me concerning you kids."

"I know that, Dad. It wasn't what I meant. As you hadn't said anything I thought perhaps—"

"I'm not going to come on the heavy father," Jim interrupted. "But you need to think about what you are doing."

"I have thought about it. I want to go as soon as I can."

"You're jumping the gun. You probably won't be allowed a visa while the war is still on, and, what's more, you don't know how things will be out there. I think you'll have to face the fact that David won't be the same young soldier you knew over here. For a start, he's been badly wounded—"

"I can put up with that!"

"Can you? Listen! You haven't seen him. To you, he's just as he was when he was over here."

"I've seen his photograph!"

"A photograph is nothing. You don't know how the war has affected him mentally, let alone losing his eye."

"But if I don't go, he'll think I've rejected him!"

"I'm not asking you not to go. I'm just trying to put you in the picture about what you may have to face, and if you get out there and find that all you feel for him is pity—"

"It isn't pity, Dad, it isn't."

Jim looked at her earnestly, and when he spoke again, it was in a softer voice. "Ina, you're a young girl. You don't know what you may have to cope with. His mother has already told you that he hasn't settled down. It is one thing to say he'll be better when you get out there but another for you not to be prepared for what you may find. David has been through a war. He has seen things no young man should see. He's been in action. He's seen his mates killed or horribly wounded. He's seen them with terrible injuries—"

"Jim!" Hilda broke in. "You'll terrify her!"

"Hilda! I want to get over to her why he's like he is and what she's in for—why he hasn't settled and why he's having nightmares." He turned to Ina. "Don't forget; I've been in a war. I didn't settle when I came home. I had nightmares; ask your Gran. I wasn't even badly wounded. You don't think about it at the time. You're too busy fighting your way through, and you have your mates around you. You're all in the same boat. When you get home, everyone wants to make a fuss of you—slap you on the back and buy you a drink. You feel like a hero. Then, when the fuss dies down and you and your mates go your separate ways, you start to think about things—all the things you had to see, all the things you had to do. It takes a long time, Ina, to get back on track. I had no trouble getting a job on the railway, thanks partly to your granddad. David doesn't even know what his disability will allow him to do. It looks like the turkey farm is out for a start."

Jim's lengthy speech came to a halt. He looked at his daughter's face and saw that it was pale and set. Had he gone too far?

"I know what you're telling me, Dad, but I can help him get over it. I know you're putting obstacles in my way because you don't really want me to go."

Jim sighed. "If you are really set on going, then I will not stand in your way. I'd rather you went than tell me in a few years time that I ruined your life. As for the money to pay for your fare, well, I suppose we'll scrape it up somehow."

"Dad!" She ran over to his chair and hugged him.

"Now, don't go getting daft. I'm going to make a condition."

"What is it?"

"That you wait until this war's over, and if by then, you are eighteen."

"Yes. All right, Dad."

"Then write to David and tell him. If he wants you that much, he'll wait."

"He'll wait for me. I know he will."

"Well, I'll say no more. You realise you'll be doing me out of taking you down the aisle?"

"You'll still have Avril to give away."

"I should have liked to have given both my daughters away."

Ina, whose every thought had been centred on her eventual reunion with David, now realised what a wrench it was going to be, not only to leave her family but also to have her leave them. America was a long way away.

She wrote to David and told him all that had transpired between her father and herself and was surprised when a letter came from him only a few days later. He wrote.

I do appreciate what your dad said, I understand his attitude. I'd maybe feel the same if I had a daughter. I wish I could get to England and marry you, but if I'm going to college to get myself some qualifications to get a decent job, money is going to be tight. And I don't want to be a burden on my mom while I'm living at home. I guess it makes sense to wait, but it seems so long since I saw you, and I do need you in my life.

He also wrote to Jim and Hilda. He told them he was going to take a business course at college and that he would wait for Ina no matter how long it took, and he thanked them for taking him into their family.

***

November, with all it's dreariness, its dampness, and its foggy weather, crawled slowly by. There were days when Ina felt depressed. She sometimes thought her world was gradually changing; only David's letters brought her any relief. Perhaps she was in the doldrums as Stella had suggested.

For Stella herself, her own life seemed to be in contrast. "Jeff's come back to Larkhill," she had informed Ina one morning.

There had been no more news from or about Joe.

"Did Joe ever tell you about his family?" asked Ina

Stella frowned. "No," she answered. "He never did."

"Nothing at all? Did you never ask him?"

"I got the impression that he was on his own. As he didn't say much about his life in America, I didn't press him. Anyway, it wasn't important enough to me."

Avril's occasional weekends home came as some relief to Ina, although, with working Saturdays and Avril having to visit her future in-laws, they could not spend a great deal of time together.

Stella's free time was spent with Jeff. He met Stella from work one Saturday night, and Ina was introduced to him. He was a pleasant enough person but not a bit as Ina had imagined. Excepting in the case of David and Joe, Stella had always managed to secure for herself the best-looking and the more outgoing of any two boys she and Ina had gone out with. Jeff was not all that much taller than Ina and, although he had a nice face, wouldn't have been called particularly handsome. His handshake was warm enough. From the way he spoke to Stella, he seemed to be fond of her. Ina could only wish them well; nevertheless, she could feel that something was missing from the relationship between Stella and herself. Once they had had David and Joe in common; now, with Stella's interest in Jeff the main topic of her conversation—where they had been and what they had done and the friends of his she had met—discussions about David had been limited to relating the odd items from his letters. Ina became aware that, although to her, he was real and near, to Stella, he was far off in another land; he was in the past, where she had left Joe. She was now in another time in her life, and whatever had been before did not have a place in it now.

They still walked around the town but not when the weather was bad, which was more often than not. Then they sat eating their lunch by the warmth of the gas fire. Stella brought the girl, Iris, into her conversations.

It was perfectly natural, Ina supposed. Iris was going out with Jeff's friend. It stood to reason they would make up a foursome.

Ina confided all this to Avril one Sunday morning when the two of them were in their bedroom, sorting out their winter clothes.

"I suppose Stella is about the only friend you've really had since you left school, isn't she?" Avril asked.

"Yes, she is. Do you have a special friend at Upavon?"

"No. Not really. A group of us go about together—pictures, shopping, and that. Sometimes we have camp dances or we get invited to other stations."

"Does it worry you that other blokes might make a pass at you?"

"No. I put them straight if they get any funny ideas. When was the last time you went dancing?"

"Oh, ages ago."

"You used to like dancing. Is that what you're afraid of? Someone might ask you for a date and you'll have to turn them down?"

Ina told her about the British soldiers in the café at Tidworth and how embarrassed she'd felt and about the woman in the shop the day they'd heard about Vera's fiancé, who had become totally unsympathetic when Ina had told her that her own boyfriend was an American soldier.

"I wish, sometimes, that he would come over here and marry me and find a job and stay over here."

"That's not likely is it?"

"No. If Stella ends up marrying Jeff, there won't be any problems for her. No having to get a passport; no having to get a visa; no having to scrape money up for a boat to take her to him. It's the same for you and Brian and Maureen next door and her Keith. You're all English. You'll all be getting married here with all your family around you."

"Are you having second thoughts?"

"No! I want to go!"

Avril studied her sister's face. She saw the same hopeless look in her eyes that had been there when they had looked over the wall of the Castle Keep and Avril had said she would like to spend her honeymoon in Guildford.

"You'll get there," she said. "We'll all help. You can come back to see us. You and David can go to an English Church and take your vows again."

"What! And wear a white wedding dress and have Dad take me up the aisle? Now that is a pipe dream."

Hilda called up the stairs to tell them tea was ready.

"Just think," Avril exclaimed. "After tea, I don't have to go up to the station and take that dreary train journey."

"I'll come down and see you off on the bus, if you like."

"Yes, all right. It'll be dark though," Avril warned.

"Don't worry. I'll get the bus home."

Chapter 34

Five years into the war and, despite the rationing and the shortages, there was still a determination to keep, wherever possible, the traditions of the English Christmas. Ina came home one Wednesday afternoon to find Hilda standing by the dining room table with an array of pudding ingredients, basins, and cloths surrounding the big floral washbasin, which normally stood on the washstand in her parents' bedroom but was brought down each year to be used as an outsized mixing bowl.

"Good!" Hilda exclaimed as Ina came into the living room. "You're just in time to give me a hand."

Ina went into the hallway, hung up her coat, and came back in.

"What do you want me to do?"

"Help me prepare all the stuff that has to go in. You can start stoning the raisins while I grate the suet."

None of this preparation was a chore to Ina. She had loved to help her mother with the pudding making even when she was small and had to kneel on a chair to reach the table. They worked steadily together—peeling, mixing, chopping, and grating. Propped up in front of Hilda for her to refer to was a cookery book, *Cooking for the Home Front*. It read on the cover, "Wartime Recipes". It gave alternatives for what was now unobtainable or in short supply. Now, with all the various items weighed and in the bowl, Ina fetched the bottle of stout that her father had brought home from the legion and took the top off. The brown liquid fizzed and bubbled as she poured it into the contents of the bowl. They took turns in stirring the mixture until Hilda was satisfied it was ready to go into the greased basins.

"I managed to get tomorrow off," she said, "so I can spend all day steaming them."

When they had cleared away and washed up, Hilda made sandwiches and a pot of tea. They sat in the armchairs either side of the fire.

"Have you decided what you are getting David for his twenty-first birthday?" Hilda asked.

Ina sighed. "No, I haven't yet. I just don't know."

"You'll have to hurry up, or it won't get there in time."

"I'll send it airmail," Ina replied.

"It'll have to be something small then, or it will cost you a fortune."

"I'll go out dinner time tomorrow and see what I can find. I'll buy his card at the same time."

"Don't forget to buy one from us."

"No. I won't forget."

***

Directly Ina went into the staffroom at lunchtime the next day, she put her coat on and got ready to go out.

Stella looked up at her. "Are you going out now?" she asked.

"Yes. I've got to get something for David's birthday while there's still time to post it."

"What are you getting him?"

"Lord knows. I shall just have to walk round until something comes to me."

"What about your sandwiches?"

"If I don't get time to eat them when I get back, I shall have to come in here later on and have a crafty nibble."

It was a miserable day. The pavements were wet with low-lying mist, and the sky was leaden. There was a damp chill in the air. People were walking along the streets, muffled up to their eyebrows in scarves. Ina thought of Stella, sitting by the gas fire eating her sandwiches, and she had a sudden urge to be back with her. Time was against her, and David would be lucky to get his present on his actual birthday.

Several ideas came into her mind as to what to get him, and then she quickly discarded as being unsuitable. He didn't smoke, so a cigarette case and lighter were out of the question. Hankies, then—linen ones, with his initials on and marked, "Made in England". Not much, really, for a twenty-first birthday present. Stationery! Writing paper and envelopes did not look like a present without being in a writing case, and the only ones she could see were very expensive leather, way beyond the range of her slender means. She paused outside a jewellery shop and searched the window for inspiration. Cuff links! Did he wear shirts that needed cuff links? Did he wear shirts like her father did when he went out anywhere? Or did he wear the check shirts like the country people wore in the American films? She realised that she knew nothing of his preferences regarding his clothes; in fact, she did not know all that much about his preferences for anything.

She could feel tears of frustration prick the back of her eyes. Then she saw it—tucked among the silver rose bowls, candlesticks, and christening mugs—a silver filigree photo frame. She went into the shop and asked the price.

The shop assistant reached into the window and drew out the frame. She looked at a little white ticket that was fastened to the frame. "It's 7/6d," she told Ina.

Ina gulped but said, "I'll take it."

She fished her purse out of her handbag and took a ten shilling note from it.

The assistant took it from her, rang the till, and handed Ina the change.

"It comes with a box," the woman told Ina. She dived under the counter and produced a flat white box. She then proceeded to open the box from the side, put a finger and thumb in, and draw out a piece of folded tissue paper and a piece of corrugated cardboard. The assistant then placed the cardboard over the glass frame. She then wrapped it in the tissue paper and put the whole lot into the white box. Once outside the jeweller's, Ina reflected on her purchase—7s.6d. in one go! The 10s was supposed to have been for the present, the airmail postage, and the birthday cards. It wasn't that she begrudged it to David, but with Christmas looming towards her, there wasn't much money to spare.

She went to the paper shop on Milford Street and managed to get two presentable cards with "21st Birthday" on that were different from each other and a sheet of brown wrapping paper; she decided that she would cut off a piece of string from the roll at work.

***

She showed Stella the photo frame, having very carefully extracted it from its wrappings.

"Oh, nice," commented Stella. "Are you going to put a photo inside it?"

"Oh, Lord!" Ina exclaimed in some consternation. "I hadn't thought of that! I suppose he could put in the one he already has."

"Not the same though. Is it?"

"Well. There's not much I can do about it now."

"Haven't you got another one at home? What about the little ones we had done in that place over the chemist shop in the Blue Boar Row? Haven't you still got the ones we had enlarged?"

"That was ages ago. There's only one left at home, and that's in Mum and Dad's bedroom. Anyway, I've changed a bit since then."

"Not all that much. That was a really good photo. Surely your mum will let you have it when she knows it's for David?"

"I can ask her, can't I?'

***

The pudding boiling was well under way when Ina came round the back way to put her bicycle in the shed. The back door was wedged open, and puffs of steam wafted through into the garden. Inside, Clive was busy with his homework but still bemoaning the draught coming into the living room whenever the door into the kitchen was opened. Ina received the full force of his displeasure as she came into the room.

"All right, narky!" she answered. "I've got to come through the door unless you want me to climb through the window."

"You can put that away now, Clive," called Hilda from the kitchen. "I want to get the table laid for tea."

"I don't know!" Clive grumbled. "I don't think anyone wants me to get on at school. If I fail my exams next year, everyone will want to know why, and I shall tell 'em it's because I can't get on and do my homework."

"Clive! For heaven's sake! The paraffin man will be here tomorrow. I'll light the stove and put it in the front room directly I come in from work, and it will be nice and warm in there when you get home from school."

A little mollified, Clive put his books into his satchel and helped Ina lay the table. Jim came downstairs into the room. He had no collar or tie on, and his shoes were in his hand. He sat in his chair and bent down to put the shoes on his feet.

"Strewth! Hilda!" he exclaimed. "How much longer are you going to have that copper boiling?"

"I'm just taking the puddings out now."

"Thank God for that! I don't know why we have to put up with this performance every year. Lord knows how much gas it's using, and Joe Soap here has to pay the bills."

"I can see you haven't got up in a very good mood!" Hilda retorted crossly. "You'd be the first to moan if you didn't have pudding Christmas Day!"

"That steam will be in the kitchen for ages," Jim muttered. "I just hope Cissie Daley comes barging in through the back door and gets a face full."

***

Hilda picked up the photo frame from the chest of drawers. It was made of Bakelite. Two grooved side pieces held two small sheets of glass, which in turn, held the photograph, the whole, fitting into a wide-grooved base. She studied the photograph for a while and then withdrew it from the frame. Downstairs again, she handed the picture to Ina.

"Here you are," she said.

"Thanks, Mum," Ina replied. "I've written my card. Do you want to write yours?"

"Yes, please. Let's borrow your pen."

Ina passed her fountain pen to her mother, and Hilda wrote her message on her card.

"You'll have to wrap it well," Hilda advised Ina.

"I thought I'd put the cards inside the parcel," Ina replied. "It will probably save on postage as well."

Hilda took her purse from her handbag and put 1s.0d on the table.

"That will pay for the card and help towards the airmail."

***

Stella volunteered to go to the post office with Ina on their lunch hour the next day. Having sent the parcel off, they decided they would take a walk

341

around the town. The day was sunny but cold. There were still signs of the early morning frost on those parts of the pavement that were shaded from the sun.

"What are you and Jeff doing tomorrow night?" Ina asked.

"Nothing," Stella answered. "He's on duty this weekend."

"Why don't you come in and stay? We could go to the pictures—"

"Oh. Sorry. I promised to babysit."

"That's okay; perhaps some other time."

"Yes. I'll let you know when Jeff's on duty again."

They walked in silence for a while, until Stella said, "I expect you get lonely sometimes, don't you?"

"Yes. It's not so bad when Avril's home and we can see a film."

"But not dancing."

"No."

"You're not really worried about other blokes trying to get off with you are you? It wouldn't do any harm for you and Avril to go to a dance, would it? You could look out for each other."

"I'm not all that bothered about going dancing."

"Well," Stella mused, "David wasn't a dancer, was he? Not like Joe, but you did dance with that Virgil once or twice at the Red Cross. David didn't mind, did he?"

"No. I suppose not."

"I used to think he had a soft spot for you."

"Virgil?"

"Yes." Stella sighed. "You know, Ina, I do miss those days a bit—all the places we used to go and all the people we met. Don't get me wrong; I like Jeff a lot. But . . . the Yanks . . . they were different—different uniforms . . . different accents. They'd come from the other side of the world."

"I don't think they we're all that different underneath, Stella."

"But they seemed different. They have a different life back in America, don't they? You see it on the screen at the pictures—big houses, all those electrical gadgets. They're all on the phone. They all have cars and fridges."

"I expect some of them are poor and don't have all those things."

"Not many of them, I bet! Just think! You'll be going out to all that! You'll have nice dresses and nice underwear and live in a nice house. You'll be eighteen soon. You'll be able to go over there. You won't have to hang around waiting for David to get demobbed like a lot of girls will. He'll be over there already."

"I can't go if the war's still on."

"I don't see why not."

They had reached the shop, and as they walked through the door, Stella said "I'm trying to cheer you up!"

Ina smiled, "I'm not really such a misery, am I?"

"No, of course you're not. But you do look as though you could do with a good night out."

Chapter 35

Hilda stood in front of the wall mirror in the living room putting on a modicum of make-up. She wore a long-sleeved blue wool dress that went well with her short dark curly hair. She is quite attractive for her age, Ina thought. Even though her waistline was disappearing a little, her figure was still trim.

Hilda caught sight of Ina's reflection in the mirror. "Why don't you come down the legion with us tonight?" she asked.

"Oh . . . I don't know . . ."

"Come on! It will do you good to get out. I expect David goes out. He must have a few friends back in America."

"He never says anything about what he does at home. Don't forget, he maybe a little self-conscious about . . ." She paused.

"Yes," Hilda said, quietly, "of course." She turned away from the mirror and put her make-up in her handbag. "I expect you miss Stella's company," she said.

"Stella's got other fish to fry." There was a faint note of bitterness in Ina's voice. "When her Jeff's on duty weekends, she's babysitting . . . or so she says."

"Don't you believe her then?"

Ina shrugged, "I do and I don't. I think she goes to Amesbury with that Iris girl."

"It's a pity you hadn't kept friends with some of the girls you used to know instead of keeping to Stella."

"I suppose we just got used to going around together and having boyfriends who were mates."

Jim came down from upstairs into the living room. He had on his best navy blue suit. Ina could not remember him going anywhere special not wearing his navy blue suit, except in the summer when he wore grey flannel trousers and a sports jacket.

Ina said suddenly, "Do you mind if I come with you after all?"

Jim looked at her. "There's nothing to stop you if you want to come."

"I'll just go up and change."

"Don't be long!" Jim warned. "We don't want to be walking in as the place is closing."

"Tell Clive to get a move on," called Hilda as Ina raced up the stairs.

Dressed and ready to go, Hilda, Ina and Clive waited in the hall while Jim made sure the back door was locked.

"I hope you're all wrapped up warm," he said when he joined them. "It's pretty cold out there."

Clive was wearing the balaclava helmet his grandmother had knitted for him with his school cap perched on top.

"You look stupid!" Ina commented.

"I don't want my ears covered in chilblains!" Clive retorted. "Anyway, what about you, then—with that scarf around your head, you look like a Russian peasant."

"Now that's enough you two!" scolded Hilda. "Clive, walk in front with Dad."

***

The night sky was brightly moonlit and criss-crossed with searchlight beams.

"Just the night for a raid," commented Jim.

"I thought the air raids had all stopped now, Dad," Clive said.

"Well . . . I suppose they've tailored off a bit, but the Jerries are still capable of launching their doodlebugs."

"What, even though we're nearly in Germany?"

"Germany's a big place, son, and the war's not over yet by a long chalk. We've been lucky here—just that bit of bombing a couple of years ago."

"Jim!" Hilda called to him, "stop putting the wind up us."

"Sorry! Just saying; that's all."

***

There were quite a few people in the legion when they arrived. Cissie came towards them.

"We came down early," she explained. "Alb had a few things to see to. Hello! Ina! We don't see you down here much these days."

"I thought it would do her good to get out for a while," Hilda answered for her.

Ina just smiled.

They found four seats and sat down while Jim fetched drinks for them.

"Nell and Sid aren't coming tonight then?" Cissie enquired.

"Sid's working," Hilda told her.

Jim came back, joined by Alb.

"We're going to have a bit of music in a minute," Alb said. "Jack's playing the piano for us and what's 'is name is bringing the accordion."

"Oh ah! You mean Charlie Gibbons," put in Jim.

"Yes, that's him. We can have a bit of a dance."

Bully for us! thought Ina.

She had never heard of Charlie Gibbons, but she had heard Jack's piano playing before. He had quite a good tune as far as melody was concerned, but his bass was haphazard and was often out of synchronisation with the rest of his playing. There again, he did only play by ear and asked for no payment except for a steady supply of beer.

"I don't expect you go dancing these days do you, Ina?" Cissie asked.

"No. I'm not bothered about it."

"You don't see your little friend much now, do you?"

"No, only when we're at work. She has a boyfriend she sees on weekends."

"Has she forgotten her American boyfriend already?"

"She's only had one letter from him since he left the hospital and went back to France. It wasn't serious, anyway."

"She had a letter she wrote to him come back," Hilda said quickly. "She's heard nothing from him since then." She added quietly, "Jim said the most likely explanation was that he had probably been killed."

"Yes . . . I expect that's it." Cissie sighed. "Such a shame."

The dancing began. The accordion managed to dampen down the jarring notes of the piano, and people started to take to the floor. Jim stood up. Hilda likewise, and together they glided across the floor. Ina liked to see her parents dance with each other. Her mind went back to the first time she managed to get David to his feet to dance with her in the bar at the American Red Cross club. Then there had been those times when she had been whirled around the dance floor by Virgil. Had he really had a soft spot for her as Stella had said? She smiled to herself.

"What are you grinning at?" asked Clive.

"Nothing really. Would you like me to teach you how to dance?"

"Me!" Clive answered horrified. "Not blooming likely! You won't get me hopping around a dance floor like a fairy on a rock cake!"

A voice by the side of her startled her. "As you've been so rudely turned down," said the voice, "perhaps you'd dance with me."

Ina had not noticed him before. He was a young man of about eighteen or nineteen. He was not very tall and inclined to be a little skinny. Nevertheless, he had a nice face, and she guessed that under all that Brylcream he had ginger hair. She got up out her seat and let him lead her to the dance floor. Jack and Charlie were playing a waltz. The boy was not the best dancer Ina had ever danced with, but he kept to the tempo and didn't step on her toes.

"I know your dad, Jim," he said by way of conversation. "He's my driver sometimes."

"You're a fireman then?"

"That's right—it's the first time I've been in here. My dad booked me in."

"Your Dad?"

"Arthur Potter. He was in the Wiltshire Regiment in the last war. He carries the banner at the Armistice Day parades."

"Oh. I see."

"Your name's Ina, isn't it?"

"How did you know?"

"I heard someone call you."

She didn't answer him

After a while he said, "My name is Norman."

She smiled but still did not speak.

"Have you got a boyfriend?" he asked her.

"Yes; I have as a matter of fact." She hoped that would be the end of the conversation going in that direction, but it seemed Norman was the persistent type.

"Is he in the army?"

"No." (Well that was the truth.)

"Does he live in Salisbury?"

"No."

"Would he mind if you came to the pictures with me one night?"

"I—"

Ina's reply was cut short. There came a wailing sound, loud enough to be heard over the music. Everyone on the dance floor stood stock still.

"Excuse me, please," Ina said and, leaving him standing, went over to where her parents were sitting.

"This is your fault Jim Welland!" Hilda said. "You and your predictions!"

"Wasn't wrong, was I?" Jim grinned back.

People were leaving the dance floor and standing in groups by the tables, muttering between themselves.

"I thought we'd heard the last of them," Cissie said. "Alb? What are we going to do?"

Alb stood up. "Listen, everybody!" he called out. "We can carry on or call it a day, in which case we might as well go home."

Jack shut down the lid on his piano, and Charlie put his accordion back in its case.

"Want me to close down, Alb?" the steward called from behind the bar.

"Drinking time's not up yet!" a voice protested.

"If you want to stay here, then I suggest we go down to the cellar," Alb told them.

This brought more howls of protest.

"There's not enough room for all of us in the cellar."

"We shall be packed in like sardines."

"There's no place to sit down there."

"We can take some chairs down."

"Take the chairs down! All down those steep steps! Not likely!"

"Then I suggest we pack up and go home," Alb told them. "It's ten to ten; the bar will be closing anyway."

"We might as well have the last ten minutes, Alb."

Alb shrugged his shoulders. It was the last voice he was prepared to listen to. He sat down again and drank up the last of the beer in his glass.

"Want another, Alb?" Jim asked.

"No. Do you?"

"No," Jim said. "I'm all for going."

"It's spoilt our evening." Hilda sighed.

"I thought we'd finished with all this." Alb grumbled, "I thought the perishers would cave in once we got near to Germany."

"We took it for granted," Jim said." We didn't reckon on them digging their heels in like this."

"I haven't heard any planes go over," put in Clive.

"Just let's hope you don't," Jim told him.

"It could be buzz bombs," Clive persisted.

"Oh! Shut up, Clive! "Ina cried crossly.

"I hope Maureen's all right." Cissie's voice was full of anxiety.

"Is she at home?" Hilda asked.

"No. She's gone to the pictures with a girl from work."

"She'll be all right, Cis," Alb said. "There are plenty of places she can shelter in."

"I can't help worrying." Cissie now sounded near to hysterics "I worry about Harold being sent to Germany, and I wouldn't know where. I don't know what danger he'd be in. I don't like this war!" she cried vehemently. "I don't like what's happening to us all! Harold, Keith going over on that bomber, Avril's boy going over there, and Ina's boy being wounded like he was."

Hilda put her hand on Cissie's arm. Alb leaned towards her and put his hands on her shoulders. "Come on, Cissie," he said, comfortingly. "This isn't like you."

"I'll see if there's a spot of brandy behind the bar," Jim said.

The steward was just pulling down the shutters when Jim reached the bar.

"Can I have a drop of brandy please? Jim asked him.

"Yes. Sure, Jim. How much?"

"Just a tot. It's for Alb's missus."

"Is she poorly?"

"No. She's just having a bit of a bad spell."

Jim took the brandy back to the table and put it in front of Cissie. "There you are; get that down you," he told her. "It will make you feel better."

Cissie sipped the brandy.

"Get it all down!" said Alb. "Go on! One big gulp!"

Cissie downed the brandy, coughed a little, and wiped her mouth on her handkerchief.

"Let's get our coats and push off home," Jim suggested.

They had barely got outside when the all clear sounded.

"There you are," said Alb. "It's all over and no sign of enemy action!"

***

Indoors, the living room fire still glowed, sending out a little warmth. Jim took the fireguard away and stoked the ashes.

"Ina, would you fill up the hot waters bottles and take them up please? I'll make some cocoa and some sandwiches," Hilda said.

Ina walked into the kitchen where the hot water bottles were laid side by side on the table—two tin ones shaped like barrel loaves and a large stone one that went in her parents' bed. She turned on the Ascot and let the hot water dribble over the sides of the bottles before she filled them. Hilda was busying herself with sandwich making. By the time Ina came back, the sandwiches were on the table and her father and brother were helping themselves.

"Tonight was a bit of a damp squib wasn't it?" she said.

"Never mind," Jim told her. "We'll make up for it share-out night."

"Do you think the war will be over soon, Dad?" Clive asked.

"Your guess is as good as mine, son, but something tells me we've still got a long way to go."

"A lot of the older boys at school want the war to go on so they can fight when they leave."

Hilda put a tray of cocoa on the table. "I hope you haven't got any ideas about joining the army when you're old enough," she said sternly.

"Me? No. I'm not going to join the army. I want to do something with my life, not chuck it away in some silly old war!"

Ina looked at him and said, with a slight tremor in her voice, "Then let's hope you never have to!"

Chapter 36

December 1944

Old Mrs Welland had stopped going to the whist drives. She could no longer cope with walking up the hill, and there was a hill whichever way she chose to get to or from the legion whist drives.

"Why don't you come with us?" Hilda asked Ina. "It will do you good to get out a bit more instead of being stuck indoors all the time, now you don't see so much of Stella."

"I can't play whist, Mum. Not that well anyway."

"I worry about you being on your own so much."

"Don't worry about me. I'm all right, really."

Then, feeling she might be letting her mother down, she asked tentatively. "Has Auntie Nell got another partner?"

"Yes—one of the women from the milk factory."

"You're still playing with Mrs Daley, then?"

"Oh, she's not so bad, really. She seems to have quietened down since Harold went into the commandos. I expect she worries about him, especially if he goes overseas to fight."

"He's not a general yet then."

"Ina!" her mother admonished.

"Well, she's got nothing to boast about. He'll probably miss the war altogether."

"He's had some stiff training to get where he is, and the war doesn't seem to be anywhere near over."

"I didn't think it would go on this long," Ina said.

"No. Neither did a lot of people. At least you know David's out of it."

"The Americans don't seem to be doing too badly in the Pacific."

"No," Hilda agreed. "I just wish your Auntie Nell could get some news of Teddy. I hope to goodness he's still alive."

***

At the shop, slippers had long replaced sandals. The windows had been decorated with strips of red, green, and white crêpe paper. They and the glass shelves sported cardboard cut-outs of Santa Claus among cotton wool "snowballs" and imitation holly and mistletoe. Even Vera came out of her shell a little and took an interest in her window. There were no ceiling decorations. Mr Phillips did not feel he could stand on the steps for long reaching upwards, and he would not risk the girls injuring themselves should they fall. Anyway, they agreed the trimmings were too old and would probably not stand up to even the slightest draught coming through the door. Nevertheless, there was a certain sense of festivity, especially as all the other shops had made some effort to make the best of the season.

"I'm dreaming of a White Christmas!" carolled Stella.

"I hope it doesn't snow!" muttered Mrs Gray, who, in spite of the annual stocktaking, which came after the Christmas holiday, had been granted a few days' extra leave. "I don't want to get stuck up north."

"Well, if it snows anywhere, it's most likely to be up there," Stella told her.

"Thanks a lot!" replied Mrs Gray and waddled away quite oblivious to the sprig of holly stuck on the lower back of her overall. As it was fixed in place with a sticking plaster, she would not be aware of until she sat down for her morning break. Stella, the culprit, along with Ina and Vera, served their customers with deadpan faces, who in their turn held back their mirth until they were outside the shop.

Presents and cards became the main topic of conversation between Ina and Stella. They confined their discussions to break times in deference to Vera, who had been so recently and tragically bereaved.

"It's the legion share-out soon," Ina confided. "I've no idea what I'm going to send David's family. I suppose I ought to get something between all of them, except David of course."

352

"What about a calendar with scenes of Salisbury on it?" Stella suggested. "You'll probably get one in Woolworth's or WH Smith."

"It doesn't seem much, though, does it?" Ina answered.

"Don't leave it too late and nearly miss it like you did with David's birthday," Stella warned.

"I think I'll ask my dad if I can borrow some money and give it back to him when I get my share-out. I can have a good browse around lunchtime."

***

Ina broached the subject after they had eaten that evening.

"Where do you think I get money from? Money doesn't grow on trees, you know. You seem to think I'm made of money," Jim grumbled.

He finally agreed to lend her £3.0s.0d on the understanding that it would be repaid when she received her legion money. Mr Phillips had already told them they could have an hour off to do their Christmas shopping, as long as it was not busy in the shop, and they would have to decide between themselves when their time off would be. It made sense for Ina to have first choice because of her deadline.

So it was that on the next Monday morning, armed with her precious £3.0s.0d, she deposited her bicycle at work with the promise of getting back at ten o'clock. She set out to tour the shops of Salisbury, looking for gifts that were reasonably priced but not cheap-looking or took too many coupons. She had brought from home one of her mother's shopping bags, not very elegant but roomy, and into this went her sundry purchases. She arrived back at the shop just before ten o'clock, red faced from the chilly wind and struggling with her burden.

"Hope you've left something for everybody else!" remarked Stella as Ina trudged her way through the shop.

At lunchtime, Ina laid out the contents of the shopping bag on the table.

"You seem to have had a good morning's shop." Stella remarked. "What have you got?"

"Well." Ina replied. "I thought I'd do as much as I could while I had the chance. I got Olivia a bottle of Devon Violets from Boot's and a headscarf. I got one for David's sister as well." She held the scarves up for Stella to see.

"Oh. They're pretty," said Stella.

"I've got David's stepdad and his brother some white hankies in a box with 'Made in England' on it. I bought a writing case and a fountain pen for David; I thought it might encourage him to write more often."

"Did you remember the wrapping paper?"

"Yes and a box of cards from Woolworth's. Tonight I can do my American parcels up and ask my mum to post them for me. They should go out about tomorrow morning."

"What have you got for me?" Stella grinned.

***

Ina went to the legion on share-out night with her parents and Clive, who had saved sixpence a week from his 1s.0d pocket money. The hall had been decorated earlier in the day with paper chains that had seen better days but were considered to be serviceable enough to fit the requirement of the day, which was to make do with what was available. Paper balls and bells hung from the ceiling, and a Christmas tree stood on the stage, planted in a large tub covered in crêpe paper. The tree was draped in silver tinsel, which showed signs of tarnishing but still glittered in the light. On top of the tree was a fairy doll—tired and jaded but still performing her duty.

Cissie had come down earlier with Alb, who now sat behind a long wooden table with another man. In front of them was a wooden box containing small brown envelopes and a large opened cash book. People were already lining up by the table. Alb took their names and gave them their envelopes, which they opened to check the contents, and then, having satisfied themselves and Alb that all was correct, they put a few coins in an ashtray, to be shared later by Alb and his partner.

Ina took her envelope, checked it, signed the book, and put some loose change into the ashtray. She rejoined her family and gave her father the £3.0s.0d that she had borrowed. They were sat with Cissie and were joined by Nell and Sid. An old lady, Mrs Drew, was sat near them and leaned towards Nell. "Your mother's not coming down tonight then?"

"No," Nell replied. "She has a job with the hills."

"Oh ah. You don't have to tell me about legs. Mine give me jip all the time. I'm glad I live on York Road; otherwise, I wouldn't be here myself."

Mrs Drew drained her glass before continuing. "It's what happens when you get old."

She looked over at Ina, who was drinking a small glass of beer shandy, and Clive, studying the bubbles rising up in his glass of Tizer.

"You young 'uns have got all that to come!" She caught Hilda's frown and went on hastily, "Still, it's not fun for you spending your childhood through a war."

The old lady swirled her empty glass around. When silence fell over the group she said, "Oh. There's Mrs Parker over there. I must have a word with her."

She got up and left, taking her empty glass with her.

"I think she was waiting to be asked if she wanted a drink," said Sid.

"Ah!" replied Jim. "She's caught me like that before. Sits there with her half a bitter and, if anyone asks her if she'd like a drink, she catches them for a port and lemon!"

***

A man was playing the piano; it was not Jack. Ina could not remember seeing him before. He played very well, and several couples got up to dance, including Jim and Hilda. The young man she had danced with on the previous occasion when she had come here was nowhere in sight. In fact, there were no young men of her age there. She contented herself by dancing with her father and then Uncle Sid.

She was glad when the interval came. Most of the women, including her mother, aunt, and Cissie, had managed to make sandwiches and fancy cakes. These were laid out on a long table covered with a white cloth. Alb was stood nearby and called to them all to come up and help themselves.

Ina did not feel particularly hungry. She got up out of her chair and walked towards the pianist. He was a tall lean man, probably in his middle thirties, and she wondered momentarily if he had been in the forces. She didn't think he was a railway man. He was still sat at the piano but turned sideways, facing the room and sipping beer from one of the many glasses that were lined up on top of the piano. He saw her approaching slowly and a little self-consciously. He smiled at her. It was a nice smile, and she smiled back.

"I hope you don't think I've a cheek," she began, "but do you write music as well as playing it?"

355

"Yes. I do as a matter of fact." He was still smiling at her.

"I . . . um . . . I wonder if you could write down some music notes for me?"

"What is it? A song you have written?"

"No. Not exactly."

She opened her handbag and took out a sheet of notepaper. "It's what someone used to sing to me. I've got the words, but I don't know anything about writing music."

He took the paper from her and scanned it. "So you'd like the music as well?"

"Yes. Yes, I would."

"Well. I don't very often have a request like that," he said.

She looked at him apprehensively.

"Important to you, is it?" he asked.

"Yes."

"Well. It will give me a chance to brush up on my skills. I wanted to be a concert pianist once."

"What stopped you?"

"The war," he said quietly but gruffly and then, on a more cheerful note, "Sing it to me, and I'll pick it up as we go. What key do you want it in?"

She looked at him in some surprise. "I don't really know," she told him.

"I haven't got any proper sheet music paper," he went on, "but I can scribble the notes down if you sing them. Never mind about the key; I'll sort that out later."

He took some paper out of his music case, on which he drew some horizontal lines. As Ina sang the tune, he dotted a series of notes along them.

When she had finished singing, he played it back to her. It was note perfect. "There!" he said. "Is that okay?"

"It's fine. Thanks so much."

"Tell you what," he offered, "if you've got a copy of the words, I'll set them to music properly. I can't say when I can get it done; it's my busy time—Christmas and New Year. Put your name and address down on the bottom of this piece of paper, and I'll make sure you get your song."

He turned back round to the piano keyboard and ran his fingers over the keys. "I'm going to play some more dance music now, so you can join in and enjoy yourself."

Ina rejoined the group at the table.

"What were you talking to that bloke at the piano about?" Jim asked.

"I wanted to know if he knew a song." She had flushed slightly.

Even after all this time, she tried never to get into any deep conversations with her father about David. Before he could question her further, she changed the subject. "He told me he wanted to be a concert pianist, but the war stopped him."

"I think he'd won a scholarship to some sort of music academy but was called up," put in Alb. "He was in the Terriers, and they were among the first lot to go. He went to France; got caught up in the Dunkirk lot. It was something to do with the Germans bombing the beaches while the boats were trying to get the men off. Don't know what happened to him exactly. He got home but was unfit for military service."

"Couldn't he go back to the music academy?" Ina asked.

"Bit late in the day by the time he got over it. Anyway, he had to do war work. He's in the NAAFI somewhere, just takes on these jobs to keep his hand in. Maybe when the war's over, he'll be able to pick up where he left off."

***

Ina recounted her story of the young piano player putting David's song down in written music to Stella when she met her off the bus the next morning.

"Working at the NAAFI? Whereabouts?"

"I don't know. Why?"

Stella shrugged. "Oh, I just wondered; that's all."

The conversation seemed to close, and Ina did not pursue the subject any further. So, when at lunchtime, she and Stella were toasting their tomato sandwiches in front of the popping gas fire, she was quite unprepared when Stella said, "I'm going to give my notice in to Mr Phillips at the end of this week."

A small piece of tomato fell from Ina's toast and landed at the bottom of the gas fire, where it sizzled before the flames. She scooped it off with a knife and turned to Stella. "It's a bit sudden, isn't it? When did you decide all this then?"

"I've been thinking about it for some time."

"And you never said?"

"I wasn't sure. Don't say anything to anyone. I don't want them to know before I've spoken to Mr Phillips."

"So you won't be coming back after Christmas then?"

"I shall come back for stock taking. I wouldn't leave you in the lurch for that."

"What are you going to do, join up? You're not old enough yet."

"Two months is nothing. Anyway, I'm joining the NAAFI. I don't have to be eighteen."

"Does it have something to do with this new boyfriend of yours?"

"Well, I do have more chance of seeing him if I go to Larkhill or Amesbury, don't I?"

"What if he gets sent overseas or you get sent to Land's End or John O'Groates?"

"I'll cross that bridge when I get to it."

Ina sighed. "We should both have been called up in a few months time and we would have probably gone our separate ways, anyway."

"Then he would have to find replacements for us both," Stella said. "At least he can advertise for another girl to train before I leave."

For some time, Ina had been aware of the growing rift between her and Stella. At least, this way, there would be no animosity. They would not be parting on bad terms. It was all coming to an end—this life she had been living for the past three and a half years. With Stella gone, there would be no one with whom she could share her memories of David.

Chapter 37

Ina came home from work that evening to be told by an excited Clive that a parcel had arrived from America.

"Are you going to open it, Ina?" he asked.

Ina looked at her mother.

"Don't look at me!" Hilda said. "It's addressed to you!"

"All right, then," Ina agreed, as anxious to see the contents as Clive.

She took the wrapping paper off and lifted up the lid of the cardboard it revealed. Inside were various packages with names on, wrapped in the quality of Christmas paper the onlookers had not seen since the start of the war.

"Can we open them, Mum?" Clive was hopping from one foot to the other in excitement.

"Don't you want to wait until Christmas Day?" Ina asked.

"Don't you want to see what you've got?"

"Oh . . . Go on then."

Jim, who had been sitting in his chair listening quietly to what was going on, said, "No need to open the parcels. If it's come from America, it should have a list of contents on the outside wrapping in case something in it could be liable to excise duty."

Clive made a dive for the discarded wrapping. He picked it up and examined it.

"Can't see anything on here, Dad."

Jim held out his hand for the paper and looked for himself.

"Ah!" he remarked. "Here—where the stamps are. 'Duty paid.' No. You're right. No list."

"Wonder what he had to pay duty on?" Hilda said.

"We shan't know till we look," Jim told her. "These customs people are pretty hot off the mark."

Hilda handed him the packet with his name on. Jim opened it, and exclaimed, "Well I'll be darned!"

They all turned to him. He held two packets of Virginia tobacco in his hand.

"I just don't understand," he said. "I thought something like tobacco would have to be paid to customs this end!"

"Well, if anyone comes knocking on the door, you'll have to hide it up the chimney." Hilda laughed.

"Gran always says that cigarettes are money going up in smoke!" Ina said.

"Wow. Look what I've got!" Clive held up a construction kit of a Sherman tank.

"That will keep you out of mischief for a while," Jim told him.

Clive turned to Ina. "Is this the kind of tank they had in the 2nd Armoured Division?"

Ina had given Hilda her parcel and was trying to reach a flat cardboard box that lay on the base of the larger one. For a moment, she paused. In her mind's eye, she could see him walking near the tank that had suddenly erupted into a mass of flame, smoke, and shards of metal that had killed or wounded so many.

Hilda caught the look on her daughter's face. "I expect they had a lot of different ones, like our boys did," she told Clive quietly. Turning to Ina she said, "Look what I've got," and held out a silk scarf with pictures of Florida printed on. "And look! A diary! There's a verse for each month!"

"Open yours, Ina." Clive was hopping about with excitement again.

Ina gave up trying to get the box out and just lifted up the lid. She pushed aside a layer of tissue paper and drew out a pink satin nightdress trimmed with lace.

"Phew," whistled Jim.

"Oh! Ina!" Hilda cried. "That's beautiful!"

Ina went back to the box and, this time, found a matching negligee.

"That must have set him back a bob or two," observed Jim.

Ina's thoughts went back to that day at Tidworth; he'd said he'd buy her pretty underwear . . .

***

Clive busied himself making paper chains from strips of coloured paper stuck with a paste of flour and water. Hilda had got some holly from the market and had put some behind the pictures on the wall. Jim tacked the paper chains to the ceiling as Clive finished them. There was enough to go into the front room as well. The festive decorations were rather sparse, but in wartime England, they had at least made the effort.

Avril came home Christmas Eve. Brian, of course, would be spending the holiday in Germany, but she would be going to his parents' Boxing Day. A kind neighbour of old Mrs Welland had offered to take her to her son's Christmas morning. Going back would be downhill all the way. The old lady was now sitting in an armchair in the front room, a small table beside her, on which was a glass of port and lemon. Jim had cleared the top of the sideboard, which now held an array of bottles of port, sherry, and Babycham. Bottles of stout and pale ale were being kept cool in a crate outside the back door. Nell, having been told by Hilda that she had plenty of help in the kitchen from the two girls, sat opposite her mother, holding a glass of sherry. Clive and Terry were on the sofa, two glasses of beer shandy on the small table in front of them. Jim put his head round the door; the smell of roasting chicken and boiling pudding wafted through behind him.

"Are you ladies all right?"

"Yes, thanks," they told him.

The door opened wider, and Sid came through, followed by Hilda and the two girls. Jim poured out sherry for them and one for himself.

"Let's drink a toast," he said. "Let's hope that next year, we shan't be spending Christmas at war."

They chorused their agreement.

Old Mrs Welland looked around her; her family—her children and her grandchildren—all together to celebrate Christmas. All except one—her eldest grandson, Teddy, whose coming into the world had caused so much acrimony, recrimination, and grief; whose life had brought so much happiness; and now, whose unknown fate was bringing heartache like no other.

***

There was never a lot of trade after the Christmas break. The whole town seemed quiet after the Christmas rush. The staff were able to concentrate on the stocktaking without too much interruption. The area manager had come down to go through the books; pronounced them satisfactory; and departed, wishing them a happy New Year and taking with him a packet of coffee beans, which Stella had obligingly purchased for him from Stoke's. It was one of the last acts she did before she left.

Mr Phillips had already advertised for a girl, and she came the day Stella left. She was fourteen years old and pretty, with ginger hair and a slightly freckled face. Ina had been taken back to the days of Tidworth Hospital and her meeting with Red. A tinge of sadness came over her. It seemed years ago that it had all happened. Stella's departure would leave a gap in her life.

"You can show Miss Baker the ropes, can't you, Miss Welland? She can share her break times with you."

Ina showed the girl the shelves, pointing out the things Miss Baker should familiarise herself with. Mr Phillips seemed satisfied with the way things were progressing. He hoped this new young girl was a quick learner. Soon he would have to fill Miss Auden's place. Shy at first, the young girl had, nevertheless, been a keen listener to all that Ina told her. Ina remembered the eager-to-learn young girl that she had been when she had arrived there as a fourteen-year-old in her first job.

"Don't try to take it in all at once," Ina advised

"By the way," the young girl said, "my name is Freda."

"Mine's Ina, but in the shop we have to call each other 'Miss'."

Freda noticed Ina's ring. "You're engaged. Is your fiancé in the army?"

"Yes. He was. He was wounded . . . in France . . . last August. He's American. He's gone back home."

"I am sorry. Was he badly hurt?"

"He lost an eye."

"Poor man! Will you go to America to get married?"

"Not until the war is over."

"Will you go over all by yourself?"

"I expect so."

"I think you're brave to go all that way." Freda gave a small sigh and said, "I think it's so romantic. By the time I'm allowed to have a boyfriend, all the Yanks will have gone home!"

"I think there's still one or two left mooching around." Ina smiled.

Chapter 38

January 1945

Ina and Hilda stayed up to see the New Year in; Jim was working, and Clive, tired, went to bed at half past ten. At midnight they heard the train whistle blowing up. Although Jim was nowhere in the vicinity, they both wished him a Happy New Year.

There was no partying; it was hardly worth it these days. Perhaps the young ones went to the New Years' balls, but as far as most people were concerned, Christmas had been enough. Staying at home and quietly celebrating the dawning of a new year was all that was needed. Hilda could remember the times before the war started, when neighbours had come out of their homes to call on each other, wishing each a happy new year. The Wellands had usually gone to the legion earlier in the evening. They had partied, and at midnight, the train whistles had blown and all the church bells had rung, and they had walked home arm in arm in the bright starlight. Now, only a few trains blew; the church bells were silent, as they had been all during the war, except for that one time when the battle of El Alamein had been won.

Would those days ever return? Would things be different after the war? Now, all there was in the night sky were searchlight beams criss-crossing and the silvery sheen of the barrage balloons.

***

New Year's Day, a letter came from David. He wrote:

I start college for a business course next week, a bit late; but I got in. I'm travelling back and forth, as I can't really afford to live on campus. I have to buy the books I need.

***

It was still quite dark when Ina reached the bus stop. The Purdy girls were there.

I wonder, she mused, *what they do for entertainment now that most of the Yanks have gone.* Then admonished herself. *I'm beginning to sound like Cissie Daley.*

It was cold on the bus. Either the heaters weren't working or they'd been turned off. She walked briskly across the market and was glad to get into the shop.

"It snowed this time last year as I recall," Mr Phillips remarked. He had followed Ina into the staffroom.

This time last year! What had she been doing?

Little Freda came in on the bus from Waters Road. She was bound up in a thick coat, fur-lined boots on her feet, a scarf wrapped around her neck, and a "pixie" hood pulled over her head.

"You don't intend to get cold." Ina laughed.

The shop was warm, and during the course of the morning, little pools of water formed on the floor where customers had come into the shop with snow on their shoes, neglecting to wipe them on the mat inside the door.

"One good thing," Ina said as she and Freda were on their morning break. "I don't think it snows in Alabama."

"Is that where you're going?"

"Either Alabama or Florida. I don't know yet."

"You are lucky." Freda paused and then continued, "I don't know much about American States, except they've got cowboys in Texas and film stars in California. What do they have in Alabama and Florida?"

"I don't know really," Ina replied. "I know they grow oranges in Florida."

"Wish they'd send some over here. It's ages since I had an orange."

"Perhaps the war will be over this year," Ina said.

"They said that last year and the year before!"

Ina got up. She picked up the two cups they had used.

"Do you want me to wash them up?" Freda asked.

"No. It's all right. I can do them. You go on back into the shop."

Freda left the room, and Ina followed her into the little workroom. She ran water over the cups.

Mr Phillips came in with a pair of shoes and a packet of stick-on rubber soles.

"You're nearly eighteen, now, Miss," he said. "You'll be getting a 5s.0d raise."

"Yes," Ina answered. She went on wiping up the cups and then said hesitantly, "I shall be getting my call-up papers."

Mr Phillips had put one shoe on the last and was now scoring it ready for the rubber solution to go on. "Yes. I am aware of that, Miss, and I shall have to find another girl I suppose. How do you think Miss Baker is shaping up?"

"Very well, I think, considering she hasn't been here long."

"It wouldn't be a bad idea to let her find her way around the children's department. She can fill the stock order sheets in, but under your guidance, mind."

"Yes, I don't think she'll be long picking it up. She's interested; that's the main thing."

"Good. I think that's why you've done so well."

Ina felt herself blushing.

"I relied on you a lot to keep things ticking over, you know," he went on.

Ina took the cups back into the staffroom. When she came back out into the workroom, Mr Phillips had gone back into the shop. The shoes had been soled and were lying on their uppers, surrounded by the aura of gum solution.

She went back quietly into the shop. There was only one customer there; Freda was serving, supervised by Vera. Ina looked around at the familiar shelves and the boxes of shoes, dusted and neatly stacked. She had taken a pride in her job ever since she had first started working here—fresh from school and in her first job. She remembered that time, Easter 1941. Vera, two years older than Ina, was already there, and two other girls. Joan, who had married just before the war started, had been expecting her first baby and had been allowed to stay on until she "showed". The other girl, Molly, had no desire to go into any branch of the women's services and had left to work in a factory.

Then, Stella had come, about a year after Ina. There had been an instant rapport between the two of them. They had become firm friends, sharing leisure times and confiding in each other their young, girlish hopes and dreams. Then had come that day in March (was it really almost a year ago?) when they had strolled together around the town on that Sunday afternoon in the winter sunshine, pausing to look in Bloom's window and were asked the way to the cathedral by two American soldiers.

Chapter 39

Hilda had washed up the lunch things and brought in a tray of tea. She didn't usually cook at midday, but Jim was on at two o'clock, so she had catered for the two of them, although it meant cooking again later for Ina and Clive.

Jim, already dressed in his railway clothes, sat by the small fire. "There's hardly enough fire to keep the room warm," he said.

"The log man should be around soon," Hilda told him.

"I shall have to see if I can get hold of some sleepers," Jim went on.

"It would be such a help if you could, Jim."

"I'll try, but they disappear like magic the moment the word gets around that there's some going. And that's it! Everybody's after them. We drivers don't get a look in. The station staff are the lucky ones. They're on the spot."

There came a loud knocking on the front door.

"Who on earth can that be?" said Hilda. "I'm not expecting anyone!"

"Whoever it is, they want you to know they're there," Jim replied.

Hilda hurried to the front door and came back into the living room.

"Well? Who was—?" He caught sight of the telegram in her hand and the paleness of her face. He stopped short and rose up, out of his chair.

"Jim!" she said, in a small voice. "It's from America!"

"Oh, it's for Ina then."

"It's addressed to us. It's from his stepfather."

"Perhaps it's to say he's coming over—"

"Why send it to us? Why not to Ina?"

"Get on and open it. You won't learn anything until you read it."

368

With trembling fingers, Hilda opened the envelope. "I know it's bad news," she said as she took the slip of paper out. She read it and passed it to Jim. He took it from her silently and read the contents.

Regret to inform you, David died yesterday evening. Stop. Please break the news to Ina. Stop. More details in letter to follow.

"Oh, dear God!" Jim said. "Out of the blue . . . just like that! How the hell are we going to tell her?"

After Jim had left for work, Hilda played with the idea of not going back to work herself but thought she'd be better off among her workmates, although she was a minute or two late. She confided in Nell.

"I don't understand!" Nell exclaimed. "I thought he was discharged from the army and was on the mend."

"So did we," Hilda answered. "Something's gone wrong somewhere. We shan't know until we get the letter."

If Hilda thought being at work would ease the situation, she found in the course of the afternoon that she could not concentrate, and the last straw came when the bottom fell out of a box of coffee she had lifted from the conveyor belt and the tins had rolled across the floor. The forewoman came over and Nell, intercepting her, told her of Hilda's distressing news.

"Hilda, I am sorry. Why don't you go on home? It's nearly four o'clock. An hour won't make any difference."

"Yes, all right. Thanks."

Hilda went to get her coat and handbag.

Nell called after her, "I'll come up later on tonight."

***

The clock on the sitting room mantelshelf struck a half past four as Clive came in the back door.

"You're early!" Hilda remarked.

"We came out of school early because the weather didn't look too good," Clive answered. He went through to the hall and hung up his outdoor clothes. He came back to the kitchen and stood by the sink, watching his mother as she peeled potatoes.

"I've something to tell you," she said, solemnly.

"Yes?"

She put the last potato into the saucepan, lit the gas under it, and pushed him gently through to the sitting room.

"We've had some bad news. A telegram came from America this afternoon. It was from David's people. It was to say . . . It said . . ." She paused, went to the sideboard, and started to take cutlery out of the drawer. "Clive . . . I'm afraid David died."

There was silence from Clive. She looked at him. His face was contorted into a deep frown. When he spoke, his voice quivered. "But he was better, Mum! He was out of the army! Why did he die, Mum? I was going to Florida after the war to see his turkey farm!"

"I think he had to give up that idea for a while."

"It won't happen at all now, will it? What's Ina going to do? She won't be going either, will she?"

"Ina doesn't know yet."

Clive went out into the hall and came back with his coat on.

"Where do you think you're going?"

"Down to Gran's. I don't want to be here when you tell Ina. I don't want to be here when she starts crying and that—"

"Take your coat off, Clive. You're not going anywhere. You go bursting into your gran's, and you'll give her a heart attack!"

Clive took off his coat and hung it up once more. He sat in his father's chair, hunched up, with his arms crossed, gazing into the fire.

"We shan't know anymore until we get a letter from America. They will know more themselves then. Do you want to get on with some homework? It might take your mind from it."

"I wish it was tomorrow; all this will be over, and everyone will know!"

Hilda sighed. "It won't be over for a long time, Clive. For me and your dad, the worst bit's to come."

Chapter 40

"How is she?" Nell enquired.

Hilda, sat at the table opposite her, poured tea into a cup and replied, "It's hard to tell, Nell. It didn't seem to sink in. She didn't cry or anything. I should have known what to do if she had." Hilda stifled a sob and took a gulp of her tea. "She just went very quiet . . . Didn't say a word . . . I know she's hurting. When she was a little girl . . . if she fell and hurt herself . . . when she was ill or had a nightmare, I could hug and kiss her, make it better, but now I can't. I just have to watch her suffer. I don't know what she's thinking. I don't know what to do!"

Hilda rested her elbows on the table and put her head in her hands. She cried, but her crying was silent.

Nell put her hand out and touched Hilda's arm. "Where is she?"

"She's up in her room. She must be cold up there," Hilda said.

Nell's mind went back to that day in 1917. She had not heard from Eddie for nearly a month, and she was sure now that she was carrying his baby. Then one Sunday afternoon, that knock had come on the front door. Her mother had gone to answer it and had come back with Johnnie, Eddie's friend, one sleeve of his greatcoat hanging empty by his side. He'd held a letter out to her. Their eyes had met, and she had seen the immeasurable grief in them.

"He wrote this while we were having a break, and then the shell came . . . I don't think he finished it. They gave it to me at the hospital. They found it on him. They put it in an envelope when he . . . I said I'd give it to you when I got back to England, I'm so sorry, Nell. He was my best mate . . ."

So, Eddie would never know he was going to be a father and Teddy would never know his dad.

Nell turned her attention back to Hilda. "Shall I go and have a word?"

Hilda nodded, "You can try, Nell."

Nell opened the door to Ina's bedroom and went inside. Ina was lying on the bed. The room was in darkness, although the curtains weren't drawn.

"Ina?" Nell whispered. "Its Auntie Nell."

Ina sat up and leaned back against the headboard.

"Do you want to put your light on?"

Ina reached over to the table lamp. Nell drew the curtains across the window and then came back and sat at the foot of the bed.

"We're so sorry about David," she said. "He was such a nice young man. To think he went home and—"

"I want to write to his mother," Ina broke in. "But I don't know what to say. Mum said there was a letter following. Do you think I should wait till then?"

Nell hesitated and looked at her. The lamp didn't give much light. What fell on Ina's face did not show any trace of tears. Nevertheless, she looked wan and strained. *She's not going to let go*, thought Nell.

She said, "Yes, that might bc best."

"Auntie?" Ina's voice quiet and with a slight tremor made Nell look at her intently. "Yes, dear?"

"How did you feel? You know, when you heard about Teddy's dad?"

Nell took a deep breath. Ina wanted to know how she felt. "Well," she said, "perhaps the way you're feeling right now. I didn't want to talk about it because, if I did, then that would make it real, and I didn't want it to be real."

"How long did you feel like that?"

"A long time—quite a while. I pretended that he was still in France or Belgium, wherever it was he had been fighting. I just went on as though nothing was wrong, except I didn't seem to want to laugh anymore. It was a big mistake. When Teddy was born it hit me—suddenly. My blood pressure went up, and I wasn't at all well. But, after that, I found I could think about Eddie, all the nice things that had happened to us and, although the sadness was still there, the hurt gradually went away. Don't hold it in too much, Ina."

"You had Teddy to help you through it."

"Yes, but I didn't know then if it was a good thing or a bad thing."

"But you could talk to him about his dad."

"Yes. I could do that, not that he understood me."

Ina looked at her and then said, "The last time I saw David, when I said goodbye to him, I told Stella I would never see him again . . . I never will now, shall I?"

There was nothing Nell could say to this.

Ina went on, "Everything has been wiped out—going to America, meeting his family, getting married, having children . . . I wish . . ." She paused.

"What do you wish, Ina?"

"That we'd . . . you know . . ."

"Don't wish that, Ina. David died loving you, and he knew you loved him. No one can ever take that away from you. You've had your share of grief early in your life. But you've got your mum and dad and Avril and Clive, and we're all here to help you."

"But I might have had some part of him left, like you had Teddy."

"No, Ina. You don't know how hard it was for me. No one takes the fact that you loved someone into account. You're just a bad girl, and you're treated with such contempt. I was lucky. I had your gran and granddad to help me. The manager let me stay on at the milk factory. Your mum was a brick, although she was much younger than me. She supported me all the way through, and she made such a fuss of Teddy. But others . . . They made things hard for me and your gran. Even Teddy at times."

"I'm sorry. I didn't know how awful it was for you. I've never thought about Teddy like that. He was just my cousin."

"I was lucky to have Uncle Sid."

"I won't ever forget David."

"I know. Now, why don't you try to get some sleep?"

"I do feel a bit tired."

***

Hilda looked up as Nell came into the living room.

"She's going to try and get some sleep," Nell said.

Hilda nodded

"How did she seem to you?"

"I think it's gone deep with her. She's not going to get better overnight; she's seen all her dreams shattered." Nell looked up at the clock. "I'd better get on," she said, "or Mum will wonder what's going on. She's upset over this for Ina's sake, like we all are."

"Thanks for coming, Nell."

***

Hilda tried to coax Ina into not going to work the next day.

"I'd rather go in, Mum. I don't want to sit around here all day. I'd rather be doing something."

She went in early so that she could tell Mr Phillips before Vera and Freda came in.

"I'm so sorry, Miss," Mr Phillips sympathised. "It seems most unfair, seeing that he was out of the army and at home. Are you sure you wouldn't rather be at home?"

"No. I'd rather be here."

"Well. If you want any time off you've only to ask."

Back in the shop, everything seemed so unchanged and normal that Ina had a job for a while to understand why the world around her had not stopped. But she got on with her work and found herself relating to her customers with the same ease and politeness that she always had. Only the dullness of her eyes and the drawn set of her mouth betrayed her to those who knew her.

Vera, happening to come near her, put a hand on her arm and whispered, "I'm so sorry, Ina."

Ina looked at her and saw a glint of tears in her eyes. *She knows what it's like*, she thought. And in that instant, Vera's expression had meant more to her than all the words of sympathy. She nodded and smiled. "Thanks," she murmured.

When they were sat at the morning break, Freda said, "I'm ever so sorry, Ina. I had a little brother, Peter. He died of diphtheria four years ago. I still cry for him sometimes. He would have been ten, now." She gave a sigh. "You'll never forget your David, but you'll have lots of nice memories of him, like I have of Peter."

In spite of herself, Ina smiled. *Dear little Freda—"old head on young shoulders". But I'm young myself; only I feel so old. If only the pain would go away.*

If Ina thought Mrs Gray would show some feeling or concern, she was mistaken. Mrs Gray lived in her own tight little world—smug and self-satisfied, ready to impose her own narrow view on everyone near to her, and at a loss to understand why anyone should take misfortune so seriously. Her inability to put herself in another's place was complete.

Vera was in her window with Freda, showing her the finer points of window dressing. Mr Phillips was serving a gentleman customer. Ina was putting shoes away in their boxes when Mrs Gray came up to her.

"I'm sorry to hear about your young man," she said. "Never mind, you're very young. You'll get over it. It might be a blessing in disguise, you know. You might have gone to America and decided you didn't like it. Then where would you have been? No. You take my word for it. You're much better off in this country with your family. Just remember him as he was the last time you saw him."

Ina looked at this unimaginative tactless woman. With a dark frown on her face and her eyes glinting angrily, she almost spat her words of reply. "The last time I saw him, he was standing in a field in Tidworth dressed in his combat gear, ready to go to war!"

Chapter 41

February 1945

It was a week after the telegram had arrived that the letter came. This time it was addressed to Ina. She read:

Dear Ina,

I cannot tell you how devastated we are at David's death. It does still not seem real. We grieve for you being so far away. We know you loved him and he loved you. He talked of you all the time. I don't suppose we will ever meet up now, and that will be our loss. He died of a brain haemorrhage, but until they do an autopsy on him, we shall not know for sure. My husband and children have given me much support, but I do wish Todd was near. I pray that he will soon be home from the Pacific. I hope this war will be over before it takes my other son. I will let you know about the autopsy as soon as I have news; I know your people will be of comfort to you. Give them our regards,

God Bless you my dear.
Olivia.

Ina passed the letter over to her mother. Hilda read it and passed it to Jim.

"Poor woman," she murmured. "She's already lost one of her sons, and the other is still fighting the Japanese."

"It happens a lot in wartime," Jim commented. "Do you remember the Bakers who lived somewhere around Scott's Lane? One son captured at Dunkirk and the other going down on the Hood."

He read the letter and gave it back to Ina.

"What happened to them, Dad?"

"The Bakers? They moved away. I don't know where to."

***

Stella paid a surprise visit the following Sunday afternoon. Hilda showed her into the front room, where Ina was sitting by a small log fire.

"I'll go and make some tea," Hilda said, leaving the room.

"I got your letter," Stella said. "It was quite a shock hearing about David. Do they know what happened?"

"He had a haemorrhage—a brain haemorrhage."

"Was it anything to do with losing his eye?"

Ina shrugged. "I don't know," she said, "perhaps. They're doing an autopsy on him—what we call a post-mortem. Olivia is going to let me know."

"I am sorry, Ina."

"How's your boyfriend? Is it still on?" Ina seemed keen to change the subject.

"Yes. He may be going to Germany soon. It's still early days for us, but I do like him a lot."

"Do you still like being in the NAAFI?"

"Yes. It's a bit different from what I thought. I'm serving behind the counter, but I cut sandwiches as well. And there's always washing up! But we have some fun. I suppose you'll be getting your call-up papers soon. Where do you want to go?"

"Into the ATS."

"Not the WAAF like your Avril then."

"No, if soldiering was good enough for David, then it's good enough for me."

"What if they put you into something else?"

"I'm going to volunteer. I thought I'd go to the recruiting office tomorrow dinner time. Only I haven't said anything to Mum and Dad yet, so don't say anything, will you?"

"No, I shan't say anything." Stella paused for a second or two and then asked, "How are things at the shop?"

"Oh, all right. We have a new girl. She's fourteen, and she's getting on quite well. Mr Phillips is interviewing another girl tomorrow, ready for when I go."

"What about Vera?"

"Vera's surprised us all. It's as if she's suddenly woken up. I think she realises how much Mr Phillips depends on her. She's really good with Freda, showing her the ropes, and I think she's more interested in the job now."

"I think Mr Phillips relied on us a lot, especially you."

Ina's mind went back to what Mr Phillips had said to her.

"We had some fun though, didn't we, Ina?" Stella went on, breaking into Ina's thoughts.

"Yes. We did," Ina agreed.

"Remember when we used to go up the dance hall and those boys smuggled those bottles of beer in and they took us home on the crossbars of their bikes? Remember that day when Sharkey and his mate came into the shop and put the wind up Vera so she hid in the lav? And that time you had the row with him at Tidworth?"

"I think the best times were when we met the boys," Ina said, "going to the Red Cross and that football match at Tidworth . . ."

Her voice trailed off, and Stella noticed the shadow across her face. She stood up. "I suppose I'd better be going. Don't want to miss my bus."

She put her empty tea cup on the tray. Ina rose as well. Picking up the tray, she followed Stella into the sitting room.

"Just come to say goodbye, Mrs Welland," Stella said to Hilda.

"Oh, off then Stella?"

"Don't want to miss my bus." Stella smiled.

Hilda glanced at the clock. "You should just catch the bus to town now."

"I'll see you off," Ina told her.

They walked to the front door, and Ina walked to the gate with Stella. The faint headlights of the bus came into view.

"Just in time," Stella remarked, walking the few paces to the bus stop. "Goodbye," she called over her shoulder.

"Goodbye," Ina called back. "Thanks for coming."

She stood there for a while after the bus moved on and watched it until it was out of sight. "Goodbye," they had both said; neither had said, "Keep in touch" or "See you soon."

***

The light was fast fading, and already, the sky was beginning to take on the dark hue of night. It was cold. She turned and went indoors. She suddenly felt alone. For a long time, even before Stella had left, they had more or less gone their own ways, but the shop had still kept the bond between them. They had no common ground now. It was all gone, all part of the past—their history.

She walked into the sitting room. She stood in the doorway, looking at her family, her father rolling a cigarette, her mother darning socks, and Clive with his head stuck into the inevitable comic.

"Mum, Dad."

Three heads turned in her direction. Three pair of eyes looked at her.

"I've decided what I'm going to do. I'm going to the army recruiting office tomorrow and sign on for the ATS."

For a while, there was silence. Hilda took the darning mushroom out of the sock she had been working on, broke the thread, and reached for another sock. Clive gave a slight shrug and went back to his comic.

Jim said, "Why the hurry? You'll be getting your call-up papers soon."

"I want to make sure I get into the ATS and not in some factory or something I don't like."

"You know we'll have to sign something giving our permission, don't you?"

"I shall be nearly eighteen by the time I get accepted."

"We shall still have to sign the enlistment form."

"Will you sign, or will you stop me?"

Jim gave a sigh. "Well. I don't think we have much choice. If the services are going to take you anyway, it might just as well be now as later. You may have more choice of what you want to do if you volunteer, I don't know . . ."

"Mum?"

"I shall be going along with your father," Hilda said. "It makes no difference now, the ATS or America. You were going off anyway."

"I shan't be going to America now, shall I?"

Hilda caught the slight touch of bitterness in her daughter's voice. "I'm sorry, Ina. I didn't mean—"

"It's all right, Mum." Ina put her hand up, interrupting her. "It's all right."

Chapter 42

The letter came from America. The report of the autopsy concluded that the haemorrhage was caused by a small splinter of metal, which must have been overlooked during the operation to remove the pieces of shrapnel from his eye socket. Olivia had written.

You will never believe, Ina, I have someone from the Defence Department come see me. Because his death was the result of his wound, he is having a military funeral.

***

The buff envelope was put before her as she sat at the table; she felt a slight chill come over her. She remembered the OHMS letter that Avril had had when they had come back from Guildford. Avril had moved stations a few times since she had joined the WAAF. She must be used to the routine by now and going to different places. How long did it take to get used to the idea that your home would now be some Nissen hut somewhere in the wilds of the country instead of a brick house with a front and back garden, a room to oneself, and a mother who cooked and cleaned for you and washed your clothes? Would she be homesick? Had Avril been homesick? She'd never said so. Had David? Had he just wanted to be home when he left America with his regiment to fight in foreign countries? She knew he must have seen some terrible things—even been scared sometimes. And when he was wounded and in that hospital in Ireland, did he want his mom?

But the die had been cast. She had had her medical—been poked and prodded, had her eyes tested, and taken her ability test. Had she passed? Or had she been rejected?

"Are you going to open that?" Hilda asked.

Ina slit the envelope open with her table knife and read the contents.

"Well?" Hilda enquired.

"It's a travel warrant and a list of things I need to take with me. I'm not allowed to take any civilian clothes other than the ones I'm wearing, except pyjamas. I have to take my book, identity card, and writing materials."

"What do they say about underwear?" asked Hilda.

"I suppose that's included in with no civilian clothes," Ina replied.

Clive broke into song. "She'll be wearing khaki bloomers when she comes . . ."

"That's enough, Clive," said his mother. She turned to Ina again. "Does it say where you'll be going?"

"I have to catch a train to Woking. Someone will meet me there and take me to my camp, where I have to do six weeks of basic training."

"Does it say where the camp is?"

"A place called Camberley in Surrey. That's where Guildford is, isn't it?"

"Surrey? Yes. But I don't think I've heard of Camberley," Hilda said. "Perhaps Dad will know."

Ina helped her mother clear away and wash up.

"I think I'll go and have a bath," she said, after she'd put the cutlery and crockery away.

"Don't use too much hot water," Hilda replied.

Ina had just left the living room when the back door opened and Cissie called her customary, "Coo-e-e."

"Come in," called Hilda.

Cissie came in to the living room. "I just came in to see how Ina is."

"I'm a little worried about her actually," Hilda told her.

"Oh. I am sorry. Isn't she getting over it very quickly?"

"I don't think it is something you get over quickly, Cissie."

"No. Oh, no, of course not. It's still early days, as they say."

"It's just that she hasn't cried or anything. I'm worried it will hit her suddenly, and she will break down at her army base, where I won't be there to help her," Hilda went on.

"Perhaps she didn't think as much of him as she thought, and she hasn't seen him for such a long time."

"I don't think it's that. All she thought about was going to America and seeing him again."

"Well," Cissie went on, "it's solved one problem for you; she won't be leaving you to go to the ends of the earth, and you'll know where she is when she's in the ATS."

"I admit Jim and I weren't too happy about it, but the last thing I would have wanted was David to have died."

"No. It was such an awful shame. His poor mother! All the same, I'm glad Maureen settled for a nice English boy. I've no worries there. I just hope Harold is as sensible."

Hilda gritted her teeth and, forcing her lips into a smile, said, "Any chance of Maureen getting married? They've been courting some time, haven't they?"

She saw the faint reddening of Cissie's cheeks. "They don't want to get married until the war is over. Keith said he's seen too many women widowed to bring it on Maureen." She hesitated and then said, "I think they may be getting engaged soon . . . but I'm not sure . . . so I shouldn't say anything, really . . ."

Hilda did not reply. She had heard that before.

An awkward silence lay between them. Cissie said, "Well. I ought to be getting back." She walked towards the back door. "See you tomorrow night when we go to the legion, then."

And she was gone.

"There are times when I could cheerfully throttle that woman!" Hilda told Clive.

***

Ina, meanwhile, had shed her clothes and was sat on the bath stool, watching the water flowing from the geyser and into the bath. She reached for the jar of bath crystals and poured out a handful, scattering them across the bathwater. They slowly dissolved and thin, coloured threads spiralled deep into the bath. She put her hand into the water, swishing it around until the spirals merged and became one rosy whole. She stepped into the bath, stood up, and washed herself and then, sitting down, rinsed the soap suds off as well as she could in the shallow water. She lay back, trying to keep the warm water over her body as much as she could, but it barely covered her legs or her hips.

Bet they didn't have five inches of water in their baths in Alabama. Coal probably wasn't rationed there. Anyway, they all had central heating, and they had big bathrooms with showers and air conditioning and refrigerators. What was the good of thinking about all that now? She was never going to be part of it.

She suddenly remembered her earlier home, before Clive was born and there was just herself and Avril. The living room was called the kitchen. It boasted a built-in dresser and a black leaded kitchen range. The kitchen was called the scullery. In the corner was a large whitewashed brick copper, in which her mother boiled water for baths and the washing. She remembered bath nights then—the tin bath taken off the wall outside the back door and placed in front of the kitchen fire, she and Avril getting into the bath together and feeling the prickle of the hot water and the heat from kitchen range. Afterwards, there was the drying with the warm towels that had been draped over the fireguard surrounding the range. Dressed ready for bed—a nice warm bed—she had lain there and watched the circle of light from the oil lamp flickering on the ceiling.

Clive had come along when she was four. The little house, with just two bedrooms, would soon be too small. Her father had bought the little house with the money due to him when he had been demobbed from the army and the small amount that his father had left him. The house was sold and the money put towards the house in Devizes Road. Then her father became a driver. Luckily, he had not had to move away from Salisbury as many drivers did—like Uncle George at Guildford and Mr Daley.

Was she going back in time—remembering things she had long forgotten? Was it because she could not see her future clearly? Old people, like Gran, talked about the olden days because they didn't have many more days in front of them.

The water grew cold. She got out the bath, dried herself, dressed, and then went downstairs. Tomorrow would be her last day at the shop, and suddenly, she wanted to stay home where it was warm and safe.

Chapter 43

The warmth from the gas convector heaters, with their own peculiar (though not unpleasant) smell, greeted Ina as she walked through the shop door. Mr Phillips stood behind the cash desk opening the mail with a paper knife and laying the unfolded contents in a neat pile to be mused over and dealt with later. He looked up and, in his customary manner, said "Good morning, Miss."

She answered him and wheeled her bicycle on through the shop and out into the yard. Back in the staffroom, the gas fire had been lit and a small fireguard placed in front of it. Ina took off her coat and put her overall on, took a comb from her handbag, and combed her hair. She looked into the heavy old mirror over the mantelpiece with its wooden frame and flyblown surface.

This is the last time I shall ever do this, she thought, *the last time I shall come in here to have my breaks. No more toasting sandwiches in front of the fire.*

How they had looked forward to their breaks—she and Stella! Going around town before it was time for work again. Looking in the clothes shops, thinking of what they would buy once the war was over and there were no more coupons. Or perhaps they would just sit quietly talking—about the boys they had met or the films they had seen or what they would wear to the Saturday night dance. Then they had talked of David and Joe.

In that short year, she had gone through so many different emotions. There had been the excitement of getting ready to meet David and then the anxiety of wondering if he would turn up and the overwhelming sense of relief when she saw him standing by the bridge. The places they had gone to, the conversations they'd had, the first little "spat" they'd had over the American Civil War, and making up afterwards. So many memories! In this room, she had opened her heart to Stella. There was no one now.

Freda came into the room, followed by Dolly.

"Crummy!" Freda exclaimed. "Are we late?"

"No," Ina told her. "I'm early."

She had just gone into the shop when Vera came in.

"You're eager," Vera commented with a smile.

"Spinning out my last day." Ina smiled back.

***

Mr Phillips was obviously in the back toilet, as there was no visible sign of him. Ina was in the shop all by herself. She stood in front of the hosiery showcase, looking out of the only window that was low enough and big enough to see outside the shop. It wasn't an inspiring scene, just the small backyard enclosed by the backs of the buildings in the next street. On this gloomy day, at the beginning of February, there was no glimmer of sunlight to brighten the bleakness. On the wall at the bottom of the yard, probably from a blocked gutter, water ran unchecked. She turned away from the window as Mr Phillips came through from the back. He went up to the front door, unlocked it, and turned the "closed" sign to "open". The last day had begun.

The morning passed quickly. Shoes were taken out of boxes and tried on; some sold, and others rejected, put back into their boxes, and replaced on the shelves.

At lunchtime, Ina and Freda were sitting together in the staffroom. "Are you sorry to be leaving?" Freda asked, looking intently at Ina.

"Yes, I am in a way," Ina said. "I've been here four years. I've never had any other job. I've never wanted to go anywhere else. I like it here."

"So do I! I wonder if I shall be here in four years' time. Just think, I shall be eighteen, same age as you."

"I'm not eighteen until the end of the month."

"You weren't a leap year baby were you?"

"Not quite. I was born on the twenty-seventh. My friend, Stella, was born on the fifteenth; she was just too late for Valentine's Day."

"How old is she?"

"Eighteen."

"Did she get her calling-up papers?"

386

"No. She volunteered for the NAAFI. She left just before you came."

"Oh. Yes. Stella."

"That's right. She came nearly a year after I started."

"Now she's gone and you're going."

It was time to go back into the shop. Just as they were about to leave, Mrs Phillips came through the door. "I hope I'm not disturbing your break."

"No," Ina said. "We're just going back to work."

Mrs Phillips dumped her shopping basket on the table and sat down in one of the chairs. "This shopping!" she commented. "It doesn't get any better. It's a nightmare wondering what to get for a change."

Freda had already left the room, and Ina was just about to follow when Mrs Phillips said, "Miss Welland?"

Ina turned and looked back, "Yes?"

"You know, Mr Phillips will miss you quite a lot when you go. He relied upon you and Miss Auden," Mrs Phillips sighed. "Now this blessed war has taken you both . . . and so many young people."

"I think," Ina replied in a small voice, "I'd rather not be going at all, but I know it really isn't up to me."

"No, of course it isn't. And you might enjoy the life once you have settled in and made new friends. You'll learn new skills and see new places, but you won't forget what you've left behind and you mustn't expect to . . . not all at once. You'll be all right, you see. Don't forget to come and see us."

Ina smiled and nodded to her and then went through to the shop. What Mrs Phillips had said to her meant more than all the words of consolation she had heard from anyone else no matter how well meaning. Mrs Phillips had bent from her loftier position as the manager's wife, to let Ina know that she knew how she was feeling. Perhaps, in the past, there had been something in the older woman's life that she, too, had had to come to terms with.

***

As the morning had passed quickly, so now did the afternoon—too quickly, Ina thought. Not that she didn't want to go home, but the idea of saying goodbye to four years of her working life, not to mention the growing up she had done, was beginning to make her wish to stay among these things familiar to her. She became aware of Vera talking to her.

"Are you all right?" Vera asked.

Startled Ina said, "Yes."

"You looked far away."

Ina smiled. "I was far away."

Vera walked over to the cash desk, unlocked the drawer, put a one pound note in, and gave the woman she'd been serving her change. Ina watched her. Vera seemed to be transformed these days. There was a marked assurance about her. Her attitude towards the customers had somehow changed. Gone was the faint air of timidity; she smiled more often and joined in a repartee with them. Freda and Dolly hung on her every word, which was more than she and Stella had done. She now felt a bit guilty about the way they had sometimes joked about Vera behind her back. She realised that she had followed where Stella had led. She remembered the overwhelming sense of pity she had felt for Vera when her boyfriend had been killed.

A woman came up to Ina. She had seen a pair of shoes in the window. Did they have her size?

Ina went outside with her, and the woman pointed out the shoes. Two soldiers were passing by. They wolf whistled at Ina. She took no notice.

"That's right, my dear; you just ignore them," the woman said. "Decent young men don't whistle after young girls."

Ina led her back into the shop. "If only you knew!" she said, under her breath. A year ago, she would have smiled at them and Stella would probably have laughed.

Trade began to slacken off. Mrs Gray announced that she was leaving and went out to get her coat. The others took advantage of the lull to clear up the discarded shoes. Mrs Gray came back through, dressed in her outdoor clothes. "I'm off, now, then. See you all Monday."

She had nearly reached the door when she turned and came back to where Ina and Vera were straightening the shelves.

"Oh, Miss Welland," she said. "I shan't see you again, shall I? So, good luck. You'll have the time of your life in the ATS, you see. No paying for your clothes or food, your fares paid when you come home on leave. Just think! All those camp dances you'll be going to! All those British soldiers you'll meet. You'll soon forget about your Yank and going halfway round the world—"

Ina's face paled. The two young girls looked at Mrs Gray, open-mouthed. It was Vera who sprang suddenly to life. Her eyes were bright and her hands clenched. She came up to Mrs Gray and hissed, "When are you going to learn to keep your mouth shut?"

Mrs Gray looked at Vera in horror. She opened her mouth to speak and then changed her mind, wheeled round, and went out the door without a word to anyone. Vera went back to tidying up the shelves. Ina cast a glance in Mr Phillip's direction. His face gave no sign that he had heard Vera's outburst. But was it her imagination? Or had there been a slight "twitching" at the corners of his mouth?

***

At six o'clock, Mr Phillips told the young ones they could go. He locked up and then began to cash up the day's takings. Vera and Ina added up the sums on the carbon copies of the receipt books. Freda and Dolly, dressed for home, came back into the shop, Freda carrying a small flat parcel wrapped in brown paper and Dolly, an envelope. They laid both on the small counter in front of Ina.

"This is from all of us," said Dolly.

Ina picked up the envelope and drew out a card. It bore the message "Good Luck" on it, with the picture of a black cat and a sprig of heather. Inside were the signatures of all of them, including Mrs Phillips', but not, she noticed, Mrs Gray's. The parcel was next. She opened the package and took out a red leather writing case. Inside of that was a writing pad on one side and envelopes on the other, while nestling in between was a fountain pen. Ina touched it, running her fingers over it gently.

"It's lovely," she said. "I'm so pleased with it. Thank you all so much."

"You can write to us and let us know how you're getting on," Freda said. Then she and Dolly left.

Ina's last day had come to a close. She and Vera went out to the back to get ready for home. Outside, the darkness had closed over the yard. Ina wheeled her bicycle carefully into the staffroom.

"Well," she said, "this will be the last time I shall be in this room. No more tea and toast in front of this fire . . ."

"I shall miss you Ina," Vera said. "It won't be the same without you."

"Oh," Ina said, "from what I've seen of Freda and Dolly, I reckon things will get lively enough."

She looked at Vera seriously—this Vera who had suddenly blossomed—and the old Vera, shy and lacking confidence, seemed to have gone.

"Do you still grieve for your boyfriend, Vera?"

"Yes. But it doesn't hurt quite as much. I just think about the good times we had together. You're not expected to forget them, Ina."

Back in the shop, Mr Phillips opened the door for Vera to go through. She said goodnight to them and, again, wished Ina good luck and then went out into the night.

Mr Phillips said, "Before you go, Miss Welland, I have something for you." He held out a small brown envelope. "This is a little something from the firm and me."

She took the envelope, her face slightly flushed.

"It's just to show our appreciation," he went on.

"Thank you, very much." She felt emotions swelling up inside her.

He held the door open once more, carefully, because of the blackout. "Goodbye then, and all the best. Come to see us when you can."

Outside, the street lamps shone their meagre light upon the damp pavements. There was a chill in the air, and a fine drizzle fell against her face. She checked her dimmed headlamp and rear light, mounted the bicycle, and rode out of Market Street and into the canal. She cycled past the homeward bound workers and the last-minute shoppers, hurrying along to catch their buses. She would no longer be among them. They would all be going home for the weekend, and Monday morning, they would start all over again. She would be on a train, going to Woking. And, what else, she didn't know.

Chapter 44

Hilda was straining potatoes when Ina came through the back door into the kitchen; the steam was rising from the hot water as it poured into the sink.

"Well?" asked Hilda. "How did your last day go?"

"Not too bad," Ina replied. "They gave me a present." She took the parcel from under her arm.

"That was nice of them. What is it?"

"It's a writing case."

"Well, that'll come in handy." She nearly said, "You sent David one," but changed her mind. Instead, she said, "Tea's nearly ready."

Ina went through to the living room. Her father and Clive were already sat at the table. She put the parcel and card on the sideboard.

"What you got there?" asked Clive.

"A farewell present from work."

"Cor! Let's see."

"After tea!" Hilda told him, bringing in two plates of food. "You can go and get the other two plates for me."

Ina went into the hall and hung her raincoat on the hall stand. She came back into the living room and took her place at the table.

"I expect you'll miss the shop, won't you?" Jim asked.

"It'll seem strange doing something else after four years."

"You'll soon settle in and make new friends. You're not worried about Monday, are you?"

"No. Not really, Dad. But I wish I was there so I'd know what I have to do. I don't know what to expect."

"There'll be other girls going there. Just join in with them. I expect they will be feeling like square pegs in round holes, too."

"Can we see your present now, Ina?" Clive asked, his impatience getting the better of him.

"For heaven's sake, Clive!" Hilda said. "It's a writing case not a box of chocolates."

Ina reached for the parcel, opened it, and passed the case over for scrutiny.

"It's very nice," Hilda said. "A fountain pen as well."

"It looks like real leather," Jim remarked." You'll be able to take it with you. No excuse for not writing home!"

The card was passed round and the signatures read.

"I see that friendly Mrs Gray didn't sign it!" Hilda laughed.

The meal over, Ina helped her mother wash up.

"I've gone through the list of what you have to take. I've marked your things so you don't lose them," Hilda told her. "Dad can get the case down off the wardrobe and clean it up a bit. It's got a bit shabby. We ought to have got you a new one. I didn't think. Still, never mind; it's a lot stronger than the utility ones."

"It's all right, Mum. Don't worry about it. It's just as likely that none of the others have new suitcases."

"Maybe we can get you a nice one for your birthday; I'll have a look round when I go to town."

"Yes. All right, Mum. I'd like that," Ina said.

"You can pop down and see Gran tomorrow morning." Hilda turned to Clive. "What are you doing tonight? Are you going down to the Turners?"

"Yes, I said I'd take some comics down for swap."

"All right, then. Back for half past nine, mind. No later."

"Do you want to come with us down the legion, Ina?" Jim asked.

"No thanks, Dad. I want to write to Olivia."

"You'll be here on your own."

"I don't mind. I can have the wireless on. I'll be all right."

Jim nodded and got up out of his chair. Turning to Hilda, he said, "I'm going to get ready. You're not going to be long, are you?"

"No," Hilda answered. "I'm coming now." She followed him up the stairs.

Ina went to the radio and turned it on. She automatically tuned it into the AFN. A Glenn Miller song was being played:

Tonight . . . I found the love of my life in someone else's arms . . .

Ina thought of the inscription on the gravestone of little Georgie who'd died—"Safe in the arms of Jesus". Is that where David was now? Safe in the arms of Jesus?'

She turned the radio off and opened her new writing case. She took out the pen and unscrewed the top. Finding the bottle of Stephen's blue black at the bottom of the sideboard cupboard, she filled the pen and then sat down and began to write.

I miss David so much . . . I can't bear the thought that I'm never going to see him again . . . I want everything the way it was . . . I wish he would come back . . . I wish he hadn't gone to war . . . Why did that tank go over that mine? . . . Why did they let him walk near that one? Why did he die, when he was already home and safe?

She stopped writing and looked over the page; she couldn't write that to Olivia! Olivia was mourning her son!

She tore the page off the pad, screwed it up, and threw it on the fire. The flames licked across it, curling up the edges and then, always ready for more fuel, devoured it.

Hilda came into the living room. She wore her dark green, crêpe dress with the V neck, soft pleats falling in front from just below the waist, and a black belt. Ina watched her as she creamed her face with Pond's Vanishing Cream and then dabbed on her face powder and drew lipstick gently across her lips. *She's still attractive*, Ina thought. Hilda was slim, her hair was dark and naturally wavy and curly, like hers and Avril's, only she wore it short.

Clive's hair was fair, like her father's and her auntie Nell's.

∗∗∗

Jim had come into the room carrying his shoes. Ina wondered why he always brought his shoes downstairs to put on. He sat down in his chair, pushed his feet into the shoes, and bent down to tie the laces. She noticed his hair was beginning to thin out, and he would probably become bald in time, like Uncle Sid and Alb Daley.

Jim looked up at Hilda. "You ought to put a cardigan on over the top of that dress; it's nippy out there. I don't expect it will be all that warm down the legion tonight."

"I'll have to put my fawn one on," Hilda said. "It's the only one I've got that will go with this dress."

"Shall I go up and get it for you, Mum?" Ina offered.

"Yes, please, if you don't mind."

Ina went upstairs and into her parents' bedroom. The cold in there struck her. Her father had said that, after the war, he would have gas fires put in the bedrooms. She wondered what kind of place she would be sleeping in, if it would be barracks or a wooden hut somewhere in the wilds. Avril had been in a wooden hut and a barracks and, at one time, a hut made of "breeze" blocks.

"It was just like an air raid shelter," Avril had remarked.

She wished Avril had been home that weekend.

She took the cardigan downstairs. As she walked into the living room the sound of voices came through the party wall between the Wellands' and the Daley's and almost at once turned to angry shouting, although the words were indistinct. Somewhere, a door slammed.

"It's unusual for the Daley's to make a noise," Jim remarked.

There came the unmistakeable sounds of sobbing and, again, slamming of doors.

"Should I go round there to see what's happening?" asked Hilda.

"No," said Jim, "best keep out of it."

Again, they heard the slamming of a door, this time, the front door. Jim went into the hall, opened his own front door, and stepped out onto the path. He came back indoors, his face stern. "Whatever it is, it's got Alb in a tizzy," he said. "He's gone off marching down the road."

"I thought they were coming with us." Hilda sounded concerned. "Are you sure I shouldn't go round there, Jim?"

"If there's anything they want to tell us," Jim replied, "they'll let us know soon enough. Let's get going, if you're ready. We can't solve other peoples' problems unless they ask. If Alb wanted us to know, he would have come round here and not gone storming off down the road."

Ina went to the front door with her parents.

"Make sure the back door's locked and bolted," Hilda told Ina. "Clive's got a key. I've made some sandwiches for you both. There's a bottle of

Tizer in the cupboard, or you can make some cocoa. Not too heavy with the milk, mind."

They went on through the gate. Ina watched them as they walked down the road. Her father was about four or five inches taller than her mother. His strides were long, and Hilda, in her Cuban heels, was trotting beside him, taking two steps to his one.

***

It was chilly outside. Her father had been right. But the drizzle had stopped, although there were a few dark clouds hiding much of the starlight. The barrage balloons had gone up, even though there had been no siren. They hovered about in the sky on their cables. Ina watched them for a while. They were like big silver elephants, minus their legs and trunks. She turned and went back indoors. It was nice and warm in the living room. She sat in her father's chair and watched the flames as they crept up on the log fire. She picked up the poker and thrust it into the flames. Immediately, they sprang higher. A shower of sparks rose from the log, and then the flames settled again.

Ina sat gazing at the fire for a while going over the events of the day. She could not recall Stella having been given a leaving present. It struck her, suddenly, that she had not opened the envelope Mr Phillips had given her. She got up and fetched her handbag, opened it, and drew out the envelope. Inside was a brief note thanking her for her hard work and loyalty and, with the note, four new crisp one pound notes, one for each year's service with the firm—£4.0s.0d! On top of her wages and holiday pay! Ina put the money away and sat down again.

After a while, she became restless. She needed to be doing something. Try writing to Olivia once more? No. Better wait until she was settled in at Camberley; she would have more to say. She switched on the radio and listened to a comedy show, but somehow, she felt unable to join in the laughter.

After a while, her eyelids drooped, and she drifted into sleep.

Chapter 45

A loud knock on the front door awoke Ina. For a moment, she could not collect her thoughts. She glanced at the clock. Half past eight. Clive was not expected to come home until after nine. Perhaps he was early. Maybe he had lost his key. The knocking came again.

She got up from the chair and made her way to the front door, opening it cautiously. On the doorstep was a young boy of about fourteen or fifteen years of age. He was holding a large brown manila envelope.

"Miss Welland?"

"Yes?"

He held the envelope out to her.

"My dad asked me to give you this. He said to tell you that he's sorry he hasn't sent it before, but he's been busy."

She took the envelope. "Your dad?"

"Len Palmer. He played at your club just before Christmas."

Realisation dawned on her. "Thanks," she murmured.

"There's a note inside," he went on.

She nodded and thanked him once again.

"Goodnight," he said.

She watched him walk through the gate, get on his bicycle, and ride towards town. She sat at the table and opened the envelope. Inside was a large sheet of paper, about A3 in size, folded in half. As she drew it out, a piece of paper flew out. She managed to catch it before it fell to the floor. She read the note:

Dear Miss Welland

I'm sorry you haven't received this before. I am with the band, and it has been a busy time for us. However, I have managed to get down to it at last, and I hope it is what you wanted. I've called it "David's Song," as that was what you had written on the piece of paper Do not think you owe me anything; it has been a pleasure to do.

Yours truly,
L. Palmer

Ina looked down at the sheets of paper—obviously preprinted with the lines and symbols. He had written the notes himself and had fitted the words in under the notes. There it was, just as she had told him, "David's Song".

She stared at it and gave a dry sob. She felt her eyes burning, and sharp prickles of pain were under her lids. Then the tears that had been kept back began to spill over, running unchecked down her cheeks. She started to cry audibly, not caring if the Daleys could hear her. Her sobbing shook her body, and she called his name, over and over again, wanting him back.

Presently, the tears ceased to flow; her body, shaking with the pouring out of grief, was now still. In the kitchen, she splashed her face with cold water, drying it on the roller towel. She stood by the sink for a while, quietly. There was no sound coming from next door now, and she could not imagine what the rumpus had been about. She could feel a headache coming on. Reaching up to the small cupboard by the sink, she took out a strip of Aspros, broke it open, and took two of the tablets with a drop of water.

Back in the sitting room, she sat once more in her father's chair, picked up a copy of the woman's magazine that her mother received on a weekly basis, and glanced through the pages, not that there were many pages these days to scan through. She saw a few articles that were not of much interest to her—tips on how to juggle the meat ration so that it spread as far as their recommendations would take it. Hilda had tried something similar once, but it had turned out to be a glutinous tasteless mess, and the whole lot had gone in the pig swill bin with the vegetable peelings.

There was the weekly serial in which the characters followed the set trend for all characters. The heroine was always painfully thin, had a heart-shaped face and large blue eyes, and wore her blonde hair in naturally curly waves. The hero was required to be tall, dark, handsome, and rich; he was always in a senior capacity or a Harley Street doctor. There was the true to form villainess, also dark and expensively dressed, with red painted fingernails and her mouth a slash of scarlet across her face. She would go to extreme lengths to get her claws into the hero. These tales were always set prewar, so that the characters would not disrupt their storyline by having to be called up. Utter rubbish!

Ina put the magazine down and lay back in the chair. She closed her eyes. The clock on the mantelshelf ticked softly, the logs crackled in the flames, and Ina felt a drowsiness creeping over her; she gave into it willingly, not trying to sort out the jumble of emotions going round in her head.

She heard Clive come in, heard him close the front door. She did not look round when he came into the room, carrying a bundle of comics.

"Mum left some sandwiches and Tizer for you in the kitchen, unless you want cocoa."

"Do you want cocoa?" Clive asked.

"Not particularly."

"I'll have Tizer then."

Clive put the comics down on the table and fetched his sandwiches and drink from the kitchen. As he came back into the living room, he glanced at her and said, with a typical boyish candour, "You been crying? Your eyes are red and puffy."

She did not answer but got up out of the chair and went out of the room and into the kitchen. She filled the kettle with water and put it on the gas stove. She went to the cupboard and took out four hot water bottles. When the first spirals of steam were coming from the spout, she turned off the gas and filled each bottle, very carefully, with hot water. Going back to Clive, she said, "I'm going on up to bed."

Clive replied, "Oh. Yeah . . . All right . . . G'night," and bent his head over his comic.

Ina went firstly into her own room and put a bottle into her bed. Then she put two in her parents' bed and the other in Clive's. She went back into her room. She did not draw the curtains or switch the light on. She undressed in the dark with only the feint glimmer of light coming through the window. She slipped into bed, nestling against the propped-up pillows.

Lying there, she could feel her head clearing. Turning towards the window, she watched the low, dark clouds as they scuttled across the night sky. She could hear the lowing of a cow from the farm not far away, and somewhere, a dog barked. There were sounds of tyres swishing along the Devizes Road—cars, a lorry, a bus, a motorcycle. She wished, once more, that Avril had been home this weekend; she had no idea when, she would see her sister again.

***

Hilda and Jim came home. Clive heard the front door close and their footsteps in the hallway. He pushed his comic away and sat back in his chair.

"Haven't you gone to bed, yet?" Hilda sounded surprised.

"I've had my supper," he told her. "Ina's gone on up to bed. She's put the bottles in."

Jim sat down in his chair and took off his shoes, unknotted his tie, and removed the front and back studs from his shirt.

"Not too long, now, son," he said to Clive.

"No," Clive answered. "I'm going up now." He got as far as the door and then turned and said, "Our Ina's been crying." Then he went into the hall and up the stairs.

"Well!" commented Jim. "That's what you've been waiting for, isn't it?"

"Yes. I suppose so, but why wait until she was alone? We could have given her some comfort."

Jim sighed. "Sometimes it isn't comfort people need but to just be left alone and let it all out without anyone being there. I've seen blokes bawling their heads off in the first war because a mate had been killed. We just walked away. We weren't being callous; we knew they had to come to terms with it in their own way."

"She never really confided in us at all, did she? About David, I mean? Do you think it's because she thought we didn't approve?"

"Who knows what goes on in a young girl's mind? Perhaps now she'll be able to get it out of her system. Perhaps going into the ATS will help."

"You didn't mind her volunteering and leaving home?"

"She would have gone anyway sooner or later. We were ready to let her go to America."

Hilda asked, "Do you want anything?"

"No. I'm for bed. I'm just going to make sure the back door's locked and there's no taps left on."

"I'll go on up then. I'll pop in on Ina to make sure she's all right."

The room was still in darkness when Hilda opened the door. She could just make out the silhouette of Ina propped up against the pillows, "Ina?"

"Yes?"

Hilda crossed the room and sat on the bed. "Anything you want—a drink or anything?"

"No thanks, Mum."

"Clive said . . ." She hesitated.

"That I'd been crying?"

"Yes . . . He waited up. I expect he was concerned. Do you feel a little better?"

"I don't know how I feel. I shall be glad when Monday is over. At least I shall know by then where I am and what I'm supposed to do."

"I expect there'll be other girls starting. It'll be like your first day at school or the first day you were at the shop."

"Except that I shan't be coming home at the end of the day."

Hilda had the feeling she was getting out of her depth with Ina. "Perhaps we could come and see you. Dad could put in for a 'priv'. We could be up there in no time."

"I shall have to find out if we're allowed out of camp." Ina's voice was toneless.

"You'll have to let us know." Hilda tried to sound bright.

Silence fell between them while Hilda struggled to say something that wouldn't sound as if she had no idea of her daughter's inner feelings. Ina had received a shattering blow, and it was still very early days. It was Ina herself who gave her mother a chance to avoid further comment on the subject. She asked, "Did you find out what the row next door was all about?"

"Yes," Hilda said. "It seems Brian was right. Keith was married. I always wondered why he never asked Maureen to go with him to meet his auntie. Cissie hinted that they were going to get engaged last Easter, didn't she? Then, when I asked her when they were getting married, she said they were waiting till the war was over.

"How did they find out, Mum?"

"Apparently, Maureen had a letter from his wife. She'd found a letter from Maureen in with the washing he'd brought home. They have a couple of children too. I'm sure he was a lot older than Maureen. And that's not the end of it. Maureen confessed to Alb that she's expecting!"

"Oh! Mum! Poor Maureen! After all her mother said about other girls! I was sure sometimes that she was waiting for you to tell her I was in the 'family way'."

"Well. There it is. Things have a habit of rebounding on you. I just hope people are kinder to her and Maureen than some were to your auntie."

"No wonder her dad went up the wall."

"He was all for going to see Keith's commanding officer, but I think your dad managed to talk him out of it. There's nothing the RAF can do. They can't force him to stand by her."

"Has Maureen heard from him?"

"No. He was supposed to have come last Wednesday evening, but he didn't turn up. Now she knows why."

"Not even come to tell her? That's mean."

"I don't suppose she'll hear from him again." Hilda sighed. "I expect there are hundreds of girls up and down the country that have found themselves in the same boat."

Hilda got up from the bed. "Get some sleep now," She said.

***

When she had gone, Ina pushed the pillows down flat and laid her head upon them. She remembered the time when she had almost wished that David had left her with a baby. Now she was glad that they had never done anything wrong. She couldn't have put her mother and father through the anguish that Maureen's parents were going through. She closed her eyes. Suddenly she felt very tired.

Chapter 46

On the rooftops, lawn, and hedges; on the walls and kerbs—wherever the warm sunrays had not fallen—lay the sprinkling of sleet that had come with first light. Ina, although having been persuaded by her mother to wear a long woollen scarf over her head and over her shoulders, still felt the coldness of the air on her ears and at the back of her neck. She had walked to her grandmother's sooner than ride her bicycle and catch the icy draught on her legs. She walked along the passageway and around the back. The garden looked forlorn and forgotten by nature. The leaves on the Michaelmas daisies and the dahlias were black and lifeless. The fruit bushes were bare, as were the apple and pear trees. Ina knocked on the back door and opened it.

Nell was stood at the sink, cutting up a cabbage and putting the sections into a small bowl of water. She looked up as Ina came through the doorway. "Hello!" she greeted her. "Come to say your goodbyes?"

Ina smiled. "I thought I'd just pop in for a minute or two."

"Uncle Sid and Terry are both working today," Nell said. "Anyway, go on in and see your gran. I'll make some cocoa. You'd like a cup, wouldn't you?"

"Yes, please."

Ina went on into the living room. Her grandmother was sat in her armchair, close to the fire. "Ah. Ina. I thought I'd heard your voice."

Ina unwound her scarf, slipped out of her coat, and hung them both on a hook behind the door. She sat down opposite her grandmother feeling the warmth of the fire, small that it was.

"You're off tomorrow, then? All set, are you?"

"Yes," Ina replied. "I've done my packing, although I'm not taking much with me, only what they've asked me to take."

Nell came in with the tray and put it on the table. She handed her mother a cup of cocoa and one to Ina. Ina was going to get up, but Nell said, "No. Stay where you are. I expect you are cold, aren't you? It's not very nice out there today, is it?"

"No. It's quite miserable," Ina agreed.

"Never mind," said the old lady. "It's your birthday next week, and then it will be the end of February, and we'll have spring to look forward to."

Spring Ina thought. *March, that sunny Sunday afternoon, was it almost a year ago?* Why did she keep on remembering it?

"You'll have to let us know your address so we know where to send your birthday cards."

"Yes. I'll do that directly I find out what it is," she answered.

"Looking forward to going tomorrow?"

"I am . . . and I'm not. It will be good to be among a crowd, but I shall miss everyone."

"Yes. Of course you will," put in her grandmother. "You're sure to be a little homesick at first. I left home when I was a lot younger than you. I was only twelve, and I'd been put into service in a big house a long way from home. No going home for a weekend in those days. Half a day off once a week and one day off once a month, but it couldn't be a Sunday. Not long enough to go home and get back in time, even if you could afford the train fare. I was there a whole year before I had a week off to see my parents . . . and I had to lose that week's pay! Even when my young sister, Dora, died—she was only ten—they weren't happy about me going to the funeral. They didn't think the likes of us had any feelings. We were never supposed to feel sad when we lost someone . . ."

Her voice trailed off, and Ina said, "What did you do, Gran?"

"I was a scullery maid and that was about as low as you could get in those days. I was up at five o'clock in the morning to light the fire in the old kitchen range, taking Cook in her morning cup of tea. Ruled that kitchen she did, and us! We'd peel the vegetables, and the Lord help you if the peel was too thick! And the saucepans had to be scoured with salt. Our fingers were always sore. I had to light the fires in all the rooms. Then it was all day scrubbing and polishing . . . I was lucky if I got to bed before midnight."

"How long were you there?"

"Two years. Then I got a job on a farm nearer home. It was still hard work, but I was better fed and paid more, and it was within walking distance of home."

For a while, she was silent, and then she said brightly, "Of course, things are better now. In those days, feelings were only what the upper classes had."

"Is that why you put me to dressmaking, Mum?" Nell asked with a smile.

"Yes. I didn't want you to go through all that hardship."

"Being in that workshop when I first went to work there was a bit like slave labour" exclaimed Nell.

"Ah yes. But it gave you a trade, and you can still make yourself a bob or two besides what you get at the milk factory!"

"Yes, Mum!" Nell agreed.

The old lady turned to Ina. "You'll be all right, deary. Just do as they tell you. You'll meet lots of girls from all sorts of backgrounds, and they won't all be like little Stella or the girls from the shop, so don't let yourself get led astray by any of them. Just look after yourself and don't bring any hurt to your mum and dad. Remember, it's not the bad girls who always get caught; it's the good ones. The bad ones know what to do!"

"I'll remember, Gran." Ina looked at the clock. "I think I'll be making a move," she said. "I still have a few things to do."

"Yes. You get on. Thanks for coming to see us before you leave."

Ina stood up. Nell took Ina's coat and scarf off the hook and helped her into it. Ina wound the scarf around her neck once more.

"Before you go"—Old Mrs Welland pointed to an envelope on the mantelshelf—"Fetch that down for me."

Ina reached for the envelope and handed it to her.

"It's for you!" her grandmother told her. "Open it."

Ina opened it. Inside was a one pound note. "I can't take that, Gran!"

"Yes you can; it's for your birthday . . . from all of us. You may be glad of a bit of money. I don't expect you'll get paid very much."

Ina mumbled her thanks.

"Come on out the front way," said Nell.

She followed Ina through the front door and up to the gate.

"Well," she said. "Goodbye and best of luck. Keep in touch."

"Yes. I will, Auntie."

Nell watched her niece as she walked up the road. She was so young, poor little mite, yet she'd suffered at her age what so many women suffered in war—the heartache and knowing all the tears in the world won't bring him back to her.

"Will all my tears bring you back, Teddy?" she murmured, quietly.

Ina had reached the top of the road. She turned, and they waved to each other before she disappeared into Devizes Road.

***

Hilda knocked on the bedroom door and opened it. Ina was standing by the dressing table, dressed in her old dressing gown and rubbing her hair vigorously with a towel.

"Don't get cold up here," Hilda said to her. "Is all your packing done?"

"Yes, Mum."

Hilda glanced around the room, noticing as she did so David's photograph in its frame.

"You're not taking David's photo, then?"

Ina paused in her rubbing and then said, "No . . . Something might happen to it."

"Come on down by the fire then. Make sure your hair's dry before you go to bed."

Ina looked around her room after Hilda had gone, to make sure there was nothing she had overlooked. Her eyes rested on David's photograph. Why didn't she want to take it? She could have taken it out of the frame and kept it in her writing case. No. David belonged here. Her mother would look after it, keep it dusted when she cleaned the bedroom. David did not belong in that alien place she was going to. This was the last night she would sleep in this bed, in this room for some time . . . How long?

When Avril had joined the WAAF, it had been six weeks before she came home.

Ina felt her hair; it was nearly dry, and she could finish it off by the fire. She put her towel over the rail in the bathroom and went downstairs.

***

405

How gloomy and depressing it was standing on the station platform. Ina looked at the railway lines, damp in the mist. Along the platform, porters were trundling their trucks, pushing their trolleys, their voices echoing as they called to each other. People milled around or sat on suitcases. Bicycles were lodged against the iron stanchions, parcels waiting to be put into the goods wagon, so different from when she and Avril had waited for the train to Guildford. And David . . .

A bell clanged and the announcer's voice came over the tannoy telling them it was the Waterloo train, stopping at Basingstoke and Woking.

"Fast up," said Jim. "You won't be long getting there."

A long, drawn-out whistle sounded in the distance. Jim took his watch out of his waistcoat pocket. "Looks like she's on time."

The train thundered into the station and stopped with the grating of steel on steel. It gave a loud belch, and a jet of steam ran along between the underbelly and the edge of the platform. Doors opened and passengers got out. Jim found a carriage with just a few people in it and helped Ina aboard. When she was settled and her suitcase on the rack, Jim climbed down to the platform and closed the carriage door firmly behind him. Ina leaned out of the window. He looked up at her.

"You'll soon be off."

"Now don't forget to write and let us know you've arrived all right," Hilda told her.

"No, Mum."

"Give our love to Auntie Grace and Uncle George if you get to Guildford."

"Yes, I will."

"Just do as everyone in charge tells you," put in Jim. "Some of it might not make sense, but they know what they're doing. Don't get lippy or anything, even if some of the other girls do. It's not clever, and they'll get back at you."

"No. I won't."

"Try to get in with some nice girls," Hilda added.

The conversation seemed to end there. Hilda and Jim looked up and down the platform, then at each other, then at her, and smiled. *I hate this*, Ina thought, *no one knowing what else to say. I wish the train would go.*

She suddenly remembered that Avril had once told her that this was how she had felt. Ina had thought her hard; now she knew what her sister had meant. As if in accordance with her wishes, the guard blew his whistle and waved his flag. The train started to move, people waved and, as the train gathered speed, heads and arms were drawn in and the windows closed.

***

Hilda and Jim watched until the train was lost to view around the bend.

"Well, there she goes. Another bird flown the coop," remarked Jim.

"She didn't take David's picture with her," said Hilda.

"No? Well, I expect she had her reasons."

"I suppose getting right away will help her get over him, won't it?"

"It'll probably blunt the edges," Jim replied.

"It's not so much now as later, when the girls who have married American soldiers go to America; it's bound to be on the newsreels at the pictures," Hilda sighed.

"That's a long way off yet."

They turned and walked away off the platform.

"We haven't done so bad, have we, Jim? By the kids I mean?"

"No. Of course not. They've had a good start in life. They won't let us down. That's up to you, more than me, what with being on the turns I work and leaving you to deal with them."

"Oh, I don't know. You've done your share."

"I think you'll find Ina will cope. She's learned one valuable lesson," Jim said. "She's learned never to take life for granted. There's always something waiting round the corner. She'll take whatever it is in her stride, you see. This time last year," he said, reflectively, "she was not much more than a young girl. Now, bless her, she's a young woman."

They walked through the main door, feeling the cold draught that came from the street.

"Tell you what," Jim said, "why don't we take a taxi home?"

They climbed into a waiting taxi, and Jim gave the driver the address. The taxi moved away from the station and went under the bridge into Fisherton Street. A pale ray from the weak sun came through the window and fell across their laps. Jim put his hand on Hilda's and squeezed it gently. She turned to him and smiled.

"You still have one chick at home," he told her.

"We can be proud of him, can't we?" she replied. "He might even get to university one day."

Jim smiled back at her and said, "I wouldn't be at all surprised."

Chapter 47

June 1945

Although it was late afternoon, the sun still had enough heat to bring discomfort to anyone not sheltered from its rays. Crossing the road onto High Street and making her way towards the canal, Ina wished she had taken her mother's advice and changed out of her uniform into a cotton dress. But it was getting late and she wanted to reach Bloom's before the store closed. Besides, she felt she must call in at the shop. She had promised; it would be churlish not to when they had given her a farewell gift. It wasn't something she looked forward to; she knew that whatever bond she had had with the shop had gradually faded. It would have, like most of her life in Salisbury, gone on without her.

It was cooler in the canal, where a slight breeze drifted along, unimpeded, from as far away as Milford Hill. The shops still had signs of the festivities to mark VE day; cardboard cut-outs of the king and queen nestled among the red, white, and blue backdrops. Large framed photographs of the royal family on the balcony of Buckingham Palace vied for attention with those of Winston Churchill, complete with cigar and his unforgettable V sign. From some of the buildings hung the allied flags, and a few gradually deflating balloons hung limply from windows.

She had left off her jacket and had her sleeves rolled up to the regulation width above her elbows; nevertheless, she felt damp around her waist and inside of her collar and tie. She knew that, when she took her hat off, her hair would be a moist flat cap against her head. And goodness knows what her feet would be like after being enclosed in lisle stockings and clumpy shoes.

The interior of Bloom's looked dark after the bright sunlight of the street. Ina climbed the carpeted stairs into the gown department. There was another woman being served. In a loud voice she was proclaiming her wish to have something suitable to wear for the Victory Ball she was attending. "Have you something in velvet? Satin backed Moroccain? Twilled silk?" She already had this and that. She couldn't possibly wear the same thing twice—not at the balls she was invited to.

Ina browsed through a rail of dresses in her size. She had no idea what she wanted; only that she would know it when she spotted it. When she saw the pale pastel pink dress, she knew it was the one. She took it from the rack, held it up by the hanger, and gazed at it. She could not tell what material it was, only that it was lightweight and silky. The crossover bodice was gathered at the shoulders and then pleated into the waistband that rose into a point. From a dropped waist fell soft, unpressed pleats.

"Does madam wish to try the dress on?"

Ina turned. Unheard, a shop assistant had come up to her and now stood beside her. The woman was tall and had an air of elegance. She must have been in her forties. Her greying hair was in a roll around her head, in the same style as Stella had so often worn hers. The woman showed Ina to a cubicle, pulled back the curtain, and switched on a small, rather dim light. Ina took off her outer garments and slipped the dress over her head. As she gently eased it around her hips, the material seemed to slip through her fingers like silk. She could only gauge in the dim light how much it suited her. She had lost a little weight, all that PT and square bashing! Her hair had been cut, not that she had particularly wanted to lose her long tresses. But the "put on top" style she had adopted was not very successful, wisps of hair had escaped from under her hat onto her shoulders.

"We do not wear our hair like a cobweb cape, Welland!" her sergeant had bawled, so she had gone to the camp hairdresser and come out leaving her crowning glory on the floor. At the first sight of her newly cropped hair, tears had come to her eyes.

"Never mind," she had been consoled, "it'll be better when it's washed, and it will grow again."

So she had mixed an Evan William's shampoo, washed her hair, and been pleasantly surprised to discover that the hairdresser had, after all, known what she was doing. When it was dry, the waves came back and the ends of her hair curled around her head.

Coming out of her daydream, Ina stepped out of the cubicle and went to the nearest long mirror. Now she could see the effect of the dress. Was that really her? What would David say if he could see her now? Would he have said she looked a million dollars? That's what they said in the films, wasn't it? She could wear her pink necklace; the one David had given her that day at Tidworth . . .

For a split second, her face clouded over but brightened up again when the sales assistant said, genuinely, "It looks very nice on you, madam." Ina smiled at her as she continued. "It's a new line, just in. Still utility of course, but they seem to have been a little more generous with the cut."

Ina turned from side to side and felt pleased. It looked a little incongruous with the thick stockings and heavy shoes, but it was the dress that counted.

"I'll take it," she said.

It was when the dress was laid in the tissue paper on the counter that Ina realised she hadn't asked the price.

"Four guineas, madam,"

Four guineas, *four guineas*! She had drawn £5.0s.0d from her savings and had a few shillings in her purse, but she would have to be frugal for some time. The dress was wrapped in brown paper and placed in a carrier bag. Once it would have been in a box. But perhaps the carrier bag would be easier to cling onto. Ina put her fingers through the string handles and went out into the street.

***

The doors of the shop were open. The familiar smell of new leather wafted towards her as she walked in. Mr Phillips was standing by the cash desk talking to a tall slender young man wearing horn-rimmed spectacles. The two young girls were serving at the end of the shop. Mr Phillips turned and saw her.

"Well! Miss Welland! It's nice to see you."

Ina went towards the desk.

"I must say, you look very smart. Are you keeping well?" he went on.

"Yes, thank you."

"Are you settling in all right?"

"Yes. I like it very much—now I've got used to the routine and the rules. I found it confusing at first—learning all the different ranks and who to salute."

Mr Phillips turned to the young man.

"This is Miss Welland," he said. "She was with us for four years."

The young man nodded and smiled at her.

"This is Mr Pearce. He is going to take over when I leave at the end of this month."

"You're leaving?" There was a faint note of regret in Ina's voice.

"Yes. I'm retiring at last. Mrs Phillips and I will be heading for Devonshire."

"They're going to miss you, Miss Jenner and Mrs Gray."

"Yes. Well. I'm sure they'll settle down well with Mr Pearce."

Vera came into the shop. "Ina!" No need for formality now. "I'm glad you called in. How are you?"

"I'm fine, thank you."

"How long are you home for?"

Funny, thought Ina, *how everyone asks that.* "I'm on a long weekend pass. My sister's coming home tomorrow, so we're having a family get-together."

"Have you heard anymore of Stella?"

"No, I haven't. We seemed to have lost touch."

"That's a pity. I suppose these things happen."

"How are you, Vera?"

In spite of the fact she now had an air of assurance about her, Ina could see there was a trace of sadness in her eyes. How long did it take before the smiles reached them?

The two young ones, having now finished serving, stood smiling at her.

"We got your letter," said Freda. "Are you glad the war is over and you don't have to fight?"

Ina laughed. "I don't think the army would have put me in the front line."

Mr Phillips had shown the last two customers out of the door, and Ina took her cue from that.

"I'd better be going," she told them. "You'll be wanting to cash up."

Mr Phillips remained by the door. As she stepped into the arcade, he held out his hand. "Goodbye, Miss Welland, and good luck."

She shook his hand. "Thank you. I hope you and Mrs Phillips have a happy retirement in Devon."

He smiled at her.

She reached the pavement and heard the faint click of the door as it closed behind her. She had kept her promise, although she knew that she had said her final goodbye to the shop. She looked back along the street. All the canopies had been pushed back, all the outside displays taken in. She heard St Thomas's Church clock strike the hour. Soon, the shop workers would be leaving, cycling home or catching buses. Tomorrow they would be back and starting all over again. She would not be part of it, and just for a while, she felt a slight feeling of nostalgia. There again, she was no longer a shop girl; she was a soldier. She squared her shoulders and, by the left, walked briskly towards the market square. Her sergeant would have been proud of her!

Chapter 48

The American soldier was standing by the War Memorial, his back towards Ina, watching some children dancing around the pigeons. There was something familiar about him—the way he wore his cap and the way he stood, although he had crutches underneath his arms. One trouser leg was pinned up to the inside of his thigh. Ina felt a stab of pity for him and a sudden need to cry. She walked slowly towards him.

As if he had sensed her presence, he turned his head towards her, his face lighting up as he did so.

"Hello, Virgil," she said quietly.

"Ina! Am I pleased to see you. Never thought I would, and here you are. And a lady soldier, no less. I thought you'd be all packed up and set, ready to get the boat to Alabama!"

"David died . . . last January."

His expression changed "Dead . . . Dave? Why . . . I knew he'd been badly hurt, but I didn't reckon on him dying."

"It was a blood clot. They thought it might have been a result of losing his eye."

"I'm so sorry, honey. It must have been pretty tough on you. He was a really nice guy."

"I'm getting over it now." She put out her free hand and gently touched his arm. "What happened, Virgil?"

"The leg? It was the darnedest thing, you know? I spent the whole of the war getting in and out of tanks, and then this one time, I jumped out just as a hand grenade landed by my side. The war was supposed to be over, but somebody forgot to tell this Kraut. He was put right pretty damn quick."

"I'm so sorry."

"Well . . . it's done; could have been worse. Guess I've come out of this war better than a lot of guys . . ." His voice trailed off. He looked at her and said quietly, "Do you have a few minutes?"

"Yes. I'm in no hurry to get home."

"Would you come and have a drink with me, in that pub by the bus depot? I'm going home Monday." He grinned at her. "It could be my last glass of warm English beer!"

She laughed. "Going home, eh? I'm so pleased for you, and I'll come and have a drink with you."

Together, they made their way to Endless Street, Ina matching her pace to his. As yet, there were not many people in the Woolpack. The pair took a seat near to the door.

"What'll you have?" Virgil asked.

"No. You sit down. I'll get them. You've bought me enough in your time."

"Shandy, as I remember."

"Yes. But this time, I'm having half a pint with you. I'm eighteen now, so I can go into a pub and have half a beer."

"Eighteen and all grown up!" he said.

She came back to the table carrying the drinks and sat down opposite him.

"Do you have something nice in your package?" he asked her.

"It's a new dress. I bought it for our Victory Ball at the camp next week. It's a bit late to celebrate, but they say these things take time to organise."

"Well. That's the army! You have yourself a good time."

"Thanks."

"Do you like being in the army?"

"It's all right now I'm getting used to it. I was homesick at first."

"Guess we all are to start with. What are you doing?"

"I'm with a signals group."

"Oh, I see—running around waving little flags."

"There's a bit more to it than that. But . . . I like it. We have a good Yeoman. I've put my name down to be a driver."

"You don't drive now?"

"No. I never had the chance to learn. Now I can have some lessons free."

"I hope you make it."

"Thanks."

He took a drink, looked at her, and said, "Do you still see that girlfriend of yours? What was her name? Sheila . . . Shirley . . ."

"Stella."

"That's it, Stella—used to be Joe Smith's girl."

"No. I haven't seen her. We've lost touch. She left the shop after Christmas. Joined the NAAFI. I don't know where she is now. She came to see me when I wrote and told her about David. She didn't stay long. We didn't have much to say. I haven't seen her since."

"You know what happened to Joe?"

"I know he was wounded. Stella had a letter from him asking her to go over to Tidworth and take me with her. He told me about David."

"Was he at the hospital, David I mean?"

"No. He was sent to a hospital in Northern Ireland. He went back home from there. I never saw him again. We wrote to each other until Christmas. Just after, his stepfather sent a telegram, and then I had a letter from his mum. It was very sudden . . ."

"I'm really sorry, honey."

Ina smiled ruefully. "I'd like to have seen him again . . . just once more."

"Did you know Joe got killed?" he asked quietly.

"No. No, I didn't. Stella couldn't have known. We went over to the hospital one day, and they'd sent him back to France. She had one letter from him and never heard anymore."

"We were in Belgium when it happened. He hadn't been back long. There was a bit of hand-to-hand fighting. I wasn't there, but I heard . . . Joe got shot."

Ina could feel the prickle of tears in her eyes. "Poor Joe," she murmured.

"Sorry to give you bad news," Virgil said.

Ina swallowed hard and changed the subject. "What about your friend, Bob?"

"Bob? Oh, he's okay. Kicking his heels up; waiting to get the boat home. We all thought we were on our way when we heard about the ceasefire."

"And you weren't."

"Nope! Mopping up and waiting for reinforcements, so we had to sit tight, except I got messed up. An' old fat Sharkey won't be going home either. Got himself run over by a tank."

"A German tank?"

"No. One of ours. He'd got hold of some hooch from somewhere and was pretty tight. It was last winter. We were making for the Ardennes. The ground was pretty frozen, and he tripped over a rut right into the path of the tank. The guy had no chance of stopping in time, so it was goodbye Sharkey."

"It must have been horrible."

"Guess it was. Didn't see anyone cry, though."

They sat in silence for a while, until Ina broke it. "What are you going to do when you get home?"

"Well, that kind of depends on how soon I get fixed up with a new leg. I shall have to stay in the army until I'm ready for discharge."

"Will you have a job to go back to?"

"Don't rightly know. I may get on one of those GI Bill of Rights schemes."

"That's what David was going to do. What did you do in civvy street?"

"I worked in a radio assembly plant. I put radios together. That's why I operated radios in the tanks. Don't know if I care to do that again."

"I expect your family will be glad to have you home."

"Yeah. It'll be great seeing the folks again after all this time. Guess I'll spend a lot of time with them, tuck into my ma's cooking; maybe see a ballgame with my dad."

He paused a while, looking reflectively into his glass and running his finger around the rim. When he spoke, he did not look at her. "Guess," he said quietly, "I'll try to get it back together with my wife . . ."

"I didn't know you were married!" exclaimed Ina.

"I wasn't exactly the faithful husband, was I?"

He took another drink from his glass. "We hadn't known each other very long. We got married about a month before we were shipped out of the States. We wrote to each other, pretty often at first. Then, I don't know, ran out of things to say. I didn't know her folks, and she didn't know mine. We sort of lost the common ground. Letters got shorter and further apart . . ."

"Does she know about your leg?"

"Yeah. I told her. She said to wait till I got home and we'd sort things out."

"If she loved you long ago, she'll not love you less I know," Ina quoted.

"Pardon me?"

"It's from a song David used to sing to me, about a boy named Jack, who had to go to war and told his girl, Mary, to wait for him. He was wounded—lost an arm. And that's when his friends told him that she would still love him."

A frown came to Virgil's forehead. He leaned forward and snapped his fingers. "I think I know that song," he said. "Don't know where I heard it. One of those songs you grow up with. Doesn't he come back and she'd died? Got buried under a tree?"

"Yes! Ina said. "That's it!"

"'Mary Dear,'" Virgil said. "That's the name of it, 'Mary Dear'."

"I just call it 'David's Song'." There was a slight catch in Ina's voice.

"Then if old Dave sang it to you, I reckon that's as good a name as any." He smiled. He looked at his watch. "My bus is due in."

Ina felt a small twinge of regret. He was going back to Tidworth and, Monday, would be going home. They both stood up. She helped him steady himself on his crutches and remembered when she had helped Joe. Poor Joe! The bullet with his name on had found him after all.

Outside the sun still shone. The bus was in and a queue had already formed. Virgil got into line with more people coming on behind him. He turned to Ina. "I suppose this is goodbye, honey. It sure was nice seeing you again."

"And you, Virgil." She gave a short laugh. "It's all I seem to do these days—say goodbye to people."

"I know. I've said goodbye to a lot of good guys. Maybe that's what war is, honey, a whole heap of goodbyes." He leaned forward and kissed her on the cheek. "I'll always remember you as the last girl I danced with when I had two good legs."

"You'll dance again someday."

"You boarding, buddy?" came a voice from behind. "C'mon, then. Let's get you up the step."

Together, the GI and the conductress helped Virgil to mount the step and make his way along the interior of the bus. People crowded on behind him, and Ina lost sight of him among the throng. She looked up and down, but could not see him. Probably, he was sat in the far aisle, hidden by a few passengers who were standing. The last passenger got on, and the conductress rang the bell. The bus moved, snaked its way out of the bus station into Endless Street, and disappeared down Chipper Lane. For a while she stood there, people milling round her, coming into Salisbury or waiting for the arrival of the bus to take them home.

When she did move, it was not towards the marketplace to catch her own bus but across the road, onto Chipper Lane and then onto Castle Street, following the route taken by the Tidworth bus. She crossed again and walked briskly towards the railway bridge. Around the entrance to the lorry park, girls were already gathering. Soon the trucks would come rolling down Castle Road bringing more GIs—more Davids, more Joes, more Virgils and Bobs . . . even more Sharkeys; who knew?

The doors of the Rising Sun were open, and the sound of merriment spilled through into the evening. On, under the bridge, across the road, through the trees, and she was there. She seemed to see him waiting, head slightly to one side, smiling as she walked towards him. She went up to the little bridge and put her hand on the slim rail. Just over a year ago, she had met him on this bridge for the last time. She remembered the first time she and Stella had met him and Joe here. Then, there were wild daffodils on the banks, violets and primroses; the trees were coming into leaf, the brambles were in flower, and mallard chicks scrambled down the banks and *plopped* into the water. Now, there were buttercups, cow parsley, ragged robin; trees were in full blossom, and bramble bushes were showing small green fruits. And the dog roses were blooming.

Dog roses! She remembered that last day—the field at Tidworth—when she had been ready to open her very soul to him. She let the memories flow unchecked into her mind—when they had met, what they had shared, the places that had been special to them. Now, she would never again meet him here, never sit beside him in the cinema or the Bib and Tucker or the Red Cross Club. She would never again go to Tidworth and feel the excitement of seeing him standing there at the bus stop, waiting. He would never sing to her again. Now everything was gone.

The shop was behind her; Stella had gone from her life and, along with her, all the intimacies they had both shared. There was nothing left of the short life she had had with David. Perhaps Virgil had been her last link with him. Now, he too had gone.

419

She would never forget David. Somewhere, deep inside her, he would remain, to come back to her when some faint memory was stirred. But her young mind and her young body would not hold her back from the life she would live. In time, the pain of loss would lessen, and she would remember only the happiness of his closeness and that sweet time when she had loved and been loved.

Vera had said, *You're not expected to forget them, Ina.* And those were the ones she would hold dear. She leaned over the bridge. What had he said? *"Did you know that if you look at the flowing water long enough, it seems like you are moving forward?"*

Well, she had moved forward. She was living a new life, meeting new people, gaining new skills. She had grown up—gone through that door of girlhood into womanhood. It was time to take everything life had to offer her and, for now, make it on her own.

She stretched out her hand, plucked the head of a dog rose, and let the petals fall spiralling down to the water. She watched as the current swept them under the bridge and out of sight.

"Goodbye, David." she whispered. "Goodbye, my love."

Then she turned away from the bridge and went home.

.

The soldier from the wars returns,
The sailor from the main;
But I have parted from my love,
Never to meet again,
My dear—Never to meet again.

Robert Burns
"The Farewell"

Biographical Synopsis (as at 2004)

Jim Welland	born 1896, Salisbury	died 1978, Salisbury
Hilda Welland	born 1902, Alderbury	died 1991, Salisbury
Old Mrs Welland	born 1871, Chalfont St Giles	died 1947, Salisbury
Nell	born 1898, Salisbury	died 1982, Salisbury
Sid	born 1897, Walthamstow	died 1980, Salisbury
Teddy	born 1918, Salisbury	died 1945, British Military Hospital, Aldershot
Cissie Daley	born 1900, Salisbury	died 1965, Salisbury
Alb Daley	born 1898, Woking	died 1970, Salisbury
Maureen	born 1924, Salisbury	died 1945, Salisbury (died in childbirth with infant son)
Harold	born 1926, Salisbury	died 1951, Korea (killed in action)
David Easton	born 1923, Alabama	died 1945, Alabama (as a result of wounds from WWII)
Joe Smith	born 1920, Georgia	died 1944, Belgium (killed in action)
Virgil Romano	born 1919, New York City	died 1990, Georgia
Ina	born 1927	still living
Avril	born 1924	still living
Clive	born 1932	still living
Terry	born 1923	still living
Brian	born 1922	still living
Stella	born 1927	???
Vera	born 1924	still living

Time, like an ever rolling stream, bears all its sons away.